A HISTORY OF MODERN BRITAIN
VOLUME 1

A History of Modern Britain confronts head-on the victory of shopping over politics. It tells the story of how the great political visions, and rival idealisms, of a second Elizabethan age came to be defeated by a culture of consumerism, celebrity and self-gratification.

In each decade, political leaders think that they know what they are doing, but find themselves confounded. Every time, the British people turn out to be stroppier and harder to herd than predicted.

Throughout, Britain is a country on the edge—first of invasion, then of bankruptcy, then on the vulnerable front line of the Cold War and later in the forefront of the great opening up of capital and migration now reshaping the world.

A HISTORY OF MODERN BRITAIN

Volume 1

Andrew Marr

BBC LARGE PRINT

First published 2007
by
Macmillan
This Large Print edition published 2007
by
BBC Audiobooks Ltd by arrangement with
Pan Macmillan Ltd

Hardcover ISBN: 978 1 405 64877 6
Softcover   ISBN: 978 1 405 64878 3

British Library Cataloguing in Publication Data available

Printed and bound in Great Britain by
Antony Rowe Ltd., Chippenham, Wiltshire

PART 1

HUNGER AND PRIDE:
BRITAIN AFTER THE WAR

The Democratic Bombshell

Many of us find our innermost fears or hopes take arms while we sleep, ready to strike at the moment of wakening. Churchill recorded that, on the morning of 26 July 1945, he woke up with 'a sharp stab of almost physical pain' to find himself sure that he and the Conservatives had just lost the general election. There was a long delay for the votes to be brought back from battlefields around the world. Few people thought the war leader could lose power. Most Labour leaders assumed he would be returned. So did the apparently well-informed City experts, the in-touch trade union bosses, the self-certain press, the diplomatic observers passing back the latest intelligence to Washington and Moscow. Churchill was at the very peak of his personal triumph, outshining the King and Royal Family when he appeared on the famous balcony to wave. Never in British history has military success been so personally associated with a civilian leader – not the two great Pitts, not Disraeli at his peak, not David Lloyd George, could rival Churchill's radio age charisma. True, 1945 had been a most unusual election. The Parliament it ended had begun in the middle of the thirties – nine years, six months and twenty days earlier, making it the longest UK Parliament ever, a Parliament of old men unused to raw party conflict. Churchill would have liked it to go on longer, at least until Japan was defeated. Never quite a party man, he had a coalition cast of mind. It had been Labour which insisted on the election. Now, no one knew what

3

was coming: the scattered and disrupted nature of the electorate meant accurate polling was impossible. The new electoral roll was inaccurate, too, having been based on ration book records. Among those who found they had no vote because of clerical errors was the Prime Minister himself.

For those with ears to hear, there were intimations of what was about to happen. During the war a high-minded religious socialism had become fashionable at home. As the carnage ground on overseas, an almost Utopian determination to build a more Christian country took root. As early as 1940 the great wartime Archbishop of Canterbury, William Temple, had called for 'extreme inequalities of wealth to be abolished'. Going rather further, his Council of Clergy and Ministers for Common Ownership declared private ownership of industry 'contrary to Divine Justice'. In the forces compulsory discussions about Britain after the war had been led by the Army Bureau of Current Affairs, ABCA, organized by a left-leaning educationalist called W. E. Williams. Conservative-minded officers complained about the tone of the pamphlets sent round the army and that Williams had 'smothered the troops in seditious literature'. One general burned 10,000 of the 'wretched pamphlets' in front of his men and warned that they were 'rank treason'.[1] To this day many Conservatives believe that socialist propaganda foisted on the troops was to blame for their defeat in 1945. In fact, the numbers do not add up; the minimum voting age was 21, which cut out many of the more malleable troops and in any case, there were fewer than two

4

million service votes cast in a total electorate of 33 million.

The change was happening among civilians. A strong sense that it was time for a fresh beginning had been reflected in a series of by-election defeats of Tory candidates when vacancies were caused in the Commons by the deaths of sitting members. (Twenty-two MPs were killed fighting, all but one of them Conservatives.) At Maldon in Essex, the left-wing journalist Tom Driberg had won, standing as an independent. By 1943 candidates for the piously socialist Common Wealth movement, founded by our English traveller J. B. Priestley and by Sir Richard Adand, were winning upset victories up and down England. In April of that year the Battle of Britain pilot John Loveseed won a Cheshire seat; Lt Hugh Lawson won Skipton in the Yorkshire Dales. Most sensationally of all, in April 1945 in Tory Chelmsford, Wing Commander Ernest Millington, a pre-war pacifist and socialist who had then joined the RAF and turned his attention to bombing Germany, defeated the Conservative candidate. Millington, standing for Common Wealth and supported by local vicars, had fought a remarkably aggressive campaign whose tone can be summarized by a banner he put up in the middle of the market town which read, 'This is a Fight between Christ and Churchill.' By 1945, there was a whiff of Oliver Cromwell in the air.

The Labour conference which kick-started the election campaign one hot afternoon in Blackpool is still remembered for the youth of the delegates. Denis Healey was there, in battledress and beret, fresh from the battlefront in Italy, preaching red-hot socialist revolution. Across Europe the upper classes were 'selfish, depraved, dissolute and decadent' he told the cheering hall. Roy Jenkins, who had helped crack the German codes at Bletchley Park, was there too, a slim and dapper soldier. There was even a socialist Rear Admiral. Labour's manifesto, well written and snappily designed, would be distributed to nearly two million people, backed by powerful posters, 12 million leaflets and huge numbers of party volunteers. Its most popular passages could hardly have come as a shock. They relied on the blueprint for a fairer, more planned country which had been worked out by the coalition government before the war ended. Labour had the support of only a minority of the national press. Apart from the *Daily Mirror* and its in-house *Daily Herald,* the big-circulation papers were all pro-Tory and the two upmarket leftish newspapers, the *Manchester Guardian* and the *News Chronicle,* both backed the lost-cause Liberals. Different parts of the country found very different audiences for Labour's meetings. Attlee was rushing about in his little Standard car, rapping out around eight speeches of a terse twenty minutes apiece every day. He thought his reception was excellent. In some towns the election seemed quiet. In others, huge and attentive crowds turned up to listen and argue back. In Birmingham Roy Jenkins recalled 'seas of faces looking up in the twilight, a mixture of exhaustion, hope, some kind of doubt. A sea of tired faces looking up in hope, that's the best phrase I can make of it.'[2]

Churchill meanwhile was fighting one of the bad campaigns of his life. His theme was that Labour was a sinister socialist conspiracy. In a badly misjudged radio broadcast kicking off his campaign, he let his florid wartime language loose and struck entirely the wrong note. No socialist system, he said, could be established without some form of political police, a British Gestapo. Instead he offered a vision of bucolic good cheer which would have seemed dated in the aftermath of the Boer War: 'Let us make sure that the cottage home to which the warrior will return is blessed with modest but solid prosperity, well-fenced and guarded against misfortune ...' Attlee answered him with gentle irony. The Gestapo suggestion was grossly offensive but the Labour leader disarmingly replied that it was no doubt Churchill's way of demonstrating the gulf between his qualities as a great war leader and those of a mere party leader, and that the attack had probably been devised by the press baron Lord Beaverbrook. It was in fact all Churchill's own work. His wife Clemmie had strongly warned him against it and his party's chief whip had commented that 'it is not my idea of how to win an election'. A second line of Tory attack was that Attlee was the mere frontman for extremists. The Labour chairman Harold Laski was portrayed by Conservative candidates as hell-bent on revolution. Laski did use wild language and was on the left of the party, though his father campaigned for Churchill and had recently suggested that a public fund be raised to show Churchill the nation's gratitude. (The Prime Minister said a better monument for him would be a public park for the children of London on the south bank of the Thames 'where they suffered so grimly from the Hun'.[3] This was never followed up.)

Churchill had based himself in Claridge's Hotel

in London and used a private train and a cavalcade of cars to make his speeches around the country. Mostly he won an enthusiastic enough reception, though he was dumbfounded to find himself booed by a large section of the crowd in his final rally at Walthamstow. This was not quite the respectful British nation of myth. Despite these warning signs, the brutal rejection of Churchill for Attlee caused amazement around the world. Before the election result was declared the two men had been together at Potsdam in Germany negotiating the future of post-war Europe with Joseph Stalin and President Harry Truman. Where would Poland's borders be? How hard should defeated Germany be squeezed? Whose was Greece? Returning to London for the results, Churchill had not even bothered to say goodbye to the Soviet dictator or Washington's new man. He did not properly pack. He would be back.

Attlee was by then somewhat more optimistic. He thought it would be close. About that, at least, he was wrong. In 1935 the Conservatives had won 585 seats. In 1945 they won just 213. Labour won more votes than the Tories for the first time ever, giving them 393 seats and a majority of 146. When Attlee returned to Potsdam alone without Churchill, Stalin's right-hand man, Molotov, was incredulous. He suspiciously cross-questioned the Labour leader about why he had not known the result in advance. Such democratic sloppiness would not have been tolerated further east. Churchill, brooding at home, found it a terrible personal shock. When Clemmie tried to cheer him up with the thought that it might be a blessing in disguise he grunted that, just at the moment, it seemed quite effectively disguised. Yet he quickly spirited a silver lining out from the cloud.

The years ahead would be a terrible trial to the British people, Churchill believed. Might not Labour be better left to cope with the disappointments to come? At last, discovering the generosity of spirit that had gone absent without leave during his election campaigning, the old man rebuked one of his aides: 'This is democracy. This is what we have been fighting for.'

What had Labour been fighting for? The party's new MPs arriving in London by train, car and bus were a mixed bunch. Most were inexperienced in the ways of Parliament, as they would soon show by giving a raucous rendition of the Red Flag in the temporary chamber – the historic one having been demolished by the Luftwaffe. There were Fabian intellectuals, wartime rebels, trade unionists and civil servants such as the podgy, moustachioed Harold Wilson, soldiers and teachers, cautious moderates and – so the Communist Party believed – at least nine secret communist plants. All of them had stood on a manifesto written by Herbert Morrison and a young idealist called Michael Young who would go on to found the Consumers' Association. It called for the establishment of 'the Socialist Commonwealth of Great Britain – free, democratic, efficient, progressive, public-spirited'. It contained a long list of ideas but it was as realistic as (in private) Churchill had been about the difficulties ahead: 'The problems and pressures of the post-war world threaten our security and progress as surely as – though less dramatically than – the Germans threatened them in 1940. We need the spirit of Dunkirk and of the Blitz sustained over a period of years.' In the years ahead this fighting bulldog tone would quickly grate.

Some of the new Labour MPs felt they had been elected to overturn the class basis of the country, others that they simply had a difficult list of domestic reforms to get through. As they introduced themselves to one another for the first time, gossiping and exchanging campaign stories, a sizeable minority also believed they had better get rid of the conventional-sounding Attlee and elect a proper leader while there was time. Herbert Morrison, a popular minister who had organized London's defence against the Blitz, had warned Attlee that he would stand against him in a party contest. The plot gathered force in the corridors and urinals of Westminster Central Hall. At the same time, Attlee, Morrison, the burly ex-trade union leader Ernie Bevin and the party secretary met: at Transport House, the party headquarters a few hundred yards away. As Morrison nipped out to make a call to another supporter, Bevin leaned across to Attlee and growlingly gave him the best advice of his life: 'Clem, you go to the Palace straight away.' Clem did. He took tea with his wife Vi and family at Paddington, hopped into their little car and was driven to Buckingham Palace where the King, a staunch conservative taken aback by the turn of events, duly handed him control of the British Empire. Morrison and the other Labour plotters left half a mile to the east had underestimated Attlee. Many people had. He would go on to become one of the two genuinely nation-changing prime ministers of modern British history.

Hiroshima and Keynes:
the Limits of Wit

The Labour government of 1945–50 is remembered today as among the greatest British administrations ever. Some of the glory is justified. As we will see, it changed the health and welfare structure of the country, nationalized sections of the economy and managed to survive a series of terrible external shocks. But if its aim was to create a British socialist commonwealth with different values and different people in charge – to make a social revolution – then Labour failed. No significant changes to the British class system came about as a result of the work of the Attlee government. Nor was there any loosening of the ties to Washington, ardently desired by many on the left who thought Labour could deal better with Moscow on the dubious principle that 'left can speak to left'. Labour hoped to keep Britain free and independent, going her own way between the Great Capitalism on the other side of the Atlantic and the Great Communism now in possession of half Europe. Yet under Attlee Britain became dependent on the United States. She could not match America's overwhelming military power around the world, symbolized by an atomic bomb that Britain had helped create but was not allowed to share. The weakness of Britain's dying imperium meant her world role would have to shrink dramatically. Attlee understood this much faster than most of his colleagues.

Britain had arrived blinking into a new world still cloaked in the archaic nineteenth-century grandeur of imperialism. The Americans were busy creating their own commercial empire, moving into markets vacated by defeated or exhausted rivals. The Soviet Union was equally busy extending its political empire, funding local dictators and occasionally lurching towards more dramatic confrontation. These two new empires were very different. America's empire came informally dressed talking about freedom and equality. Outside its Asian wars and its support for vicious South American regimes these words did not ring hollow – but those are large geographical exceptions. Moscow, meanwhile, was busy repressing and imprisoning in the name of History and the working class, one eye always on the even more bloodthirsty tyranny of Mao's China challenging it for Third World leadership. Against these new empires, the moth-eaten pretensions of a mild-mannered king-emperor, a few battleships and a modest number of colonial governors in baggy shorts barely seemed relevant.

Britain's dilemma from 1945 until today has been easy to state, impossible to resolve. How do you maintain independence and dignity when you are a junior partner, locked into defence systems, intelligence gathering and treaties with the world's great military giant? At times Britain has had real influence in Washington, above all in the talks with the Labour government which produced the North Atlantic Treaty Organization, NATO, and in the first Gulf war when Margaret Thatcher urged George Bush senior not to wobble. At other times her dependence has been embarrassing, in big ways such as the Suez fiasco; and small ways, such as the American refusal to share intelligence assessments in Iraq, even when the raw intelligence was gathered originally by British agents and passed on. Yet when one country, the United States, is both leader of a large alliance of other countries, and has strong national interests which may conflict with those of her allies, there is bound to be friction. Periodic bouts of anti-Americanism inside the Foreign Office and in Whitehall generally have been the result. Anti-American feeling has been the Establishment's secret vice. In public, successive foreign secretaries and mandarins spoke reassuringly of the British 'punching above our weight' and the vital importance of the Churchill-hallowed 'special relationship'. In practice this meant sharing intelligence with the Pentagon and CIA, the intertwining of nuclear strategy, large US bases on British soil, the leasing of British bases to America, and a posture towards American presidents that is nearer that of salaried adviser than independent ally.

For there was another reason for Britain's new dependency politics. The country was broke. Attlee's government had little time to contemplate all this. The military and economic weaknesses of the country were tested with devilish symmetry just a fortnight after the new government was formed. On 14 August 1945, eight days after the atomic bombing of Hiroshima and five after the attack on Nagasaki, Japan surrendered. A week after that President Truman reached across and briskly placed his signature on a paper ending the wartime Lend-Lease agreement with Britain and other countries. Lend-Lease, which dated from 1941, had allowed the US government to lend, sell, lease and give countries fighting Germany and Japan whatever they thought was needed. Britain was by far the largest recipient, getting more than $30bn of the $50bn spent. She had become dependent on the huge pipeline of aid, and not only for fighting. About a fifth of people's food needs came from America. When the pipeline was suddenly cut off, and a bill presented for whatever was still being used, it was brutal cold turkey indeed. Truman, acting in strict accordance with American law, stopped Lend-Lease without warning his allies and without, it seems, realizing the implications of what he was doing.

The effect on Attlee's new government was instant. Britain did not have enough dollars left to feed the country. Nor was there any way to earn the money quickly. The shattered economy was exporting only around a fifth of what it had before the war, yet non-military imports were five times higher than in 1938. In the words of one historian Britain had by now declined into 'a warrior satellite of the United States, dependent for life on American subsidies' and had, by waging total war, destroyed the basis of her economy on which she had flourished for the previous hundred years. Through the war years America had been open-handed but Britain, fighting also to prevent a German victory which would have threatened the global influence of the United States, spent proportionately far more of her energy on the common struggle. The official historians of the wartime economy, writing in the dark post-war years, allowed their feelings to show: 'In a war allegedly governed by the concept of the pooling of resources among Allies, the British had taken upon themselves a sacrifice so disproportionate as to jeopardise their economic survival as a nation.'[4]

In his memoirs Truman said he had learned the lesson from his signature of the ending of Lend-Lease 'that I must always know what is in the documents I sign'. But the economic crisis which the action caused in Britain in many ways served American interests. At the time, with the victory celebrations a recent memory and patriotic films pouring from the British cinema industry, pessimism about the future would have seemed outlandish to most people, a kind of moral treason. This after all was the Britain of – to quote Labour's 1945 election manifesto – 'scientists and technicians who have produced radiolocation [radar], jet propulsion, penicillin and the Mulberry Harbours', the Britain whose Empire had mostly survived, the Britain occupying swathes of Germany and Italy, the Britain whose leaders sat with those of the new superpowers, apparently shaping the world.

The historian Correlli Barnett summarized the situation with brutal clarity: the post-war British people had 'the psychology of the victor although their material circumstances approximated more to those of a loser'.[5] That was a perception gaining ground in Whitehall at the time, where they had the figures. In August 1945, the economist John Maynard Keynes told Attlee that the country 'is virtually bankrupt and the economic basis for the hopes of the people non-existent'.

Attlee's cabinet duly sent Keynes, the world's most famous economist, to Washington to get help. What followed was as important in the history of modern Britain as any minor war to be fought in the decades to come. As beggar, Keynes may not have been a good choice. He was over-optimistic about his powers of persuasion, indeed startlingly arrogant, a trait not unknown among Bloomsbury intellectuals. He sailed off assuring Attlee that he believed he could get a free gift of some $6bn from the Americans, a large proportion of what was left in the Federal Reserve. Once in Washington, he ran into a stodgy defensive line of conservative bankers, bolstered by public opinion which was 60 per cent against giving the British a loan, never mind a gift. Keynes responded by dazzling but also irritating the American negotiators with wit, high-minded arguments and occasional mockery. One US banker retorted, 'He is too brilliant to be persuasive with us Americans ... how many trust him? How many will accept his sales talk? No one.' Up against Keynes, who arrived ill via a troopship to Canada, was William Clayton, a gangling cotton manufacturer from Texas, and Fred Vinson, a former professional basketball player and lawyer. For four solid months, based in his Washington hotel and supported by the British ambassador Lord Halifax, Keynes haggled and chiselled. Keynes's biographer said this of their marathon argument: 'The Kentucky lawyer and the Bloomsbury intellectual were like chalk and cheese ... Vinson and Clayton were no match for Keynes in argument. But they always held the whip-hand. It was a case of brains pitted against power.'[6]

London had a completely unrealistic notion of what might be won. Attlee's cabinet refused the early US offers and held out, vainly, for better ones. Keynes, ill with a heart complaint and surviving on icepacks and sodium amytal capsules through a sweltering autumn, was trapped by the exuberance of his earlier self-confidence. He described the mood as 'absolute hell'. The core of the trouble was

16

that the Americans did not quite believe how broke the British Empire really was. Nor did they much care. Powerful players in Washington may have been sentimental about the common struggle that had just ended but were unsentimental about empires and the new world that must now be built. This was not a game of equal players. Every time the British turned down an American offer, the next offer was worse. An angry Keynes wrote back to his mother: 'They mean us no harm but their minds are so small, their prospects so restricted, their knowledge so inadequate, their obstinacy so boundless and their legal pedantries so infuriating. May it never fall to me to *persuade* anyone to do what I want, with so few cards in my hand ... I am beginning to use up my physical reserves.'[7]

Eventually, though the effort would contribute to his death early the following year, Keynes's hoped-for gift or interest-free loan of around $6bn had shrunk to a 50-year loan of $3.75bn, at 2 per cent interest. In addition, the Americans required that within a year of the loan starting, pounds should be freely exchangeable for dollars, so removing a traditional protective wall from London. Alongside British agreement for the new Washington-dominated international financial system, this placed the country firmly under the economic control of the United States, which through the later forties and early fifties would also be steadily advancing into former British markets round the world. It was a moment of truth for the country as stark as the fall of Singapore, or Dunkirk. The loan was not finally paid off until 2006, well into Tony Blair's time at

Number Ten. So part of the story of post-war Britain was set. The new financial system made future financial crises inevitable and they duly followed under Attlee, Eden, Macmillan, Wilson and Callaghan. Each time, Britain's weak economy meant another 'run on the pound' as the world, and particularly the United States, sold Sterling, causing inflation and a slump in investment. Neither the starkness of the crisis nor the inevitable long-term repercussions were ever fully grasped by the country. This was the moment when the British government could have honestly explained to the people how grave the country's situation really was.

Instead, Attlee and his ministers hid their dismay about the underlying weakness of Britain's hand – the brutal treatment of Lord Keynes in Washington and, later, the equally brutal repudiation of Britain's claim to nuclear cooperation. War-trained, and proud, they put on a good face. The new Chancellor, Hugh Dalton, claimed that he valued the settlement 'very highly' and instructed MPs to 'welcome' it. *The Economist,* generally the most pro-American British publication, retorted: 'We are not compelled to say we like it. Our present needs are the direct consequence of the fact that we fought earlier, that we fought longest, and that we fought hardest.' But in Parliament, after the devastating events of the past few years, it seemed there was little energy left for outrage or debate.

One action was taken immediately. Within months of the end of the war the characteristic sounds of the Royal Navy changed. The thunder of guns and the pounding of turbines gave way to a great clanging, from Portsmouth to the Clyde, a smashing of hammers and hissing of flame, the thud

18

and the sparks of destruction as, one by one, the great ships were destroyed. By 1946, when the Russians were beginning to build an even bigger surface and submarine fleet than they had had during their 'Great Patriotic War', 840 British warships had already been struck off the Navy List, and a further 727 in various stages of construction had been abruptly cancelled.[8] By the time the new Admiral of the Fleet, Lord Fraser, took over in 1948 a total of 10 battleships, 20 cruisers, 37 aircraft carriers, 60 destroyers and 80 corvettes had been sent to the scrapheap. This was an extraordinary rate of destruction. Fraser, who had worked with the US Navy in the Pacific and survived a kamikaze attack and who therefore understood the need for modernization, now had to deal with a demoralized and stunned Royal Navy. Battleships whose names read like a history lesson – *Nelson, Rodney, Valiant* – were broken up. New battleships and aircraft carriers whose names read like an optimistic prospectus for a revived empire, which had been ordered to project British power around the world into the sixties, ships such as *Lion, Malta, New Zealand, Eagle, Gibraltar* and *Africa,* were abruptly cancelled. Britain's very last battleship, HMS *Vanguard,* was completed on the Clyde. Too late for the war, she survived to take the King and future Queen Elizabeth to South Africa for an unsuccessful Commonwealth-boosting trip, and then functioned as a training ship before she too was towed away and broken up.[9] Ninety British warships were towed out to sea and used for target practice until they broke up and sank. Hundreds more were taken to the breakers' yards and painstakingly disassembled back into piles of torn, rust-softened steel.

Some were sold to small countries which had hardly had navies before. The US Navy had proved that aircraft carriers were an indispensable part of modern global war, but Britain could afford only a few, relatively small ones. So one British carrier was given to the French as a free loan until they could pay for her. Another was loaned to the Dutch and two were offloaded at half price to the Australians. The inaptly named *Terrible* ended as an uncompleted hulk sitting in the Gare Loch, near Glasgow. Some smaller ships were 'mothballed' – shrouded with nets, which were then sprayed with plastic and treated with electrolysis to stop their bottoms rotting. Initially, seagulls proved worryingly keen to eat the plastic. Meanwhile, inside their cocoons, the ships' poor-quality wartime steel rotted anyway.[10] Vessels which had protected the convoys which helped keep Stalin's Russia fighting, or shepherded food and fuel convoys across the Atlantic, or had rescued the British army from Dunkirk, or which had been in at the kill in the Pacific, ships whose names went back to Nelson's navy and whose captains came from West Country families which could trace their service just as far – almost all of them went, and very quickly. This is little remembered. It is as if the nation engaged in a giant act of smashing, the quiet murder of its nautical self, out of sight, out of mind. Of the 880,000 men and women serving in the Royal Navy towards the end of the war, nearly 700,000 had left two years later.

The admirals fought back. 'If we are to hold our world position, we must maintain our sea power,' said the Admiralty. Using an argument already hopelessly out of date, the deputy director of naval planning, Captain Godfrey French, protested that a force of two major fleets, with battleships and carriers, was vital to sustain the British Empire's status as 'a first class power'. Battleships, he said, were needed to counter the Soviet fleet and, in the future, rather more bizarrely, the French. The Labour government was not impressed. Attlee argued forcefully that Britain was no longer America's rival on the high seas and could not maintain large fleets. Hugh Dalton, his Chancellor, ordered the dockyards to give up the electricians and woodworkers he needed for the post-war home-building programme. By 1948 the defence statement said that it was necessary for manpower to be brought down as quickly as possible, even though this meant 'a degree of disorganisation and immobility'. Naval campaigners in the Commons were horrified to discover that the Home Fleet was down to a single cruiser and a few lesser ships.

Reports came into the Admiralty of 'strangely apathetic crews' and occasions of 'outright disobedience'. In time, of course, the navy readjusted to a far smaller role, particularly once the nuclear deterrent was based in its submarines, not on the RAF's airfields. But finally, the 336-year history of the Admiralty itself ended, when it was swallowed up by the Ministry of Defence. On 31 March 1964 the Queen saved a salary by becoming her own Lord Admiral. The Admiralty's historian expresses institutional hurt as eloquently as it can be told:

No department of state survived so long,

through so many metamorphoses and vicissitudes, as the Admiralty. When most of the great departments of state were born, it was already ancient ... Monarchs and dynasties, statesmen and ministers, came and went, the tides of war and revolution washed over and around, constantly altering but never submerging the Admiralty, and it survived them all, counter, original, spare and strange to the last.[11]

It was the last act in the ruthless liquidation of the organization that had been central to British identity for as long as Britain had been a single nation.

Falling behind in military technology and without the strength to keep hold of her empire, the Royal Navy's time had gone. What might have happened without the extremity of the financial crisis after the American cancellation of Lend-Lease is unknowable. The government's failure to involve the country in the full grimness of the situation was made more palatable two years later with the generous American Marshall Plan aid, as Washington finally realized how far Soviet Communism might advance over bankrupt and demoralized Western European nations. Britain got the largest share of that, and the immediate crisis eased. The Marshall Plan helped put all Europe back on its feet. It is still remembered as Washington's 'most unsordid act'.

Optimism about the British economy's ability to export its way back to health returned. There was a great national drive for more exports at the expense of consumption at home. The post-war world, in which so many industrial countries had been devastated, was starved of goods, so it was not hard to find export markets, even for outdated British cars and unsuitable British clothing. But the politicians' habit of embarrassed deception about how things really stood would continue. Successive British prime ministers treated the country's weakness as a personal failing which could be hushed up.

A Meeting of Remarkable Men

Keynes's deal bought Labour time. Yet the Attlee government was not well prepared to use it. In London in 1945 there was nobody with experience of how to take over and then organize a peacetime economy. Ministers agreed that central planning was the way to create a more efficient economy but the way British administration was structured made efficiency a distant dream. There was a vast sprawl of overlapping Whitehall committees which meant slow decision-making and fudged choices. By one count the Attlee administration employed just ten fully qualified economists – and this from a government which promised 'rule by experts'. It is often and rightly said that the problems Labour had to grapple with were awesome and so they were – the demolished housing and the archaic economy, the demand for swift Indian independence, the crises in Palestine and Greece, the need to demobilize so many people, the danger of starvation on continental Europe and the need for some kind of new world order, even as the first

23

intimations of the Cold War began. But the eventual failure of New Jerusalem's architects and orators, remarkable men and women that they were, was also caused by their inability to agree what it was they really wanted to do.

The people who took charge of Britain in 1945 were as mixed a bag as any democratic government has seen. First comes Attlee himself, the model of suburban Pooter, speaking so little and so tersely it drove everyone around him mad. He was the butt of some often retold Churchillian insults: 'an empty taxi drew up at the House of Commons, and Attlee got out' (though Churchill later denied that one) and 'a modest little man with much to be modest about'. Yet if Churchill had been formed by imperial dreams and his grand family history, Attlee was just as determined a product of Edwardian England. He had merely taken a different course, good works and mean streets, not cavalry charges and country houses. His father was a hard-working lawyer of advanced Liberal views. He grew up surrounded by prayers and poetry. After his rough public school, Haileybury near Hertford, he studied law but was diverted by the chance of being asked to help out at the Haileybury boys' club in the sooty, impoverished east London borough of Stepney. He stayed and eventually joined the Independent Labour Party. Never a great speaker he was a dogsbody and organizer, cutting up bread for children, helping suffragettes, distributing leaflets and carrying banners on marches. After brave service in the First World War, he returned as Major Attlee and threw himself into London politics again, becoming Mayor of Stepney and then an MP. He became

Labour leader in 1935 almost by accident. There were so few other plausible candidates in the wake of Labour's shattering election defeat of four years earlier, he was almost the last plausible leader left standing – a stopgap.

He would become the most effective stopgap in British political history. No intellectual, he was a man who held things together, the ultimate chairman. He was reassuring, thoroughly English, addicted to the *Times* crossword, cricket and as fond of his old public school as Churchill was of his. Before the war he had steered the Labour Party towards moderation and away from pacifism. During the war he tolerated Churchill's long-winded egotism and quietly directed the civilian ministries. After it he became the watchful ringmaster for elephantine egos roaring and bellowing around him. He was never a charismatic character – one sympathetic historian judges him to have had 'all the presence of a gerbil'[12] – but that was part of his attraction. He defended himself against the charge that he was too moderate, quietly insisting that practical measures to boost employment, share resources fairly and plan the economy were as socialist and radical as any revolutionary could wish. Yet he was weak on economics, and when his cabinet was arguing over deep practical problems, such as the troubled programme for steel nationalization, he had a tendency to pull back and let ministers struggle without his support. He had shafts of clear analytical insight, into Britain's overstretched military commitments, and the importance of house-building. But his analysis of domestic change, above all what nationalization was really meant to achieve, was pretty thin.

He did not offer the cheering-up that ministers sometimes require and his put-downs became legendary. When one hapless minister was summoned to be sacked and asked, appalled, what on earth he had done wrong, Attlee looked up, pulled out his pipe and remarked, 'Not up to the job.' Interviewed at the start of the 1951 election campaign, he told the journalist just that he hoped to win and now was off to a committee meeting. The interview finished thus: 'Interviewer: Is there anything else you'd like to say about the coming election? Attlee: No.'[13] This was an entirely characteristic exchange and there are literally hundreds of similar examples. Yet despite all this, Attlee has gone down as a great man, loved for his limitations, not despite them. He was a staunch believer in the monarchy and if he had misgivings about the class system he rarely voiced them. His political conservatism is well described in a touching limerick he wrote long after losing office. Though he embodied the opposite of spin, sleaze, self-importance or swank, he did allow himself a famous pat on the back:

> Few thought he was even a starter
> There were many who thought themselves smarter
> But he ended PM
> CH and OM
> An earl and a knight of the Garter.

What is touching about this is, of course, that it could equally well have been written by a hostile satirist. Clement Attlee was a strange mix of radical and paternalist; he would have made a good Liberal reformer under Gladstone. Yet half a century on, he was the right man for the time. Wartime magnifies some personalities. Similarly, peace discovers its own people. Attlee was the chairman of the peace party, but what about the rest?

There were the class rebels. Sir Stafford Cripps was an intensely religious vegetarian, brilliant lawyer and sometime Marxist. Obstinate, politically naive and worryingly convinced that he was, at any given time, doing God's work, he was the most controversial upper-class socialist until the heyday of Tony Benn. In the thirties Cripps had fallen under the spell of the charismatic leader of Britain's Communists, Harry Pollitt. A colleague said of him that he started to go wild in 1931. Then stimulated by attacks from the Tory press 'and by eager cheers from our own lunatic fringe, he went wilder and wilder'.[14] He had advocated emergency powers to deal with the coming 'capitalist dictatorship' and zigzagged over whether rearmament would be a betrayal of the workers. In 1939 he was thrown out of the Labour Party for advocating a Popular Front with the Communists. Yet a year later the same Cripps was sent as Churchill's special envoy to the real Communists in Moscow. He was brought into the war cabinet, then put in charge of aircraft production, sent to negotiate the end of British rule in India and by the end of 1947 was Chancellor – a job he performed with great grit, patriotism and determination. It was about as strange a change as any in natural history. Throughout the war, as a former rebel, he was not even in the Labour Party but was already famous for his rimless glasses, regime of cold baths and doctrinaire views. He got the Churchill treatment too, famously in the cutting remark, 'There but for the grace of God, goes God.' In ruder mood, Churchill was said to have been approached while in the toilet by an official, knocking on the door and nervously insisting that Cripps, then Lord Privy Seal, needed to see him immediately. The Prime Minister is said to have replied: 'Tell Sir Stafford I am in the lavatory and can only deal with one shit at a time.'[15] He may have been affected by rumours that Cripps was plotting to replace him, the war being at a low ebb then; Cripps would later go on to suggest to Attlee that he too should quit as Prime Minister but was quickly bought off.

Then there was the loud, haw-hawing Hugh Dalton, a useful reminder of how small and interwoven Britain's political class was in the middle of the twentieth century. He was the son of the canon at Windsor, a clergyman so ferocious he was said to have terrified even Queen Victoria. He tutored the King-Emperor, George V. His son, George VI, loathed Dalton and begged Attlee not to make him Foreign Secretary. This was probably a service to the nation because of the extreme nature of Dalton's anti-German feelings but the King saw merely Dalton as a turncoat, an Etonian who rebelled against his class and monarch. Dalton had started out as a Tory and switched, partly as an act of rebellion against his father. He was sexually repressed and easily depressed. The poet Rupert Brooke had been one of those he adored. 'My love', he said much later, 'is the Labour movement and the best of the young men in it'. Beyond anything,

28

though, Dalton loved conspiracies. As Chancellor he paused on his way to deliver the crucial 1947 Budget and told a lobby correspondent some of its key points, allowing a London paper, the *Star,* to scoop his speech. This indiscretion – in Dalton's customary ear-splitting whisper – led instantly to his resignation, a blow from which he never really recovered. But Dalton had had a difficult and unsettling day until he leaked the Budget, having just come from unpleasant and confrontational talks at the Palace about how much money Philip and Elizabeth, the new Royal couple, should get from the Civil List. Perhaps he simply saw the journalist concerned – a man he knew very well – as the first friendly face of his day.

The silent, anti-intellectual Attlee, the Christian ex-Marxist Cripps and the confused Dalton do not sound like the core of a coherent vision for the new Britain of 1945. But alongside them were some remarkable figures who had known rather more of life at the coalface. Attlee apart, nobody was as important in the new government as the hulking figure of Ernest Bevin, the most influential man British trade unionism has ever produced. Orphaned at eight, 'Ernie' began as a Somerset labourer and worked his way up to become the organizer of dockworkers, until in 1921 he helped merge those men into the new Transport and General Workers' Union. A powerful figure in the General Strike, he ran the union until he was brought into the Churchill cabinet in 1940, a parliamentary seat being hurriedly found for him in Wandsworth. As the most powerful trade union leader of the inter-war years, Bevin was a passionate anti-Communist and a patriot who believed 'my boys' in the T & G were the very best of Britain. In the wartime government he had almost dictatorial powers to direct workers into factories, mines and fields. If total war consisted in gathering together a country's total human and physical resources and then directing them at the enemy, Bevin was the Great Director. Described by one newspaper of the time as 'a bad mixer, a good hater, respected by all', he could be rude enough, even to Stalin who once hilariously whined that Mr Bevin was 'no gentleman'.

In the post-war government Bevin ruled almost in alliance with Attlee, both of them describing the other in fond, almost devoted terms. Attlee called it 'the deepest relationship of my political life'. Bevin chortled about Attlee, after he had shrewdly seen off another attempted coup against the Prime Minister, 'I love the little man.' After cabinet meetings, they would stay on together, charting the government's course. He always mistrusted intellectuals, particularly socialist ones. Reportedly, when he bumped into the famous Kingsley Martin, editor of the *New Statesman,* after the 1945 victory celebration, he greeted him: 'Ullo gloomy, I give you about three weeks before you stab us all in the back.' When Bevin died right at the end of the Attlee years, the loss was more than symbolic. He was probably the only person who could have stopped the party splitting over the rows which engulfed it because of the Korean War and military expenditure, but by then he was too sick to help.

His achievements as Foreign Secretary were enormous and controversial. The North Atlantic Treaty Organization, NATO, founded in 1949, depended on America's military power to provide a shield against Stalin for the shattered European democracies. Something like it would have happened, given the United States' growing fear of Soviet expansion, but the timing, precise form of the treaty and its basic principles owed a lot to Bevin. In 1948 he began calling in private letters for 'an Atlantic approaches pact of mutual assistance'. Its purpose was clear: 'to consolidate the West against Soviet infiltration and at the same time inspire the Soviet government with enough respect for the West to remove temptation from them and so ensure a long period of peace.'[16] And so it would be. Now, it all seems inevitable but at the time Bevin was particularly clear about the nature of the Soviet threat and withstood a storm of bitter attack from the USSR and its allies at home. More than a hundred Labour MPs abstained when the Commons voted first on NATO, and only a year before Bevin's first proposal Cripps, for instance, had been telling officials that 'we must be ready at any moment to switch over our friendship from the US to Russia.'

Bevin is less happily remembered for his role in the bitter arguments and fighting that led to the creation of the state of Israel. Most unfairly, he is still traduced as an anti-Semite. He had in fact been numbered as a friend of Zionism during the war, until faced with the impossible contradictions in Britain's position in the Middle East afterwards. There, the UK was both in charge of Palestine under international mandate, and had wider links to surrounding Arab countries. British officers ran the Jordanian Arab Legion, one of the instruments of Arab anger against Jewish migration; yet British officials were in charge of the Jewish homeland too. There is no doubt that the desperate migrations of Jewish refugees were handled very badly by Britain, determined to try to limit the settlement to a level that might be acceptable to Palestinian Arabs. The worst example was the turning-round of a refugee-crammed ship, *Exodus,* as she tried to land 4,500 people in 1947, and the eventual return of most of them to a camp in Hamburg, an act which caused Britain to be reviled around the world. This was followed by the kidnap and murder of two British soldiers by the Irgun terrorist group, which then booby-trapped their bodies. But Bevin was pressed very hard by the United States, which wanted far larger migration, and his instinct for a limited two-state solution now seems sensible. The British forces in Palestine were entirely ill equipped for the guerrilla and terrorist campaign launched against them by Jewish groups; in the circumstances of the later forties, Bevin's position was entirely impossible. It is worth recalling, if only for a bleak balance, that Bevin was reviled by Arab opinion as vigorously as by Jewish opinion.

The key to Bevin, from NATO to directing the British fight against Communist insurgents in Greece, was that he believed in liberty as essential to the building of a fair society. He believed in a welfare system to keep the wolf from the door, and full employment for unionized workers, which could be delivered by taking some of the economy into public ownership. Because of his huge wartime powers, he was a great believer in the State. He once told some American correspondents that he believed it was possible to have public ownership and liberty: 'I don't believe the two things are inconsistent ... If I believed the development of socialism meant the absolute crushing of liberty, then I should plump for liberty because the advance of human development depends entirely on the right to think, to speak, and to use reason, and allow what I call the upsurge to come from the bottom to reach the top.'[17] He was a wonderful man, on a huge scale. He had faults too, of course: he was as easily entranced by the old Britain of smooth mandarins and Palace receptions as anyone.

This was not, on the whole, the weakness of the next of the extraordinary men who made up the 1945 government. Aneurin, or Nye, Bevan was wild, rebellious, radical, and above all, Welsh. Not since the days of Charles James Fox, champion of the French Revolution, had the British public been confronted by a minister as divisive and flamboyant as Bevan. Like Bevin, he had been a trade union leader. Born in Tredegar in South Wales into a mining family, he too was largely self-taught, in his case mopping up thrillers and Marx in workmen's libraries and at college in London. Like Bevin, he had been an excellent organizer during the 1926 General Strike. But there the comparisons between the two near-namesakes end. After entering Parliament a few years later, Bevan established himself as one of the few truly great orators of the time, rare in being a worthy opponent of Churchill – who Bevan described as 'suffering from petrified adolescence'. Unlike Attlee, Cripps, Bevin or Dalton, he had been outside the wartime coalition government and on many issues had seemed like a one-man opposition to it. Partly because of this, he had a far fiercer attitude to the Tories than his colleagues, and a clearer determination that Labour must build a completely new world. The nationalization and public control of almost the whole economy was his aim.

Nye Bevan spoke for the grassroots of the Labour Party, the people who expected a genuine socialist takeover of Britain. He did not believe there could be any compromise between capitalism and 'democracy'. The Commons was 'an elaborate conspiracy to prevent the real clash of opinion which exists outside from finding an appropriate echo within its walls. It is a social shock absorber placed between privilege and the pressure of popular discontent.'[18] Unlike most of the other leading figures, Bevan was, at least in theory, dangerous to the established order, even if in office he would turn out to be shrewder and subtler than his ranting public performances suggested. People prejudiced against him often came away from a first meeting seduced and bewitched. Like Bevin, he showed that a trade unionist could turn into a successful national leader. Unlike Bevin he had a vision of what Britain ought to become which went far beyond better pay and free spectacles. He would eventually be destroyed by the hard choices and compromises ahead, resigning when spending cuts were needed and dividing himself from most of his natural supporters over the issue of nuclear weapons. Beautifully dressed, witty, sibilant, wide-ranging, sarcastic, poetic and at times very alarming indeed, Nye Bevan represented everything that the old upper classes most feared after the 1945 election.

The final great shaper of post-war Labour Britain is Peter Mandelson's grandfather. Herbert

Morrison was a Cockney policeman's son, the third working-class boy to set against the Labour 'aristocrats'. Like Gordon Brown he was blind in one eye and an obsessive reader. He started out working in a shop, weighing out the tea and sugar. His devotion to politics took him up through the London party machine until he eventually became the minister in the first Labour government, responsible for the capital's early integrated transport system. Had he not lost his seat in 1931 he would probably have become leader instead of Attlee (and hence Prime Minister), a loss he never ceased to regret. Instead he went on to become the first Labour leader of the London County Council and the most prominent voice of the rising new class of public servants, small traders, teachers and shopkeepers who would become key to Labour's successes. This meant that he was a moderate – enough of a moderate for the young Tory MP Harold Macmillan to suggest that he lead a new Centre Party in the late thirties. None of this, and his long career as an organizer and fixer, endeared him to the romantics in the party. Nor was he exciting. He lived a quiet suburban life with a quiet wife he rarely spoke about and pootered around in a small car. Michael Foot described him as a 'soft-hearted suburban Stalin'. In government Morrison was responsible for directing the astonishing torrent of legislation – seventy bills in the first year alone. He was not, however, a great economic planner and was far too obsessed with his reputation in the press, keeping great piles of cuttings to complain about when he met editors. He was also, like his grandson, a rotten intriguer, the boy always spotted and called to the front of the class the minute he starts whispering. Yet he was popular, passionate about his voters and hugely admired by Labour members. Had Morrison become Prime Minister, he might have been a good one.

Patriots First, Socialists Second

These were the six men who set Britain on its post-war course, a chaotic platoon, sentimental, reactionary, revolutionary, patriotic, moderate and extreme all at once. A small book could be devoted just to the disobliging things they said about each other. They believed in a socialist society but few of them seemed able to agree in detail what that meant – whether widespread nationalization was really needed, what should be done about the public schools, whether rationing was basically a good thing or a bad thing. Marching behind them was an equally divided crowd of intellectual socialists, practical middle-class people who believed in planning, trade unionists who thought it was time for the workers to get their share, and a few committed Marxists. And behind them, watching, there were millions of Labour voters who merely hoped for a better life. This meant, in practice, welfare plus nationalization, a consolidation and extension of the wartime directed economy and the 'fair shares' of the previous few years. Labour would apply the lessons of the war to the peace. After so many later disappointments it is hard to recapture quite the sense of hope that was clearly present in the mid-forties. Nor is it easy to recall how openly and passionately proud of Britain people were.

This was a government of patriots first and socialists second. In this Attlee set the tone. The historian Peter Hennessy said of him that he was 'certainly the most understated and, perhaps the most deeply, almost narrowly, English figure ever to have occupied Number Ten'. Bevin, rooted in his union and its members, ran Attlee close. He had a deep understanding of British political history and his predecessors in government, as the American Secretary of State Dean Acheson later recalled:

> He talked of them as slightly older people whom he knew with affectionate respect. In listening to him, one felt strongly the continuity and integrity of English history … 'Last night', he said to me, 'I was reading some papers of Old Salisbury. Y'know, 'e had a lot of sense.' 'Old Palmerston' too came in for frequent and sometimes wistful mention … With George III he was very companionable. When sherry was brought in, he would twist around to look at the portrait. 'Let's drink to him,' he would say. 'If 'e 'adn't been so stoopid, you wouldn't 'ave been strong enough come to our rescue in the war …'[19]

Like Dalton, Bevin hated the Germans and thought little of the Russians and, though no imperialist, profoundly believed that Britain should take a lead role in the post-war world. The rulers of post-war Britain were far keener on the Empire than one might expect of socialists. While Attlee was sceptical about the need for a large British force in the Middle East, his government thought it right to maintain a massive presence sprawling across it, in order to protect both the sea-route to Asia and the oilfields Britain worked and depended on. Restlessly active in Baghdad and Tehran, Britain controlled Gibraltar, Malta, Cyprus and, at the tip of the Red Sea, the world's second-busiest port after New York, Aden. Throughout the forties and fifties, British conscripts and professional soldiers baked and sweated to little purpose in garrisons which bled the British Treasury. When they finally went home, they left behind an unstable, unhappy part of the world, with borders like wounds scored across it.

When it came to Indian independence the whole government agreed there was no holding back. Beyond that, the Labour ministers felt strong kinship with Canadians, Australians and New Zealanders and assumed that most of the African colonies were decades away from self-government. They were dubious about European integration, above all because it might compromise Britain's freedom to set her own political destiny. Attlee, in characteristically terse mode, later explained his feelings about Western Europe coming together: 'The so-called Common Market of six nations. Know them all well. Very recently this country spent a great deal of blood and treasure rescuing four of 'em from attacks by the other two.' Herbert Morrison, for his part, declared that the new socialist government of Britain was 'friends of the jolly old Empire; we are going to stick to it'.

Such views were widely shared. The left dreamed of a distinctly British socialism which would in turn become a beacon to other nations, a fantasy almost imperial in its ambitious assumption. It falls oddly on the ear now but it touched great writers such as George Orwell, fine journalists like the young Michael Foot and many idealistic Labour footsoldiers. Virtually all the Labour family, from Attlee to the radicals at *Tribune* believed that the Empire should be eventually be turned into a free association of democratic countries; but they assumed this could become the basis for a different kind of British power. The sterling area of countries using the pound included about 1,000 million people and was therefore seen by Whitehall as roughly equivalent to the areas of the world under American influence. There was talk of a new Commonwealth airways system, linking the social democratic worldwide web of the future. (An echo of this lost dream can be found in the writings of the fantasy novelist Michael Moorcock, who speculated about a liberal, anti-racist British commonwealth linked by huge fleets of airships.)

The question was how aggressively socialist was the government's post-war agenda to be? After 1940, many local Labour branches had wanted to retain robust party politics in pursuit of class war. Even as the German armies drilled on the coast of Normandy, the Labour conference had a unanimous motion sent to it from the Halifax branch calling for a negotiated peace with Germany because this would be less disastrous 'for the workers' than a military victory 'by this or any other capitalist government'.[20] Such sentiments were mostly squashed by the mood of national crisis, but there was a lively debate about what should happen after the war which could not be subdued. The centrist PEP (Political and Economic Planning) pressure group said with evident pleasure that wartime conditions 'have already compelled us to make sure, not only that the rich do not consume too much, but that others get enough ... new measures for improving the housing, welfare and transport of the workers ... the end of mass unemployment.' In the debate about the country's war aims in 1940, the generally understated Attlee complained that while the Germans were fighting 'a revolutionary war for very definite objectives' Britain was fighting a conservative war: 'We must put forward a positive and revolutionary aim admitting that the old order has collapsed and asking people to fight for the new order' – a view much modified by the time he came to power. But he was not alone in 1940 in thinking that the stronger government needed for fighting total war could usefully lead a peacetime revolution afterwards. As the *New Statesman* put it, 'We cannot actually achieve socialism during the war, but we can institute a whole series of Government controls which after the war can be used for Socialist ends.'

For Labour, there had been no conflict between the inspiring story of an old nation rallied against Hitler, and the rational organization of a future society; they were the same thing. As Orwell had written in 1941, in a famous essay describing England as a family with the wrong members in control, 'This war, unless we are defeated, will wipe out most of the existing class privileges. There are every day fewer people who wish them to continue.' But it would not become Russianized or Germanized: 'The Stock Exchange will be pulled down, the horse plough will give way to the tractor, the country houses will be turned into children's holiday camps, the Eton and Harrow match will be forgotten, but England will still be England, an everlasting animal ...'[21] Orwell put it far more beautifully and persuasively than most others and of course the Stock Exchange, the Eton match and the country houses survived. But his dream of a third way, building on British parliamentary traditions, plus a national instinct for restraint and fair play to make a new kind of socialist society, unknown in Russia or elsewhere, was widely shared among Labour supporters.

A vision of Britain as an almost ungoverned, self-regulating place, whose people got on with their lives without interference, had survived from the eighteenth century, through Victorian liberalism to the instincts of many of the National government politicians of the thirties. But by 1945, in a Britain of identity cards, ration books, regulations and high taxation, it seemed to be dead. The mood was for big government, digging deep into people's lives to improve them. Yet the extraordinary thing was that, within a couple of years, Attlee's 'peacetime revolution' had lost momentum too. The optimism shrivelled under economic and physical storms, and though much of the Attlee legacy survived for decades, it was nothing like the social transformation Labour socialists had hoped for.

In Deepest Secret

On the morning of 11 December 1941 over the Gulf of Siam, a stretch of sea between Malaya and Vietnam, a single Japanese torpedo-bomber flew out of the cloudless sky. Piloted by Lieutenant Iki, it dipped down towards the waves and dropped not a bomb but a single wreath of leaves and flowers, left floating amid the oil stains and debris. Nothing like this would happen again in the bloody Far East war. The wreath was a rare sign of Japanese respect for nearly a thousand dead British sailors, blown to pieces or drowned when two great warships, the 'unsinkable' new *Prince of Wales* and the rather more elderly *Repulse,* had gone to the bottom in less than two hours, thanks to brilliantly precise and lethal torpedo attacks by the Japanese. The defeat had shocked Britain and plunged Churchill into despair. These ships were, in the words of one naval historian, 'symbols of the men and nation that had dominated the sea lanes of the Pacific since the days of Anson and Cook'.[22] The fall of Singapore, the psychological death-blow to the British Empire and the single worst defeat in the war for British forces, followed swiftly. But Lt Iki's gallant action was not simply a tribute to the sunken ships, the Royal Navy generally, or even to that expiring British Empire the Japanese had long admired. It was also a tribute to an Aberdeenshire aristocrat, William Francis Forbes, the Master of Semphill.

Semphill is one of those Britons forgotten here, remembered over there. He had been a pioneer aviator who served in the Royal Flying Corps in the

First World War and made a once-famous early solo flight to Australia. When the two warships were sunk he was serving with Britain's Fleet Air Arm. A child of the British Establishment, the son of an aide to George V, Semphill would live on until 1965, honoured as a veteran of air warfare. So why the Japanese wreath? A quick inspection of the honours Semphill received after the war would have turned up the Order of the Rising Sun. The fact was that Semphill can be blamed or credited for some of Japan's awesome skill in destroying warships with torpedo-carrying aircraft, not only off Malaya but at Pearl Harbor. He had been sent to Japan on a British mission in the twenties to help build the Japanese naval air force, teaching the latest torpedo bombing techniques and advising on the design of aircraft carriers. Another British engineer had obligingly helped design one of the aircraft, which eventually developed into the feared Mitsubishi Zero. Semphill was impressed by the determination of the Japanese pilots and was thanked by the then Japanese Prime Minister who called his work 'almost epoch-making'. By 1942 it certainly was. When Semphill had trained his Japanese friends the two countries were linked by a treaty of friendship. More recently it has been revealed that Semphill went on to spy for the Japanese as well. He was not a one-off, nor was the passing over of a vital technology from Britain a rare event. Repeatedly in the past century Britain was involved in the early development of a breakthrough in military or industrial thinking which went straight to enemies or rivals who developed it further and used it better. The sinking of those battleships should have caused even more soul-searching than it did.

43

In the early years of the twentieth century the Royal Navy had been well ahead of the Germans, Americans and French in developing a modern submarine with guided torpedoes, despite the objection of one admiral who found it 'underhanded, unfair and damned un-English'. The Second Sea Lord, Jack Fisher, a brilliant, restless, terrifying man, widely rumoured to be half-Asiatic himself, pressed ahead. Yet it was Germany, first under the Kaiser and then under Hitler, which developed the U-boat to its logical and lethal conclusion, coming very close to starving Britain into submission in both world wars. Again, it was a Royal Navy engineer and a British company, Fosters, who produced the first workable tank in 1915 (they were originally called 'landships' but to keep their purpose secret, factory workers in Lincoln were told they were mobile water-tanks for the desert and this was shortened to simply, tank). Yet it was the Germans who turned the tank two decades later into an instrument of a new kind of warfare, by which time British tanks were comparatively outdated. As Semphill demonstrated, Britain had also once been ahead with torpedo-attack aircraft. In the mid-forties Britain was far advanced with jet engines, too. But again and again, deploying the new idea, actually getting it to work, was something that foreigners seemed better at.

The greatest example of all is the atomic bomb. We now know that Hitler's scientists were working hard on this new doomsday weapon, and hoped to test it as early as 1944. Scientists from Italy, France and Hungary were struggling with the physics throughout the thirties. The anguished private warning of Albeit Einstein to President Roosevelt in a letter of 1939 about 'extremely powerful bombs of a new type' has gone down in history. Less well known is the work of two émigré scientists a year later in a laboratory at Birmingham University. Otto Frisch and Rudolf Peierls were working on the effects of using the isotope uranium 235 for a nuclear weapon. They made the theoretical breakthrough for building an effective bomb and in 1940 hurriedly typed out a memo for the British government, an obscure paper which has been described as one of the most significant documents of the century. The government, as governments will do, set up a committee of scientists and military advisers and reported back that 'the scheme for a uranium bomb is practicable and likely to lead to decisive results in the war'. This was shrewd enough. Thanks to Hitler's persecution of the Jews Britain had the know-how to get ahead of Germany. But this was the year when the Blitz was at its height and the threat of invasion very real. Britain's economy was already vastly overstretched. The huge effort needed to create a nuclear industry, to turn the mathematics into metal, was beyond the country's technical and economic strength. So the news about the bomb was passed to the Americans. Out in the New Mexico desert, they soon leapt ahead. A new world order would swiftly follow.

For a short while after the war it looked as if Britain would stay out of the nuclear race, which seemed to the Attlee government expensive and difficult. Key ministers argued against trying to join it. Had Ernest Bevin, Britain's post-war Foreign Secretary, not been a prickly patriot, perhaps Britain would have stayed non-nuclear. But after being patronized by his American opposite number, Bevin told his colleagues that he wanted no British Foreign Secretary to be treated that way again. It was a matter of national status, said Ernie. 'We've got to have this thing over here, whatever it costs. We've got to have the bloody Union Jack on top of it.'[23] This was an agonizing struggle, far harder than was admitted. Churchill had had a private wartime deal with President Roosevelt. Both countries would seek the other's permission before using nuclear weapons. Information would be shared. Britain would not develop civil nuclear power without Washington's agreement. This was effectively torn up by the Americans in 1946 with the McMahon Act, which prohibited the sharing of nuclear information or technology. When Attlee tried to revive nuclear cooperation after the war, the White House ignored his letter and the US copy of the secret Churchill–Roosevelt agreement was conveniently lost in the wrong file. A few years after that early breakthrough by the refugees in Birmingham, Britain was far behind the Americans, without access to their work.

The decision to develop the first A-bombs had been a secret even from Churchill in opposition, who later told the Commons: 'I was not aware until I took office that not only had the Socialist Government made the atomic bomb as a matter of research, but that they had created at the expense of scores of millions of pounds the important plant necessary for its regular production.' Though private assessments of the threat posed by the Soviet Union were drawn up within months of the end of the war, right from the start in the cabinet committee papers there is the curious and unmistakeable fact that the Soviet menace is rarely at the top of the argument about the British bomb. It is all about the Americans. First, in the Bevin years, it is about status and old-fashioned bulldog pride.

Then it becomes a matter of global strategy, something needed as leverage to influence US policy. Answering the appeal of the defeated Admiralty after the war, the mandarins bluntly admitted: 'The UK has ceased to be a first-class power in material terms. The United States and Russia already far outstrip us in population and material wealth, and both have vast untapped resources. Canada, India and China, to name only three ... in time will certainly outstrip us.' But, they pointed out, the much more powerful hydrogen bomb was transforming the military situation around the world: 'If we possess these weapons, the Americans will be prepared to pay attention to our opinions in a way they would otherwise not. The same applies to our standing in the eyes of other countries, such as Germany. And our lesser potential enemies, such as Egypt, will feel that we might, if pushed too far, use nuclear weapons against them.' 'These', concluded the mandarins rather chillingly, 'are great advantages ... '[24]

From early on, Whitehall intelligence reports to ministers identified the peril of war being triggered by a pre-emptive strike from America, hitting the Russians, before they had devised their own nuclear systems at a level which would allow them to properly retaliate. With British troops on the vulnerable front line in Germany, Britain would be thrown into the midst of the new war for which she was not prepared. Persuading the Americans to stay their hand might be easier, the British policy-makers suggested, if Britain was herself an independent nuclear power. In the summer of 1947 work began in deepest secret to build a plutonium-producing plant at Windscale, a little place on the coast of Cumbria, and work started on designing a bomb under the guidance of one of the British scientists who had been at Los Alamos, William Penney. A few years later, the tiny Berkshire village of Aldermaston, with its twelfth-century church, brick labourers' cottages and ancient Roman defences, which had been looking forward to quieter times with the closure of an airbase, was chosen as the site for Britain's nuclear weapons programme. More money spent on defence and status was of course less money available for a New Jerusalem.

A Winter Landscape

The winter of 1947 has gone down in history and personal memory as a time of almost unendurable bleakness. For three months, Britain seemed more like one of the grimmer scenes in a medieval Flemish painting. It was not only the shortages of almost everything in the shops, and what was described as a virtual peasant diet, heavily based on potatoes and bread – though by then even the bread had now been rationed, and potatoes ran short. It was not only the huge state bureaucracy still interfering in so much daily life, controlling everything from how long you could turn your heater on, to what plays you could see and whether or not you could leave the country. It was not the 25,000 regulations and orders never seen in peacetime before, administered by a government which though anti-Communist, still urged people to learn from the 'colossal' industrial achievements of Soviet Communism.[25] It was not the smashed and broken homes. It was not even all those war dead – for this war had involved far fewer soldiers than the First World War, and far fewer dead – 256,000 as against nearly a million, as well as the 60,000 British civilians who had died in air-raids. Relief at the final victory was still strong across the country, and pride in Britain's part in it. No, the crisis of 1947 was set off by that most humdrum of British complaints – the weather.

At the end of January with an efficiency the Red Army could not have mustered, a great freeze had swept across from Siberia and covered the country in thick snow, a bitter cold which brought the exhausted British very nearly to their knobbly, ill-clad knees. The country still ran on coal. But at the pits, the great piles of coal froze solid and could not be moved. The winding-gears ceased to function. Drifting snow blocked roads and closed the rail lines. At the power stations, the remaining coal stocks ran swiftly down until, one by one, power stations began to close. Lights flickered off. Men dug through snowdrifts, tramping for miles to find food to carry back to their neighbours and homes. Cars were marooned on exposed roads. With shortages of power, factories across the South and Midlands of England had to stop work and within a week two million people were idle. Attlee suspended that still unusual middle-class diversion, television. Much worse, electric fires were banned for three hours each morning and two each afternoon.[26] Everywhere, people shivered, wrapped in blankets in front of barely smoking coal fires, or those rationed electric ones. Around London, commuters were completely unable to reach the capital. Scotland was cut off from the rest of the country. Then things deteriorated further. It was the coldest February for 300 years. Another half million people had to stop work. One young office worker from Slough, Maggie Joy Blunt, recorded herself sitting in her house, the water in washbasins frozen, looking out at the ice-blue sky: 'I am wearing thick woollen vest, rubber roll-on, wool panties, stockings, thick long-sleeved wool sweater, slacks, jacket, scarf and two pairs of woollen socks – I am just about comfortable.'[27] The sun was so little seen that when it came out briefly, a man rushed to photograph the reassuring sight for the newspapers. Green vegetables ran out in the shops. 'CHRIST IT'S BLEEDING COLD' howled the future novelist Kingsley Amis to the poet Philip Larkin, from his Oxford student rooms.

After a short thaw March had brought terrible storms and snowdrifts thirty feet high. People talked about snowflakes the size of five-shilling coins. There were ice-floes off the East Anglian coast. Three hundred main roads were unusable. Still to come were the worst floods in memory, cutting off towns, inundating huge areas of low-lying England, and destroying the crops in the fields. On the hills the sheep were dying. Their carcasses would be piled into pyres, causing foul-smelling smoke to hang over rural Wales, a precursor to the foot-and-mouth and BSE episodes of later decades. It was, in short, about as near as this country has been to experiencing at first hand a truly Siberian winter, though without the sturdy boots, furs and vodka that help the Russians get through. It would be followed by the real political storm – the run on the pound made inevitable by the Keynes deal in Washington, and a balance of payments crisis. As people were digging out frozen vegetables from fields and despairing of the empty shops, the Treasury was finally running out of dollars to buy help from overseas. This was the moment when the optimism of 1945 shivered and died among many voters.

Summer did come, as summer does, and it was a good summer. The sun shone, cricketers blazed away at Lords and a nation sweltered. Economically, though, Hugh Dalton's year of misery continued. The clauses negotiated by Keynes insisting that sterling should become freely convertible to American dollars were triggered, and the inevitable happened. The world rushed to change pounds into greenbacks, and such was the outflow that convertibility had to be hurriedly stopped. The economy was simply too weak – a message that echoed round continental Europe's finance ministries too. British housewives might have been more worried still had they known of a secret plan during the sterling crisis drawn up by the civil servant Otto Clarke (father of the later New Labour minister Charles Clarke). With Britain running out of dollars to buy food from America, Clarke drew up preparations for a 'famine food programme', including taking children out of school to help in the fields.[28] It never came to that but the rationing of bread, which had not been necessary during the war was now in place. There was not enough cash left to buy wheat supplies from the United States, yet British ministers had to ensure there was no actual famine in other parts of the world for which they were responsible, including India and defeated Germany.

The answer, bread rationing at home, was hugely unpopular and long remembered. Along with the sterling crisis and the subsequent devaluation of 1949, a further but necessary humiliation, it gave Churchill's Tories the essential ammunition they needed to turn Attlee out. Their manifesto would later remind voters that 'In 1945, the Socialists promised that their methods of planning and nationalization would make the people of Britain masters of their economic destiny. Nothing could be more untrue. Every forecast has proved grossly over-optimistic. Every crisis has caught them unawares. The Fuel Crisis cost the country £200 millions and the Convertibility Crisis as much.'

The next year, though, the government did try to cheer the country up, holding the 1948 London Olympics. Cost over-runs were trivial. Security was barely an issue. The games were a triumph of determination in a war-scarred, rubble-strewn city, during which the athletes were put up in old army camps and hospitals, and the Union Jack was missing for the opening parade. And though the medal toll for British competitors was very meagre, holding the games was a genuine sign that Britain was back. For all its weaknesses, this was still a country that could organize itself pretty well.

The Sun Also Sets

The deep nostalgic vision of Empire was dented too in 1947. The King ceased to be Emperor. The jewel in the imperial crown, India, was moving towards independence long before the war. Gandhi's brilliant insight that through non-violence the British could be embarrassed out of India more effectively than they could be shot out, had paid off handsomely in the inter-war years. London was dragged to the negotiating table despite the attempts by Churchill and others to scupper every deal from the thirties to the late forties. The war delayed independence but showed how much goodwill there was on the subcontinent, if Britain was wise enough to withdraw gracefully. During the conflict some two million Indians fought on Britain's side or served her forces directly, their contributions being particularly strong in the campaigns in North Africa against the Italians and defeating a pro-German regime in Iraq. Gandhi himself was sentimentally fond of Britain and saddened by the Luftwaffe attacks on London. While Nehru was in prison, he kept a picture of his old school, Harrow, in his cell.

Yet many Indians had become frustrated by endless delays and the watering-down of plans for more autonomy. Leaders out of jail organized a massive wartime protest involving the burning of police stations, the beating of British residents, the cutting of telegraph lines and the blowing up of a railway line. For a while, British control of India hung in the balance, though the true story of what was happening was kept out of newspapers at home. Less dangerous if more spectacular, was the formation of an anti-British Indian National Army under Subhas Chandra Bose, armed and supported by the Japanese. Indians were used to guard captured British troops, a humiliation designed to spread the Japanese line that this was essentially a war of Asian people against colonial Westerners. When the pro-Japanese Indians returned home after the defeat of Japan, Britain wanted them prosecuted as traitors but they were greeted as heroes by Gandhi's Congress Party.

As soon as Attlee took power, his government organized talks on withdrawal. Anti-imperialism had been a genuine strand in Labour thinking since the party's formation, but now there were other motives too. There was gratitude for Indian support for the Empire at its worst moment. There was also fear – the clear evidence that delaying independence would result in mass and probably uncontrollable protest. Attlee wanted a united, independent India, Muslims and Hindus in one vast state connected by trade and military agreement with Britain. Apart from anything else, he believed this would function as a major anti-communist bulwark in Asia, at just the time when the Russians were looking south and China was in revolutionary turmoil.

Attlee would get some of what he wanted, but not all. Sir Stafford Cripps led the first Labour delegation to post-war India but it was not socialist politicians who negotiated the end of British control in India. That job was begun by Field Marshal Wavell, a veteran of the Boer and First World Wars who had served with the Czarist

Russians before fighting the Italians (successfully) and Rommel (less so) in the desert. He had come to India as commander-in-chief just ahead of the most decisive Japanese advances, and had succeeded as Viceroy in time to free the Congress leaders from prison. But this poetry-loving and mildly pessimistic soldier was unsuccessful in trying to reconcile Hindus and Muslims. Sectarian mobs began to attack one another, the first flickers of the communal violence which would soon ravage the subcontinent. Early in 1946 there was a major mutiny by the Royal Indian Navy, when about a quarter of its strength aboard ships off Bombay, Calcutta and Madras raised Congress flags. It was put down, with hundreds dead, but trouble spread to the Royal Indian Air Force and the police, and it looked as if authority was finally crumbling. Wavell's last-ditch plan involved British withdrawal without any political agreement, evacuating whites from the country and handing it over to local state governments. This was regarded in London as likely to lead to civil war and fundamentally dishonourable.

Attlee passed the job to Lord Louis Mountbatten, who had been supreme commander in South-East Asia, organizing the reconquest of Burma. It was a wily choice. Mountbatten was a member of the Royal Family and his nephew, a naval officer, Prince Philip of Greece, was about to marry the young Princess Elizabeth, so he was a hard man for the imperialists at home to attack. Dashing and arrogant, he shared Attlee's determination to get a swift deal with the leaders of the Muslim and Hindu peoples, which meant with Mohammed Ali Jinnah's Muslim League and

Nehru's Congress Party. Jinnah was always hard for the British to deal with or like, and was by now close to death; but Nehru proved an easy partner, forming a famously close attachment to Mountbatten's wife, Edwina. Partitioning the subcontinent was by now inevitable. Muslims would not accept overall Hindu domination and yet across most of India the Hindus or Sikhs were in the majority. British India was duly split into Muslim Pakistan (a made-up name, an anagram of Punjab, Afghania, Kashmir, Sind and Baluchistan, the key provinces) and Hindu-dominated India. The line was drawn up by a British lawyer, Sir Cyril Radcliffe, and kept secret until after the handover of power.

Mountbatten announced to widespread surprise and shock that independence would happen ten months earlier than planned, on 15 August 1947. Churchill was so appalled that his former Foreign Secretary and friend Anthony Eden had to keep him away from the chamber of the Commons. Having listened to the parliamentary statement, Enoch Powell was shattered enough to wander the streets of London all night, squatting in doorways with his head in his hands. No doubt millions of other British people felt equally that their familiar world was coming apart. And while the speed of British withdrawal may have been a political necessity, the consequences were appalling. By some counts a million people then died, many of them women and children as Muslims and Hindus caught on the wrong side of the new border fled from their homes. Sikhs rose against the Muslims in the Punjab, Muslims drove out Hindus. Rather as in Yugoslavia after the collapse of Communism, it turned out that the old central power had merely frozen and held in suspension older religious and ethnic rivalries which revived at a moment of crisis. As some 55,000 British civilians returned home, the Indian Army was hurriedly divided into two. Mountbatten had hoped for a close military alliance to continue and Karachi had even been earmarked as a base for British atomic bombers to use in attacking Russia. But no military deal could be agreed. Eventually, Pakistan broke up, with Bangladesh declaring herself independent, and succumbed to a history of coup and dictatorship. Today India and Pakistan face each other with nuclear weapons and large armies across their Kashmiri frontier.

Britons have been told that as compared to the war in Algeria which tore post-war France apart, or the Americans' desperate war in Vietnam, Britain managed decolonization rather well. It is too comfortable a conclusion. Who was to blame for the horrifying number of Indian deaths – far more, for instance, than have died during the mayhem in Iraq? British post-war weakness probably meant that it would have been impossible to impose a single state at the time of independence. Yet Jinnah's Muslim League and Congress had been nearer to a mature deal before the war; had Churchill and others not stymied independence in the thirties by cynically supporting the cause of the semi-independent Indian princes, then perhaps the slaughter would have been averted. Against that, the story of the Second World War would have been very different too. And today's India, linked by English and a growing democratic superpower, stands as one of the more successful of Britain's old imperial possessions. Indian independence was a trauma to some, a relief to many more.

Labour ministers were less enthusiastic about dismantling the Empire in Africa. Officials wrote minutes to Attlee's ministers informing them it might take many generations before some of the colonies were ready for independence. Herbert Morrison, the deputy leader of the Labour Party, agreed. He said that to give the African colonies their freedom would be 'like giving a child of ten a latch-key, a bank account and a shotgun'. Attlee himself speculated about creating a British African army, on the lines of the lost Indian one, to help project British power around the world. The Colonial Office described Africa as the core of Britain's new world position, from where she could draw economic and military strength. In the early fifties, the Colonial Office itself grew in numbers and was even hoping for a large new headquarters opposite Parliament Square, promised to it by Churchill. There was a grand scheme for growing groundnuts in Tanganyika, to provide cheap vegetable oil for Britain – though that was a swift and embarrassing failure. For a while it seemed that the Raj would be transplanted, in fragmented form, to Africa.

White People

Back in the mother country in 1947, who were those people who were just beginning to adjust to a post-imperial world? They were sparser and whiter. In the years after the war Britain contained about ten million fewer inhabitants than live here today. The thirties had seen a fall in the birthrate and there was much official worry about another kind of national shrinkage. In William Beveridge's famous 1942 report launching the modern Welfare State, he suggested that a bit of fast breeding was needed: 'with its present rate of reproduction, the British race cannot continue.' To Beveridge and his generation 'the British race' meant white natives of these islands. Before the war, around 95 per cent of people in Britain had been born here, and the other 5 per cent was mostly made up of white English and Scots whose parents had happened to be serving the Empire in India, Africa or the Middle East when they were bom. There were black and Asian people in Britain but very few. In the thirties the Indian community numbered perhaps 8,000 at most – a tenth of them doctors, intriguingly – and there were a few Indian restaurants and grocery stores in the biggest cities. There had been a tiny West Indian presence. No detailed surveys were done, but there were at most a few thousand, many of them students. Black sailors and mixed-race Lascars, along with Chinese, had been settled in dockland areas of Liverpool, Cardiff, Bristol and London for a long time. Again, though, the numbers were small.

During the war, men from the Caribbean began to arrive, serving with the British forces. There was a Jamaica Squadron and a Trinidad Squadron in the RAF and a West Indian Regiment in the British Army. Others came to work in factories, in the countryside and on radar stations. But once the war was over, most were sent straight home leaving an estimated permanent non-white population of about 30,000. It had been the 130,000 black American troops who made the most impact on British public opinion during the war. Despite official worries about 'fraternization' with coloured soldiers, they were widely welcomed and lionized. There are well-attested incidents of white GIs who tried to apply the American colour bar being mocked and challenged.[29] After the war, almost unnoticed by the general public and passed in response to Canadian fears about the lack of free migration around the Empire, the 1948 British Nationality Act dramatically changed the scene. It declared that all subjects of the King had British citizenship. This gave some 800 million people around the world the right to enter the UK. Though it seems extraordinary now after so many decades of new restrictions on immigration, this was uncontroversial at the time for a simple reason – it was generally assumed that black and Asian subjects of the King would have no means or desire to travel to live in uncomfortable, crowded Britain. Travel remained expensive and slow. Why would they want to come, anyway? Until the fifties so few black or Asian people had settled in Britain that they were often treated as local celebrities and officially it was not even considered worth while trying to count their numbers.[30]

There were other immigrant communities. A Jewish presence had been important for a long time, in retailing, the food business and banking – everything from Marks & Spencer to Rothschild's Bank. But in the five years before the war, some 60,000 more Jews from Germany and Eastern Europe arrived here, many of them highly qualified, helping transform the scientific, musical and intellectual life of forties Britain. When Hitler came to power in 1933 it was agreed at cabinet level to try 'to secure for this country prominent Jews who were being expelled from Germany and who had achieved distinction' in science, medicine, music and art. Beveridge himself helped set up an organization to help Jewish refugees, the Academic Assistance Council, which, using public donations, helped 2,600 intellectuals escape. No fewer than twenty of them later won Nobel prizes, fifty-four were elected Fellows of the Royal Society, and ten were knighted for their academic brilliance.[31] In their invasion plans for 1940, the German SS reckoned the Jewish population of Britain to be above 300,000, and hugely influential.

Then there were the Irish, a big group in British life after a century of steady immigration, the vast majority of it from the south. It continued through the war, despite government restrictions, as Irish people came over to fill the labour shortage left by mobilization. Ireland's stony neutrality and her expression of sympathy at Hitler's death at the end of the war, had made Eire very unpopular with the British. Popular prejudice against the Irish continued, as it always had, and would for a long time to come. Yet none of this seemed to affect immigration, which carried on at a great rate through the forties and fifties, running at between 30,000 and 60,000 during any given year. Whenever cabinet committees turned to the issue of migration, the Irish were excluded from debate because they were regarded as effectively indigenous. There were other more exotic groups. By the end of the war, Britain was home to 120,000 Poles who had fled the Soviets and Nazis, many of them then serving in the British forces, notably the RAF. Most chose to stay on and by the end of 1948, with the energetic help of government settlement officers, 65,000 had jobs, in everything from coal-mining to factory work. Similar tales can be told of Czechs and many other nationalities. All these, of course, were white.

It would be wrong to portray Britain in the forties as relaxed about race. Despite the horror of the concentration camps, widely advertised in the immediate aftermath of the war, anti-Semitism was still present. The assumption that 'they' dodged queues or somehow got the best of scarce and rationed goods, erupts from diaries and letters of the time. After Jewish terrorist attacks on British servicemen in Palestine in 1947, there were anti-Jewish disturbances in several British cities, including attacks on shops and even the burning of a synagogue, mimicking the actions of Nazis in the thirties. More widely, trade unions were quick to express bitter hostility to outsiders coming to take British jobs – whether they be European Jews, Irish, Poles, Czechs or Maltese. The government itself spoke without self-consciousness or embarrassment about the central importance of 'the British race'.[32] The multilingual, multi-hued Britain of today, with its greengrocers selling baskets of yams and its scents of turmeric and incense, in which more than 90 per cent of us do not think you have to be white to be properly British, would have left a visitor from the immediate post-war years utterly astonished. Then, Jews and passing American servicemen apart, the composition of the country in 1945 was not much different from late medieval times.

62

Proper Drains and Class Distinction

Patriotic pride cemented a sense of being one people, one race, with one common history and fate. But to be British in the forties was to be profoundly divided from many of your fellow subjects by class. By most estimates, a good 60 per cent of the nation was composed of the traditional working class – that is, they were factory workers, agricultural labourers, navvies on the roads, riveters, miners, fishermen, servants or laundrywomen, people in a thousand trades, using their muscles; and all their dependents. The workers were paid in cash, weekly – cheque-books were a sign of affluence. People did not move, much. War aside, most would spend all their lives in their home town or village, though the thirties had produced modest migrations such as from industrial Scotland and Wales to the English Home Counties. The sharp sense of class distinction came from where you lived, how you spoke; and it defined what entertainments you might enjoy. The war had softened class differences a little and produced the first rumblings of the coming cultural revolution. Men and women from widely different backgrounds found themselves jumbled together in the services. On the home front, middle-class women worked in factories, public schoolboys went down the mines and many working-class women had their first experiences of life beyond the sink and the street. In uniform or in factories, working-class or lower middle-class men could find themselves ordering former well-spoken toffs around. 'Blimps' – the older, more pompous upper-class officers – became a butt of popular humour, a symbol of dying old Britain.

With skill shortages and a national drive for exports, wages rose after the war. The trade unions were powerful and self-confident, particularly when the new Labour government repealed the laws that had hampered them ever since the General Strike of 1926. Three years after the war, they achieved their highest ever level of support. More than 45 per cent of people who could theoretically belong to one, did so, and there were some 8.8 million union members. In other European countries at this time, trade unions were fiercely political, communist, socialist or Roman Catholic. In Britain, they were not. The Communist Party, deprived of any real part of parliamentary politics, spent much of its energy and money building support inside the unions, and was beginning to win elections for key posts, but in general British trade unionism remained more narrowly focused on the immediate cash-and-hours agenda of its members. This did not mean British trade unions were quiet. Because so many of their most experienced and older shop stewards and organizers had effectively gone to work for the government during the war, or had joined up to fight, a new generation of younger, more hot-headed shop stewards, men in their twenties or even teens, had taken control of many workplaces. The seeds of the great British trade union battles of later decades were sown and watered during the forties.

The core of the old working class which had depended for jobs on coal, steel and heavy manufacturing would eventually have a grim time as these industries first struggled, and then failed, in the decades to come. But this was not obvious after the war. The shipyards of the Clyde, Belfast and the Tyne were hard at work, the coalfields were at full stretch, London was still an industrial city, and the car-making and light engineering areas of the West Midlands were on the edge of a time of unprecedented prosperity. We were a nation of brick terraces. It was not until the next two decades that many of the traditional working-class areas of British cities would be replaced by high-rise flats or sprawling new council estates. The first generation of working-class children to get to university was now at school, larger and healthier than their parents, enjoying the dental care and spectacles provided by the young National Health Service. But for the most part working-class life was remarkably similar to working-class life in the thirties. No televisions, cars, foreign holidays, fitted kitchens, foreign food, service sector jobs had yet impinged on most people's lives. Politicians assumed most people would stay put and continue to do roughly the same sort of job as they had done before the war. Rent acts and planning directives were the tools of ministers who assumed that the future of industry would be like its past, only more so – more ships, more coal, more cars, more factories.

The class who would do best out of the wartime changes was be the middle class, a fast growing minority. Government bureaucracy had grown hugely and would continue to do so. Labour's Welfare State would require hundreds of thousands of new white-collar jobs, administering national insurance, teaching, running the health service. Even the Colonial Office vastly expanded its staff as the colonies disappeared, giving one of its officials, C. Northcote Parkinson, the idea for 'Parkinson's Law' – that work expands to fill the time available. Studies of social mobility, such as the major one carried out in 1949, are notoriously crude and have to be taken with a pinch of salt. But they suggest that while working-class sons generally followed their fathers into similar jobs, there was much more variation among middle-class children. Labour might have intended to help the workers first, but education reform was helping more middle-class children get a good grammar school education. A steadily growing number stayed at school until fifteen, then eighteen.

So, perceptibly, the old distinctions were softening. The culture was a little more democratic. Increasing numbers would make it to university too, an extra 30,000 a year by 1950. The accents of Birmingham and Wales, the West Country and Liverpool would challenge the earlier linguistic stamp of middle-class respectability. The culture of public radio would bring literature and music to much wider audiences; the post-war humour of Tommy Handley and *Round the Home* would be as enjoyed by the suburbs as by the palaces. Churchill himself had told Harrow schoolboys that one effect of the war was to diminish class differences. Sounding almost like a New Labour politician, he said to them as early as 1940 that 'the advantages and privileges that have hitherto been enjoyed by the few shall be far more widely shared by the many.'

The Old Order

But not quite yet. The ruling class was still the ruling class. Despite the variety of the 1945 cabinet, Britain in the forties and fifties was a society run mostly by cliques and groups of friends who had first met at public schools and Oxbridge. Public school education remained the key for anyone hoping to make a career in the City, the Civil Service or the higher echelons of the Army. Schools such as Eton, Harrow and Winchester might educate only some 5 per cent of the population, but they still provided the majority of political leaders, including many of Labour's post-war cabinet. Parliamentary exchanges of the period are full of in-jokes about who was a Wykehamist and who an Etonian. Briefly, it had seemed such schools would not even survive the war: boarding schools had been in enough of a financial crisis for some to face closure through bankruptcy. Churchill's own Harrow was one, along with Marlborough and Lancing, though all struggled on. More generally there was a belief that public schools had contributed to failures of leadership in the thirties and right up to the early defeats of the war. When the Tory minister R. A. Butler took on the job of education reform during the war, he contemplated abolishing them and folding them all into a single state school system. Had that happened, post-war Britain would have been a very different country. But Butler, intimidated by Churchill, backed off. A watered-down scheme would have seen Eton and the rest obliged to take working-class and middle-class children, paid for by the local authorities, but this quickly fizzled out too. The public schools stayed. Attlee, devoted to his old school, had no appetite for abolition. Grammar schools were seen as a way of getting bright working-class or middle-class children to Oxbridge, and a few other universities, so that they could buttress the ruling cliques. One civil servant described the official view as being that children were divided into three kinds: 'It was sort of Platonic. There were golden children, silver children and iron children.'[33]

The problem for the old ruling order was whether the arrival of a socialist government was a brief and unwelcome interruption, which could be sat out, or whether it was the beginning of a calm but implacable revolution. The immediate post-war period with its very high taxation was a final blow for many landowners. Great country houses like Knole and Stourhead had to be passed over to the National Trust. It was hardly a revolutionary seizure of estates, yet to some it felt that way. Tradition was being nationalized, with barely a thank-you. In 1947 the magazine *Country Life* protested bitterly that the aristocratic families had been responsible for civilization in Britain: 'It has been one of the services of those currently termed the privileged class, to whom, with strange absence of elementary good manners, it is the fashion not to say so much as a thank you when appropriating that which they have contributed to England.' Evelyn Waugh, an *arriviste* rather than a proper toff, sitting in his fine house in the Gloucestershire village of Stinchcombe, straggled with the dilemma. In November 1946 he considered fleeing England for

Ireland (many richer people did leave Britain in the post-war years, though more often for Australia, Africa or America). Why go? Waugh asked himself. 'The certainty that England as a great power is done for, that the loss of possessions [he is talking of the colonies], the claim of the English proletariat to be a privileged race, sloth and envy, must produce increasing poverty ... this time the cutting down will start at the top until only a proletariat and a bureaucracy survive.'

A day later, however, he was having second thoughts. 'What is there to worry me here in Stinchcombe? I have a beautiful house furnished exactly to my taste; servants enough, wine in the cellar. The villagers are friendly and respectful; neighbours leave me alone. I send my children to the schools I please. Apart from taxation and rationing, government interference is negligible.' Yet the world felt as if it was changing somehow. Why, he wonders, is he not at ease? Why does he smell 'the reek of the Displaced Persons Camp'?[34] Many more felt just the same; Noël Coward said immediately after Labour's 1945 win, 'I always felt that England would be bloody uncomfortable in the immediate post-war period, and it is now almost a certainty.'[35] These shivery intimations of change would have some substance, though it would happen more slowly and have little to do with Attlee or Bevan. The old British class system, though it retained a medieval, timeless air, much exploited by novelists, depended in practical terms on the Empire and a global authority Britain was just about to lose. 'Disgusted of Tunbridge Wells' would soon become shorthand for the returnees from Malaya or Rhodesia. A pervasive air of grievance and abandonment would hang about the right of British politics for decades.

Meanwhile, old society events like the 'Varsity' rugby match, the Boat Race, the Henley Regatta and Ascot, quickly returned after the war and indeed reached the height of their popularity. Young Conservative dances were where the better-off went to find partners. The most famous actors and actresses were able to carry on a lavish lifestyle, hidden from the taxman. London clubland carried on almost as in the twenties. The capital's grandest restaurants, some which are still going, such as the Savoy Grill and the Ivy, were again crowded with peers, theatrical impresarios, exiled royalty and visiting American movie stars. In the upper-class diaries of the day there are complaints about a rising tide of 'common' behaviour, the end of good taste and the regrettable influence of Americans and Jews.

Under Attlee, Britain remained a country of private clubs and cliques, ancient or ancient-seeming privileges, rituals and hierarchies. In the workplace, there was a return to something like the relationships of pre-war times, with employers' organizations assuming their old authority and influence, at least some of the time, in Whitehall. Inside the new nationalized industries the same sort of people continued to manage and the same 'us and them' relationships reasserted themselves remarkably easily. In the City, venerable, commanding merchant bankers with famous names would be treated like little gods; stiff collars, top hats and the uniforms of the medieval livery companies were still seen, even among the grey ruins of post-Blitz London; younger bankers and accountants deferred utterly to their elders. Newspaper owners would sweep up to their offices in chauffeured Rolls-Royce cars and be met by saluting doormen. *The Times* was soon full of advertisements for maids and other servants. Lessons in speaking 'the King's English' were given to aspiring actors and broadcasters; much debate was had about the proper way to pour tea, refer to the lavatory and lay the table. Physicians in hospitals swept into the wards, followed by trains of awed, indeed frightened, junior doctors. At Oxford colleges, formal dinners were compulsory, as was full academic dress, and the tenured professors hobbled round their quads as if little had changed since Edwardian times. All of this was considered somehow the essence of Britain, or at least of England.

Gnasher George and his Girls

So too was the last grand monarchy in Europe, the only remnant of the extended family of former German princelings which had once enjoyed power from Siberia to Berlin, Athens to Edinburgh. After the national trauma of the Abdication crisis, George VI had established a reassuringly pedestrian image for the family which now called itself simply the Windsors. In private the King expressed fiercely right-wing views, falling into rages or 'gnashes' at the pronouncements of socialist ministers. In public he was a diffident patriarch, much loved for his tongue-tied stoicism during the Blitz, when Buckingham Palace received several direct hits. There had been cautious signs of Royal modernization, with Princess Elizabeth being used to make patriotic radio broadcasts and later joining the ATS, photographed in battledress and even mingling anonymously with the crowds on VE Day. The King and Queen, though, ran what was in all essentials an Edwardian Court well into the fifties. Every March teenage virgin girls from aristocratic or merely wealthy families would be presented to the Queen wearing three ostrich feathers in their hair. Then they would begin 'The Season', a marathon four-month round of balls and dinners during which, it was hoped, they would find a suitable man to marry. These debutantes would often have been sent to 'finishing school' in Switzerland where they would have learned how to walk properly, speak French and run a household according to the old manner. The Royal presentation dated back to 1780 and would eventually be ended by the Queen in 1958: Prince Philip opined that it was 'bloody daft' while Princess Margaret complained: 'We had to put a stop to it. Every tart in London was getting in.' It continued at a nearby hotel where, in eccentric British fashion, the girls still arrived to curtsy to a six-foot-tall birthday cake, rather than the monarch.[36]

Initially, it was unclear how well the monarchy itself would fare in post-war Britain. The leading members of the family were popular and Labour ministers were careful never to express any republicanism in public – indeed, there is almost no sign of it in their private diaries either – but there were many Labour MPs pressing for a less expensive, stripped down, more contemporary monarchy, on Scandinavian lines. Difficult negotiations took place over the amount of money provided by cash-strapped taxpayers. Yet the Windsors triumphed as they would again, with an exuberant display which cheered up many of their tired, drab subjects. The wedding of the future Queen Elizabeth and the then Lieutenant Philip Mountbatten in 1947 was planned as a public spectacle. Royal weddings had not been so organized in the past. This was an explosion of colour and pageantry in a Britain that had seen little of either for ten years, a nostalgic return to luxury. Presents ranging from racehorses to cigarette cases were publicly displayed, grand cakes made and a wedding dress by Norman Hartnell created out of clinging ivory silk 'trailed with jasmine, smilax, seringa, and rose-like blossoms,' encrusted with pearls and crystals.

There had been interesting arguments before the wedding about patriotism, complaints about the silk having come from Chinese worms, and a rather over-effusive insistence on Philip's essential Britishness. The nephew of Lord Mountbatten was sold to the public as 'thoroughly English by upbringing' despite his being an exiled Greek prince, a member of the Greek Orthodox Church, and having many German relatives. In the event, Philip's three surviving sisters were not invited to the wedding, all of them being married to Germans. He showed himself wryly prepared to accept all this, though he was reported to have annoyed the King by curtsying to him at Balmoral when he saw him wearing a kilt.[37] The wedding was a radio event, still, rather than a television one, though newsreel films of it packed out cinemas around the world, including in devastated Berlin. In its lavishness and optimism, it was an act of British propaganda and celebration for bleak times, sending out the message that despite everything Britain was back. The wedding and the later Coronation reminded the club of European royalty how few of them had survived as rulers into the post-war world. Dusty uniforms and slightly dirty tiaras worn by exiles were much in evidence: the Queen's younger sister Princess Margaret remarked that 'people who had been starving in little garrets all over Europe suddenly reappeared'.

The Look of the Forties

History is mostly written about wars and politics and then, after that, about the lives of people as expressed through schools, employment and so on. Outside official history are the lives we actually lead, more marked by births, love affairs, illnesses, deaths, friendships and coincidences, than by public events. Those are the personal histories depicted in novels, films and poems. But something is missing, because we also live surrounded by stuff – rooms, chairs, plates, curtains, bags of pasta, bowls, televisions, and beyond that, offices, shopping centres, roads cluttered with signs, adverts and cars – all of which changes constantly and colours or shapes the world in which our smaller histories happen. For the consumer society, changing brands and ads are the scents which suddenly bring back a moment in childhood or later: we walk through life marking it off with a new rug, or the tune for a drinks commercial.

In the forties, there were far fewer brands and a glaring insufficiency of 'stuff'. There was a shortage of furniture, cups, plates, lights, curtains, towels, bicycles, radios – you name it, you couldn't find it. The famous brands from before the war, whether for soap, cooking materials, clothes or cars, were rather desperately still reminding people that they would return, as soon as possible. There was a natural tug back to the lost world of pre-war Britain, the designs and flavours people had been familiar with – art deco moulds from ten years earlier were pressed back into manufacturing service; old pot and pan designs were given a lick of cheerful paint and put back on sale; the vacuum cleaners and toasters which did arrive in shops had a sturdy, clunky, almost defiantly ugly look. But there was a strong push in the other direction, towards a new Britain that would look and feel brighter, cleaner, more rational, more open. This was partly driven by politics. Ministers wanted the slums replaced by airy communal housing and schools which would be three-dimensional expressions of a less fusty, cluttered nation. Labour believed in the public sphere and in planning; that meant straight lines and big spaces. In these years, public housing far outpaced private housing; and taste followed the money.

Changes in technology and the shortages of traditional materials like wood after the war drove architects and designers to express those political beliefs through brick and concrete, steel-framed windows and flat roofs. The prefab homes being hastily built in former aircraft factories may have been a stop-gap, but something about their simplicity chimed with the mood; it was the coming, cut-price British version of the modernist architecture, sculpted from the new concrete and steel-rod systems developed on the continent before the war, and brought here by refugee, generally left-wing, architects. But what would go into these flats and houses? The designer Robin Ray, a key figure at the time, noted that the Council of Industrial Design had been formed in 1944, but its power remained until the early fifties, partly because of tax incentives: 'We naively felt that modern town planning and enlightened design of buildings and products would transform the environment and enhance the lives of people. Progress was made in many areas, helped by the socialist government.'[38]

This meant a stream of new-looking furniture, fabrics, crockery and rugs designed to fill the new-looking homes. There was not a surplus of much after the war, but there were surpluses of materials intended for warplanes or landing-craft, or indeed troops. So perspex, developed for gun-turrets in bombers, was tried out for table tops and even women's shoes. Royal Air Force uniform material was dyed green or brown and used to cover sofas and armchairs. There was a great amount of aluminium which could be effectively used for lightweight chairs and tables. Laminated wood techniques, steel rods and latex became popular. After the drab colours of wartime, there was a yearning for brightness; designers responded with abstract, whimsical and cubist patterns in primary colours.

Better-looking cooking pots, mugs, lights and cutlery were advertised, the first of them in the 1946 *Britain Can Make It* exhibition at the Victoria and

Albert Museum, which had been emptied of its treasures during wartime. The show was quickly nicknamed 'Britain Can't Have It' by disgruntled citizens but its design work was hugely influential, not least on Scandinavians, who returned home and started manufacturing similar designs which would be bought in large quantities by the British over the next decade – a less familiar version of a story that would be repeated with cameras, motorcycles and aircraft. The result of the new designs, on show again in the Festival of Britain in 1951 at the end of Labour's era, was to decorate austerity with a sharp-edged, spindly, brittle and optimistic look, one that is now as securely of its era as lava-lamps or beanbags stamp the seventies. Some of the design now looks rather cold; perhaps it never truly caught on. But some of it, from the Roehampton flats overlooking Richmond Park, to the famous Jason stacking chairs, just like some of the young designers, including Terence Conran, would last.

What Did We Look Like?

Study photographs or film of a reasonable number of Britons of the mid-forties, and you are likely to notice striking physical differences; above all, bulky, creased clothes, tired-looking faces and bad teeth. From working-class women with great gaps and sharp edges in their smiles, to landed politicians with buck-toothed smirks, this was not a country able to take care of its appearance in the modern way. For good practical reasons, the male 'short back and sides' was almost universal. Women struggled to put on a show. American troops coming over here during the war had been warned that English girls would be a bit grubby and 'often cannot get the grease off their hands or out of their hair'. Women were advised to rub their hair with dry towels when they could not get shampoo, or to steam it over boiling water. Spongeing with lukewarm water had replaced regular baths for millions of people. To put it bluntly, many British people in the forties would, by our sensitive standards, have smelt a little. Cosmetics were hard to get, too. Women had used everything from cooking fat and shoe polish to soot and baby powder to make themselves up – though bought cosmetics were still regarded as a little racy by many older women and men.[39] Others put up with squints, semi-blindness or ugly, heavy-rimmed spectacles, which were not yet free. Buck-toothed, squinting and not overly clean: we were, in the mid-forties, very far from the scented, freshly dressed and sometimes surgically enhanced narcissists of modern Britain. People looked older at any given age than they would today – except the children who, dressed in shorts, dresses and buckle shoes, looked younger.

The dirtier air of coal-fuelled city life, and long traditions about respectability meant coats and umbrellas were much more often worn. In the City, on the football terraces and among women shopping, hats were almost universal. Photographs are a vivid reminder of how creased and rumpled the clothes of even quite well-off people looked. It was not only the war. These were still the days before easy dry cleaning and almost universal washing machines at home. In a country whose workforce was overwhelmingly manual, men's clothes were a straightforward marker of class and occupation; heavy jackets, thick wool trousers, leather boots for most; three-piece suits, also heavy by today's standards, with detachable collars, for the middle classes. Leisurewear was hardly known for most – simply a matter of using an older shirt, or swapping a suit jacket for a tweed one. Clothes had to last longer, so were inevitably patched and mended more frequently. During the war, most of the civilian clothes produced were so-called 'utility clothes', with special labels, and designed to save material; they had fewer pockets, seams and buckles. Turn-ups on men's trousers, then fashionable, were banned. The result of utility designs could be seen on every British street well into the fifties. Richer people still had their well-made clothes from before the war, but for the working classes, clothing rationing, which arrived in 1941, meant a struggle to stay warm and decent.

Because rationing affected the quantity of clothes you could have, but not their quality, it hit the poor harder. Government campaigns about how to reinforce or reshape old clothes, ranging from well-meant advice about reinforcing 'underarm areas', to unravelling old woollens and re-knitting them as something else, did not improve the mood. For women, faced with an almost impossible struggle to replace laddered stockings or underwear, the wartime fashions felt boxy and unattractive – service-style caps, or flat bonnets, with short skirts and masculine jackets, what was called 'man-tailored'. The dominant colours were dull, greys or dark blues or dark browns. On their feet women wore the heavy soled, heavily-strapped 'wedgie', or laced-up black leather shoes, endlessly repaired. If pregnant, they were encouraged to adapt their ordinary clothes – the ethos of 'make-do and mend'. Their children, they complained, tended to grow far too fast for the coupons. It was a time of ankles protruding from short trousers, jackets that would barely do up, mottled wrists hanging from outgrown jerseys. It wasn't that the post-war British did not know how to look smart. The imported American films showed immaculately dressed icons and the newspapers showed the richest, flashiest Britons, from Anthony Eden to the King, still beautifully tailored. But they could not afford to look smart. Some men found themselves avoiding invitations to drinks parties because they were ashamed of the state of their clothes. Women avoided brightly lit restaurants when their stockings had gone, and been replaced with tea-stains and drawn-on seams.

Under the hats or umbrellas, below the coats and suits, the British of the forties were also considerably leaner. Wartime rationing had actually increased the health and strength of the working classes whose diets had been nutritionally dreadful before it. By 1945, children were growing measurably taller. Fair and effective rationing of food and clothing was a prime domestic achievement of the wartime government. Organizationally, it was as complex and difficult as moving armies around the world, building instant harbours and invading Europe. Though there was some experience from the very end of the First World War to recall, it had been done almost from scratch, replacing the market with the queue and the ration book, distributing the same amounts of protein and starch to families on hill farms, in industrial Northern terraces and in Home Counties villages. If wartime opinion-polling is to be believed, it was even popular in the first few years. Some 44 million ration books, in buff, green or blue, were distributed. Regional offices were set up across the country and 1,400 local food control committees were organized. Everyone had to register with a local shopkeeper, who would get supplies of the rationed meat, ham, sugar, butter, margarine and the rest from centrally bought supplies accumulated by the newly formed Ministry of Food. With more people working away from home, more people ate out too, though in a frugal and strictly controlled way. There was a huge expansion of school meals; children were allocated free orange juice and codliver oil; works canteens and 'British Restaurants' were opened throughout urban Britain, serving plain and limited but nourishing food. A system of 'points', which allowed people to get tinned foods, dried fruits and other extras when they were available, had proved one of the great successes of wartime rationing.

For socialists, of course, this was more than sad necessity. It showed what could be done to achieve a fairer country. Yet if Labour thought rationing provided any kind of popular lesson for peacetime this would soon seem a great mistake. For though rationing was fair, it was also dull, monotonous, time-consuming and by the end infuriating. A portion of meat each week little larger than an iPod was not an existence the beef-eating British could endure for ever. During the war people had resorted to all sorts of bizarre concoctions to keep up their interest, everything from haricot beans flavoured with almonds making do as marzipan, to mashed parsnips masquerading as bananas, 'mock goose' made of potatoes, cooking apples and cheese, or jam made from carrots. The rich, particularly in London or when they had access to country estates, managed to avoid some of the effects of rationing: Boodles Club in London, for example, enjoyed a steady supply from hunting-and-shooting members of venison, hare, rabbit, salmon, woodcock and grouse – none of these things was rationed – though it failed to sell many portions of a stuffed and roasted beaver served on one occasion.[40] For most, rationing was the prime example of the dreary colourlessness of wartime life. After the guns had stopped, it went on unbearably long. It was still biting hard at the end of the forties. Meat was still rationed until 1954. And though the poor were better fed, most people felt hard done-by. Many doctors agreed. Shortly after that horrific 1947 winter was over, the *British Medical Press* carried a detailed article by a Dr Franklin Bicknell which argued that available foods were 400 calories short of what women needed each day, and 900 calories short of what men required: 'In other words, everyone in England is suffering from prolonged chronic malnutrition.'[41] This was angrily disputed by Labour politicians, keen to point out the effect of all that free juice, codliver oil and milk on Britain's children. But people were on the side of Dr Bicknell.

Under the Skin: Belief

Below the skin, though, were the British of the forties fundamentally different to the British of today? This was then a religious society, though less so than in any previous time. In surveys people overwhelmingly described themselves as Christian, but communal worship and knowledge of the Bible was falling away. The Church of England saw one of the sharpest declines in membership in the decade from 1935 to the end of the war, losing half a million communicants, down to just under three million. (Another half million would be lost by 1970 and more than a million by 1990.) The Roman Catholics rose in numbers after the war, perhaps because of Polish, Irish and other European immigration, while the Presbyterians and the smaller churches also suffered decline. Though the first mosque in Britain had been built in Woking, Surrey as early as 1889, there were few Muslims or Hindus. North of the border, the Church of Scotland, which had only finally won full independence from the British State in 1921, was more popular than the English established church, and continued to grow until the early sixties. In the absence of a Scottish parliament, debates at the Kirk's ruling body, the General Assembly, had an authority and produced a level of newspaper interest unthinkable today. Scotland's higher religiosity – for the Catholics were strongly represented too – had its darker side in the persistence of Orange marches, bigotry and mutual suspicion on a scale which almost matched that of Northern Ireland. To the visitor, Britain would have seemed a very obviously Christian nation, with its State and Royal ceremonies, its famous and often controversial bishops, its religious broadcasting and above all its spires and towers in every suburb and village. The churches below those spires were at least thronged for marriages, funerals and the special services such as Christmas and Easter. Girls and boys were likelier to be in the Christian Scouts or Guides; schools had prayers at morning assembly; Sunday schools were busy; the Army had its Sunday parade.

Some of the most eloquent cultural moments in the life of post-war Britain had religious themes, from the rebuilding of Coventry Cathedral, with its tapestries by Graham Sutherland, to the popularity of Benjamin Britten's wartime choral work *A Ceremony of Carols.* Perhaps Britain's best-loved serious painter was Stanley Spencer, who was turning out work in the forties and fifties based on his own idiosyncratic interpretations of biblical events – the Resurrection, Christ calling the Apostles, the Crucifixion. John Piper was famous for his watercolours and etchings of medieval churches; John Betjeman celebrated later, Victorian ones. Post-war Britain's major poet, the American-born T. S. Eliot, was an outspoken adherent of the Church of England. His last major book of poetry, *Four Quartets,* is suffused with English religious atmosphere, while in his verse drama *Murder in the Cathedral* he addressed an iconic moment in English ecclesiastical history. He would win the Nobel Prize for Literature in 1948. C. S. Lewis had become a nationally known Christian broadcaster during the war, with his

Screwtape Letters, and for children there was soon to be the religious allegory of the Narnia books, the first of which, *The Lion, the Witch and the Wardrobe,* appeared in 1950. It could fairly be said that in this period, there still existed an Anglican sensibility, a particularly English, sometimes grave, sometimes playful, Christianity, with its own art and thought. It may have been wispy and self-conscious but it was also alive and argumentative, as it is not today. It was of course a limited and elite movement. Already, saucy revelations in the Sunday papers were where most people turned when they thought of immorality, not to sermons.

Were the British of the forties any more moral, or at any rate any more law-abiding, than the modern British? This is one of the hardest questions to answer. Conventions and temptations were just so different. On the surface, it was certainly a more discreet, dignified and rule-bound society. Divorce might have been becoming more widespread, but it was still a matter for embarrassment, even shame. Back in the early thirties, the average number of divorce petitions filed was below 4,800 a year. During the war, it jumped to 16,000. By 1951, with easier divorce laws, it was more than 38,000. In the forties and fifties, it still carried a strong stigma, across classes and reaching to the highest. As late as 1955, when Princess Margaret wanted to marry Group Captain Peter Townshend, the innocent party in a divorce case, a Tory cabinet minister, Lord Salisbury, warned that he would have to resign from the government if it allowed such a flagrant breach of Anglican principles. Divorced men and women were not welcome at Court. Homosexuality was illegal and vigorously prosecuted. Pornography was, for most people, almost unknown – 'dirty books' were on sale in a very few bookshops but 'smut' was still considered something mostly available for foreigners.

The censorship of the theatre, dating back to Walpole's time, was taken extremely seriously. Playwrights had to submit their plays to the Lord Chamberlain's Office at St James's Palace, which would strike out double entendre or vulgar language. John Osborne had a letter back about his play *The Entertainer* in March 1957, with sixteen alterations, such as 'Page 6, alter "turds". Page 9, alter "camp" ... The little song entitled, "The old church bells won't ring tonight 'cos the Vicar's got the clappers". Substitute: "The Vicar's dropped a clanger".' Yet behind the firewall of censorship and law, there is plenty of evidence of a country just as sex-obsessed as it is now, and probably always was. The scatological outpouring in private letters and diaries is amazing, presumably the flip-side of public discretion. The war had involved years of disruption to family life, broken relationships, a lot of quiet domestic adultery, and a boom in homosexual activity, as tens of thousands of young, frustrated servicemen were let loose in darkened cities. One thing which would shock many people now, if they could be transported back, was the huge number of prostitutes working openly on the streets in the 'red light' areas of the cities, around Manchester city centre, Edgbaston in Birmingham and Edinburgh's Leith Walk. In London, the so-called Hyde Park Rangers and Piccadilly Commandos were gangs of prostitutes working almost unmolested by the police and earning small fortunes from horny soldiers.

Street crime had boomed particularly in London and in the words of one of the capital's historians by 1945 'the country was awash with guns, illegally sold by American servicemen for £25 for a handgun, or brought back by British servicemen from abroad'. Over the war years, though the population of London had dropped by some two million, the number of serious offences per head had doubled.[42] The immediate post-war years saw real problems, partly because of the size of the black market, armed racketeers, and the continued presence of deserters, of whom many thousands were hiding out, including an estimated 19,000 from the US Army. Because of frustration at the slow pace of demobilization, desertions increased after hostilities ceased. Films of the time sometimes reveal a semi-anarchic wilderness territory of bombed-out homes and urban wasteland, which may be policed by gangs. Memoirs confirm that many children and adolescents, lacking parents or simply profiting from the shaky administration of a great city returning to life, more or less ran wild.

Yet to get the tone of the times right, it is important not to forget that, among the rebellions against rationing and official incompetence, Britain was basically law-abiding. In a country awash with cheap handguns, struggling with profound resentments about shortages and a thriving black market, and still containing many deserters on the run, by virtually every count available, serious crime then fell. The guns did not lead to spates of shootings. Croydon did not become Chicago. Armed crime in London involving guns fell from a high of forty-six incidents in 1947 to just four cases in 1954. The number of people sentenced to prison fell by 3,000 between 1948 and 1950. The murder rate fell.[43] Indeed, overall serious crime fell by nearly 5 per cent per head of population in the five years after the war. One historian of British crime concludes: 'Perhaps the most peaceful single year was 1951, with a low level of crime, especially violent crime, following a brief increase in bad behaviour following the war.'[44] Bearing out the tricksiness of all statistics, this year is cited by others as a post-war crime peak, yet the general picture holds up. People respected the police and came across serious crime rarely. The various scares about violent racketeers in London, or lawless youths, were mostly confined to the papers. Foreign observers talked about the orderly, calm, law-abiding nature of British society as something rare in Europe or around the world. All of this matters enormously to Britain's self-image now, since commentators and politicians often point to the post-war era as a time of Edenic peace and order, far removed from the world of machine-gun-toting police and drug gangs. Why was Britain so well-mannered and lawful?

Some argue that tougher penalties are the most obvious reason. It is true that from 1946 until the year hanging ended, 1964 (though it was legally abolished two years later), some 200 murderers were executed. Other grim punishments, notably flogging, were on the wane; they were ordered infrequently in the fifties. The last judicial birching was approved by the Conservative Home Secretary, R. A. Butler, as late as 1962, though the practice continued in the Isle of Man and very occasionally in Scotland. Yet violent crime was on the increase again well before hanging was abolished. Its abolition cannot be the only reason. One obvious factor is that so many young men, the people who commit most crimes, were in the Armed Forces, latterly doing National Service. This did not simply take people off the streets. It provided discipline and the habit of obeying – and issuing – orders. Two generations of boys were marched off for short haircuts and taught to polish their shoes by fathers who had been in the services. Then there was the relative lack of opportunity. A society in which people barely have enough to eat and possess few movable goods is rather less prone to street crime than one in which every teenager totes an expensive mobile phone, and every urban street is lined with parked cars. Finally, not to be underestimated simply because it cannot be measured, there was the spirit of the times. The war had shaken everyone's sense of security – not just serving troops but the bombed and the evacuated and the bereaved as well. The Cold War would not diminish an underlying sense that life had become fragile. In these circumstances, it is hardly surprising that there was a profound post-war turn towards hearth and home and a yearning for security, order, predictability – in the street, in the neighbourhood, if it could not be there in the wider world.

These then, in all their variety, patriotism and hope, were the people whose fate was now in the hands of Clement Attlee and his ministers. We have looked at the difficulties facing the country and at the confused hopes of the new government. We know that the dream of a New Jerusalem, a socialist commonwealth, was never realized and that some historians see the 1945 government as a wasted chance. It is time now to look at what this government actually did.

What the Romans Did For Us

The post-war Labour government did the following things. It created the National Health Service. It brought in welfare payments and state insurance 'from the cradle to the grave'. It nationalized the Bank of England, the coal industry, which was then responsible for 90 per cent of Britain's energy needs, and eventually the iron and steel industry too. It withdrew from India. It demobilized much of the vast army, air force and navy that had been accumulated during the war. It directed armament factories back to peaceful purposes and built new homes, though not nearly enough. It oversaw a rationalization and shake-up in the school system, raising the leaving age to fifteen. It kept the people fed, though, as we have seen, not excitingly fed. It started to fight Communism in Korea and to develop the atomic bomb. It did these things against the background of the worst financial crisis that could be imagined, at a time when its own civil servants were drawing up plans for starvation rationing if the money ran out, and while meeting its obligations to the malnourished people of other countries, left bereft by war or crop failure. It harangued people to work harder and consume less. In its dying months it did its best to amuse and entertain them too, with the Festival of

Britain. This combines to form the most dramatic tale in our peacetime history of a State organization doing things it actually meant to.

Without the war, clearly, there would have been no 'Attlee government' as we remember it. With the war, though, some major social reform programme became inevitable; wars shake up democracies violently, whether they win or lose. France and Italy saw a huge rise in Communist influence after the war. Britain did not. But had a post-war British government tried to shrug off the hopes for a brave new world shared by so many and encouraged by everyone from archbishops to newspaper editors, what damage would have been done to Britain's political system? There could have been no return to the thirties. After the privately run chaos and underinvestment of pre-war Britain people from almost all parts of the political spectrum thought central planning essential. Churchill's Tories would have done many of the things Labour did, just a little less so, and more slowly. By the time the old man returned to power again in 1951, he was promising to do more in some areas, such as housing. The historian of the Welfare State puts it like this: 'A country which had covered large tracts of East Anglia in concrete to launch bomber fleets, and the south coast in Nissen huts to launch the largest invasion the world had ever seen, could hardly turn round to its citizenry and say it was unable to organise a national health service; that it couldn't house its people; or that it would not invest in education.'[45] What was done after the war to remake Britain was not inevitable. There were lots of battles and individual decisions on the way. But some such quiet revolution, some big grab of state power, or extension of political will, was bound to have occurred.

Beveridge: Spin Doctor and Sage

If there is one man who deserves a place in the pantheon of reform, outside party politics, it is that cadaverous, white-haired, publicity-mad, kindly, harsh, determined and entirely impossible man, William Beveridge. He had left his wealthy upper-class circle to become a social worker in the East End of London, just like Clement Attlee. He then became a journalist and a civil servant before the First World War, a friend of intellectual socialists. He worked with the young Winston Churchill in the Liberal government, was one of the architects of rationing in 1916 and was later a Liberal MP. He knew Whitehall inside-out but left to become an academic, using the young Harold Wilson as his dogsbody. This was a hard life. Beveridge was fanatically hard-working, rising at six for a cold bath before spending the rest of his day icily wallowing in cold statistics, writing and dictating. When war came again, Beveridge decided that government could not properly function without him and pestered the Churchill team for a job. He was bitterly disappointed when Bevin, who disliked him intensely, finally shut him up with the offer of a review into the confusing array of sickness and disability schemes for workers. It was hardly glamorous or central to the war effort and Beveridge apparently wept tears of rage and frustration when he was told. He set to work, however, and quickly decided there could be no coherent system of work benefits without looking too at the plight of the old, women at home and children. Workers were not alone, self-sufficient. They had families. They aged. He would have to devise a system to include everyone, while keeping the incentive to work. There would have to be family allowances, and a National Health Service, but all this would be undermined if Britain returned to the era of mass unemployment; so the State would have to manage the economy to keep people in work. Giving Beveridge a limited remit and telling him to get on with it was like giving Leonardo da Vinci some paper and telling him to doodle away to pass the time.

Earlier we noted that the spirit of Oliver Cromwell was abroad in the England of the mid-forties. Beveridge was urged by his helper, soon to be his wife, Jessy Mair, to adopt the language of Cromwell too. Soon he was stomping around telling anyone who would listen that he intended to slay five giants – Want (he meant poverty), Disease, Ignorance, Squalor and Idleness. Beveridge was addicted to what a later Britain would call 'spin'. He used his position as a well-known broadcaster, and his contacts with the press, to drip out advance hints of the great report he was preparing, which he clothed in millennial language. He was also lucky in his timing. After the bleakest of the war years, Britain's fate was on the turn. There were, inevitably, plenty who were nervous or hostile. Leading industrialists protested that Britain was fighting Germany to keep the Gestapo out of our houses not to build a costly Welfare State. The Conservative Chancellor, Sir Kingsley Wood,

93

briskly told Churchill that Beveridge's plan would be unaffordable. Whitehall mandarins resented his egotism and self-promotion. But he had the wind at his back. Popular expectations were too high and memories of the thirties were too vivid for the white-haired giant-killer to be stopped.

Beveridge's was a long, detailed, number-filled report, longer than this book, with no pictures and very few adjectives. Yet there were queues in London on the day of publication waiting to grab copies. It sold like no government report before, and very few since. Within a month, 100,000 copies had been bought; eventually six times as many were sold. It was distributed to British troops, snapped up in America, and dropped by Lancaster bombers over occupied Europe as propaganda – 'Look, here's the kind of thing a democratic society promises its people.' A detailed analysis of the Beveridge Report was discovered in Hitler's bunker at the end of the war, ruefully describing it as 'superior to the current German social insurance in almost all points'.[46] At home, unaware of the impact he was making in the unlikeliest places, Beveridge lectured. He wrote columns. He filled halls. He broadcast. A few months later the cautious Churchill acknowledged that, far from distracting attention from the war effort, the Beveridge Report was greatly boosting morale. He gave his first broadcast on domestic issues, accepting 'a broadening field for state ownership and enterprise' in health, welfare, housing and education, noting that Britain could not have 'a band of drones in our midst', whether aristocrats or pub-crawlers; and in a splendidly Churchillian twist announcing that 'there is no finer investment for any community than putting milk into babies'.

The inevitable tumble that follows a Report and White Paper – the watering-down, haggling, legislating and organizing – had to take place before the new National Insurance system was finally brought into being in 1948. Yet it was a fantastic feat of organization which puts modern government to shame in its energy and speed. A new office to hold 25 million contribution records was needed, plus 6 million for married women. It had to be huge and to go up quickly. Prisoners of war were used to build it in Newcastle; meanwhile a propeller factory in Gateshead was taken over to run family allowances. The work of six old government departments was brought into a new ministry. More than half the staff who were transferred were still working away with typewriters and fountain pens in the bedrooms of 400 Blackpool hotels and boarding houses where they had been sent for the war. Forms were printed, box files assembled, new teams picked. Jim Griffiths, the Labour minister pushing it all through and refusing to take no for an answer, wanted a thousand local National Insurance offices ready around the country, decently decorated and politely staffed. After being told a hundred times that all this was quite impossible, he got it. Britain has been a subtly different and slightly less dangerous place to live in ever since. The level of help given was rather less than Beveridge himself would have wanted, and married women in particular were still treated as dependents; there was a lot to be argued about over the next fifty years. Still, from Beveridge's first rough notes in an office where he was thought to be safely out of harm's way, to a revolution in welfare, sweeping away centuries of complicated, partial and unfair rules and customs, it had been just six years' work.

The NHS: Nye's Simple Idea

The creation of the National Health Service, which Beveridge thought essential to his wider vision, was an angrier task. Britain had had a system of voluntary hospitals, raising their own cash, which varied wildly in size, efficiency and cleanliness. Later, it also had municipal hospitals, many growing out of the original workhouses. Some of these, in go-ahead cities like London, Birmingham or Nottingham, were efficient, modern places whose beds were generally kept for the poor. Others were squalid. Money for the voluntary hospitals came from investments, gifts, charity events, payments and a hotchpotch of insurance schemes. Today we think of ward closures and hospitals on the edge of bankruptcy as diseases of the NHS. The pre-war system was much less certain and wards closed for lack of funds then too. By the time the war ended most of Britain's hospitals had been brought into a single national emergency medical service. The question was what should happen now – should they be nationalized or allowed back to go their own way? A similar question-mark hung over family doctors. GPs depended on private fees, though most of them also took poor patients through some kind of health insurance scheme. When not working from home or a surgery, they would often double up operating in municipal hospitals where, as non-specialists, they sometimes hacked away incompetently. And the insurance system excluded many elderly people, housewives and children, who were therefore put off visiting the doctor at all, unless they were in the greatest pain or gravest danger. The situation was similar with dentistry and optical services, which were not available to anyone without the cash to pay for them. Out of this Labour was determined to provide the first system of medical care, free at the point of need, there had been in any Western democracy.

Simplicity is a great weapon. Nye Bevan's single biggest decision was to take all the hospitals, the voluntary ones and the ones run by local councils, into a single nationalized system. It would have regional boards but it would all come under the Ministry of Health in London. This was heroic self-confidence. For the first time, a single politician would take ultimate responsibility for every hospital in the land, bar a tiny number of private ones. Herbert Morrison, the great defender of municipal power, was against this nationalization but was brushed aside by Bevan.

A more dangerous enemy by far were the hospital doctors. What followed was the most important, most difficult domestic fight of the post-war Labour government's life. The doctors, organized under the Conservative-leaning leadership of the British Medical Association, had it in their power to stop the NHS dead in its tracks by simply refusing to work for it. They were worried about their standing in the new system – would they be mere state functionaries? And they were suspicious of Bevan, quite rightly. He had wanted to have the doctors nationalized too, all employed by the state, all paid by the state, with no private fees allowed. This would mean a war with the very men and women trusted by millions to cure and care for them. But Bevan, the red-hot socialist, turned out to be a realist and diplomatist. He began by wooing the top hospital doctors, the consultants. The physicians and surgeons were promised they could keep their lucrative pay beds and private practice. Bevan later admitted that he had 'stuffed their mouths with gold'. Next he retreated on the payment of the 50,000 GPs, promising they could continue being paid on the basis of how many people they were treating, rather than getting a flat salary. This wasn't enough. In a poll of doctors, for every one who said he would work in the new National Health Service, nine said they would refuse to take part. As the day for the official beginning of the NHS drew closer, there was a tense political stand-off. Bevan continued to offer concessions while also attacking the doctors' leaders as 'a small body of politically poisoned people' sabotaging the will of Parliament. Would the old Britain of independent professionals, with their cliques, status and fees, accept the new Britain of state control? They did, of course. More concessions and more threats brought them round. In the end, Bevan was backed by a parliamentary majority and they were not. But it had been a long, tight, nasty battle.

When the NHS opened for business on 5 July 1948, there was a flood of people to surgeries, hospitals and chemists. Fifteen months later, Bevan announced that 5.25 million pairs of free spectacles had been supplied, as well as 187 million free prescriptions. By then 8.5 million people had already had free dental treatment. Almost immediately there were complaints about the cost and extravagance, the surge of demand for everything from dressings to wigs. There was much anecdotal evidence of waste and misuse. There certainly was waste. The new bureaucracy was cumbersome. And it is possible to overstate the change – most people had had access to some kind of affordable health care before the NHS, though it was patchy and working-class women had a particular difficulty in getting treatment. But the most important thing it did was to take away fear. Before it millions at the bottom of the pile had suffered untreated hernias, cancers, toothache, ulcers and all kinds of illness, rather than face the humiliation and worry of being unable to afford treatment. There are many moving accounts of the queues of unwell, impoverished people surging forward for treatment in the early days of the NHS, arriving in hospitals and doctors' waiting rooms for the first time not as beggars but as citizens with a sense of right. If there was one single domestic good that the British took from the sacrifices of the war, it was a health service free at the point of use. We have clung to it tenaciously ever since and no mainstream party has dared suggest taking it away.

The People's Economy?

The same cannot be said of some of Labour's other nationalizations. The first, that of the Bank of

England, sounds dramatic but had almost no real impact. Exactly the same men stayed in charge, following just the same policies. Nationalization of the gas and electricity industries, themselves already part-owned by local authorities as well as many small private companies, caused few ripples. Labour had talked about nationalizing the rail system from 1908, almost from the moment it became a party. The railway system had been rationalized long before the war into four major companies – London & North-Eastern; Great Western Railway; Southern Railways; and London, Midland & Scottish. By the mid-forties there was almost no real competition left in the system and periodic grants of public money had been needed for years to help the struggling companies out. The distance between rationalized and nationalized is longer than a single letter, of course, but since the government had taken direct control of the railways from the beginning of the war it was an easy letter to replace.

This did not produce a transport system of delight. Labour had the ultimate Fat Controller world-view. It wanted everything from lorries and ships to trains and barges under one giant thumb. The new British Rail would be only one part of an empire comprising the London Underground, canals slicing through the England of the industrial revolution, the grimy trucks of thousands of road haulage companies, the major ports and harbours and even travel agents and hotels. All this came under a single British Transport Commission. For the railway system, which had been the glory of the country, this meant a subsidiary position, answering to a new Railway

Executive and his regional managers who would oversee the 632,000 staff, 20,000 steam locomotives and more than 4,000 electric commuter trains in the country. Among the stock were battered, rackety gas-lit carriages from the days of Queen Victoria and 7,000 horses used to pull rolling stock around shunting yards.[47] The post-war train system was more powerful than the pre-motorway road network, but it was now in dreadful condition and, because of the economic crisis and the shortage of steel, it would be starved of new investment. Unpainted bridges and dripping tunnels nearly a century old, creaking and failing signalling systems, clapped-out locomotives, rusted and broken lines, the lack of electrification and cold, uncomfortable carriages – none of that was the fault of nationalization. But nationalization without new investment was no answer to it either. The only people who did well out of rail nationalization were the original shareholders of the railway companies who were, to their surprise, rather well compensated.

In the forties, coal and steel stirred up more emotion even than transport. Coal provided nine-tenths of Britain's energy. Its smoke and smell hung heavily over every town and city. When the coal industry fell behind its quotas, or was interrupted by bad weather, the factories closed and the people shivered. Coal was also central to Labour's story. The 1926 General Strike had begun and ended with the miners and 'hard-faced colliery owners' were the group most despised by Labour MPs. Coal was red-hot. The ambitious young Harold Wilson, looking for a way to make a mark, wrote a book about how to modernize the industry. Socialist writers such as Priestley and Orwell used the awful conditions of the miners to rub readers' noses in what was wrong with Britain. So for Labour MPs, nationalizing the coal industry was what they were in politics for, as well as sweet revenge. The job was given to one of the government's older and more ideological members. Manny Shinwell had been a tailor's boy in London's East End before moving to Glasgow and emerging as a moving force on 'Red Clydeside'. He was a stirring speaker and veteran MP but when handed the task of nationalizing coal and electricity, he found there were almost no plans or blueprint to help him. All anyone could dredge up was a single Labour pamphlet written in Welsh.

Shinwell managed the job by the due day, 1 January 1947. But his timing was catastrophic. As we have seen it was just then that the freezing weather stopped coal being moved and the power stations began to fail. You can hardly blame socialism for snow but, along with the food minister, John Strachey, Shinwell became a demonized figure for promising that there would be no power cuts. 'Shiver with Shinwell and Starve with Strachey' said the papers. More important in the longer term was the lack of planning about how to modernize the industry that kept Britain working, warm and fed. Many mines, operated under Victorian conditions by families which had owned them for decades, simply needed to be closed. In other parts of the coalfield, new mines needed to be sunk for, by 1947, Britain was producing a lot less coal than before the war. Modern cutting and winding gear was desperately required everywhere. So was a better relationship between managers and miners to end the history of mistrust and strikes. The miners got new contracts and a five-day week but the first major strikes spread within months of nationalization. On inauguration day, signs had gone up outside most collieries proudly announcing that they were now managed by the National Coal Board 'on behalf of the people'. In some cases, 'people' was scored out, and 'miners' written in. Over time, relations between local managers, most of them from the pre-nationalization era, and the miners did improve a little. Over time, investment did come in, and the worst pits were shut down. But the naive idea that simply taking an industry into public ownership would improve it had been punctured early. What matters is the quality of the managers. The historian Correlli Barnett was unkind, not unfair, to complain that Whitehall chose for the nationalized boards 'administrators of their own kidney, sound chaps unlikely to rock boats, rather than innovative leaders strong in will and personality'.[48] Coal was under Viscount Hyndley, a 63-year-old marketing man from the industry, an Etonian ran the gas boards and transport was overseen by Sir Cyril Hurcomb from the Ministry of War Transport, 'a man whose entrepreneurial experience and knowledge of engineering were nil'. The political symbolism of taking over great industries on behalf of the people was striking but as politicians discover anew, every few years, talking about change and actually imposing it are very different things.

By the time the last big struggle to nationalize an industry was underway, the steel debates of 1948–9, the public mood was already turning. Labour did nationalize the iron and steel industry, which differed from coal and rail in being potentially highly profitable and having good labour relations. But it did so with a nervousness that showed the government felt a change in the weather. Labour had worked itself up, proclaiming that 'the battle for steel is the supreme test of political democracy – a test which the whole world will be watching'. Yet the cabinet agonized and went ahead only because of a feeling that, otherwise, they would be accused of losing their nerve. In the debates in the Commons, bright young Labour backbenchers rebelled. The steel owners were organized and vigorous. Labour had a torrid time and the Tories seemed to be regaining their spirits.[49] An over-excited Cripps told the Commons: 'If we cannot get nationalization of steel by legal means, we must resort to violent methods.' They did get it, but the industry was little shaken. Steel needed new investment almost as much as the coalmines and railways did – new mills, coke ovens, new melting furnaces. Again, though, nationalization helped not at all. Within just a few years more, it was largely returned to private ownership.

Nationalization would give Britain a kind of modernization, but a thin, underfunded and weak variety, nothing like the second industrial revolution its planners hoped for. Reversing it would give Margaret Thatcher some of her greatest victories, in the programme of privatization that followed some forty years after Attlee's government. The coal industry would virtually disappear after catastrophic strikes. The railways under BR would become a national joke, but then fall further after a botched privatization. The whole notion of state planning would fall from fashion.

Squatters and Prefabs

The first stories began to appear in newspapers in July 1946. Out of the blue, fed up with having nowhere decent to live, around forty-eight families had marched into disused army camps at Scunthorpe. Then it happened again, in Middlesborough when thirty families moved into a camp. Homeless people in Salisbury took over thirty huts there. At Seaham Harbour, just up the coast from Newcastle, eight miners and their families chalked their names on empty huts and began unrolling bedding. Then squatting began in Doncaster. In picturesque Chalfont St Giles in Buckinghamshire, a hundred families declared themselves the 'Vache Park Estate committee' and took over a military base. They elected a Mr Glasspool as chairman, who declared in best Ealing comedy mode, 'by sticking together, we can do it. If the local authorities try to move us out, they will have a bit of a job now.' Through August, the squatting gathered pace – Ashton, Jarrow, Liverpool, Fraserburgh in Aberdeenshire, Llantwit Major, one of the oldest towns in Wales. In Bath, an RAF aerodrome was seized. At Ramsgate, miners and their families took over gun emplacements. Families marched into an unoccupied Cardiff nurses' home. A London bus conductor and his family occupied an empty nursery in Bexleyheath. Some 500 people took over camps outside Londonderry. A Sheffield anti-aircraft battery was taken over. Most of the invasions were peaceful, but the squatters were determined. At Tupsley Brickworks army camp outside Hereford, where German prisoners had been housed, *The Times* reported that 'A British corporal refused them admission, but he was overpowered, the gates were forced and a party of about twenty men and a number of women entered the camp. They found ten empty huts, which were promptly allocated.' Six couples moved into a Royal Artillery camp in Croydon. At Slough, where thirty-two empty Nissen huts stood in the football stadium, squatters waited until the guards were distracted and infiltrated through hedges. Birmingham people took over flats.

By early autumn it was estimated that 45,000 people had illegally taken over empty huts, flats or other shelters. It was only then, however, that the spreading revolt really hit the headlines.

On the wet Sunday afternoon of 8 September, about a thousand people began to converge on Kensington High Street in London. They were mainly young married couples with children, including babies. Most carried suitcases. Taxis piled with bedding, and the odd furniture van, joined them. A carefully choreographed operation, it was organized by London Communist Party officials such as Tubby Rosen of Stepney and Ted Bramley, the party's London boss. They had been identifying and marking up empty properties in the capital. A reporter from *The Times* takes up the story: 'Those who could not find accommodation stood patiently in the rain while the scouting parties were sent out to inspect neighbouring property ... Consultations were held under lampposts in the rain and there appeared to be an elaborate system of communications by messengers.' Around town, properties were duly taken over: Lord Ilchester's former London home and Abbey Lodge in Regent's Park, a building just round the corner from Buckingham Palace and flats in Weymouth Street, Marylebone, Upper Phillimore Gardens and further afield, in Ealing and Pimlico.

The authorities' initial reaction was superbly British. The Women's Voluntary Service (WVS) brought hot drinks, and the police, rather than trying to evict the families, supplied tea and coffee from Kensington Barracks. The press was sympathetic and so, it seemed, was much of the public. As the squatting continued, crowds gathered outside and formed human chains to pass food and drink through windows. In some streets, the police picked up the food parcels and brought them to the squatters themselves. Blankets, money, food, chocolates and cigarettes were collected for the families. Students from London University marched through the streets with banners declaring 'Homes for Everybody before Luxury for the Rich'. Some squatted properties soon had too much food to cope with. But as the rebellion went on, the official mood hardened. Electricity supplies were cut to some of the seized properties, local authorities were warned not to help them and mounted police were used to disperse sympathetic crowds. Squatters in Buckingham Palace Road wrote to the King to protest. A deputation went to Number Ten but was met by the Prime Minister's housekeeper, who told them Attlee was too busy to see them. The cabinet had decided the revolt had to be stopped. Nye Bevan, in charge of housing, announced that this was now a confrontation to defend social justice and led the government response against 'organized lawlessness'. The Communist leader Harry Pollitt retorted that 'If the Government wants reprisals, they will get them. The working class is in a fighting mood.' In the end, the squatting revolt fizzled out and the Communists led the retreat. The clinching argument seems to have been a threat that people who squatted would lose their position in the queue for new council homes.

Housing was the most critical single post-war issue, and would remain near the top of the national agenda through the early fifties. Half a million homes had been destroyed or made uninhabitable by German air-raids, a further 3 million badly damaged and overall, a quarter of Britain's 12.5 million homes were damaged in some way. London was the biggest single example. Films of the post-war years, such as the Ealing comedies *Hue and Cry* and *Passport to Pimlico,* show vividly a capital background of wrecked streets, a cityscape of ruins, inhabited by feral urchins. But the problem was nationwide. Southampton lost so many buildings that during the war officials reported that the population felt the city was finished and 'broken in spirit'. Coventry lost a third of her houses in a single night. Over two nights, the shipbuilding town of Clydebank, which had 12,000 houses, was left with just seven undamaged.[50] Birmingham had lost 12,000 homes completely, with another 25,000 badly damaged. By the time people began to pour out of the armed forces to marry or return to their families, the government reckoned that 750,000 new houses were needed quickly. This was far more than a country short of steel, wood and skilled labour could possibly manage, at least by ordinary building. Worse, though there had been slum clearances, the old industrial cities, including London as well as Glasgow, Manchester, Liverpool and Newcastle, still contained hideous slums, blackened grimy terraces lacking proper sanitation, and in some cases lacking any gas or electric power supply too.

This was about a lot more than bricks and mortar. The war had separated husbands and wives, deprived children of their parents and in general shaken the family fabric of the country. Some 38 million civilians had changed address, a total of 60 million times. Many marriages had broken up under the strain of the war. Yet people wanted a return to the warmth and security family life can offer. There were more than 400,000 weddings in 1947 and 881,000 babies born; the beginning of the 'boom' that would reshape British life in the decades ahead.

With both marriages and births, these were really big increases on the pre-war years, a million extra children in the five years after the war. There were not nearly enough individual homes to go round, so hundreds of thousands of people found themselves living with their in-laws, deprived of privacy and locked in inter-generational rows. It was, admittedly, a time when people were prepared to live more communally, more elbow-to-elbow, than they would be later. Wartime queuing had revived a kind of street culture, as women spent hour upon hour standing together, inching forward, sharing their grumbles as they waited for the shutters to snap up. Cinemas and dance-halls were crammed with people trying to escape the cold and monotony of their homes. Without television, or central heating, and severely short of lighting, people were in it together. It was the least private time of all. With wartime requisitioning, evacuation and the direction of labour, many were lodging in unfamiliar rooms. So the sharing of toilets and squeezing past each other in small kitchens that so many new families had to put up with in the late forties, was not a shock. It was just a disappointment, like the dreary and meagre food, and the ugly, threadbare clothing. Some believe the popularity of the mother-in-law joke in British variety and television comedy, well into the seventies, was forged in the cramped family homes of the immediate post-war period. Public support for the squatters was perhaps not so surprising. What could ministers do?

The most dramatic response was factory-made instant housing, the 'prefabs'. They were designed for a few years' use, though a few of them were still being lived in sixty years later. Between 1945 and 1949, under the Temporary Housing Programme, a total of 156,623 prefabs went up, far fewer than the total of new homes needed, but a welcome start. They were a lot more than mere huts; the prototype 'Portal' bungalow, shown outside the Tate Gallery and in Edinburgh in 1944, came with a cooker, sink, fridge, bath, boiler and fitted cupboards too. Though, at £550, it cost fractionally more than a traditional brick-built terraced house, it used a fraction of the resources – it weighed, for example, just under two tons, as compared to about 125 tons for a brick house.[51] The houses were typically built in hastily converted aircraft factories – the Bristol Aeroplane Company made many – and then loaded onto lorries, with bags of numbered screws, pipes and other fittings. When they arrived at cleared sites, ready-painted, they would be unloaded and screwed together on a concrete plinth, often by German or Italian prisoners of war. Within a couple of days, they could be ready for moving into. The thirteen designs, such as Arcons, Spooners and Phoenixes, had subtly different features – some had larger windows, some had porches, some had curved roofs, some looked almost rustic – but they were all weatherproof, warm and well lit. People did complain about rabbit hutches or tin boxes but for many they were hugely welcome. The future Labour leader Neil Kinnock lived in one, an Arcon V, from 1947 until 1961, and remembered the fitted fridge and bathroom causing much jealousy: 'Friends and family came to view the wonders. It seemed like living in a spaceship.' As they spread around the country, in almost all the big cities and many smaller ones too, they came to be regarded as better than bog-standard council housing. Communities developed in prefab estates which survived cheerfully well into the seventies.

Dirty Stubs to Rich Spikes

The great grey stubs of the tower-block boom which ran from the fifties to the late sixties litter most of urban Britain. Never has newness turned dark so quickly. Rarely has revolutionary optimism been so quickly and abjectly confounded. This revolution was born, like others, on the European continent and imported to Britain a generation after the prophets of concrete modernism had spoken. Mies

111

van der Rohe, Le Corbusier, Auguste Perret and Walter Gropius were idealists of the twenties and thirties who dreamed a new world of light, tall, glass-covered buildings springing up to free humanity. This was about more than architecture. It was to be social revolution accomplished with concrete and prefabricated steel, bringing hygiene and sunlight to the masses who had lived and worked in the dark, grimy and above all messy streets of industrial Europe. With the arrival of the Nazis many of the idealists fled, particularly to the United States, where their towers would glorify not socialism but American capitalism in its age of triumph. Some, however, came to Britain. Berthold Lubetkin designed beautiful white modernist structures for London, early multistorey concrete flats, a famous health centre and the Penguin Pool and Gorilla House at London Zoo. Erno Goldfinger on the other hand went for vast towers to house human gorillas and managed to offend Ian Fleming sufficiently to be used as a Bond villain's name.

In other circumstances, avant-garde artists from Germany, Russia, France and Switzerland might have had limited impact in Britain, a country whose architecture had see-sawed between classicism and revivalism, and where the prefix 'mock' was not a term of mockery. But from the end of the Second World War through to the seventies, the shortage and foul quality of much older working-class housing meant a desperation for speed and short-cuts. Scotland alone had 400,000 homes without indoor toilets in the mid-fifties. Glasgow's slums were so bad they had been formally denounced by the Roman Catholic church as inhuman. The great industrial cities of the Midlands and the North of England were in almost as bad a way. Politician after politician promised more new houses, ever faster. Britain would end up building a higher proportion of state-subsidized houses than almost any comparable country – beating, in fact, most of the Communist-run countries of Eastern Europe. The idealist architects offered scale and speed – huge streets in the sky, thrown up fast. The local bosses of British cities seized these foreign dreams with both hands. There is a photograph from the late fifties and sixties endlessly reproduced. Actually, it is many photographs, taken in different cities at different times. But they all show the same thing: eager, powerful men in suits staring down, or pointing, at a small-scale nnodel with cardboard blocks set across it.

The architectural visionaries and the scores of ambitious, modern-thinking British architects who worshipped them, drew their towers set against rolling fields, surrounded by trees, on sunny spring days. In Britain's cities, the municipal bosses were generally hostile to decanting populations out beyond their borders to entirely new settlements where they might have more space. People would want to stay in their own communities, they reasoned. Also, they wanted to keep the tax base and the votes. So instead, the towers tended to go up right in the middle of towns, on waste ground, or where old Victorian terraces had just been bulldozed. From 1958 councils got a central government subsidy for every layer over five storeys, a straightforward bribe to build up, not out. The new towers, which were only ever a minority of the total new housing, offered working-class families real benefits, though – fitted kitchens, underfloor heating, proper bathrooms, enough space for children to be able to stop sharing beds. The more ambitious and refined tower-block plans rarely got built: shortage of money and haste, plus a lot of local corruption, favoured quick-build thrown up by local companies.

Once, the different regions, counties and countries of Britain had boasted their own architectural traditions. Glasgow had her red sandstone tenements, London her ornate dark crimson brick apartments, Manchester her back-to-backs. Now, under the influence of a single modern aesthetic, identical-looking towers appeared, often bought off-the-peg from builders. The architect Sheppard Fidler recalled a boozy day out with Birmingham's Labour boss, the 'little Caesar' Harry Watton, when they went to inspect a prototype tower-block by the builder Bryant. It gives a flavour of the time: 'in order to get to the block we passed through a marquee which was rolling in whisky, brandy and so on, so by the time they got to the block they thought it was marvellous … As we were leaving, at the exit, Harry Watton suddenly said, "Right! We'll take five blocks" – just as if he was buying bags of sweets! "We'll have five of them … and stick them on X" – some site he'd remembered …'[52] Watton was a right-wing, anti-immigrant, pro-hanging Labour boss (not lord mayor, but chairman of the key committee in Birmingham). He was not corrupt but he was autocratic and self-righteous. There were Wattons everywhere. Some, like Newcastle's T. Dan Smith, working with the massive architectural practice Poulsons, were corrupt. Others, like the puritanical socialist Bailie David Gibson of Glasgow, were certainly not. One of Gibson's colleagues remembered him as frightening: 'white-faced, intense, driving idealist, absolutely fanatical and sincere … He saw only one thing, as far as we could see: how to get as many houses up as possible, how to get as many of his beloved fellow working-class citizens decently housed as possible.'[53]

Scotland and the North of England saw the most dramatic examples of the prefabricated mania. On the outskirts of Dundee, under the city's controversial Bailie J. L. Stewart, more new housing was thrown up per head than anywhere in Europe, including the vast hexagonal nightmare of the Whitfield estate, built by Crudens, Under Gibson in Glasgow, the huge thirty-one-storey Red Road flats went up, the tallest in Europe, and at astonishing speed. As time went on, lessons were learned and more dispersed, varied and decorated concrete developments appeared. Newcastle had a late example, the giant wriggle of the Byker Wall, as if the emperor Hadrian had turned residential developer. Mostly, though, the stubby blocks were much the same everywhere. West Ham or Kidderminster, Blackburn or Edinburgh – who could tell? And everywhere the same problems quickly began to crop up. Dispersed local communities did not easily reform when stuck vertically in the air. The entrance halls and lifts, so elegantly displayed in architects' watercolours, were vandalized and colonized by the young and the bored. Asbestos, it was discovered too late, was dangerous. Hideous condensation problems appeared. Walls were too thin for decent privacy. Shops were too far away.

In many cases, blocks were popular and well run in the early days, when people were proud of their new homes. The deterioration was human as well as concrete. A single drunken, fighting family could spread misery throughout many floors of a block. Two or three could wreck it. Councils who simply crowded tenants in, without considering problems such as those caused by having large numbers of children high up in the blocks, were at least as much to blame as Le Corbusier or Mies van der Rohe. It is true that some of the prefabricated, hurriedly flung-up blocks were dangerous. In May 1968 part of the Ronan Point tower block in east London, built with concrete panels, simply collapsed. Since the four deaths then, nobody else has been killed by a collapsing tower block and the craze to condemn them as inherently unstable matches the original craze to throw them up everywhere. Just as the slimy brick slums of the forties and fifties were blamed for producing hooliganism, so the new vertical slums were blamed for the vandalism of the sixties and seventies – even though some were being vandalized well before they were finished and open. Perhaps the bleakly uncompromising shadows they cast did have a demoralizing effect. You would have to be a very naive rimless-glassed modernist to love those dully repetitive lines.

Opinion began to turn against the towers, even among architects. Smaller-scale projects came into fashion during the seventies except in a few isolated and well-managed cities, such as Aberdeen. Tower blocks began to be blown up. Rochester destroyed all of its blocks to improve the look of the town. Later, Birmingham promised to do the same. Even Glasgow's Red Road flats were being discussed for demolition. In other places, such as Wandsworth in London, the blocks were repackaged, covered with brightly coloured panels and given a more decorative silhouette. Left-wing councils, which in the sixties had championed the blocks, began to champion cottage-style housing instead. Council house sales meant blocks in the most favoured areas began to be improved from the inside, by their new owners. Many were sold to housing associations, others were left to house asylum seekers, drug addicts and the most desperate of the poor. Through her history, Britain has seen many building crazes, most notably the vast sprawl of brick terraces during the industrial revolution and then the ribbon-development suburbia of the inter-war years. Yet not even they have marked so much of the look of Britain as quickly and nastily as the tower block revolution. The concrete jungles have become the most easily despised, most universally rejected aspect of the British experiment in modern living.

So it is worth remembering that some survived with contented tenants. It is worth recalling that even some graffiti-stained tower blocks, if they have heating, hot water and working lifts, may be better places to live than the leaking, rat-infested terraces, with outside toilets and small gas fires that they replaced. We can add to the small credit side that had Birmingham, Glasgow, Manchester and London not built high then much less of the countryside within fifty miles of these cities, and others, would exist today. The new homes had to go somewhere. Tower blocks were said to be good because they prevented 'sprawl' – the very shabby-Tudor ugliness deplored in the thirties. And some sprawl certainly was stopped. Today, it seems, we are wiser. Architects are as keen on high density as ever but now want to devise street patterns, squares and low-rise homes on a human scale. By the early eighties Britain's housing shortage was, in general terms, solved by the concrete boom: some 440,000 homes were created in tower blocks alone. But migration and the break-up of families since then have created a new housing crisis and once again skyscrapers are coming back in fashion. They are different now. From Manchester's new forty-seven-storey Beetham Tower, with its queasy-making overhang, to plans for a 66-storey shard-shaped London Bridge Tower, these are chic palaces for the urban rich, not upended slums. They are as close to Harry Watton's off-the-peg blocks as the drug habits of supermodels are to the ravages of heroin in prison. Architecture matters; but it does not matter as much as class.

Rebellion: No to Snoek!

Back in the forties, Labour's idea of Britain was beginning to take shape. This would be a well-disciplined, austere country, organized from London by dedicated public servants, who in turn directed a citizenry which was dignified and restrained. Sanitation, reason, officialdom and fairness; it was a Roundhead vision, without the compulsory psalms and military dictatorship. Unfortunately for Labour, the real country was nothing like this. It was (and is) a more disordered, self-pleasuring, individualistic place. Labour's ethic was about restraint and fair shares. Ministers viewed consumerism with disdain, a personality defect of Americans. Yet consumerism would soon erupt with a strength never known before. People were pleased with the free spectacles and the more generous insurance arrangements, and they took to the prefabricated houses, and accepted Indian and Pakistani independence without much problem. It was just that they loathed the restrictions, the queues and the shortages, and disliked being lectured about Dunkirk seven or eight years later. And so the British did what they always do, in their way. They rebelled. They did this not in the French fashion, violently, with flying cobblestones and wild manifestos, but quietly and stubbornly. As we have seen, they rebelled over housing shortages. They refused to wear the clothes they were told they should. And they would not eat what was put in front of them, either.

Diaries and letters of the time show a country utterly obsessed by food. There had been a general assumption that as soon as the war was over pre-war variety and spice would return to the shops. Instead rations were cut and the disappointment was bitter. One response was the rise in popularity of that wartime character, the spiv. The later BBC television comedy *Dad's Army* featured in the fictitious platoon, one Joe Walker, played by James Beck (who was even wilder than his character, and died at forty-four from alcohol poisoning). Walker is a double-breasted-suit-wearing, pencil-moustached, perky villain with a heart of gold, forever upending the moral pretensions of his betters by slipping them an illicit bottle of whisky, a carton of cigarettes or a pair of stockings for the missus. Walker is the service economy in guerrilla form. He is a criminal but one whom everyone relies on. After the war the real-life spivs, the traders and dealers on street corners or in cafes, came out of the shadows and became a recognized part of life under Labour.

Moral confusion about people taking the law into their own hands features in two of the hugely popular Ealing comedies, both first shown in 1949. In *Passport to Pimlico,* the citizens of an area around a bombsite find out they legally belong not to the United Kingdom but to the Duchy of Burgundy. As Burgundians, they are free from the rationing and petty restrictions hemming in other Londoners. Almost as soon as they have finished celebrating their freedom, they are swamped by a plague of spivs, jostling, threatening and causing a breakdown of law and order. They represent the suppressed greed and wild consumerism that socialists feared was always present under the surface – as indeed it was. When the British State responds by cutting off Pimlico with barbed wire, the Burgundians hold out, in a comic mimicry of the country's stand in 1940. The people of London take their side and throw them food to keep the 'Burgundians' from having to surrender. It seems clear that this was directly copied from scenes in the real-life squatting revolt eighteen months earlier. In a comic conclusion the tensions are resolved, just as in a Shakespeare comedy. The rebels reach an amicable agreement with the authorities and return to the ration-card Britain where everything is fair and ordered, if somewhat frustrating.

Whisky Galore!, shown a few months after *Passport to Pimlico,* comes down on the other side of the argument. It relates what happens when a cargo ship full of whisky, tellingly called the SS *Politician,* runs aground off the Hebridean island of Todday. The story is fictional, taken from a comic novel, but was based on real wartime events; the actual ship was called the SS *Cabinet Minister.* The islanders, like the rest of Britain, are whisky-starved and opportunistic. The film tells the story of how the island community steals and hides huge quantities of whisky which had been intended for North America, foiling the authorities in the shape of the English Home Guard commander Captain Waggett (played by Basil Radford; a precursor to Arthur Lowe in *Dad's Army).* In the film, the puritanical British State is subverted by a tightly knit and determined island community who end with a great dance of celebration and liberation. In Todday, unlike Pimlico, the people's yearning for good things triumphs. In real life, the rather heroic struggle of a lone exciseman to recover the whisky divided the islanders, led to convictions for theft and produced a poisoned atmosphere between families which lasted for many years. The fantasy, however, is remembered and the truth forgotten.

One can see the tension between the Burgundians returning to ration books, and the islanders of Todday beating the authorities to keep the stolen whisky, as a filmic version of the political tension between wartime-style controls championed by the Labour government; and the frustrated hostility exemplified by pro-free market Tories. Eventually the controls would be partly dismantled, rationing would end and the first great consumer boom would begin, more or less in parallel with Labour's loss of power in 1950–1. In the meantime, however, a surprising degree of petty criminality was tolerated in an otherwise law-abiding country, not just on the part of spivs but the shopkeepers bending rules to help old customers, or the people who filched a little from work, or the ordinary men in pubs who would buy an extra pair of stockings for their wives. This criminality, however, would not have existed without the privations of the time, and the impertinence of officialdom. A novelist looking back a decade later caught the mood:

> Ludicrous penalties were imposed on farmers who had not kept strictly to the letter of licences to slaughter pigs; in one case, the permitted building was used, the authorised butcher was employed, but the job had to be done the day before it was permitted; in another case, the butcher and the timing coincided, but the pig met its end in the wrong building. Never had a bureaucracy so flaunted its total failure to comprehend the spirit of the times, which was low and resentful ... So really, almost everyone participated; it was a sort of pale, hangdog spivery in back kitchens and the rear of shops.[54]

There were other ways of rebelling. The British Housewives' League, formed in 1945 by a clergyman's wife to campaign against rude shopkeepers and the amount of time spent queuing, helped remove the hapless food minister Ben Smith over the withdrawal of powdered egg. Other foods brought into the country and foisted on consumers were regarded as disgusting. Horses were butchered and sold, sometimes merely as 'steak'. Whalemeat was bought from South Africa, both in huge slabs and in tins, described as 'rich and tasty, just like beefsteak'. It was relatively popular for a short while, but not long. Magnus Pyke, later a popular television scientist, explained that though it tasted fine to the first bite of a drooling mouth, 'as you went on biting, the taste of steak was quickly overcome by a strong flavour of – cod-liver oil'.[55] Then there was snoek, a ferocious tropical fish supposed to be able to hiss like a snake and bark like a dog.

One of the odder vignettes of wartime Britain has the young Barbara Castle, then Betts, working for the fish division of the Ministry of Food.[56] She was quartered in a grand London hotel, the Carlton, which boasted large bathrooms and generously sized baths. These were filled with fish, to be observed for experimental purposes. Barbara Castle, in short, lived with a snoek. Her report on its behaviour must have been favourable because in October 1947 the government began to buy millions of tins of snoek from South Africa. Protein was in short supply. South Africa would take pounds, not the scarce dollars. So ministers tried to persuade the British that, in salads, pasties, sandwiches, or even as 'snoek piquante' with spring onions, vinegar and syrup, the powdery, bland fish was really quite tasty. The country begged to differ and mocked it mercilessly, buying very little. Snoek became a great joke in the newspapers and in Parliament. Eventually it was withdrawn and sold off for almost nothing as catfood.[57]

The Conservatives would later put out pamphlets showing pictures of a horse, a whale and a reindeer to show 'the wide choice of food you have under the Socialists'. Labour tried hard to keep the country decently fed during a grim few years, when much of the world was at least as hungry. But between the black market organized by the spivs, which spread very widely across Britain in the forties; the British Housewives' League, whose rhetoric would be remembered by a young Conservative student called Margaret Thatcher; and the spontaneous boycott of snoek, the public showed that it was fed up to the back teeth with rationing. Fair or not, as soon as they could, Labour from 1948 and then Tory ministers began to remove the restrictions and restore something like a market in food. American aid began to flow again and spiritually the mildly anarchic island of Todday trumped goody Pimlico.

Rebellion: a Bit of Skirt

It took a long time for British clothes to brighten up. Well into the sixties, children were still wearing the baggy grey shorts and unravelling home-made jumpers of the forties, men were still dressing in heavily built grey suits for social occasions, wearing macs and hats on their days out, and women were in housecoats and hairnets. But the forties did see one celebrated revolution, which showed just how frustrated women had become at the dowdy, dreary life they had suffered. It began in Paris, with the arrival of a new fashion house, created by a young designer who was in love with the *belle époque* France of his childhood, the pre-First World War country of swirling skirts, elegance and luxury.

His name was Christian Dior and his revolution was christened the New Look. One of the British women who attended the unveiling in 1947 said she heard for the first time in her life 'the sound of a petticoat' and realized that at long last the war was really over.[58]

Dior's revolution was a return to billowing, deliberately unpractical skirts and dresses, what the magazine *Harper's Bazaar* described as 'a slight, slender bodice narrowing into a tiny wasp waist, below which the skirt bursts into fullness like a flower. Every line is rounded...' The long skirts and padded bosoms, the pleats and extravagance, burst like a firework display over a British womanhood described later as in a 'grey state ... weary, dispirited, cramped and cross'. It was a direct challenge to the austerity culture of the government and quickly caused a genuine political battle. The British Guild of Creative Designers complained that they did not have the materials and could not give way to French irresponsibility. Labour MPs busily threw themselves into the fight against frippery. The beefy and redoubtable Mrs Bessie Braddock denounced the New Look as the 'ridiculous whim of idle people'. Mabel Ridealgh MP said it was being foisted on women and promised that housewives would not buy it. All this padding and artificiality was bad because it made for 'over-sexiness', she added; the New Look was turning women into caged birds and removing their new freedom.

Yet from the young princesses of the Royal Family downwards, women were ignoring the political orders and doing everything they could to alter, buy or borrow for the Dior look. Ruth Adam, who worked in the Ministry of Information during the war and later became a novelist, argued that a generation of girls who had been ordered to work in factories, on pain of prison if they refused, did not see it as a liberation:

> To them, Labour MPs who lectured them about wearing 'sensible' clothing, suitable for productive work, were the same breed as the women officers who had routed them out of doorways where they were having a goodnight kiss, and sent them back to camp; and as the forewoman who had shouted at them for spending too long in the Ladies while Russia was waiting for aeroplane-parts. Now they did not have to listen to lectures about hard work and freedom any more, but could think about being feminine and glamorous.[59]

There was a pent-up yearning for the better, more colourful life that middle-class people, at least, could remember from before the war – everyone from their twenties onwards would have had a reasonably vivid recollection of mid-thirties consumerism. In a world in which men and women were still wearing roughly fitted and standardized demob suits, handed out with hats, ties and shoes as you left the forces, clothing was a powerful symbol of prosperity postponed.

Knobbly Knees and Other Fun

In and out of their homes, what were the British of the forties doing for fun? They were certainly not watching television, something owned by less than 0.2 per cent of the adult population in 1947 and by only 4 per cent in 1950. They were not travelling abroad for their holidays. For one thing, people had less time on holiday, and less money to spend too. The Holidays with Pay Act, passed shortly before the war, had hugely expanded the number of people with guaranteed paid holidays but a fortnight was more common than a month. In 1947, in the days before jet travel and with the amount of money one could take severely restricted, just over 3 per cent of people holidayed abroad, the vast majority being wealthy and going no further afield than the Mediterranean or northern France. They did not drive around the British countryside, either, or 'go motoring' in the pre-war phrase; petrol rationing had seen to that. But in that same year, slightly over half the British did take some kind of holiday. Many took the train to one of the traditional Victorian-era seaside resorts, which were soon bursting with customers. Others went for cycling and camping holidays – the roads were by modern standards almost empty of traffic. Yet more would take the charabanc or train to one of the new holiday camps, run by such early entrepreneurs of leisure as Billy Butlin.

The South African-born Butlin had come from a broken family and, on his mother's side, fairground barkers. She gave him his first taste of the showman's life with her gingerbread stall which she took around West Country market towns. After a much-interrupted education and a short spell as a commercial artist in Canada, followed by service in the war, Billy Butlin began a hoopla stall in the twenties. Year by year, he slowly built up a business in amusement parks – with haunted houses, helter-skelters, hoopla and merry-go-rounds. His big breakthrough was getting the European licence for selling the new Dodgem cars. Then, having spotted the miserable time spent by many families in seaside landladies' accommodation, he opened his first camp at Skegness in Lincolnshire in 1936.

Holiday camps of different kinds, often run for employees of a particular company, had existed before. But Butlin's Skegness was a hugely ambitious undertaking, with a swimming pool, theatre, cinema, many amusements and – crucially – creche facilities so that parents could spend time together without their children. A second camp followed at Clacton two years later and after handing over facilities to the armed forces, he ended the war with five large holiday camps just at the opportune moment. A tough little man, who had carried a cutthroat razor in his top pocket while building his fairground and exhibition business before the war, and who boasted to friends that his aims were 'money, power and women', Butlin had a shrewd understanding of what war-weary people wanted. He offered colour, fun, warm cabins, surprisingly good food and almost constant activities, from dancing to the famous 'knobbly knees' and 'glamorous granny' competitions.

Butlin, who was a millionaire within two years of the war ending and who, after various financial

128

crises, would be knighted and receive the Queen at one of his camps, was targeting the middle classes as much as the better-off workers. Italian opera, Shakespearean productions, radio stars, politicians, the odd archbishop and sporting heroes were all invited to the camps – and came. There was nothing 'naff' about the camps, certainly in the forties and fifties, their heyday; indeed, for a lot of people they were pricey. After the wartime experiences of everyone mucking in together, the morning-to-bedtime activities provided by the Redcoats, with their relentless jollity, seems to have been welcomed. Butlin had his fingers burned with an ill-timed attempt to expand into the American market with a Caribbean camp in 1948, and the mass overseas tourism which began in the sixties would end the glory days of his camps, and their rivals. But for millions of British people they would remain a synonym for summer holiday well into the age of Benidorm. And, if cheap air travel falls victim to oil price rises or worries about global warming, the age of the domestic holiday camp may yet return.

Outside the annual holiday, the traditional spectator sports made a swift post-war return. Football had been badly hit during the war years, not just because so many players were away in the forces, leaving veterans the field to themselves, but because the English Football League had been suspended, and the country simply divided into north and south. New rules meant that League players had numbered shirts, could earn up to £12 a week, and that games could be played until they produced a result (though in 1946 this meant Doncaster Rovers and Stockport County playing into the darkness after 203 minutes without a goal, there being no floodlighting then). The great soccer teams were soon back in action, to capacity crowds.

Stanley Matthews, the Stoke barber's son who was a pre-war legend, was back amazing crowds for Blackpool after the war. In 1953, when Matthews was the ripe old age of thirty-eight, some 10 million people watched him in the first televised Cup Final. By 1948–9 there were more than 40 million attendances at football matches and a general assumption that British football was the finest there was, something seemingly confirmed the previous May when Britain had played a team grandly if inaccurately named the Rest of the World (they comprised Danes, Swedes, a Frenchman, Italian, Swiss, Czech, Belgian, Dutchman and Irishman) and thrashed them 6–1. That illusion would be dispelled before long, but in other ways too this was a golden age of football. The stands were open and smelly, the crowds unprotected and the greatest stars of the post-war era still to come. But football was relatively uncorrupt, was still essentially about local teams supported in their immediate area, and was not dirty on the pitch: throughout his long career Matthews, for instance, was never cautioned, never booked.

Another famous footballer of the time was Arsenal's Denis Compton. It is just that he was still more famous for cricket, which became massively popular again after the war. Some three million people watched the Tests against South Africa in 1947 and Compton's performance then and in the following years produced a rush of English pride and mass enthusiasm. The cricket writer Neville Cardus found him the image of sanity and health after the war: 'There was no rationing in an innings by Compton.'[60] In cricket as in football, many of the players were the stars of pre-war days who had served as PT instructors or otherwise kept their hand in during hostilities; but with the Yorkshire batsman Len Hutton also back in legendary form at the Oval, cricket achieved a level of national symbolism that it has never reached since, not even in the heyday of Botham or the summer of 2005. Again, as with football, the stars of post-war cricket could not expect to become rich on the proceeds. Hutton, a builder's son who first made his name beating teams of public schoolboys on behalf of London council schools, became England's first professional captain of the century in 1952 and the dishevelled Compton, whose father had worked in a chemist's shop, first came into decent money as the face of Brylcreem adverts.

Greyhound racing, using electric hares developed before the war, was a prime working-class focus for betting. The sport had begun in Britain in 1926 at Manchester's Belle Vue stadium and spread quickly across the country; unlike horse-racing, it was something that millions of people in the industrial towns could go and watch near home, and many of the most famous dogs were bred and trained by people using a narrow back garden or local parks. The greyhound tracks were also used for Speedway – the 500cc brakeless motorcycle racing which had arrived from Australia in the twenties and which went through a big expansion after the war. So too, more bizarrely, did bicycle speedway, with men and boys pedalling furiously around bombsites throughout Britain, the courses marked out with painted lines on grass or house-bricks. Cities such as Coventry, Birmingham and London played 'Test matches' against each other and there was even an international, England against Holland, in 1950. Eventually, rebuilding removed the courses and the craze gently subsided.

But the main leisure activities of the time were more traditional. Britain was, then as now, gardening-obsessed. Pottering around in a shed was how many a British male liked to spend any spare time, not in the pub. There was a post-war boom in attending football and cricket matches. Cinema, though, was for everyone, and to give some idea of its popularity, it is worth recording that in 1947, there were around ten times as many visits to a film as there are today, with a much smaller population. At the post-war peak, there were 4,600 cinemas in the country, each showing news films alongside the main and second features. The British film industry, which extended far further than Ealing, was turning out a steady flow of wartime adventures, history films, adaptations of Dickens and romances, but was not then or ever really able to stave off the power and glamour of Hollywood.

Did It Matter, Darling?
Theatre After the War

After the war, you would not have bet on British theatre, an old national glory, surviving as something that mattered. Though television had been suspended during hostilities, cutting out dramatically during a Walt Disney cartoon, and was only reintroduced in 1946 to a small audience around London, it was clearly going to present a challenge. In 1950 there were still only 350,000 television licences but the technology and appetite were clearly apparent. The first television sit-com, *Pinwright's Progress,* had begun as early as November 1946. The first BBC attempts to produce television plays were stilted and badly lit but had already proved popular. As we have seen, cinema audiences had shot up during the war years and there was, however briefly, a thriving British film industry. For the big stars, the money was in film and if at all possible, in Hollywood. Worse, British theatre before and during the war had produced little new writing of major significance; it had become an embattled heritage theatre, with astounding Shakespearean performances, plus musical reviews and other light fare to keep people's spirits up. There had been nothing like the energy and ingenuity of the film-makers as they responded to big social and moral questions thrown up by the war and its aftermath. For these failures, history has alighted on a single scapegoat. His name was Hugh Beaumont, but his friends and his many enemies called him Binkie.

His company, H. M. Tennant Ltd, was responsible for a seemingly endless run of musical and popular hits. Later on, after the theatrical revolution of the late fifties and sixties, Beaumont, who had been born in Cardiff in 1908, would be reviled as everything that was worst about the old ways, a conventional queenie Tsar of the West End, relying on drawing-room comedies, lavish sets and star names to keep the audiences happy. He would be regularly accused of running a gay mafia for friends such as John Gielgud. Much of this is unfair. Beaumont was not so timid. He was ready sometimes to take risks, such as with the controversial 1949 production of Tennessee Williams's powerful *A Streetcar Named Desire,* starring Vivien Leigh. It was denounced by the Public Morality Council as 'thoroughly indecent ... we should be ashamed that children and servants are allowed to sit in the theatre and see it'; the Arts Council suddenly withdrew its support, and planned Royal visits were cancelled after an outcry about American 'sewage' and sex-obsession. In beautifully produced, no-expense-spared productions such as *Oklahoma!, West Side Story* and *My Fair Lady,* and gripping dramas such as Rattigan's *The Winslow Boy,* Beaumont offered the middle classes of London and the Home Counties an escape from daily life and dreary politics. He made a great deal of money for his theatres and backers, and would carry on doing so for many years to come. He was the nearest equivalent to the huge popular successes of Andrew Lloyd Webber's musicals in the final decades of the century, offensive to the intellectual elite, perhaps, but keeping the West End solvent and busy. Nor was he any kind of philistine; perhaps his closest acting collaborator was the great John Gielgud, and he was responsible for some still-famous productions of Shakespeare.

Beaumont stood in the middle of a glossy circle of talent, much of it gay, which celebrated luxury and wit at a time when the country seemed short of both. The most successful of his playwright collaborators was Terence Rattigan, born in 1911 to a diplomat father who was sacked from the Foreign Office after an affair with a Romanian princess. Rattigan had made his name before the war with *French Without Tears* but his most famous and well-made plays came in the forties and fifties – sharp, poignant studies of upper middle-class life such as *The Browning Version, The Deep Blue Sea* and *Separate Tables.* Homosexuality is a hidden theme, necessarily so at the time, but the veneer of clipped, upper-crust politeness made Rattigan an easy target when the national mood turned. In a notorious preface in 1953, he seemed to confirm all his critics' case by explaining the importance to him of 'Aunt Edna', the audience member always inside his brain when writing, a 'nice, respectable, middle class, middle aged, maiden lady with time on her hands and the money to help her pass it'. Rattigan, like Beaumont, would fall suddenly and dramatically out of fashion – the days would soon pass when entertaining Aunt Edna, rather than heaving verbal bricks at her, was what ambitious playwrights wanted to do.

Among Beaumont's other key collaborators was Cecil Beaton, the photographer and designer. Born in 1904, Beaton first made his name by photographing the 'bright young things' of the twenties. He would survive to take pictures of the rock stars of the sixties and even punks of the seventies, having a long career as a Royal portrait photographer in between. His stage work exemplified the 'ooh, aah' effect that Beaumont loved, exotic and witty designs for the pinched post-war public; his film designs would later win him a pair of Oscars. An older star in the same firmament was Ivor Novello, born in 1893 who would die six years after the war's end of a heart-attack, and who had been badly shaken by a short prison sentence in

Wormwood Scrubs for a wartime motoring offence. Novello's career had included composing, notably the patriotic First World War song, 'Keep the Home Fires Burning' and a stream of musicals, ending with *King's Rhapsody* in 1949 and *Gay's the Word* in 1951. Strikingly good-looking, Novello's homosexuality was carefully hidden from his legion of female fans; at his funeral women outnumbered men mourners by around fifty to one.

But the best-known of this group of gay stars was Noël Coward, who was forty-six by the time the war ended. By now he was acknowledged as 'the Master' after a stream of hits, such as *Cavalcade* and *Private Lives* made him one of the world's highest-paid writers. Though he had self-consciously posed as a decadent drug-taking dandy in the twenties, virtually inventing high English camp, and was briefly taken up by the intelligentsia, Coward became increasingly mainstream. His patriotism was not ironic and he bitterly regretted the passing of British imperial status; his wartime films were morale-boosters. *In Which We Serve,* the 1942 film about Lord Louis Mountbatten's destroyer HMS *Kelly,* and *This Happy Breed* helped consolidate his status as Greatest Living Englishman and although the immediate post-war years were a time of relative failure, his plays and influence would continue through the fifties and sixties. Coward showed that the British could be light, witty, amoral and yet also patriotic; he expanded the limits of the accepted national character. For this, and his devastating wit, he survived even when the kitchen-sink realism, which he loathed, took over the stage.

Though the forties and fifties saw the beginning

of a new theatre, it is salutary to remember that these decades were just as coloured by people who had been born in Victorian or Edwardian times, and carried a whiff of Oscar Wilde's London around with them. Novello, Beaumont, Coward, Beaton and Rattigan were all gay, mainstream middle-class entertainers of one kind or another, highly talented and overtly patriotic. Just because they would then be pushed aside by a new generation, the self-publicizing Angry Young Men and the producers who brought talents like Samuel Beckett and Bertolt Brecht to the British stage, does not mean their years in the sun never happened. The wit and wistfulness of the Binkie Beaumont era was another British way of facing a future of grim and guttural questions. Beyond the theatre proper, it was a tone repeated in the hugely popular novels of Nancy Mitford, and the arch television performances of Joyce Grenfell.

The other dominant figure on the British post-war stage was William Shakespeare. Rarely since the days of the earlier Elizabeth had so much Shakespeare been performed to such excited adulation. Contemporary audiences thought Laurence Olivier, Ralph Richardson and John Gielgud were the equal of any Shakespearean actors, ever. They may well have been right. The Old Vic theatre at London's South Bank, seen as an embryo National Theatre, was turning out a stream of Shakespeare; the young Peter Hall, looking back at the early fifties, reflected that 'by the time I was twenty-one, I had seen the entire canon, some of it many times, and you could not do that now.'[61] There was talk of a 'bardic traffic jam' in the West End. After the wartime patriotism of Olivier's film

137

version of *Henry V* and with a dearth of strong new writing, it was perhaps inevitable that so many directors and actors would turn to England's greatest writer, as well as to other established classics. For a literate, culture-starved public, there was nothing to complain about in that. Shakespeare probes as deeply into the human state as anyone, before or since. Audiences would reel from the latest Olivier performance as emptied and wrung-out as it is possible to be. The same goes for the few other great dramatists regularly performed at the time – Chekhov and the Greek tragedians.

Yet the question would not go away: was there nothing more contemporary, nothing more political, to be said on the stage? To ask whether the theatre matters is, in one sense, a meaningless question. If it gives people a unique insight into their situation; even if it only entertains them, then surely that is enough. Yet in other times and places the theatre has aspired to do more, to function as a social and political force. Despite censorship, it had shaken up pre-Revolutionary Russia. It had mattered in Weimar Germany, post-war Paris, and would again in the United States as the Americans experienced anti-communist hysteria and the moral impact of the world's first mass consumer society. So why not Britain? One historian of the theatre, reflecting on the early fifties, found the London stage 'completely indifferent ... to contemporary events. The heavy costs of a rearmament programme necessitated by the Korean war; the inflationary pressures that this produced in a still war-weakened country; the continued shortages caused by rationing; the dramatic impact of the welfare state ... the manufacture of the first British nuclear bomb: all failed to impinge upon the West End stage.'[62] Anyone who cares about live theatre hopes that the unique coming-together of certain actors, words and audiences, will produce a transformation of some kind. This was still, just, the pre-television age. The possibility of British theatre meaning more than a pleasant, or stirring, night out, was still open.

By far the most dogged and courageous attempt to make theatre matter was led by one of the true cultural heroes of the time, a Cockney-born outsider who fled RADA for a career of provincial poverty. Joan Littlewood had been heavily influenced by a communist-inclined Salford actor, Jimmie Miller, who would later change his name to Ewan MacColl and lead the folk-song revival. In the thirties, they had produced German-influenced left-wing or agitprop plays with their touring Theatre of Action, had been offered work in Moscow, and been blacked by the BBC. Reforming after the war, they hit upon the name Theatre Workshop ('workshop' would eventually be appended to every banal meeting in schools, businesses and colleges, but was then, used in this sense, a new coining). Touring through Kendal, Wigan, Blackpool and Newcastle, they would be the very first act to exploit the new Edinburgh International Festival as 'fringe' performers and could hardly have been a starker contrast to the metropolitan flash of Binkie Beaumont. Their first major play, created by Miller, was *Uranium 235,* an impassioned and funny account of the road to the nuclear bomb, with a strongly anti-nuclear message at a time when, as we have seen, the pro-Bomb Labour government was widely supported.

Theatre Workshop mixed its political fare which eventually culminated in *Oh, What a Lovely War!* in 1963, with half-forgotten Elizabethan and Jacobean classics. There were also new plays, including by the Irish republican and drunk, Brendan Behan, whose beer-sodden and misspelled manuscripts were first recognized by Littlewood as works of genius. In every case, her shows cast aside the overwrought, self-conscious style of West End acting and direction. The cast and the production staff lived almost on the breadline, making their own sets and costumes, even after finding a semi-permanent home in the rundown old Theatre Royal at Stratford, in London's East End. Critics began to come to the performances, and they would win rave reviews travelling to Paris and Eastern Europe; among the actors who worked with Littlewood would be Richard Harris, Roy Kinnear and Barbara Windsor. Yet the conservative-minded Arts Council kept them starved of funds, and political censorship plagued the group's history. When they had popular hits, such as Shelagh Delaney's 1958 *A Taste of Honey,* a shocking story about a dysfunctional family, written by a nineteen-year-old from Salford, or Lionel Bart's *Fings Ain't Wot They Used T' Be,* a Cockney musical a year later, these transferred to the West End and made a mint. Back in Stratford, Littlewood, with her long-time lover Gerry Raffles, struggled to pay the bills and turn good publicity into a secure future. On one famous occasion when Behan was being interviewed while almost incoherently drunk by Malcolm Muggeridge on BBC Television, Littlewood was reduced to crouching on the floor, holding onto his legs so he would not fall. She harassed and

140

harangued, campaigned and cajoled. Eventually the temptations of proper wages, and the pressures of underfunded theatre on the fringe of London, lured too many people away and destroyed Theatre Workshop.

Yet the Littlewood story deserves to come ahead of the far more famous theatrical rebellion of the 'Angry Young Men', which began with John Osborne's play *Look Back in Anger* in 1956. The 'Angries' were partly a good PR stunt by the press officer of the Royal Court Theatre. They barely existed as a group, certainly not of the theatre. Newspaper hype, picked up by historians, implied that before them there had been no fresh drama in post-war Britain beyond the odd limp verse play by Christopher Fry or a middle-class romp produced by Binkie and acted by a clique of waspish homosexuals. Though Osborne himself contributed to the legend, in bitterly homophobic tirades later in his life, it is entirely untrue. The two great critics whose energy helped drive British theatre into a new age, Harold Hobson of the *Sunday Times* and Kenneth Tynan of the *Observer,* were intensely interested in Theatre Workshop and gave some of its plays rave reviews well before Osborne came along. Littlewood's problem was that her group were too obviously left-wing at a time when the Establishment was still staunchly conservative and Cold War fever was raging. The Angry Young Men's anger was less clearly directed. Comfortingly, it had no programme, no overseas admirers, no ideology. Had Theatre Workshop emerged a decade later, in the mid-sixties, it might have found stronger financial support from an Arts Council and BBC by then leaning to the liberal left. But of course, in that case, it would have pioneered nothing.

Most of us think of the story of theatre as the story of actors, whose familiar faces and fruity memoirs entertain more mundane lives. Others, particularly in universities, think of a theatre as being succession of writers and playscripts – Rattigan, Wesker, Stoppard, Hare, Brenton – as if drama was fundamentally something written down, a wayward branch of solid prose literature. And of course, this is true: no great acting, no good words, no theatre. Yet the real driving force in a nation's theatre is often provided by the producers and entrepreneurs, the people who shape the institutions, discover the plays, coax the companies. So, if Joan Littlewood found Behan and sustained Theatre Workshop, another contemporary hero is George Devine, the man who found Osborne and created Royal Court's English Stage Company. An actor who had become increasingly enthralled by new French techniques of experimental theatre before the war, which he spent fighting in the Far East, by the fifties Devine was an experienced director. At the Old Vic Centre he had overseen a radical programme of training and production, working on Shakespeare, opera and new work too. But he felt there was something lacking, a dearth of modern plays at a time when 'there had been drastic political and social changes all around us'. He was unlike Littlewood in being already a cultural insider and certainly not communistically inclined (though he admired the German Marxist playwright Bertolt Brecht). Devine drew around him some of the best young actors in London, people like Joan Plowright and Alan

Bates. One of his closest friends was Samuel Beckett. But his great coup was picking up a manuscript by a younger actor, a rather less successful one.

On the hot afternoon of 12 August 1955 John Osborne was lounging on an old Rhine barge tied up near Hammersmith on the Thames, the cheap houseboat where he was living. He had written *Look Back in Anger* over nineteen days, consumed with revulsion about the state of the country, and sent his wispy typescript to as many agents and theatre managers he could find an address for. Every one had briskly refused it. Osborne was in a hole. He had acted his way round the more obscure theatres of provincial England and was flat broke. A vegetarian, he and his house(boat)-mate had been reduced to gathering nettles from the riverbank to boil and eat. The creak of rowlocks signalled the arrival of Devine, a fat man sweating in a small boat, before he was hauled up on deck by Osborne. Devine had loved the play, and now cross-questioned Osborne; he had a prejudice against homosexuals and in favour of working-class actors and Osborne satisfied him on both counts. *Look Back in Anger* is now almost universally regarded as a classic, perhaps the single most important English play of the second half of the twentieth century. The story barely matters here. What did matter was the stream of bright, sarky bitterness that flowed from the main character, Jimmy Porter, as he bickered and ranted in the company of his wife and best friend. It was a resentful, disillusioned young voice, frustrated with what had happened to Britain. Later it would be echoed in a hundred bitter rock songs and in countless novels of youthful angst, and in films. But it had not been heard on a stage before. When the play was finally produced by the Royal Court, the third in its season, immediate reactions were unpromising. The critics were hostile. Binkie Beaumont had come, but then walked out at the interval. Early audiences seemed unenthusiastic. Osborne's mother was told by the theatre barmaid: 'They don't like this one, do they dear? They don't like it at all. Never mind, it won't be much longer. We're having Peggy Ashcroft soon. They'll like that. But they don't like *this* one. Not a bit of it.'[63]

The history of theatre is the history of legends. No newspaper review of a British stage play has been remembered quite like Tynan's review of *Look Back in Anger* in the *Observer,* published on 13 May 1956. It is widely thought to have single-handedly saved the play from being taken off. It was certainly a rave review, describing Osborne's work as a minor miracle showing qualities Tynan had despaired of seeing on stage. He thought it would be a minority taste, but continued: 'What matters, however, is the size of the minority. I estimate it at roughly 6,733,000, which is the number of people in this country between the ages of twenty and thirty. And this figure will doubtless be swelled by refugees from other age-groups ... I doubt if I could love anyone who did not wish to see *Look Back in Anger.'* The heart-on-sleeve emotion and directness of the review made waves. Yet other newspapers had spotted it too; the *Financial Times* found it 'arresting, painful and sometimes astonishing ... a play of extraordinary importance' and the *Daily Express* felt it was 'intense, angry, feverish, undisciplined. It is even crazy. But it is young, young, young ...' Furthermore, it was not until the play was shown on television, in extract by the BBC in October and then in full by the new ITV in November, that it really became a success.

Meanwhile, if the meeting between Devine and Osborne on the houseboat provided the first act of this story, there was a much more remarkable one to come. Though the accounts differ in detail, the substance is clear. Laurence Olivier had been to see *Look Back in Anger* and, like so many, took against it as 'a lot of bitter rattling on'. But the American playwright Arthur Miller was in London because his girlfriend Marilyn Monroe was making a bad film with Olivier. Miller was intrigued by the title of Osborne's play. He persuaded Olivier to take him to see it and found it wonderful. Afterwards, Devine came over and asked whether they would meet the young author. They went to the bar. Though Osborne says the remark came later, and to Devine, Arthur Miller tells the story thus: 'a few inches to my right I overheard with some incredulity, Olivier asking the pallid Osborne – then a young guy with a shock of uncombed hair and a look in his face of having awakened twenty minutes earlier – "Do you suppose you could write something for me?" in his most smiling tones, which would have convinced you to buy a car with no wheels for twenty thousand dollars.'[64] The part would become that of Archie Rice, a fading and seedy music-hall entertainer in Osborne's savage demolition job on Harold Macmillan's delusional Britain. Osborne was quick to point out that he had been researching the declining music hall world well before Olivier asked for a part in *The Entertainer*. But it was an astonishing request. Olivier was then the sun-king of British acting.

Though his marriage was collapsing in private, he and Vivien Leigh were the royal couple of the stage and screen, courted around the world, offered the greatest parts, apparently wealthy beyond the dreams of avarice. For him to ask a young playwright at a fringe theatre for a role seemed like Lord Mountbatten of Burma rolling up and asking for a job as deckhand on a battered Hull trawler.

Yet it was one of Olivier's shrewdest career moves. This was the moment when the old theatre world, of magnificent Shakespearaan film productions, Royal Command performances and West End grandness bowed and gave way to a new, rougher Britain. It was a symbolic removing of swords, buckles and plumes in favour of loose civilian clothes and satire. Olivier was incomparably the most important figure in the story of post-war British theatre. In the thirties he had swashbuckled and starred alongside many of the great Hollywood divas. His wartime stage roles had brought him huge personal success – the scent of success, he reported back, was 'like seaweed, or like oysters' – and his knighthood and films, as well as his marriage to Leigh, made him a global star. Some idea of this is given by the guest list at a Hollywood party thrown to greet him in the late forties – Groucho Marx, Errol Flynn, Ginger Rogers, Ronald Coleman, Louis B. Mayer, Humphrey Bogart, Marilyn Monroe and Lauren Bacall turned up to pay court. Later, he would be the driving force behind Britain's National Theatre; today one of its most important venues, as well as the annual awards for acting, are named after him. Actually, to compare him to a modern monarch is slightly to undersell Olivier at his zenith. Why then did he decide to ask Osborne for a part he must have known would be shockingly different to the romantic leads and tortured princes his public expected of him? Partly, it was boredom and the crushing effect of his marriage to the increasingly mad Vivien Leigh, which he was determined to leave. After various love affairs he would eventually marry Joan Plowright, one of Devine's Royal Court regulars. He would not actually give up the great Shakespearean parts – a magnificent Othello was still to come – nor would he quite turn his back on Hollywood. But *The Entertainer* and his relationship with Plowright set him on a new direction. The answer was that Olivier was able to reinvent himself as a man of the modern world, no longer the codpiece and tights-wearing hero of mid-century.

British theatre did something similar. It found a way of mattering despite the arrival of television and the continuing huge power of cinema. It is not coincidental that, while Britain was still bleakly under provided-for in the aftermath of war, British theatre in the Binkie years was extravagant, colourful and generally shallow, while when Britain set out on a mass consumer boom, British theatre turned darker and edgier. In each case, the stage offered a contrast to what was around it. Osborne's Jimmy Porter bemoaned the lack of 'good brave causes' left in 1956; in 1946, as the Cold War began and with people still demobilizing from the army, such a sentiment would have seemed ludicrous. Similarly, the naive celebration of life which warmed London when *Oklahoma!* arrived after the war would not have made nearly such an impression on the richer city of a decade later. Live theatre would have to compete for writers and actors who found they could reach far bigger audiences and make better money elsewhere. *Look Back in Anger, A Taste of Honey, The Entertainer* and *Oh, What a Lovely War!* would all be filmed. Many of the key talents, the best actors and directors and producers, would head for the new virtual theatres at Lime Grove, Ealing and Teddington, the hangar-like television studios with no seats for an audience and a forest canopy of lights and microphones.

The West End, and the big provincial theatres, would continue to provide entertainment to the middle classes who wanted to see famous actors in the flesh, and who were prepared to try out new playwrights. Of those, Harold Pinter, whose *The Birthday Party* opened to bafflement in 1958 until it was rescued from likely oblivion by a single rave review, is widely acknowledged as the greatest. His famous pauses, mundane settings, intricate use of ordinary language and background political agenda provided a way of seeing and hearing modern Britain unlike any other. He followed earlier so-called absurdist dramatists, above all Samuel Beckett, who had been given his English premier of *Waiting for Godot* by the young Peter Hall in 1955 at the Arts Theatre Club, but Pinter was as English as Beckett was French-Irish. Yet the talent pouring out of British theatre through the sixties and seventies, from the satirists like Orton, the magicians like Stoppard, the sheer entertainers like Ayckbourn, through to the great political dramatists – Wesker, Arden, Bond, Hare – showed that television had failed to kill off live drama. Londoners, indeed any British people near a major playhouse, had the opportunity to be amused, provoked, obliged to think about the world around them, with as much live wit and anger on offer to them as in any modern nation. In the twenty-first century, as Hollywood stars make a regular pilgrimage to play or direct in London theatre-land, and with the flow of good contemporary work unceasing, theatre remains, against the odds, one of the little glories of British life.

Korea: Mao, Bugles, Tins of Cheese

In March 1946, exiled from power, Churchill had made his famous 'iron curtain' speech at Fulton, Missouri. Across Central and Eastern Europe, behind that iron curtain, client Communist parties and Russian stooges had engaged in murder, vote-rigging, threats and eventually outright putsches – notably in Prague – to put themselves in power. Crisis followed crisis. Stalin had tried to throttle West Berlin, a crowded democratic atoll inside Soviet-controlled East Germany. He had hoped to persuade the West not to form an independent West German state with its own currency, but he failed. Much encouraged by Attlee and Bevin, the Americans led a massive airlift to keep the besieged city supplied. By the time the blockade ended more than 270,000 flights into Berlin had been made, carrying in fuel, food and clothing. It was an extraordinary act of succour and a dangerous one, which was wholly successful. Meanwhile there was a strong possibility of war between the Russians and the rebel communists of Tito's Yugoslavia – Stalin had planned to assassinate Tito for insubordination. With American nuclear bombers in East Anglia, and the Russians also now possessors of the Bomb, the danger seemed all-consuming and the threat relentless. And in 1950 Britain was at war again, this time alongside the Americans and a wide alliance of other countries.

Aside from military historians, Korea has become the forgotten war. Yet it was a genuinely dangerous global confrontation in which Britain played an important if subsidiary role. It was the first and only time when British troops have directly fought a major Communist army, Mao's Chinese People's Liberation Army; and it was a long and bloody conflict. Britain and her Commonwealth allies, fighting with a mixture of professional soldiers and young National Service conscripts, lost more than a thousand dead and nearly three times as many wounded. The overall UN casualties were around 142,000. All that was terrible enough, but it could have been much worse. The American commander, General of the Army Douglas MacArthur, fresh from his role as effective dictator of post-war Japan, and considered by his President to be unhinged, was keen to open full-scale operations against Communist China itself. As they struggled against a peasant army across icy, rocky hills and through paddy-fields the US military contemplated using their new atomic bombs to lay down an irradiated dead zone between Korea and China. President Truman had no intention of allowing MacArthur to start loosing off nuclear bombs but a little later, in 1953, his successor,

President Eisenhower, did raise the possibility of using nuclear strikes directly against China.

In a memorandum to Attlee's government, the British chiefs of staff wrote with elegant understatement that 'from the military point of view ... the dropping of an atomic bomb in North Korea would be unsound. The effects of such action would be world-wide, and might well be very damaging. Moreover, it would probably provoke a global war.'[65] Labour MPs wanted the nuclear bomb to be limited to use by the UN, a somewhat strange notion, and Attlee went to Washington to check that Truman was not about to engulf the world in atomic conflict. What no one in Whitehall or Washington knew then, though they might have guessed it, was that Mao had decided to use unfortunate Korea as a 'meat-grinder' war, in which the huge numbers of Western deaths would break the morale of the capitalist West and gain him vital credit with Stalin, so persuading Moscow to share nuclear secrets with Beijing. In March 1951, Mao told the Soviet dictator that his plan was 'to spend several years consuming several hundred thousand American lives'.[66] Had he been more militarily successful, the temptation to go nuclear would have been great. Though the Cuban missile crisis of 1962 is remembered, rightly, as the moment when the world came nearest to nuclear war, there was a serious possibility of it happening earlier, in Korea and China.

The scale of the challenge in Korea after the Communist north invaded on 25 June 1950 quickly persuaded the British government that troops and ships should be sent to help the Americans and the flailing southern regime of Syngman Rhee. There

151

was little disagreement, either in the government or the Commons. Compared to Vietnam, this was a consensual war, carried out under the freshly designed blue and white flag of the United Nations. On the North Korean and Chinese side, half a million men were engaged and, by the time the war ended, three million Chinese had fought in Korea. The Chinese later told their allies that they lost 400,000 men, many of them former anti-Communist soldiers of Chiang Kai-shek's army cynically sent as useful fodder. Among UN forces there would be Australians and Canadians, Belgians, French, Dutch, Thais, Ethiopians, Greeks, Turks, Colombians and others. Wherever they came from most of those who found themselves in Korea hated the country. In winter, the front line was bitterly cold, at other times it was overrun with vermin. Human excrement was used to fertilize the fields which while hardly unknown in rural economies provided a pungent scent which remained in many veterans' minds ever afterwards.

British forces performed bravely in important battles but found the cultural divide with the Americans had grown even wider in the past five years. The most famous example was the heroic stand of the 'the Glorious Glosters' above the Imjin river in April 1951 when with other troops including Ulstermen, Canadians and Belgians, the first battalion of the Gloucestershire Regiment found itself suddenly facing the full force of the fifth major Chinese offensive of the war. Hugely outnumbered, lacking heavy artillery or aircraft support and soon cut off by the advancing tides of communist troops, Brigadier Tom Brodie called for help from the Americans, explaining that the British position was 'a bit sticky'. Not realizing that this was stiff-upper-lip for 'catastrophic', the American commander told him cheerfully just to sit tight. After the battle which followed, just 169 of the 850 Glosters were left for roll-call. Sixty-three had been killed, around 200 badly injured and the rest captured by the Chinese, who had themselves lost an astonishing 10,000 men in the attack. After four desperate days, the Glosters had been able to hold on no longer. At one point, responding to the bugles and trumpets used by the Chinese commanders to signal yet another charge, the Glosters' drum-major was told to respond with every bugle-call he could remember; so the men fought under the strains not just of 'reveille' but 'defaulters' and 'officers dress for dinner'. In another position, when the ammunition finally ran out, the Glosters were reduced to throwing tins of processed cheese at the Chinese in the (vain) hope they would be mistaken for grenades. Yet the action, for all its hopelessness and poignant comedy, did check the advance of the People's Liberation Army at a vital moment. One historian of the war concluded that at Imjin, 'the most political army in the world encountered the least political – and was savagely mauled to gain its few sterile miles of rock and paddy ... Across the breadth of the Korean front, Peking's spring offensive had failed. Never again in the war did the communists mount an all-out assault which appeared to have the slightest prospect of strategic success.'[67]

There were further brave British actions by the Black Watch and, two years after Imjin, by the Duke of Wellington's Regiment. Three-quarters composed of young National Service conscripts earning just £1.62 a week, they held back the Chinese on a ridge nicknamed the Hook. Though eighteen-year-olds were banned from Korea many lied to see some action. British troops said the two worst-paid armies serving there were themselves and the Chinese. Throughout the war, of course, it was American commanders and politicians who directed strategy, perhaps the single most important and far-sighted action coming from the top when President Truman finally sacked MacArthur. By the time of the eventual armistice in July 1953 returning British troops, including prisoners who had endured appalling torture and malnutrition, found the public largely uninterested in them. There had been a major drive by the Chinese to indoctrinate British conscripts but with the exception of a spy who was later unmasked and a single Scottish soldier who, perhaps recalling the social cheer to be enjoyed in Scotland in the early fifties, opted to remain in Red China, it was ineffective. Though the Chinese political officers included some with fluent English, there was little communication: it seems that rich Geordie, Scottish and West Country accents completely defeated them.

In some ways, Korea can be compared to the Iraq wars, the first of which had UN backing, and both of which were American wars in which Britain played a secondary role. As with Iraq, at the time of Korea half a century earlier, British public opinion found the country's regional allies unattractive and undemocratic. The Syngman Rhee regime in the south was as despotic as Pakistan or Saudi Arabia but more ruthless and vicious, as well as being spectacularly ungrateful. As with Iraq, British journalists did much to spread disenchantment about the war. James Cameron, a brilliantly talented left-wing reporter with a huge reputation, lost his job with the then-popular magazine *Picture Post* after revealing the condition of political prisoners held by the south. 'They were skeletons.' he later wrote, 'they were puppets of skin with sinews for strings – their faces were a terrible, translucent grey and they cringed like dogs.'[68] As with Iraq, Britain struggled to use what leverage she had. Attlee flew to Washington to try to persuade Truman not to use atomic weapons, as Tony Blair flew there to persuade George W. Bush to try harder for UN support. As with Iraq, British troops behaved bravely under difficult conditions and returned home to find a country that did not want to know.

East Germany's Communist leader bragged that after Korea, West Germany would be next for liberation with tanks. Stalin had indeed considered trying to grab the rest of Germany, as well as Spain and Italy, and had discussed with his advisers an attack on the American Pacific fleet. In October 1950 he told Mao that a Third World War should not necessarily be avoided: 'If a war is inevitable, then let it be waged now, and not in a few years' time.'[69] In West Germany, comfortably based in former SS and Luftwaffe barracks (the Germans had provided double-glazing, central heating, sports facilities and cinemas for the fighting men of the Third Reich), some 80,000 British soldiers were waiting for the Red Army to make a surprise attack.[70] As in Korea many were National Service conscripts. Many of the British tanks were hopelessly out of date, 1939 Valentines and clapped-out Churchills. As Soviet aircraft buzzed

Western defences to test them out, there was an assumption in Whitehall that when the attack came Nato would be able to hold out with conventional forces for only a few days. It would have been 1940 all over again with one stark difference. To protect itself against the Soviet blitzkrieg the West would have had to go nuclear at an early stage. Politicians and commentators would become obsessed by the technical detail of the arms race as it lurched forward.

The huge rearmament that followed, with the Americans leading the way, Britain and France following, had grave consequences for Britain. Having been a founding member of the UN and Nato, Britain felt confirmed as a global player, with global responsibilities. The cost was crippling. Korea itself was not the cause of the financial squeeze – the official historian of that war pointed out that 'the sum was a mite compared to the volume of British rearmament for Nato during the same period'.[71] It was, however, part of the shift of resources back to khaki and jets which meant Labour hurriedly diverting money from the new National Health Service. Some 300,000 men a year were taken out of the job market at a time of serious labour shortages. Another unplanned consequence was that West Germany was quickly back on her feet again since her new machine tool factories were desperately needed to re-equip Britain. Soon these same factories would be exposing archaic, ill-managed British industry to serious competition in other areas. But perhaps the most serious domestic consequence of rearmament was on morale or the spirit of the times. The Cold War shaped post-war Europe. In Britain it helped quickly blight the sunny optimism about a better future that so briefly bloomed in the years after the war.

Jerusalem Falls

In the 1950 general election, Labour won 13.3 million votes, not so many fewer than it did in 1997, when the electorate was far bigger. Its majority then however was slashed to just five. Herbert Morrison mordantly reflected that the British people hadn't wanted to kick out Labour, just to give it a kick in the pants; 'but I think they've overdone it a bit'. The impression of fading strength was manifested in the bad health of Labour's relatively elderly leaders. Morrison had nearly been killed by a thrombosis during the crisis of 1947; new drugs given to him caused his kidneys to pour with blood. While he was still in hospital, Ellen Wilkinson, the education minister who adored Morrison and may have been his mistress, died from an overdose of barbiturates. Though Labour succeeded in raising the school leaving age to fifteen, and embarked on an ambitious school-building programme, education had been a relative failure for the Attlee government. There was too much hunger for manpower, too few qualified teachers, shortages of everything from school furniture to modern textbooks and, in the end, too little cash. Wilkinson, a small flame-haired woman who had been on the pre-war Jarrow Crusade and was much loved in the party, became increasingly depressed at the slow pace of change. On 25 January 1947, in the middle of that icy winter described earlier, she insisted on opening a theatre school in a blitzed, open-to-the-sky building in south London. Ellen became ill and seems to have muddled her medicines, though others believe she killed herself, out of a mix of love and disappointment; the coroner recorded 'heart failure following emphysema, with acute bronchitis and barbituric poisoning'.[72]

Wilkinson was an early casualty of the brutal lives lived by ministers then but far from the only one. Attlee had to be suddenly hospitalized at a key moment in the Korean crisis, with a bleeding ulcer. Bevin, utterly broken by overwork and over-indulgence, died that April. Cripps had been extremely unwell since 1949, suffering from devastating pain caused by a tubercular abscess in the spine, which eventually killed him during one of his regular Swiss hospital visits, in 1952. By the late forties, according to one account, 'the ministers began to gossip about one another's health rather like old village women. Attlee confided to Dalton his deep concern about the frailty of both Bevin and Morrison. Bevin, himself apparently on his last legs, was in turn "alarmist about Attlee". He remarked that "his mind's gone ..." And so on, through the cabinet.'[73] By modern standards the Labour cabinet was not very old, the important players being in their early sixties or late fifties, but this was a hard-drinking, heavy-smoking and pressured time to be a politician. Most of these ministers worked late into the night, every night, and spent hours in the Commons arguing with more junior MPs. When they travelled, it was still in unpressurised, slow aircraft. Their holidays, taken mostly at home near at hand, were regularly interrupted for yet more

158

crisis cabinet meetings. Ill-health and botched operations would dog not only Labour but the Tories too through the post-war years, with Hugh Gaitskell, Eden and Macmillan succumbing to health crises. (Only Churchill, with his cigars, brandy and strange hours of work, continued into late old age. International fame, and the habit of being listened to attentively even when you are being boring, proves a great boost to longevity.)

Apart from being ill and in some cases disillusioned, the Labour leadership had begun to fracture. The row that propelled Nye Bevan and his then acolyte Harold Wilson, 'Nye's little dog', out of government was with hindsight a silly one. The economy had been doing rather better than during the dark year of 1947. Though the country was short of dollars, the generosity of Marshall Plan aid the following year had removed the immediate sense of crisis. By 1949, it was estimated to have raised the country's national income by a tenth. Responding to the national mood of revolt over restrictions and shortages, Wilson had announced a 'bonfire of controls' in 1948 and there seemed some chance that Labour ministers would follow the change in national mood and accept that the British wanted to spend, not only to queue. Labour was always divided between ideological socialists and more pragmatic people, but there was no obvious necessity for the party to have a row with itself towards the end of its first majority government, with so many whirlpools navigated, and so many rocks narrowly avoided.

The problem was the familiar one. Should money be concentrated first on Britain's overseas commitment, symbolized by her involvement in

159

founding Nato, and her large army facing the Russians across the Germany border; or on protecting the social advances at home? The new Chancellor, Hugh Gaitskell, had proposed charges for dental and eye treatment to help fund the massive cost of rearmament demanded by the Americans and accepted by London as the price for remaining a great power. Spending on defence would rise from 7 per cent of Britain's income in 1948 to 10.5 per cent four years later, an astonishing proportion for an economically weak country. In money terms the proposed charges hardly signified in the bill for tanks and planes, and were small too as a proportion of the new NHS budget. But hot blood and simmering rivalries turned this into a great struggle of socialist principle. Gaitskell wanted to establish his authority as chancellor. Bevan wanted to protect his ground-breaking achievement, the NHS. Neither position looks wise half a century later. Britain could not afford to be a great power in the old way, but nor could she afford to spend the Marshall Plan aid windfall mainly on better welfare, while other countries were using it to rebuild their industrial power. At Westminster the words grew hotter. Attlee had lost his old power to hold the ring. When Bevan and his friends resigned, a wound opened in the party which would never fully heal. Bevanites began meeting in livid little cabals. Their enemies denounced them in ever nastier terms.

And so the party, which had won by such an overwhelming landslide six years earlier, seemed to have lost the will to keep going. One journalist at the time described it as like 'an old, wounded animal, biting at its own injuries' and another

160

thought the debates in the Commons showed 'a Government suffering severe internal haemorrhage and likely to bleed to death at any moment'.[74] With hindsight, the post-war Labour years were a time almost cut off from what followed. So much of the country's energy had been sapped by war; what was left was focused on the struggle for survival. With Britain industrially clapped-out, mortgaged to the United States and increasingly bitter about the lack of any cheerful post-war dividend, it was perhaps not the best time to set about building a new socialist Jerusalem. Most attempts at forced modernization quickly collapsed. The direction of factories to depressed areas produced little long-term benefit. Companies encouraged to export at all costs were unable to re-equip and prepare themselves for tougher markets. Inflation, which would be a major part of the post-war story, appeared, rising from 3 per cent in 1949–50 to 9 per cent by 1951–2.

Again and again, Britain's deep dependency on the United States was simply underestimated by the politicians. Harold Wilson, for instance, slapped import duty on Hollywood films in 1947, when the sterling crisis made saving dollars such a priority. The Americans simply boycotted Britain, a devastating thing for a country then so film-besotted. Labour tried to encourage home-made, patriotic films to fill the gap and there were wonderful British films, and directors, but already glamour was something that came from the Pacific coast. When the tariffs and boycott were lifted, the wave of American releases swamped British studios. So the tariffs were taken off again. Then there was the dream of a 'British empire of the air', fleets of giant new commercial airliners criss-crossing the oceans in patriotic livery. Again, it was an expensive lesson in hubris. Vast aircraft like the Brabazon I and the Tudor IV proved no match for America's Lockhead planes. The best of the British jets, the Comet, was to suffer lethal commercial delays after crashes in the early fifties. Britain seemed to succeed best in international competition with a plucky, wire coat-hanger and empty squeezy-bottle approach.

But nothing sums up the paradoxes, the hope and chaos, the old State-direction and the coming consumer society, better than the famous Festival of Britain of 1951. Even now its defining images can be recalled by millions of people – the great modernistic Dome of Discovery, like a friendly flying saucer just alighted on the south bank of the Thames opposite Parliament, and the Skylon, a great aluminium spear, an anorexic rocket, seemingly suspended in mid-air – rather like, people said, the British economy. The Festival had been talked about during the war, but it was the editor of a liberal-minded, leftish newspaper, the *News Chronicle,* who championed it. Gerald Barry was in many ways like the Labour ministers he appealed to – high-minded, the son of a clergyman, radical, but also upper-crust by education. He wanted the festival to be not merely for people to enjoy but 'an expression of a way of life in which we believe'. The government liked the notion and set up an equally high-minded committee to take the project forward, including senior civil servants, an architect, a palaeontologist and a theatre manager.

In a famous essay about the Festival, Michael Frayn later said it had been devised by the 'herbivores', by which he meant the leftish post-war establishment people, 'the signers of petitions; the backbone of the BBC ... guiltily conscious of their advantages, though not usually ceasing to eat the grass' – what a later generation would call the chattering classes.[75] Luckily for the herbivores, political responsibility for the shindig was soon taken over by Herbert Morrison who, whatever his faults, was no snob and who had a robust understanding that people wanted fun and colour. A chance, as he put it later, for 'the people to give themselves a bit of a pat on the back'. It was a lesson forgotten when his grandson Peter Mandelson took charge of the Millennium Dome in the late nineties.

Eventually, 8.5 million people would visit the Festival on the Thames, and 8 million more went to the associated funfair in Battersea. Up and down the country innumerable others attended local events, everything from village pageants to a ship touring the seaports and a netball display at Colchester. The Festival showed what planning and risk-taking could achieve, and what it could not. While it lasted, a weed-covered, marshy, muddy, semi-derelict wasteland was turned into the scene of a great national display. The project had survived endless Whitehall wrangles on every issue from the materials its buildings were to be made from, to where in London they should be sited, to what the displays should be about – which turned out to be an immense display of the best of British design and manufacture, plus historical and scientific tableaux and some wonderful modern art. Airy pavilions surrounded piazzas; there was a whimsical model railway; the Ministry of Pensions hoped for a

163

modest display of artificial limbs. Right-wing newspapers, led by the London *Evening Standard,* ridiculed the whole idea as a waste of time and 'Morrison's folly'. Americans wrote to oppose it, in one case on the grounds that it was essentially un-British and tourists wanted 'England to be the same, battle-scarred but beautiful'. In the final stages of construction, the rain teemed down and work was halted by strikes. As with the failing British airliners, there was clear and vivid ambition; but often, it seemed, not quite the ability to carry it through.

Yet the Festival was carried through. It was a moment of patriotic tingle. The State directed something which, though mocked by many, did catch the national imagination. Conservative MPs came round and so, grudgingly, did most of the newspapers. High culture, represented by abstract sculptors, classical music, the latest in design, did manage to hold hands, however briefly, with popular culture, as represented by the cafes selling chips and peas, the funfair rides, fireworks and Gracie Fields in cabaret. Opinion polls eventually showed a hefty majority in favour of the Festival. Herbert Morrison, whose official title was Lord President and who had come close to being ridiculed for the looming failures, was now known affectionately in the press as Lord Festival. It had been a close-run thing, fun snatched from the jaws of depression. Perhaps after all, Labour's 1945 dream of a socialist commonwealth, high minded and patriotic, standing aside from crass American consumerism, could be built on England's grey and muddy land?

The Festival turned out: to be Labour's farewell

to the country for a long time. Michael Frayn summed it up later as a rainbow, riding the tail of the storm and promising fairer weather: 'It marked the ending of the hungry forties, and the beginning of an altogether easier decade ... it may perhaps be likened to a gay and enjoyable birthday party, but one at which the host presided from his death-bed.' If the host was a certain vision of British socialism then this grimly humorous image is spot on. Labour had made Britain a little more civilized and certainly fairer. But it had accomplished nothing like a revolution. By the time it returned to power in 1964, Britain had experienced something more like a Festival of America.

PART 2

THE LAND OF LOST CONTENT

Between the fall of old Clem Attlee's Labour government and the return of Labour under cocky, wisecracking Harold Wilson, Britain went through a time which some believe a golden-tinted era of lost content. To others they were the grey, conformist, 'thirteen wasted years' of Tory misrule. Either way, this part of our past was truly a different country. Much of it has disappeared. You might climb into your Austin Sheerline for a visit to the Midland Bank, stopping off at a Lyons to read your *News Chronicle* or *Picture Post* while smoking a Capstan, looking forward to a weekend visit to the Speedway by tram. It was possible to imagine a different way of being British. To leaf through newspapers and magazines of the time is to glimpse just how very different the future might have been. There are the unfamiliar all-British cars with their bulky, rather innocent styling – Jowett Cars of Idle, Bradford, advertise their Javelins and Jupiters; or you could be 'well-off in a Wolseley'. There is no sign that, just as the great age of the car begins, Britain's sprawling independent car industry is about to be wiped out. Nor, for that matter, that the 'freedom of the road' will soon be replaced by a maze of new regulations, fines and documents; there are no motorways, no out of town speed limits. There are drawings of the coming passenger heliports.

People still look different. Few schoolboys are without a cap and shorts. Caught breaking windows or lying, they might be solemnly caned by their fathers. Young girls have home-made smocks and, it is earnestly hoped, have never heard of sexual intercourse. Every woman seems to be a housewife; corsets and hats are worn and trousers, hardly ever. Among men, a silky moustache is regarded as extremely exciting to women, collars are bought separately from shirts and the smell of pipe-tobacco lingers on flannel.

Above all Britain is still a military nation, imaginatively gripped by the Second World War, whose generals are famous public figures and whose new jet-bombers provoke gasps of pride. Military uniforms, which would be worn ironically by sixties hippies, were much more common on the streets. National Service had been introduced in 1947 to replace wartime conscription and began properly two years later. It would last until 1963. More than two million young British men entered the forces, most of them the Army. It brought all classes together at a young and vulnerable age, subjecting them to strict discipline, a certain amount of practical education, often to privation, and sometimes to real danger. Teenagers were introduced to drill, cropped haircuts, heavy boots and endless polishing, creasing and blancoing of their kit. In due course some would fight for Britain in the Far East, in Palestine or Egypt, and in Africa. Most would spend a year or two in huge military camps in Britain or Germany, going quietly mad with boredom. Some died. An estimated 395 conscripts were killed in action in the fifty-plus engagements overseas during National Service, while a couple of dozen are said to have been killed in secret experiments using chemical weapons at Porton Down in Wiltshire. Others were used as human guinea pigs in British atomic bomb tests and some killed themselves, as they might have done anyway. National Service mingled and disciplined much of a generation of post-war British manhood and helped therefore to set the tone of the times. Some of the anti-authority anger and sarcasm in the culture of the time derived directly or indirectly from National Service but so did the civilian habits of polishing, dressing smartly and conforming to authority in millions of homes. In general, it probably kept some of the atmosphere of the forties alive for a decade longer than might have been expected.

In other countries – Germany, France, Russia or Japan – the trauma and devastation of the Forties was still plain everywhere. In Britain, the last prisoners of war were being sent home. Bomb-sites were being filled in and functional, unromantic buildings were taking their place, but the lessons of the war were still being unpicked. People today who were children then recall, inevitably, the fifties as the normal time – the way we were and by implication always had been. Yet the urge for domestic tranquillity, with women at home, making jam and knitting, while men worked orderly and limited hours, was a conscious response to the pain and uncertainty of 1939–45 and the continued fears of nuclear war. Then, it felt new; to be at home and quiet was a kind of liberation. For the middle classes, there was also the memory of the pre-war years as a time of order. The return of Winston Churchill in 1951 added to the impression Britain really could return to hierarchies vaguely recalled from before the war. By the end of this period, in 1963, there were still nearly a quarter of a million people in 'domestic service' – maids, housekeepers, valets – and more than six hundred full-time butlers. Britain was still graced with thirty-one Dukes, thirty-eight Marquesses and a mere 204 Earls.[1] Many private companies had an almost military feel at the top, with an officer class of gents and middle-ranking NCO types below them. Outside work the public was monitored by a self-confident officialdom, hospital consultants and terrifying matrons, bishops and park keepers, bus conductors and bicycling police officers whose authority was unconstrained by modern standards. Hanging, the physical punishment of young offenders, strong laws against abortion and homosexual behaviour by men – all these framed a system of control that was muttered against and often subverted, but through the early fifties little challenged. The country was mostly orderly. People were more or less obedient citizens and subjects, not picky consumers. Patriotism was proclaimed publicly, loudly and unselfconsciously, in a way that would quickly become hard to imagine.

In the mid-fifties, Britain is a worldwide player, connected and modern. Her major companies are global leaders in oil, tobacco, shipping and finance. The Empire is not yet quite gone, even if the new name of Commonwealth is around. Royal visits abroad, and delegations of exotic natives, feature heavily in news broadcasts and weekly magazines. Australia, New Zealand and South Africa are promoted as places for holiday cruises or emigration – sunlit, rich and empty. Collectively, they are a British California, a new frontier. Commercial liners, their flags fluttering, are waiting at Southampton. This is not a country which is closed to foreign influence, far from it. But the influences seem as strong from Italy or Scandinavia as from America – coffee-bars, Danish design, scooters and something promoted as 'Italian Welsh rarebit' (later known as pizza) are all in evidence. The awesome power of American culture is growing all the time over the horizon. But for a few years the idea of a powerful, self-confident Britain independent of American culture seemed not only possible but likely. Per capita, after all, Britain was still the second-richest major country in the world.

In public a front of national confidence was kept up. After the 1953 Coronation of the new Queen, there was much talk, albeit slightly self-conscious, of the New Elizabethan Age, a reborn nation served by great composers, artists and scientists. Not all of this was false, even in retrospect. In Ralph Vaughan Williams, Benjamin Britten and Michael Tippett, Britain did have some world-class musical talents. W. H. Auden and T. S. Eliot were among the great poets of the age. Then, at least, it looked to many as if the sculptor Henry Moore and the painter Graham Sutherland were world-class figures. Churchill may have been really too old to be Prime Minister during the first few years of the fifties, but he was undoubtedly one of the few great figures of the time, an ageing colossus whose books were pouring from the presses, stamping his version of history on the public mind. Along with another star author of the fifties, William Golding, he would be a Nobel Prize-winner. In popular culture, the steady rise of television brought, at first, a traditionalist English upper-crust view of the world to millions of homes. This was the age of 'Andy Pandy' and gardening tips, of Joyce Grenfell and Noël Coward. It was also the time of Roger Bannister and his four-minute mile; the conquest of Everest; triumphs in yachting and football; even in the world of adventure and sport, Britain was doing well. With Nobel Prize-winning science in physics and biology, there was no sign yet of the brain drain of scientists to the United States.

Knowing what we know now, there were signs of social change everywhere from the disaffected teenagers just beginning to be discussed, to the rise of Maltese, Italian and home-grown crime dynasties, and the first wide-eyed, optimistic Caribbean immigrants. There was also much boredom and frustration. Working-class Britain was getting richer, but still housed in dreadful old homes, excluded from higher education, unless part of a small and lucky elite, and deprived of any jobs but hard and boring ones. Eventually, the lid would blow off. Yet to be British was something to be proud of. Even the mild hooligan element was home-grown; the exotic and expensive costumes of the Teddy boys, with their velvet collars, long jackets and foppish waistcoats, were modelled on English Edwardian dress.

Balcon's Britain

Among all the people who expressed the most optimistic spirit of Britishness in this period the best example is a Jewish adventurer's son from Birmingham, brought up in radical and suffragette circles. His films have already been mentioned, for Michael Balcon was the man behind the Ealing comedies and scores of other films. He was the great interpreter of these years, second only to Churchill in crafting how the British remember themselves in the middle of the twentieth century. In a world culture dominated by the United States he was determined that Britain should be distinct and his vision of the British family blended the high-mindedness of Attlee with the impatient spirit of the coming Tory years. Had we faced nuclear annihilation then one of Balcon's Ealing comedies would probably have been the last work of art broadcast by the BBC's young television service.[2] He is worth spending a little time on because his success and failure offers a key, or guide, to the underlying uncertainties and paradoxes of the age. Balcon bottled the most pungent elements of the spirit of Britain in the late forties and early fifties, and through his films we can inhale them freshly now as if the intervening years had not passed.

The Ealing studios are still there. The white painted, functional offices and the vast hangar-like shed would be instantly recognizable to Balcon, and they are busy, being used again to make films. Even the pub across the road where Balcon's team of writers and producers drank, smoked, dreamed and fought is not much changed, though Ealing is a multi-ethnic, trendy place compared to the relentlessly suburban, indeed dull part of West London it was when the film studios were established there in 1931. They were intended to be a small British redoubt against the power of American cinema. Certainly, it is hard to imagine a more dramatic contrast to the sprawl, bright light and self-importance of Hollywood. The studios could easily be mistaken from the outside as a provincial school. In a way, they were. During the thirties Ealing had bridged the nineteenth-century culture of the music hall and the new world of cinema, making popular comedies by the Lancashire musical stars George Formby and Gracie Fields. Balcon himself had been working for a range of film-makers, including Gainsborough and Gaumont-British, struggling with the sheer gravitational force of the Hollywood system before being lured there himself. It was not a success. He fell out spectacularly with Louis B. Mayer, who once bawled that he would destroy Balcon 'if it costs me a million dollars'. Balcon is said to have replied that he would settle for less. He happily quit to rule Ealing through the heroic days of the war, the years of New Jerusalem and carry on until 1955, the year of Eden's election. He enjoyed a continuity no politican could rival and he was as passionate about national cinema as they were about the nation.

Ealing was in some ways a miniature Britain of the period. It had its autocratic, eccentric leader. It developed a robust, vaguely socialist patriotism under the conditions of the war (though Churchill was dubious about some of the war films, and half-heartedly tried to ban a couple for being defeatist). And in 1945 Balcon and his colleagues voted Labour – what Balcon described as their 'mild revolution' but they quickly became hostile to the pressing rules and regulations of post-war life. Like Britain Ealing was badly underfunded and thrived on a make do and mend approach to film-making, the cult of improvisation. It too had a rich array of political views and immigrants, people from the colonies, White Russians, semi-communists and militant trade unionists. Yet they were all expected to show total loyalty and to work for only modest rewards. Many decisions were taken round a large table at which free and frank expression was expected – the cabinet table, as it were – and these sessions were followed by heroic drinking bouts at that local pub. If Ealing had an ideology it was a misty one, something to do with fairness, decency, the importance of the little man, and of standing up to bullies, be they Bavarian or merely bureaucratic.

In the films shopkeepers and fishermen outwit Whitehall officials and excisemen; small boys and little old ladies outwit criminal gangs. There is an unmistakeable edge: so many heroes are working class, so many villains are posh. But they are also culturally and morally conservative. In its war films, thrillers, psychological dramas and adventure movies as well as the famous comedies, Ealing almost entirely avoids sex and violence. Writing at the end of the sixties when British horror films and 'sexploitation' films were taking off, Balcon wryly reflected that 'if there has been a sex deficiency in the films for which I have been responsible over the years no great or permanent damage has been done, as current films are more than making up for lost time ... there are many things in life other than sex and violence. There's love, for instance ...' In Balcon's Britain, 'love' was not yet coy code for making love. As was said of a non-Ealing film, *Brief Encounter,* the post-war British ideal seemed to be 'make tea not love'. Films of understatement, films of bitten lips and dramatic silences; and, in a phrase by the novelist E. M. Forster, films about an English nervous system which 'acts promptly and feels slowly' are a good guide to how different the country was back then. It was all very non-Hollywood. It was consciously intended as an alternative way of understanding the world. Balcon had talked about the need to project 'the true Briton' to the rest of the world. He wanted a cinema that would show the Americans, the French and the Russians 'Britain as a leader in social reform in the defeat of social injustices and a champion of civil liberties ...' It was a noble vision yet like Britain, Ealing was too weak, too underfunded and improvisatory, to live up to its ambitions. After an extraordinary flowering of creativity in the forties and early fifties, Ealing fell back into romantic, self-congratulatory guff and the rest of the world moved on.

Small Rooms: How Governments Were Run in the Fifties

Churchill was about to be seventy-seven when he returned to office, which was an older age then than it is now. When he observed to his private secretary that he had never known a prime minister so old, the well-read civil servant replied that actually Churchill had – William Ewart Gladstone. Like Gladstone, he would still be Prime Minister in his eighties. (The Grand Old Man of the nineteenth century lasted a few years longer than the Grand Old Boy of the twentieth century perhaps because Gladstone had neither led Britain through a world war nor fuelled himself the while on brandy and cigars.) The Conservatives had radically overhauled their organization and policies during the Attlee years, in a way the party was unable or unwilling to do after later defeats. They had moved decisively towards the consensus for a Welfare State, a more centrist position than ever before, and they had very effectively played on the grimness and occasional absurdities of the rationing years. Having promised the unexciting agenda of 'several years of solid, stable administration', Churchill formed a government of cronies and old muckers, reluctant generals and businessmen. The best people were his wartime allies Eden, Macmillan and the education reformer, 'Rab' Butler.

Politics in the fifties, at least on the Tory side, was unimaginably different from politics today. There were the same rackety campaigning offices, the same ambitious young researchers dreaming of becoming ministers themselves and the same underlying ruthless struggle for personal power. But many more people were party members, the backbench MPs were more independent-minded, with more status in the country, yet far lazier, too; and above all, the top of government was small social circle which operated well out of the way of lenses, microphones or diarists. Churchill himself spent an alarming amount of his time playing the card game bezique and travelling, often slowly on ocean liners and, as would Eden and Macmillan, put great strain on the notion of genuine cabinet discussion, provoking ferocious rows, walk-outs and threatened resignations. When Churchill and his Chancellor, Rab Butler, hatched a complicated plot to save the pound, ministers were presented with a take-it-or-leave-it ultimatum and furiously protested. When Churchill fired off an invitation to a summit with the Soviets after Stalin's death, sending it while sailing in mid-Atlantic, his cabinet was equally outraged and eventually forced a climbdown. When Eden bitterly protested in cabinet that Churchill was breaking yet another promise about his retirement, other ministers complained that here was an important story about which they had been told nothing. Yet Eden's Suez plot was hatched without important ministers having any clear idea of what was really happening. And Macmillan governed by playing ministers off against one another, expertly avoiding full and frank discussions in cabinet.

Most of the key political moments of these years take place like scenes on a small stage, in rooms containing a handful of people who know one another too well. As in Shakespeare, there are crowd scenes too – the rallies against Eden; the first Aldermaston marches; race riots and trade union mass meetings for yet another strike. But in terms of day-to-day power, they are noises off. Instead we have Macmillan visiting Churchill in the latter stages of his prime ministership, to find the old man in characteristic Number Ten pose, sitting in bed with a green budgerigar on his head: 'He had the cage on his bed (from which the bird had come out) and a cigar in his hand. A whisky and soda was by his side – of this the little bird took sips later on. Miss Portal sat by the bed – he was dictating.'[3]

Eighteen months later, there will be the cosy private dinner in Number Ten, interrupted when Eden gets his first message about the nationalization of the Suez Canal, and is told he must hit Nasser quickly and hard, by one of his guests, the regent of Iraq, Nuri El Said. This guest

180

will later be a victim of Eden's failure, having his guts ripped out by the Baghdad mob and dragged, still living, through the streets attached to the back bumper of his car. Later still, there will be the famous procession of ministers being asked privately, one by one, who should succeed Eden by the drawling aristocratic kingmaker, Salisbury, 'Wab or Hawold?' They choose Macmillan. Edward Heath, the chief whip, has to go and break the news to Rab Butler that, though almost every newspaper says he will be the new Prime Minister, they are all wrong and he has lost out. Again, two men in a dramatically lit room overlooking Horse Guards Parade: 'As I entered, his face lit up with its familiar, charming smile ... there was nothing I could do to soften the blow. "I'm sorry, Rab," I said, "It's Harold." He looked utterly dumbfounded.'[4] After that, Macmillan's first move is to summon Heath to dinner, to reshape the government. They have to barge through a crowd of journalists – Downing Street in those days being completely open to the public – and Heath is tripped up by one, tumbling into the car which races up Whitehall to Macmillan's haunt, the Turf Club. There another member of the club, sitting at the bar with the evening newspaper announcing the identity of the new Prime Minister, looks up, sees him and politely asks whether he had had any good shooting lately. No, laments Macmillan. Pity says the clubman. As he and Heath turn towards the dining room for oysters and steak, the man politely drawls, 'Oh, by the way – congratulations.'[5]

Much later Macmillan finally decides he too must retire. He has had great pain and difficulty pissing and wrongly thinks it might be cancer. Another

181

small room: sitting in his hospital bed wearing pale blue pyjamas, with a silk shirt and cardigan (but without a bird on his head) he tells the Queen. Later, he suggests she should summon Alec Douglas-Home to replace him. There are literally dozens of similar examples of how political life was carried on among the top Tories during this period. Of course, there have been many Labour cabals, from the paranoid huddles in Harold Wilson's Downing Street to the notorious Blair and Brown deal at Granita restaurant in Islington in 1994. But nothing quite matched the tight little world of the Churchill and Macmillan era. If they were not dining in the Commons or a handful of gentlemen's clubs in St James's – Macmillan belonged to five clubs – they were shooting grouse together or meeting in villas in the south of France. It is sometimes said that Churchill's government, stuffed with old friends and relatives, was unusual. But of Macmillan's all-male cabinet, a mere two out of sixteen had not been to a grand public school, with Eton the most heavily represented. Astonishingly, within months of his becoming Prime Minister, Macmillan was leading a government in which thirty-five ministers out of eighty-five, including seven in the cabinet, were related to him by marriage.[6]

There were outsiders too, including Powell, Heath and later Margaret Thatcher. Ernie Marples, a former sergeant-major and building contractor who would help create Britain's first motorways, was another self-made man in the government; so was Reggie Bevins of Liverpool. Most of them felt awkward and ill-at-ease, not quite officer class in the Conservative hierarchy of the fifties. The social make-up of the Tory administrations contributed to their weakness and eventually the collapse of their authority. The charmed circle of intermarried grandees were so much the country's traditional ruling order that their natural instinct was to play down crisis. Not in front of the servants, children or voters seemed to be their private motto. Because all was not well, this would fatally destroy their authority. In the 'satire boom', rule by toffs would be discredited. Their silent struggles for power would eventually spill into the public domain, giving us political catchphrases like 'Establishment' and 'magic circle'. Sex scandals and spying scandals would persuade people that there really was something rotten in the old order. Rather as New Labour connived with the press in the 1990s to mock John Major's administration to death, so Harold Wilson and old Labour would join hands with *Private Eye* and playwrights to despatch the last government of grandees.

Churchill in Old Age

When Churchill returned to power in 1951, all this was still far ahead. The old order seemed to have re-established itself far more quickly than the smashing defeat of six years earlier implied. And it was an old order. Churchill was undisputedly the greatest Englishman alive. Yet he was now fighting time. Two years into his last premiership, just after giving a speech to visiting Italians in Downing Street – always history-obsessed, he had been lecturing them on the Roman legions in England

– he slumped down with a major stroke. Hurried to bed, he nevertheless recovered enough to hold a cabinet meeting the following day, though saying little. But he then deteriorated so fast his doctor thought he would die. He lost the use of his left arm, spoke only in a slurred mumble, and was unable to stand. He was hurried to his home at Chartwell. There, over two months, he recovered. It is an astonishing story in several ways. First there is the spectacle of Churchill's amazing willpower and stamina, bringing him from near death to a position where he could make a major speech to the Tory conference and then engage in full Commons exchanges within a few months. Even more astonishing, the country did not know at the time what had happened. There were vague rumours but the Prime Minister's grave illness was kept secret to all outside a very close circle. In the end he broke the secret himself, mentioning it a couple of years later in Parliament, by which time it no longer mattered much.

Before this stroke, and indeed after it, other ministers found the old lion entirely exasperating. He had brilliant moments, both in set-piece speeches and in conversation. But he was a speaking memorial to his own greatness and therefore naturally inclined to ramble on. He was described as 'senile', 'past it' and 'gaga' in the memoirs of other members of the cabinet. They wrote of their hatred for him as well as their love. Sometimes he let his private secretary write a speech for him. Sometimes he forgot what he was going to say half-way through a sentence. Sometimes even foreign leaders such as the US President, Harry Truman, expressed boredom at his long-windedness. But the person most angered, hurt and frustrated was Anthony Eden who felt that after ten years of waiting, and half a lifetime at the top of the Tory tree, it was his turn to govern. Prime ministers always find it hard to give up. Churchill resisted Eden by frequent promises that he was likely to go at some time in the future, always then putting it off. He would reshuffle his ministers, offer Eden unsuitable alternative jobs, row with him, then raise his hopes only to dash them again.

Had the pair of them not been the most powerful men in Britain, and had it not been rather cruel, it would have been almost funny. Churchill had become increasingly doubtful as to whether Eden would be any good as Prime Minister, lecturing him about the importance of keeping in with the Americans, snapping at his suggestions and complaining to friends that he didn't think 'Anthony can do it'. If all else failed Churchill, as ever, used jokes. When the death was announced of a minister's father, Churchill greeted yet another delegation sent to urge his retirement with a mournful reference to the deceased, 'Quite young, too. Only 90.'[7] Age and illness would be a big theme of the Tory years, as they had been in the latter stage of Attlee's government. Eden was frequently ill with a biliary duct problem made worse by botched surgery. By the time he finally got the top job halfway through the decade, he was physically depleted. Macmillan later said of him that he was like a racehorse who had been trained to win the Derby in 1938 but was not let out of the starting stalls until 1955. So why did Churchill carry on for so long? Undoubtedly, part of the reason was that he simply could not bear to let go. But there was a nobler reason. The old man did have a cause.

Churchill's life had been dominated by war. He came from a grand military family, brought up surrounded by the stories and mementoes of battles won. He went to fight for the Empire in the Sudan then saw the Boer War at first hand as a war correspondent who was captured and escaped. In the First World War he was a highly controversial First Lord of the Admiralty, then a colonel in France. After it, as War Secretary, he tried to strangle the Bolshevik revolution with an entirely unsuccessful Western war in support of the Whites against Lenin. His great years were as Britain's war leader in the world fight against Fascism. Many of his critics, from socialists who remembered him sending tanks against trade union strikers to Little Englanders, reviled him as a natural warmonger. So it is interesting that his last great crusade was an attempt to stop a war, this time a nuclear one. Whether it was the wisdom of age or vanity about his unique role as global statesman, Winston Spencer Churchill became the world's leading peacenik. His speeches resounded with dark warnings of the catastrophe just ahead. As early as the 1950 election campaign, speaking in Edinburgh, he had coined the modern use of 'summit' when calling for a leaders' parley with the Russians. The arrival of the hydrogen bomb increased the sense of world panic and Churchill worried in particular about an American atom bomb strike against the Chinese in North Korea (as indeed did the Chinese).

He was struggling with a new world, understanding the nuclear threat but also thinking in a highly traditional way. As soon as he returned to power in 1951 Churchill had fired off worried requests for information about the ease with which Russian paratroopers could seize strategic locations in London, and the carnage that would be caused by different kinds of surprise nuclear attack. Above all, he thought that if the atom bomb menace existed, Britain had better be as menacing as she could manage. In December 1951 he had authorized Britain's first nuclear test and at the Monte Bello islands off Australia, HMS *Plym,* one of the war-surplus frigates which had escaped being broken up or mothballed, was instead vaporized by Britain's first nuclear bomb. Then in 1954 he gave the go-ahead, with weary resignation, for work on a British hydrogen bomb as 'the price we pay to sit at the top table'. He told his cabinet, 'If the United States were tempted to undertake a forestalling war, we could not hope to remain neutral ... We must avoid any action which would weaken our power to influence United States policy.'[8] Britain would only have a voice in restraining America if it was itself a player: 'the fact must be faced that, unless we possessed thermo-nuclear weapons, we should lose our influence and standing in world affairs.' But for Churchill it was precautionary despair; his real campaign was for a new settlement between capitalist West and Marxist East.

London and Washington did not see eye to eye on nuclear matters, as we have seen. Britain had been abruptly cut off from American nuclear secrets and in the early fifties Britain was more immediately threatened. Russian bombers could not yet reach the United States so American bases in Britain, and RAF ones, would make this country the first Soviet nuclear target. Dreadful estimates of the carnage were circulated through Whitehall. Yet for the Americans, nuclear war was still something that happened abroad. Churchill saw the death of Stalin as a heaven-sent opportunity to reopen friendlier relations with Moscow. Though as passionately anti-Communist as ever he was worried that the US President, his wartime comrade Dwight Eisenhower, was too rigidly anti-Russian. Churchill frankly thought 'Ike' stupid and unable to comprehend that nuclear weapons were far more than the latest military technology. This reflected an accurate gulf of perception. Eisenhower believed nuclear weapons were a mere extension of ordinary weaponry and would soon be regarded as conventional. Eisenhower and his Secretary of State Dulles in turn feared that in his dotage Churchill had become an appeaser; though Churchill always used the term 'easement' or 'settlement' of East–West relations as his preferred description. Again and again he tried to persuade Eisenhower of the virtues of a superpower summit, and offered to go to Moscow himself alone – at a time when the Americans would not dream of setting foot on Soviet territory – to clear the way. Dulles was strongly hostile. Churchill bitterly called him 'that bastard'. At last, having got an insincere half-promise from Eisenhower that he could at least contact the Soviets about some meeting on neutral ground, he fired off the invitation too early, became embroiled in a white-hot cabinet row, and had to watch his vision crumble. At the top of the rival powers, no one but him really wanted to make peace just then. Everybody was too busy preparing the next generation of nuclear devices, thinking more like generals, less like statesmen. Churchill was arguing for détente twenty years before it happened. Perhaps he had been doing it with a selfish tremor, hoping for a final triumph, but as visions go it was quite something for an eighty-year-old.

Churchill's other overseas initiatives were less impressive. He was losing the battle about the Empire and knew it, even as he wrapped himself in mystical prose about the new young Queen and the coming Elizabethan age. If the real conflict was with the Soviet Union and her allies, what price Britain's other post-imperial commitments? What price trying to hang onto control in Palestine, where desperate refugees were determined to settle, and where Jewish terrorists were killing British soldiers? What price Britain's piggy-in-the-middle role in Greece, trying to protect an unpopular monarchy against a communist insurgency? A little later on, trying to hold on in Egypt, or Iran, would prompt the same question. The private thinking of Whitehall was laid out in a fascinating memo from top officials to a cabinet committee shortly after the Americans had upped the ante in the nuclear race by exploding their first H-bombs. The British cabinet paper was frank about the overall position: 'It is clear that ever since the end of the war we have tried to do too much – with the result that we have only rarely been free from the danger of economic crisis.'

About Europe, Churchill had long been inclined to make dramatic-sounding suggestions. He had offered to merge British and French citizenship during the darkest days of 1940. After the war he was not averse to a fully politically united Western

189

Europe, though he assumed the British Empire could not be a full member. When he came back to power one of the most immediate issues was whether Britain would join early moves towards that united Western Europe. In 1950, the ailing Labour government had decided against, though after very little thought. When the French Foreign Minister, Robert Schuman, announced that his country intended to share sovereignty over iron and coal with West Germany, so binding the two old enemies tightly together in their industrial effort, he gave the British government an ultimatum. Attlee was out of the country and Ernie Bevin was already very ill, describing himself with no exaggeration as 'half-dead'. It was left to Herbert Morrison to give a hurried response. He had been at the theatre and was found by officials at the Ivy restaurant in London's Covent Garden. The plan which would one day lead to the European Union was explained to Morrison in a back room, piled with chairs.[9] He thought for a moment and shook his head. 'It's no good. We can't do it. The Durham miners won't wear it.' For many Tories, watching from the sidelines, this was a disastrous mistake. Macmillan, who had been observing things from Strasbourg, where he was in Bevin's vacated hotel room, thought the decision catastrophic, later telling his constituents it was 'a black week for Britain' and the country might pay a 'catastrophic price' for isolating itself under the socialists from Europe.[10] So there was general expectation that Tory Britain would change tack.

There was already a strong case for doing so. The Empire was falling away. Relations with the Americans had already been damaged over the atom bomb, as well as disputes about Palestine and Greece. Here was a moment for the Tories to decide to ride another horse too, and join the young European club. Churchill declined to do so. Offered the chance to take up common European defence, he ridiculed the notion, to the despair of Macmillan and some of the younger Conservatives. He showed no interest in deeper involvement. He was the last imperialist whose rhetoric about the 'English-speaking peoples' was more heartfelt than his suggestions of anti-Communist alliances between Italians, Belgians and the French. Washington was pivotal to his world as Paris never could be, still less Brussels. He wanted summits on the H-bomb and a place on the world stage, not local deals with provincial nations half-desolated by war and invasion. The Foreign Office, where Eden was ensconced, was also hostile to entanglements with the Europeans – not surprising, either, perhaps, since its grand embassies and worldwide reach made iron and steel deals near at hand seem parochial. The manner of Churchill's decision-making on Europe, though, was worrying to his contemporaries. It was never properly discussed in cabinet. It was as much a shrug as a decision. It was never announced. It was never thrashed through. It might as well have been taken in the Ivy. Perhaps, as with nuclear peace-making, it was just too early for the decisive move. Yet there is an unmistakeable sense of anti-climax about Churchill's last government. Outside the world was changing. New leaders were coming to prominence. Here, it seemed, Britain was being distracted by one moving curtain-call too many.

Strikes and Money:
Jack Is All Right ...

Conservatives of the fifties have had a particularly bad press for their willingness to stick with the Attlee consensus, allowing the country's underlying economic weakness to worsen. There is much in this. Churchill had fought the 1951 election promising to defend the new Welfare State and was inclined to speak wistfully of the case for coalition government in peace as in war, a theme first heard in 1945. He felt warmly towards the small Liberal Party and had half promised to help them by introducing some kind of proportional voting, though this was quickly scuppered by the Conservative hierarchy. He railed against class war and deliberately appointed the moderate, appeasing lawyer Walter Monckton to deal with trade union and labour matters. Yet there was one moment when Britain might have experienced a Thatcher-sized jolt, a British revolution thirty years early. It came on Churchill's watch in 1952 when his young Chancellor, Rab Butler, proposed cutting the pound free from the system of fixed exchange rates agreed after the war at Bretton Woods. The scheme was called ROBOT. In detail it was fiendishly complicated, because of Britain's network of obligations to so many other countries using sterling as their reserve. In essence, though, it was very simple. The pound would float partly free, or rather fall dramatically against the dollar, thus giving Britain's struggling exporters a huge one-off boost. The government would be unable to fund its old obligations, the huge overseas defence establishment, and much of the new Welfare State. Grand housebuilding projects would be put on hold and unemployment would initially rise. But on the other hand, the bleeding of reserves and the periodic balance-of-payments crises would be a thing of the past. Britain would get the chance of a fresh start, not unlike post-war West Germany. Imports would be cut, exports would rise, sterling's freedom in the world would be re-established and the alternative future of a genteel, endless decline might be averted. It was nothing less than a free-market national coup which would, among other things, infuriate the Americans. The historian Peter Hennessy has compared it to the desperation of the Suez war: 'ROBOT was the desperate and risky response of frazzled yet clever men who had run out of both caution and alternative ideas.'[11]

ROBOT, which was never revealed at the time, caused a rare row over matters of high principle inside the government and was eventually scuppered by the Foreign Secretary, Anthony Eden, and by Churchill's own growing unease about its domestic implications. It was the kind of scheme which might have been pushed through by a determined, vigorous Prime Minister armed with a mandate for change but was too much for an old man elected on a blandly consensual ticket. And it was the only example of such radical thinking for years to come, at least at this level of government. For the most part, this was a government which ran on domestic autopilot. Above all, in the eyes of later critics, it failed to take on rising trade union power. The unions had swollen in numbers to record levels of membership. Their leaders tended to be working-class men who had left school in their teens to cut coal, drive lorries or load ships before becoming full-time organizers. In the fifties, they still had personal memories of the General Strike of 1926. Bitterness about the Depression had been partly assuaged after Labour repealed anti-union legislation, giving them powerful immunities in the case of strike action.

These national leaders, men such as Arthur Deakin, Sam Watson and Bill Carron, tended to be patriotic and socially conservative, ready to back the Bomb and Nato, and aligned against the left in Labour Party confrontations. They were well able to do deals with middle-of-the-road Tory ministers. More were Catholics than were Communists. But their greatest card was the economy. Very high rates of employment, high demand from customers starved of goods, and relatively high corporate profits meant that there was an insatiable demand for skilled labour. It was easy for firms to pass on higher costs caused by generous wage settlements. And in terms of days lost to strikes, Britain's record was not bad in the fifties, better than many economies which were growing faster. Butler at the Treasury confessed that he had no wages policy, only 'Walter's friendship with trade union leaders' and when Monckton and Churchill did a deal to stop a bus-drivers' Christmas strike because it was too 'disturbing', the Prime Minister phoned Butler late at night to tell him the good news. On what terms had he settled, the Chancellor nervously asked. Churchill replied, 'Theirs, old cock! We did not like to keep you up.'[12]

Why fight the unions? It was a horribly difficult task, anyway. In a statist economy, ministers were abnormally close to the power of the public sector unions. By later standards, an astonishing number of industrial workers were employed by the State – some 1.7 million people in transport, the mines and the power industry alone. Again and again, from the railways to the power stations, from bus workers to coalminers, to engineering, Monckton and his successors bought them off. Ministers knew perfectly well what they were doing. In his diary for June 1955, for instance, Macmillan, when Chancellor, reflected on the settlement of a railway strike which had done 'much harm' to the economy. He comforted himself with the thought that the men got little more than they could have had earlier which 'may have a deflationary effect and do something to stop the see-saw of wages and prices which has begun to show itself in the last year or two'. By 1958, as Prime Minister, he steeled himself to hold out against just the kind of transport strike that Churchill would have settled with a phone call. Yet Macmillan too never quite took it seriously and anyway by then the unions were changing in ways that made it harder to cope with them, not easier.

Built up over decades by amalgamations and local deals, they were sprawling baggy monsters which bore little relation to organization by plant or industry. A single factory might have a maze of competing and mutually suspicious unions operating inside it. This led to the growth in power of the shop stewards, often younger and more militant people who had filled the power gap during the war years when their elders were away. They could get deals for the people around them which were better than national agreements. By the mid-fifties there were scores of thousands of them. It was ruefully noted that Britain now had more shop stewards than soldiers. Wildcat strikes were more common than full-scale national disputes and they caused more disruption and uncertainty. Meanwhile as the old guard died off more left-wing leaders were quietly moving up the union hierarchy. A good example was Frank Cousins, a former miner and truck-driver from Nottinghamshire who was running the road hauliers in Churchill's day and who became leader of the Transport & General Workers' Union in the year of Suez when more than half a million T&G men voted for him. He was Macmillan's antagonist in 1958 and became a major headache for successive Conservative governments, leading strikes in the car industry, among busmen and elsewhere before being brought into the 1964 Labour cabinet by Harold Wilson. For a time he was the most famous, or infamous of the Brothers; but there were plenty of Cousins.

If strikes were one small cloud on the edge of the sunny skies of the Tory years, inflation was another. It was always there in the fifties, getting worse as the decade continued, but not yet quite a crisis, although with so many older people living off annuities and savings, it began eating into the lives of many middle-class families. The problem was simple to describe, hard to sort, particularly after the rejection of radical measures such as ROBOT. The country was exporting all it could but its appetite for manufactured imports was insatiable. Britain no longer had enough overseas investments and was not earning enough through producing well-made, competitively priced goods, in order to earn the living its people now thought they deserved. In other times the gap had been easily closed by 'invisibles' – earnings from banking, insurance and shipping, where Britain remained a world leader. It might have done so in the fifties and sixties too, except that Britain was spending such an historically vast amount of money on defence in peacetime, and spending that money abroad. In effect, the weaker British economy was subsidizing the fast-growing West German one because of the huge expenditure on the British Army of the Rhine.

The entirely predictable result of the balance of payments gap was that the pound was under constant pressure. There were periodic devaluations which damaged the reputation of the politicians in charge at the time – though the 1949 Labour devaluation is widely credited with kick-starting the Tory good times which followed. Trying to maintain British power through the sterling area (not just most of the Old Commonwealth, except Canada, but other countries including most of Scandinavia and traditional trading partners such as Portugal) meant that defending the value of the pound was an issue inflamed by pride and political sensitivity. In the Tory years it was another problem postponed. Defend the pound and Britain's global self-image or let it fall and help Britain's exporters? 'Stop-go' saw sudden tightenings of fiscal policy, then a stab on the accelerator, as government tried to break into a new era of growth, before slamming on the brakes to deal with the resulting surge in inflation. Until the post-war Bretton Woods system broke down in 1971 there would be regular arguments about devaluation. For politicians at the time, it was like trying to solve a puzzle with one too many parts.

The Purge

It is 24 March 1954, late in the afternoon outside Winchester Castle. The great hall of the medieval building, with its famous fake of Arthur's Round Table – created in the 1300s and painted for Henry VIII – is now empty. It has served duty all day as a courtroom. Now guilty verdicts have been passed and long since, the prison sentences meted out. But still the prisoners have been kept in the small whitewashed cells under the castle, an elderly Rolls-Royce waiting to take them to jail. The trial that had just finished made front-page headlines for days across Britain, and there were fears of a minor riot when the guilty men were led outside. They included a young peer of the realm, Edward John Barrington Douglas-Scott-Montagu, known as Lord Montagu of Beaulieu; a *Daily Mail* journalist called Peter Wilde-blood; and a gentleman farmer, Major Michael Pitt-Rivers. Montagu had just been sentenced to twelve months in prison and the other two, eighteen months. Their crime had been conspiring to induce two RAF men to commit indecent acts – in other words, they were homosexuals.

There was a great purge of homosexuals going on in the Britain of the fifties, whipped up by the newspapers and by a clique of politicians and officials. The press had been full of salacious if untrue stories of wild orgies fuelled by champagne,

198

the corruption of boy scouts and, perhaps worse than all this, of men who had associated with their social inferiors. So there was, perhaps, some reason to worry that when the three men were led away there would be angry attacks by the good burghers and women of Winchester. And indeed there were such scenes. But the attacks, the hammering of umbrellas, yelling, hissing and shaking of fists, was directed at the car taking away the prosecution witnesses. When eventually Montagu, Wildeblood and Pitt-Rivers were seen by the women who had waited so long, the mood was rather different. As Wildeblood himself wrote later: 'It was some moments before I realised they were not shouting insults, but words of encouragement. They tried to pat us on the back and told us to "keep smiling", and when the doors were shut they went on talking through the windows and gave the thumbs-up sign and clapped their hands.'[13] Much later, when Wildeblood was finally released from prison, he found his neighbours and colleagues just as supportive. The English are often unexpected.

Homosexual acts between men had long been illegal, but so long as they happened discreetly and in private, and did not involve minors, they had been relatively rarely prosecuted. The war, as we have seen, saw an increase in homosexual activity. After it, however, the official mood changed dramatically. In the last full year before the war there had been 320 prosecutions for 'gross indecency', a common way of describing homosexual behaviour. By 1952 the number had risen to 1,626. The prosecutions for attempted sodomy or indecent assault were up from 822 to over 3,000. If these still seem relatively small

199

numbers, the ripples of fear and intimidation spread far further, and in general the number of homosexual offences known to the police had risen from 1938 to 1955 by 850 per cent. A small number of men were responsible. The crackdown had started under Herbert Morrison. But the toughest years were under the Conservative politicians of the fifties. The purge was led by the former Nuremberg interrogator of Nazi leaders, Churchill's Home Secretary, Sir David Maxwell Fyfe. With him was the Director of Public prosecutions, Theobald Mathew, who would often attend court to watch the 'buggers' be sentenced, as well as Sir John Nott-Bower, a Commissioner of the Metropolitan Police determined to rip the cover off London's 'filth spots'. They were supported by a press which ran articles on the secret world of mincing pansies, or explained to stout-hearted readers 'how to spot a homo'. There were special drives to root out buggery in the Army and worried Whitehall inquiries into alleged lesbian conspiracies in the RAF. Lesbianism was not, in itself, a crime, allegedly because Queen Victoria had refused to believe it existed, but was an offence in the armed services.

Attacking homosexuals helped sell papers and certainly played to the prejudices of many politicians and clergymen but there was more to it than that. The early fifties was also the time of maximum fear about Communism, subversion and spying. Not without reason. The atom bomb spy Klaus Fachs had caused appalling damage to British intelligence by the time he was exposed in 1950. In 1951 two of the famous KGB spies, Guy Burgess and Donald Maclean, had defected to the

Soviet Union. Though a proper version of their story would not break publicly until 1955, the British government was under American pressure to show that it was tough on subversive networks. This was not formally discussed at home but friendly overseas journalists were briefed. In October 1953, the *Sydney Daily Telegraph* reported that Cmdr E. A. Cole of Scotland Yard had spent three months in Washington consulting with the FBI after 'strong United States advice to Britain to weed out homosexuals as hopeless security risks, from important government jobs'. With the arrival of Nott-Bower as the new Commissioner of Police 'the plan was extended as a war on all vice ... ' So moralism and national security worries intertwined. The homosexual, so the thinking went, had to live a double life. He was open to blackmail. He moved in mysterious circles. He was morally weak. The homosexual was therefore by definition a security risk. Burgess and Blunt had indeed lived secret sexual lives and the habits of essential deception, the feeling of belonging to a hidden and important circle, connected seamlessly to their lives as spies. Nor was the blackmail argument ridiculous. A few years after the Montagu case, John Vassall, a homosexual clerk who worked at the Admiralty and had been photographed in Moscow by the KGB at a gay sex party, was uncovered as a spy. Vassall was a conspicuous consumer, living far beyond his means, yet no one had asked the obvious questions about where his money was coming from. Again, there was much speculation about a wider homosexual and traitorous network, this time involving ministers too.

The gap in official logic was that homosexual men

were open to blackmail and had to live a secret life precisely because of the law that was now being so vigorously and aggressively enforced. Some men were self-confident enough to survive, the Labour MP Tom Driberg for one, who used the Commons toilets to proposition an impressive array of fellow politicians as well as parliamentary staff, and Macmillan's colleague, the lover of his wife, Lord Boothby. But others, including the Conservative MP Ian Harvey, convicted of an offence with a soldier in Hyde Park, and the actor John Gielgud, arrested in Chelsea in 1953, were not so lucky. There was a very extensive and semi-open gay world in theatrical circles – Alec Guinness had been fined for importuning in 1946, for instance, but had escaped press attention by giving the false name Herbert Pocket. Other celebrities of the time such as Noël Coward and the impresario Binkie Beaumont hardly bothered to hide their sexuality. But the wave of prosecutions caused terror among those living outside the charmed circle of theatrical and political power.

Montagu had fallen into the middle of the police operation first suggested by Washington. A premier peer of the realm, he was about as well connected as it was possible to be. In his time with the Grenadier Guards, he had served in Palestine during the worst of the Jewish terrorist attacks, and had an informal supper with the King, Queen and future Queen Elizabeth. In the advertising world, he had helped launch the patriotic new comic, *The Eagle* – the idea of a north country vicar called Marcus Morris who himself, said Montagu later, had 'a distinctly unclerical sexual appetite, as he adored showgirls'. The peer would go on to become famous for his national motor museum at Beaulieu, help found English Heritage and marry twice. But he was bisexual, something he had suspected at Eton and was confirmed in the Guards. At one party in London, the aristocratic officers were entertained by a young naval rating doing a striptease who would later become a national treasure as the jazz musician George Melly. Yet Montagu always insisted that he had made no improper advances to two boy scouts, the reason for his arrest. Having been acquitted then, he was drawn into the later Wildeblood case. The prosecution stooped to forging an entry in his passport to try to discredit an alibi, used illegal tapping of phones, entered and searched private houses without warrants, and put appalling pressure on two RAF men to inform against their 'social superiors', in order to avoid many years of imprisonment for themselves. The witnesses, as they later admitted, had been carefully coached in their stories.

Peter Wildeblood's unusual response to the prosecution was to declare openly and unashamedly that he was a homosexual or, in the language of the day, an 'invert'; and had a right to be treated with respect. He declined to apologize. His language was very far from the gay liberation rhetoric of modern times but it was clear and dignified: 'I am no more proud of my condition than I would be of having a glass eye or a hare-lip. On the other hand, I am no more ashamed of it than I would be of being colour-blind or of writing with my left hand.' He pointed out that Lord Montagu had done patriotic service in the Grenadier Guards and that Montagu's co-accused cousin, Pitt-Rivers, had served bravely in the war, while Wildeblood himself, though he turned out to be a terrible pilot, had served with the RAF as a meteorologist in Africa. These were all, apart from their sexuality, entirely normal members of the patriotic, upper-middle-class Establishment, about as different from the Cambridge spies in their views as it would be possible to be. And, of course, since homosexuality is spread throughout society, some of the Establishment was gay, too. Lord Wolfenden's famous committee, formed in 1954 to consider the law on homosexuality, was headed by a former public school headmaster and university vice-chancellor, and included Tory politicians, a senior official in the Girl Guides, a judge, and so on. When Wolfenden later discovered that his own son was gay he wrote asking him to keep out of his way and 'to wear rather less make-up'. The committee, however, took evidence from Wildeblood among many others and after three years of private hearings in the Home Office, duly recommended in 1957 a change in the law, legalizing private homosexual activity between consenting adults aged over twenty-one.

By then the country's mood seemed to have changed. There was a feeling that the tactics used against Montagu and the others were unfair and underhand. The hostility to government interference and meddling, which had contributed to the fall of Attlee's Labour administration, was beginning to stretch to private matters. When Wildeblood was released from prison, he found his working-class neighbours in Islington to be cheerily friendly. When Montagu was released from Wakefield prison, where his fellow inmates had included Fuchs, he got a similar reception, though it was not universal. At lunch, in the fashionable Mirabelle restaurant in London's West End, he recalled 'one or two of the neighbouring tables disapproved. The atmosphere became unpleasant and remarks were made which were obviously meant to be overheard with intent to wound.' At this point, however, the then Leader of the Opposition, Hugh Gaitskell, who was also lunching there, intervened. 'He could see perfectly well what was going on. After a while, he laid down his napkin and crossed the room to our table. "How nice to see you back," he said, holding out his hand, which I shook with surprise and gratitude. The action silenced the surrounding hostility.'[14] There was continued hostility to homosexuals then and there is today, but the so-called permissive society of the sixties was already being forged by public reaction in the second half of the Tory fifties to cases such as these. For now, Parliament disagreed. In the first parliamentary debates on homosexual law reform, the Home Secretary, Maxwell-Fyfe, said he did not think the country would wear such a change. Had he been present in the Mirabelle restaurant, or had he stood a few years earlier outside Winchester Castle he might have realized he was already out of date.

The Spies: Tom and Guy in Moscow

Britain's spy networks were far more effectively hidden by upper-class connections than by the homosexual inclinations of a few of Moscow's men.

The full story of the Cambridge spies does not belong here but to the thirties and the divided loyalties of the anti-fascists. The tale of how a cluster of rebellious former public schoolboys came to believe that the fight against poverty and Hitler required their allegiance to the bloodthirsty regime of Stalinist Russia, and then how they infiltrated the British intelligence and diplomatic services before and during the Second World War, is well known. The sons of a diplomat, a naval officer, an Anglican clergyman and a cabinet minister, they were about as traditionalist and patriotic in their upbringing as it was possible to be. They remained quintessentially English afterwards too. The Labour MP and journalist Tom Driberg visited one of them, Guy Burgess, a few years after he had dramatically defected with Donald Maclean. (And it was dramatic: Maclean's pregnant wife had just cooked a special ham for dinner at their home near Churchill's country house, when Burgess arrived and raced him off to Southampton for the overnight ferry to St Malo.) In Moscow, Driberg found Burgess outside a hotel, 'his bird-bright ragamuffin face ... tanned by the Caucasian sun'. Burgess explained his job involved trying to get the Russians to translate and publish the novels of E. M. Forster. In his flat Burgess strummed the Eton boating song on his piano and proudly showed that his suit still had a stitched badge reading 'Messrs Tom Brown of Eton, High Street, Tailors'.[15] The Moscow defectors would die there, mildly regretful but entirely unrepentant, while two further traitors, Sir Antony Blunt, who became Surveyor of the Queen's Pictures, and the economist John Cairncross, privately confessed and were left unexposed and unpunished for much of their lives.

Did they matter, really? They did. Between them British traitors helped the Soviet Union acquire nuclear weapons earlier than would otherwise have happened, passed huge amounts of information to Stalin's secret police, were directly responsible for the deaths of scores of British and other Western agents at the hands of the KGB and, in Philby's case, managed to stymie an American attempt to create an uprising in Albania, so keeping that wretched country under the heel of one of the most primitive tyrannies of modern times. Their story has been made 'glamorous' by the gilded associations of pre-war Cambridge, and the idealism of being anti-Nazi when part of the British Establishment were not. Films and countless books, some by the spies themselves, have romanticized them. Yet the consequences of their spying were squalid and dangerous. Nor were they actually the most successful spies – less 'glamorous' characters such as Alan Nunn May, a scientist, and Fuchs, were more important. It was the Dutch-born George Blake, who escaped from occupied Holland at the age of twenty, joined the Royal Navy, was recruited by MI6 and captured by the Communists in Korea, who probably caused most damage. He had been shocked, he later said, by the effects of American bombing of Korean villages and passed the names of 400 British-controlled agents in Germany to the Russians, with predictable consequences for many of them. Some think he was brainwashed. Blake was caught and in 1961 was given a prison sentence of forty-two years, which remains the longest sentence ever imposed by a British court. He, of course, was not a dapper and well-connected Old Etonian with friends to tip him off.

What is it about the British and spying? Other Western nations had their post-war spying scandals, particularly the Americans and the West Germans. But nowhere was quite so gripped as Britain by the actions of Soviet agents. Class and sex are undeniably part of the answer. But there is another half-buried theme – British anti-Americanism. Philby claimed all his life that he was a British patriot who felt that the country was simply allied with the wrong side. Another student in the same Cambridge college as Philby at the same time (though they never knew one another) was Enoch Powell who came to much the same conclusion a few years later. This anti-Americanism was something which could bring together patriotic right-wingers and left-wingers in a common cause. Washington was constantly warning London about intelligence lapses and the possibility of traitors. But even when Russian defectors brought descriptions of Maclean and Philby to MI5, they were languidly dismissed; unless there were even more traitors, even higher in the system (and Philby was close to the top) then disdain and smugness must have been to blame for the grotesque failures of security.

Once traitors were discovered there was then a national case for not making too much of it because of the angry reaction from the American intelligence services, on whom Britain relied very heavily. Politicians were obliged to explain or failed to explain, the defections and the rising suspicions of third and fourth and then fifth men still uncovered. Macmillan, as Foreign Secretary in

1955, was obliged to knock down the idea that Philby might be a Russian spy who had tipped off Burgess and Maclean four years earlier (he was, of course, and had). Later, after yet more spies had been uncovered, Macmillan was told by an excited Sir Roger Hollis of MI5 that the organization had arrested Vassall. Macmillan seemed dejected at the news and when Hollis said he didn't seem very pleased, replied: 'No, I'm not pleased at all. When my gamekeeper shoots a fox, he doesn't go and hang it up outside the Master of Foxhounds' drawing room; he buries it out of sight.' Macmillan, by now Prime Minister, lamented that there would be a great public trial, the security services would be blamed, and 'there will be a debate in the House of Commons and the Government will probably fall. Why the devil did you "catch" him?' More concerned about harassing the press, Macmillan got two scalps when journalists refused to give their sources for allegations concerning Vassall and were briefly imprisoned. It was not surprising that people suspected an Establishment cover-up by chaps who belonged to the same clubs and did not like their dirty washing flapping in public.

Public Laughter

Had anyone been asked to define British humour in the aftermath of the war, they would probably have come up with the genteel, meticulous cartoonists of *Punch* whose neatly cross-hatched ink world stretched from Westminster and the Home

Counties to the more remote areas of the Scottish Highlands but included little in between. They might have mentioned the rude postcards of the seaside tradition, fat overhanging bosoms and little Willies. There were some rather lame newspaper comic-strips; the radio surrealism of *It's That Man Again;* the exuberance of Flanders and Swann; and on film, the warm, ultimately optimistic humour of George Formby and the Ealing comedies. From the late thirties to the mid-forties the world had been harsh enough perhaps, without harsh laughter too.

What Britain had had, above all, was music hall. Even in the fifties musical reviews were still being widely performed, weaving a little light innuendo among the songs. Few of the hundreds of once-famous double acts, singers, comedians, slapstick artists, clowns and acrobats from the Victorian and Edwardian heyday of music hall had been recorded, though they provided the main form of mass entertainment for half a century. This was a powerful culture which required skilled, physically tough and consistent artistes who could sing, dance and tell jokes, the original 'variety acts'. Some of the fun can still be glimpsed in modern Christmas pantos and seaside summer shows, though these must be a pale shadow of that lost, garish gaiety. After the war there was a surge of one-way traffic as music hall acts were taken up by the BBC Light Programme and when, in the fifties, television began to take off a final generation of people who had learned their trade in small seaside and provincial theatres, would arrive to hoof it, clown and sing for the cameras. Bruce Forsyth, Jimmy Tarbuck, Ken Dodd, Eric Morecambe, Ernie Wise and their rivals were the last products of the old musical theatre and its relentless demand for all-singing, all-dancing comic talent. In its way, music hall is as important to the smell and colour of twentieth-century Britishness as rock music. It has just had less effective PR.

Below the surface, new kinds of comedy were slouching unsteadily towards those microphones, cameras and footlights. One could write a useful contemporary history by simply asking of any particular time: what made people laugh? To be British now became bound up with a string of radio and television shows, their catchphrases, lateral logic and increasingly rude jokes. The harder tone of new British comedy came most obviously from two sources. One was the absurdity of many people's army experiences during and after the war. The other, with the later satire boom, was the absurdities of private boarding schools. No democracy had mobilized a greater proportion of its people in the world war. No country sent more of the children of its elite to boarding schools with strange rules. What followed from these two incontrovertible facts was very funny indeed. It meant elongated, grotesque faces; weird nasal voices; nonsense words that could send apparently normal people into hysterics – a private British world created some of the most chippy, eloquent people on the planet in the sixth decade of the twentieth century. One of the most idiosyncratic and energetic aspects of British culture could be called popular surrealism. It was not the surrealism of experimental film-makers or painters, but of Max Wall, Goons and eventually Pythons as well.

The name 'Goon', picked up from Popeye cartoons, seems to have begun with Spike

Milligan. In the opening stages of the war, Milligan had played childish boredom-repelling games with fellow gunners around their battery in Bexhill. Milligan was a working-class child of the British Empire. His father was Irish, and had performed in music halls as a youth, alongside another boy called Charlie Chaplin who then disappeared off abroad. He had then joined the British Army, like his father before him, so that Spike was born in India and brought up there and in Burma. It seems to have been a golden time before his father lost his army job in pre-war defence cuts and the family had to return, settling in Catford, south London. Poorly educated, Spike got a job as a clerk until he was sacked for stealing cigarettes. He taught himself to play the trumpet and dabbled in politics – joining the Young Communists and according to one report, flirting with Oswald Mosley's blackshirts too. Then in 1939, as he recalled later, an envelope arrived containing 'a cunningly worded invitation to participate in World War II'.[16] Army service bored and frightened Milligan but it was the making of him.

Tens of thousands of soldiers found that the fear of death, nutty regulations, stupid officers and the incompetence of the war machine, required a more raucous, sardonic humour than they had been used to at home. Spike was sent as a signaller to North Africa, where he was duly shelled, lost friends and was injured, always playing jokes and making up games to pass the boring times. As the fighting moved north through Italy, he saw another gunner take part in one of the Army variety shows put on to amuse the troops. This was Harry Secombe, a commercial traveller's son from Swansea, who, like

Spike, had been a clerk before the war. The two were soon working together, part of a loose association of military comedians and musicians who would eventually tickle the nation when they returned (Dick Emery, Benny Hill, Frankie Howerd and Tommy Cooper among them). Meanwhile in India, Peter Sellers, a young half-Jewish impressionist was busy impersonating Sikh officers and RAF commanders. Michael Bentine, an Old Etonian intelligence officer and actor, would later complete the quartet, the most influential act of British comedy surrealism in the fifties, and one of the most important ever. Almost all of them had some music-hall connections – Sellers's mother and grandmother had been singers and dancers, and Secombe's family was saturated in music-hall culture. But they had all added a new twist, the result of those transforming army years.

The Goon Show was subversive without being party political, or even conventionally political at all. Spike Milligan described it as 'against bureaucracy ... its starting-point is one man shouting gibberish in the face of authority.'[17] Of one of the Goons' classic villains, Milligan said that it was 'a chance to knock people who my father, and I as a boy, had to call "sir". Colonels, chaps like Grytpype-Thynne with educated voices, who were really bloody scoundrels. They'd con and marry old ladies; they were cowards charging around with guns.' And one of his producers, Peter Eton, said later: 'We were trying to undermine the standing order. We were anti-Commonwealth, anti-Empire, anti-bureaucrat, anti-armed forces.' Milligan, Secombe, Bentine and Sellers were demobilized into the rationed, bureaucrat-dominated Britain of the forties so it is hardly surprising that their humour was aimed at unthinking patriotism and official bungling. It was exactly what people wanted and needed, however nervous the BBC felt when the show began broadcasting in 1951. Older listeners found it alarming and baffling, but millions were quickly mimicking the silly voices, appalling puns and nonsense words of Goonery. Milligan remained prickly about being working class, and was political enough to support the Campaign for Nuclear Disarmament away from the microphones. His comedy was meant to sting. Yet there was a warmth about the Goons that drew some of that sting: had it been otherwise it is unlikely that the Duke of Edinburgh and the Prince of Wales would have been quite such enthusiastic fans.

All Fall Down: Suez

Some sense of the popularity of the Tories' crown prince throughout Churchill's sluggish and frustrating last government, Anthony Eden, can be gauged from his reception in the 1955 election when Churchill had at last retired. Most of the time he travelled in his own car, declaring that 'if I cannot travel in my own country without an armed guard, I would rather retire from politics.' But when he went by train, women arrived at the windows at each stop with huge bouquets of flowers. Here was the man who had stood up to Hitler, decently waited for Churchill to retire and was now a great architect of post-war global peace. Shortly after the election, Eden invited the new Soviet leader Khrushchev to London. (Despite a completely drunk translator, the visit had gone well, though at one point Khrushchev was introduced to the huntin'-and-shootin' Tory politician, Lord Lambton, as 'a shooting peer'. The Soviet leader solemnly and sympathetically shook hands with Lambton, assuming that this meant he was under sentence of death and shortly to be shot.) Eden was at root an intensely patriotic man, who thought Britain's Commonwealth links far more important than deeper entanglements with Europe. Among his weaknesses were his inherited foul temper and a racist disdain for Arabs. But for most people in 1956 Eden seemed an almost beau ideal, the man for the moment.

Suez is often seen as a very short era of bad judgement, a crisis whose origins are obscure and whose consequences are hard to discern. This sells it short. Suez was about Britain's colonial history. It had begun as something very personal, a duel between an English politician of the old school and an Arab nationalist leader of the new post-war world. Anthony Eden and what he represented for the Britain of the mid-fifties are worth dwelling on. Through most of Eden's life he had been a glittering and glamorous figure, hugely admired across the political spectrum, a global peacemaker and statesman. Remembered by one colleague as 'half mad baronet, half beautiful woman', Eden had come from a landed, if sometimes eccentric family. During the Suez crisis he was seen in Washington as the epitome of alien English snobbishness. In fact one of his forebears, a baronet of Maryland, had been a great friend of George Washington and supporter of the American Declaration of Independence. Another had written a pioneering study of the poor, warmly praised by Karl Marx. Eden was never absolutely sure of his paternity – his mother was vivacious – but it was probably the wild, spendthrift, artistic Sir William Eden. He was a baronet out of the pages of a satirical novel, much given to hurling joints of roast lamb out of windows and, when riding to hounds, jumping closed level-crossing gates without waiting for oncoming trains. He had a terrible temper and used language so bad that, when he was presiding over local police courts, Durham miners would come simply for the pleasure of hearing him swear.[18]

The boy Eden, a beautiful casket seething with unstable genes, went on to Eton. He fought bravely in the First World War, during which his oldest brother was killed in the trenches and his much-loved younger brother was killed at sea, days after his sixteenth birthday. A liberal-minded Tory MP from 1923 onwards, Eden rose to become the Foreign Office minister who had face-to-face negotiations in the thirties with Mussolini, Hitler – the two men discovered they had fought opposite one another in the trenches, and drew maps of their respective positions – and Stalin, whom Eden thought was a kind of oriental despot. After becoming Foreign Secretary and helping form the pre-war system of alliances and League of Nations agreements, he dramatically resigned in 1938 in protest at the appeasement of Nazi Germany, finally returning to serve Churchill, again as Foreign Secretary, from 1940 to 1945. A brilliant linguist, highly cultured and with a deep love of modern art, a lover of many women, a genuine diplomatist, he was familiar by the mid-fifties with most of the world's leaders. In 1954 at Geneva he had arranged a key conference to try to keep peace in the new Cold War world, a summit seen then as a last throw to prevent the Third World War.

So what of Nasser? If Eden was the model of a kind of Englishness, Colonel Gamel Abdel Nasser was the original of the anti-colonialist autocrat who would become familiar over the decades to come – charismatic, patriotic, ruthless, opportunistic. Driving the British from Egypt was the cause that burned in him from his teenage years, and not surprisingly. Egypt, though nominally independent under its own king, had been regarded as virtually British until the end of the Second World War. It had been the centre of the fight against Rommel's Afrika Corps, and the pivot around which Britain's domination of the Middle East revolved. The oil fields of Iran and Iraq which kept Britain working, the Suez Canal through which a quarter of British imports and two-thirds of Europe's oil arrived, the airfields which refuelled planes bound for India and Australia – all this made Egypt a hub; a pivot; Britain's Mediterranean naval. Most British families contained someone who had served in Egypt at some time. What was less special was the casual contempt British people tended to reserve for the Egyptians themselves, or 'wogs' as they were more commonly known. Churchill had reacted to one moment of earlier Egyptian insubordination by shouting that if they didn't look out 'we will set the Jews on them and drive them into the gutter'.

Before the Second World War Egypt had been forced to sign a treaty making it clear that the country was under Britain's thumb. Eden's head was even placed on Egyptian postage stamps to mark this humiliation. One wartime episode makes the relationship clear. In 1942, as Rommel's tanks drew nearer, and Churchill was fulminating about Cairo being a nest of 'Hun spies', the British ambassador told Egypt's King Farouk that his prime minister was not considered sufficiently anti-German and would have to be replaced. The King summoned his limited reserves of pride and refused. It was, he insisted, a step too far, a breach of the 1937 treaty. Britain's ambassador simply called up armoured cars, a couple of tanks and some soldiers and surrounded King Farouk in his palace. The ambassador walked in and ordered the monarch to sign a grovelling letter of abdication, renouncing and abandoning 'for ourselves and the heirs of our body the throne of Egypt'. At this royal determination crumbled. The king asked pathetically if, perhaps, he could have one last chance? He was graciously granted it and sacked his prime minister. Life went on, the war went on. But Egyptians took note. Down in the Sudan a young Egyptian army officer, Lieutenant Nasser, seething with indignation, complained in letters to friends about the surrender and servility shown to the British. Colonialism, he said, 'if it felt that some Egyptians intended to sacrifice their lives and face force with force, would retreat like a prostitute'.

The son of a postal worker, Nasser was soon at the centre of a group of radical army officers, Egypt's Free Officers Movement, discussing how to get the British out and how to build a new Arab state, socialist rather than essentially Islamic. At this time, and later under Nasser, the Muslim extremists, whose thinking would one day influence

218

al Qaeda, were being persecuted and even executed. Nasser was a ruthless, quietly determined man who naturally attracted followers; when King Farouk was eventually ousted by the Free Officers in July 1952 it took just two years for the young Nasser to oust the interim leader and seize control of the country himself. For him, this was good timing. After the war Arab nationalism had made things much tougher for Britain. Its oil interests began to be challenged. Visiting British ministers found themselves stoned by Arab crowds. To Churchill's fury, Iran's prime minister, the popular and independent-minded Mohammed Mossadeq, had nationalized the Anglo-Iranian Oil Company in 1951. Though he was overthrown in a CIA-organized coup two years later (organized by a president's grandson, the gloriously named Kermit Roosevelt), Mossadeq's action was a curtain-raiser for what Nasser would do in Egypt. In Iraq, a British-sponsored king and prime minister were holding on by their fingertips and would later both be murdered by mobs. In Jordan, the British soldier who had commanded an Arab Legion there since 1939, Sir John Glubb, known as Glubb Pasha, was sacked by the young King Hussein in March 1956; an Arab now wanted an Arab in charge of his army. Though it seems a small matter now, at the time it was seen as a slap across the face for London, provoked by the uppity Arabism sweeping the region. Eden blamed Nasser for this, and told a junior minister: 'What's all this poppycock ... about isolating and quarantining Nasser? Can't you understand that I want Nasser murdered?'[19]

Egypt was where the confrontation between old colonial power and the new Arab nationalism was always going to take place. Britain's military base at Suez, guarding its interest in the canal, was more like a small country than a barracks. It was about the same size as Wales, with a vast border which was expensive and difficult to defend, so much so that Attlee had considered closing it and pulling out shortly after the war. The base depended for survival on supplies and trade with the surrounding Egyptian towns and villages. But in the latter days of Farouk's reign, it was already being boycotted by nationalist Egyptians. One incident produced another. The tension rose. Off-duty British servicemen were shot. After one act of bloody retaliation involving the slaughter of poorly armed Arab policemen holed up in a building by British soldiers, the Cairo crowds turned on foreign-owned clubs, hotels, shops and bars and set them alight. Britain found herself facing a guerrilla war.

Eventually, following yet another coup, London began to negotiate a British withdrawal – there were, after all, other bases nearby, notably in Cyprus, where however another nationalist guerrilla war was going on, and in Jordan. Eden, then Foreign Secretary, came to think that withdrawal was inevitable and pointed out to his colleagues that 'we are ourselves in serious breach' of the treaty, having eight times as many troops in the country as stipulated. To start with, all was civilized enough. Nasser even briefly met Eden, though he didn't much enjoy being lectured by the British leader in fluent Arabic. He complained later that Eden in the grandiose surroundings of the British Embassy, which made the British 'look like princes and the Egyptians like beggars', treated him like a rather dim junior official. The agreement stipulated that Britain would keep her rights over the canal, a deal soon broken by Nasser.

At this stage, how great a threat was Nasser? His ability to rouse Arab opinion was impressive, and he wanted to make himself a spokesman for the non-aligned world generally. His Cairo Radio, broadcasting across the Middle East, was the al Jazeera of its day, though considerably less independent. At different times in the coming crisis Nasser would be compared by British politicians and newspapers to Mussolini and Hitler, presented as a stooge of the Soviet Union, and then as a regional Arabist menace. He was a dictator, certainly. He was also a socialist of a kind, with great plans for a healthier, stronger, better-educated country. He wanted to spread his power throughout the Arab world, beginning with the Yemen, Syria, Sudan and Jordan. Like Saddam Hussein, he had used poison gas against enemies and, like him, was regarded with alarm by other Arab rulers. Like Saddam, Nasser believed in the destruction of the then new State of Israel.

Yet he would have remained a local irritant had it not been for a catastrophic blunder by Washington. Nasser's great ambition was the creation of the so-called High Dam at Aswan, a gargantuan project which had been dreamed about since the mid-forties and which might transform Egypt's economy. Three miles wide, it would create a 300-mile-long lake which would give the Egyptians eight times as much electric power as they then had and increase the country's fertile land by a third. It was much more than just another civil engineering project. Nasser talked of it being 'seventeen times larger than the greatest pyramid'. With Aswan, here was a new Pharoah bringing a new age to Egypt after centuries of colonial humiliation. The problem was that such a dam was also far beyond the resources of Nasser's Egypt. Loans had been discussed for years and in 1956 Nasser had every reason to think that the Americans, followed by the British, were about to sign the cheques. Partly out of pique when he thought he was being given an ultimatum, Nasser's ambassador implied they could get help from the Russians and Chinese if the American terms were not good. The US Secretary of State, John Foster Dulles, abruptly cancelled the offer. Nasser was livid. To show his anger and to find a new and secure source of revenue, he abruptly retaliated by seizing control of the Suez canal, triggering the coup with code-words given to a mass public rally.

If the dam was not just a dam, the canal was not merely a canal. It was the ultimate liquid motorway, a vital artery of world trade, connecting Europe through the Mediterranean, with India, Australia, New Zealand and the Far East. In the days before mass air freight the only other way was round the Cape, infinitely further, slower and more expensive. Years before Eden had called it the jugular vein of the British Empire, and in the mid-fifties a quarter of all British exports and imports came through it. It wasn't only Britain. Three-quarters of Europe's oil came from the region, half of it through the canal. Indeed, a sixth of the whole world's cargoes went through it, some fifty ships every day, all of them paying tolls. Because of its international importance and the fact that it had been built by a French engineer, using French and British money, it had since 1888 been administered as an international facility, not an Egyptian one. It was run by a company, 44 per cent of which was in turn owned by the British government, thanks to an inspired piece of High Victorian entrepreneurship by Disraeli. It was not hard to see how this streak of colonial-owned internationalism running through Egypt felt like a violation. Nasser's plan, having seized it by military force just days after Dulles turned down his loan request, was to use payments from canal traffic to finance the next phase of his dam. The legality of the seizure was much debated around the world but to the British government Nasser's action was simple theft and a clear breach of international treaties. Worse, you couldn't leave Egyptians running something as sophisticated as a canal. Worse still, if it was allowed to stand, this act of impudence or bravado would inspire other Arab radicals and threaten the whole region.

Since Nasser's act had been provoked by Washington, and since his revenge hurt Britain and France, Washington's allies, it might have been expected that President Eisenhower would staunchly back action against Nasser. The situation turned out to be rather more complicated. For one thing Washington was pursuing a vigorous policy of trying to turf out the old colonial powers from the Middle East in favour of America herself. The US had oil of her own but was always worried about the future and acutely aware that two-thirds of the then known world reserves were in the region. Special deals had been made with the Saudis and Iranians. This economic interest was augmented by loud and pious anti-colonialism, particularly from the Secretary of

State, Dulles, a devious and sanctimonious character who hated British imperialism with a Founding Fathers fervour. He also loathed Eden, who cordially returned the feeling. Next, there was the intense worry in Washington about the Russians, who were making menacing noises about the liberal regime emerging in Hungary. Next, there was the ticklish question of the Panama Canal which was controlled by the United States in a similar way to Anglo-French control in Suez. Ike and Dulles wanted no agreement emerging from the Middle East about international control of waterways which might affect Panama. Finally, by 1956 President Eisenhower was in the throes of trying to be re-elected on a peace and prosperity ticket and was outraged by his allies' untimely sabre-rattling. For all these reasons, America would prove to be Britain's enemy in her confrontation with Nasser, not her friend.

Little of this was understood in London, where Eden's tough line with Nasser was hugely popular. The Conservative Party was roaring its support. The Labour Opposition under Hugh Gaitskell sounded if anything even more bellicose (as it would later in the opening phases of the Falklands War, under Michael Foot). With a couple of exceptions – the *Manchester Guardian* and the *Observer*– the press, commentators and cartoonists were all on-side, and demanding punishment. The new science of opinion polling, and individual messages of support pouring into Downing Street, showed that public opinion agreed. Nasser must be sorted out. But timing in politics is everything. Under American pressure, there followed months of diplomatic manoeuvring during which Eden and his passionately anti-Nasser Chancellor, Harold Macmillan, began to lose the initiative. There were international conferences, proposed compromise deals under which the countries dependent on the canal would have a new role in administering what would formally be Egyptian property, and intensive negotiations at the United Nations. Britain kept hinting that it might yet come to war. Eisenhower and Dulles insisted that a peaceful solution should be found. By saying that America would have no part in trying to 'shoot our way through' to the canal and by referring to the problem of colonialism, they encouraged Nasser, who brusquely rejected all outside initiatives. America's attitude also encouraged Moscow, which led the diplomatic charge against Britain and France. Throughout this episode and despite the crisis caused by Russia's crushing of the Hungarians, the US and the USSR stood shoulder to shoulder against London.

This all felt increasingly ominous. And then a possible shortcut presented itself through the unlikely agency of Israel. It depended on America in the mid-fifties almost as much as it does half a century later, but the Israeli government believed Nasser and his pan-Arabism was a threat to their existence not properly appreciated in Washington. Egypt had taken delivery of large quantities of Soviet bloc armaments, including the latest jet fighters and bombers; Nasser's anti-Israeli rhetoric was bloodcurdling and he was increasingly closely echoed by the Syrians and Jordanians. The Suez crisis gave the Israeli government a one-off opportunity to strike their most serious enemy, and even enjoy Western air support while they did it. Thus came about the plot finally hatched by Britain, France and Israel to finish off Nasser. Harold Macmillan, the Chancellor, had originally suggested that Israel be used to attack Egypt from one flank, and the idea was enthusiastically taken up by Churchill in retirement. When first mentioned to Eden he thought it eccentric and dismissed it. But as the international talks dragged on and the government began to lose support and momentum at home, the idea of a plot resurfaced.

We do not know all the details for the very good reason that Eden insisted no notes were taken at the key cabinet committee discussions. He even insisted that private diaries of the time, including Macmillan's, be torn up or burned. But the Israelis approached the French who revived the idea. Israel was being harassed on her borders by guerrillas. The French, fighting a vicious colonial war in Algeria, thought Nasser was a menace to their interests there as well as in the canal. The specific plot, for an Israeli attack to be followed by an Anglo-French demand for a ceasefire, which would be refused and then followed by a 'police-action' intervention, was dreamed up by the French war hero, General Maurice Challe. So cloak-and-dagger discussions began. The place at which the details were hammered out was a modest borrowed villa at Sèvres outside Paris, a house that had once been a French resistance hideout. Eden's Foreign Secretary, Selwyn Lloyd, attended, reluctantly, having tried to disguise himself by wearing a battered old raincoat as he left London. (It did not work.)

There he met his French opposite number, the Israeli prime minister David Ben-Gurion, the country's chief of staff, Moshe Dayan, and Shimon Peres from the Israeli defence ministry. It was not an easy meeting. Britain had a close defence agreement with Jordan, another enemy of Israel at the time, and it was not so long since Israeli terrorists had been killing British soldiers. For their part, the Israelis deeply mistrusted the British. The French were also suspicious after Britain's decision a year earlier to shun the new Common Market. Finally, the deep secrecy of the meetings created its own layer of mistrust, particularly since Eden was obsessive about nothing being written down. (Eventually the outline agreement was written down, at the Israelis' insistence, and initialled by a British negotiator.) At the Sèvres house, with the help of local fish and wine, a deal was finally done. Those present solemnly swore not to reveal the details during their lifetimes, and for good reason. The agreement to ensure that French paratroops from Algeria and a British invasion force from Malta and Cyprus could attack, theoretically to separate the two sides, but in fact to grab back control of the canal, was wholly illegal. It required that ambassadors, other ministers, the head of MI6 and the Commons as well as the White House, must all be kept in ignorance. That, at least, was done highly successfully. Despite leaks from Paris to the CIA, President Eisenhower never guessed what was happening until it was too late.

Meanwhile the mood in Britain had changed. Anti-colonialism, the international rule of law and the rights of young countries were all issues which enthused Labour and the left generally. The United Nations, Nato and the European Convention on Human Rights, still smelled of fresh paint. As

American hostility to military action became clearer, some MPs and commentators began to have second thoughts. Eden, rather like Thatcher and Blair later, complained that left-wing intellectuals were stirring things up against him, while 'The BBC is exasperating me by leaning over backwards to be what they call neutral and to present both sides of the case.' There was nothing quite like the drama of the Hutton Inquiry and the resignation of the BBC's Chairman and Director General in 2004, yet at a fundamental level the earlier clash went further: Eden made menacing noises about taking the BBC under direct government control. According to BBC lore, troops were placed in a building on the Strand, awaiting orders to take over the BBC's external services in Bush House: meanwhile the Corporation's engineers there had been issued with sledgehammers and told to destroy their own equipment rather than let it fall into the hands of Eden and the government. Inside the government, some ministers became uneasy about the whole escapade. Sir Anthony Nutting, a Foreign Office minister, would resign in protest, though without the public drama achieved by Robin Cook before the Iraq War. And as with the Iraq War nearly half a century later, late in the day when the opposition really organized itself, crowds turned out to protest and private unease spilled into public anger.

For the first time in modern British history, large numbers of people came onto the streets of London to challenge a government going to war. The Suez demonstrations would be followed by the great anti-Vietnam clashes of the sixties and the marches against Tony Blair's Iraq War, but in the fifties

228

nothing like this had happened before. Suez split Britain down the middle, dividing families and friends. It brought the Prime Minister into angry conflict with Establishment institutions and Establishment grandees. Lord Mountbatten is said to have warned the young Queen that her government were 'behaving like lunatics' and a former Royal aide believed she thought her premier was mad.[20] Because of Suez a generation of politically aware younger people grew up rather more contemptuous of politicians generally, readier to mock them, keener to dismiss and laugh at them. The decline of respect for the craft of politics would probably have happened anyway in modern Britain. But the events of the winter of 1956 hastened that decline.

Even the military was affected. The call-up for Suez provoked widescale desertions and minor mutinies across Britain. Some 20,000 reservists were called back and many declined to come, some scrawling 'bollocks' across their papers. In Southampton, Royal Engineers pelted a general with stones. In Kent, there were similar scenes among reservists: 'More or less to a man they refused to polish boots or press uniforms or even do guard duty. They spent most of the time abusing the career soldiers for being idiots. The army could do nothing ...'[21] It went further than Kent. In Malta, in the unpleasant surroundings of the Qrendi airstrip, Grenadier Guards 'fuelled by NAAFI tea, marched through the camp ... down to the building where the officers were housed.' They were angry about conditions as much as politics but earned a stiff lecture from their commanding officer on the dire consequences of mutiny. Shortly afterwards, though, the Reservists of the 37th Heavy Anti-Aircraft Regiment of the Royal Artillery were at it again, marching through the Maltese camp to protest and shouting down their regimental sergeant-major.[22] These were minor incidents, undoubtedly, and had much to do with boredom and irritation among reservists brought suddenly to dusty, unpleasant camps, yet headlines in the press about army mutinies and protest marches sent shockwaves through the forces.

The biggest single difference between the Suez and Iraq crises was, of course, that the Americans did not want war in 1956 and were determined for it in 2003. Anguished letters and telephone transcripts tell the story of mutual misunderstanding. From Eden's point of view, the US was preventing any real pressure against Nasser while talking grandly about international law. He gave enough broad hints, he thought, for the White House to realize that he and the French prime minister were ready to use force. At different times Eisenhower's team had given the impression that they accepted force might be necessary. Dulles had talked of making Nasser 'disgorge' his prize. So while Britain could not tip off the Americans about the dangerous and illegal agreement with Israel, or give military details, there was a general belief that the Americans would understand. This was an error. From Eisenhower's viewpoint, his old allies had dropped him in the dirt at the worst possible time, during an election and when the Russians were brutally crushing the Hungarian uprising with 4,000 tanks and terrible bloodshed. Eisenhower and Dulles had failed to pick up persistent hints and worried reports from CIA agents in Paris and

London, just as they had failed to understand the consequences of cancelling their help for the Aswan dam. America in the mid-fifties was a young superpower, still flat footed. This time, it had been fooled by both sides.

So, on the early morning of 5 November 1956, British and French paratroopers began dropping from the air above Port Said. A huge British convoy which had been steaming for nine days from Malta arrived with tanks and artillery and the drive south to secure the Suez Canal began. So far, only thirty-two British and French commandos had been killed, against 2,000 Egyptian dead. In a military sense, things had gone smoothly. The politics was another matter. When the invasion happened, Eisenhower and Dulles exploded with anger. According to American White House correspondents, the air at the Oval Office turned blue in a way that had not happened for a century. Dulles seriously compared the Anglo-French action to that of the Soviets in Budapest. Unfortunately, at much the same time as Eisenhower was hitting the roof of his office, Nasser was hitting the floor of the canal – with no fewer than forty-seven ships filled with concrete. He had done the very thing Eden's plan was supposed to prevent. He had blocked the canal. For the first and last time, the United States made common cause with the Soviet Union at the UN to demand a stop to the invasion. The motion for a ceasefire was passed by a crushing sixty-four votes to five. World opinion was aflame. India, eight years independent, sided with the Soviet Union, which was threatening to send 50,000 Russian 'volunteers' to the Middle East. In the event, as the British troops were moving south, having taken

Port Said and with the road to Cairo open to them, they were suddenly ordered to stop. An immediate ceasefire and swift pull-out was being ordered by London, not because of the views of irate squaddies in the Home Counties or the private views of the Queen, or fulminations in Moscow. Britain was being humiliated by the United States in a way that had not happened since the War of Independence.

On the ground, clear-sighted about their national interest, and uninterested in American anger, the French were prepared to keep going. Britain was in a different situation. It came down to money, oil and nerves. The pound was again being sold around the world, with the US Treasury piling in to viciously turn the screw. Fuel was soon running short and, in what seemed like a return to wartime conditions, British petrol stations briefly required motorists to hand over brown-coloured ration coupons. Britain needed emergency oil supplies from the Americans which would have to be paid for in dollars. Britain didn't have enough dollars. Another loan was needed. Harold Macmillan turned to Washington and the International Monetary Fund to ask for help. The US Treasury Secretary, George Humphrey, told him, via Britain's new Washington ambassador Sir Harold Caccia: 'You'll not get a dime from the US government if I can stop it, until you've gotten out of Suez. You are like burglars who have broken into somebody else's house. So get out! When you do, and not until then, you'll get help!'

By now, the Egyptian air force had been destroyed and 13,500 British troops, with 8,500 French troops, had landed at Port Said and were making their way south towards the canal. Rather embarrassingly the Israelis, led by Ariel Sharon, later to be a controversial prime minister, had long ago reached their destination and stopped, so there was no real need to 'separate' anyone. But the game was up by then. With the country split from Buckingham Palace to the barrack room, Eden's health and nerves gave way. To many it seemed as if Nato itself was on the verge of breaking apart. After a brutally direct phone call from Eisenhower, ordering him to announce a ceasefire, Eden called his French opposite number Guy Mollet, who was begging him to hang on. According to French sources he told him: 'I am cornered. I can't hang on. I'm being deserted by everybody. My loyal associate Nutting has resigned as minister of state. I can't even rely on unanimity among the Conservatives. The Archbishop of Canterbury, the Church, the oil businessmen, everybody is against me! The Commonwealth threatens to break up ... I cannot be the grave-digger of the Crown. And then I want you to understand, really understand, Eisenhower phoned me. I can't go it alone without the United States. It would be the first time in the history of England ... No, it is not possible.'[23]

The ceasefire and the withdrawal that followed were a disaster for Britain, which left Nasser stronger than ever. It finished Eden, though not before he had lied to the Commons about the Anglo-French-Israeli plot at Sèvres. He said: 'I want to say this on the question of foreknowledge, and to say it quite bluntly to the House, that there was not foreknowledge that Israel would attack Egypt – there was not.' This can be compared to the French copy of the protocol of Sèvres agreed six weeks earlier which begins by stating quite bluntly:

233

'Les Forces Israeliennes lancent le 23 Oct 1956 dans la soirée une operation d'envergure contre les Forces Egyptiennes ...' The canal was eventually reopened and reparations agreed, though the issue of oil security then assumed a new importance. Britain was left chastened and stripped of moral authority, Washington's rebuked lieutenant.

The effect on the US is also worth recalling. Eisenhower and Dulles had been driven by pique masquerading as high Christian principle, and their handling of the crisis encouraged the Arab nationalism which would return to haunt America in later decades. Eisenhower misled the American people about his true state of knowledge of Britain's readiness to use force. His public statement that he abhorred the invasion because the US did not approve of force to settle international disputes sat oddly with his earlier interest in using nuclear weapons in Korea. The Russians took note and were almost certainly more belligerent afterwards. As a result of Suez, the French distanced themselves from America. It led to the Franco–German axis which endures to this day. The politics of the Middle East changed radically. Britain would not again possess independent power or influence in the region. The age of American power there, based on support for Israel and the oil alliance with the Saudi Royal Family, leading to so much later controversy, properly began after Suez. Much later, according to the then Vice President, Richard Nixon, Eisenhower had second thoughts about Suez, calling his decision to crush Britain his greatest foreign policy mistake. Dulles, who was desperately ill with cancer, told the head of the hospital where he died in 1959 that he reckoned he had been wrong over Suez too.

Other consequences of Suez were less predictable. It provoked the arrival of the Mini car, designed in the wake of the petrol price shock caused by the seizure of the canal. It even affected the fast rate of decline of the shipyards of Clydeside and Tyneside, whose small oil tankers were soon replaced by supertankers built at larger yards overseas. These, it was discovered, could sail round the Cape and deliver their cargo just as cheaply as smaller ships using the canal. Had this been realized a few years earlier, Eden might never have gone to war, and might be remembered now as one of our finer prime ministers. But it wasn't and 'Suez' became four-letter shorthand for the moment when Britain realized her new place in the world.

Muddle or Logic? Two Soldiers

Harold Macmillan's arrival as Prime Minister meant a swift acceptance of American power. Was there another way? The man who was so like him and yet so unlike him, Enoch Powell, certainly thought there was. But Macmillan, devious and wily, was the better politician. 'First in, first out' was the brutal, accurate jibe about him. Having been even more gung-ho about Nasser than Eden himself, it was he as Chancellor who felt the full impact of the run on the pound and led the political retreat. Unsettlingly, Macmillan was also having a series of private meetings with the American ambassador in London during the height of the crisis, advertising himself as Eden's deputy and suggesting ways in which the ceasefire and withdrawal could be sold to Tory backbenchers.

Macmillan and Eisenhower knew each other from the war and while it cannot be said that the Americans actually replaced Eden with a complaisant Atlanticist – the switch-over was done in the old Tory way, by a cabal agreement inside the cabinet – they certainly got the man they wanted. Macmillan swiftly tried to put Suez behind him and, greatly to France's disgust, was soon pleading with Washington for help in nuclear weapons. For a brief period Bevin's belief in the possibility of a genuinely independent British bomb had been vindicated. But this period lasts no longer than five or six years, the gap between the time it took for the new British bomb, to be dropped by long-range jet bomber, to be made militarily usable, and the moment in 1958 when Macmillan realized that British bombing and missile technology was already out of date and insufficiently threatening to deter a Russian attack.

Remaining in the tiny nuclear club wasn't the only route that Macmillan could have taken but nuclear weapons seemed a relatively cheap shortcut to retaining the full fig of global swagger. Macmillan bluffed when he could, authorizing the first British H-bomb explosion, at Christmas Island, in May 1957. It was partly a fake, a hybrid bomb intended to fool the US into thinking its ally was further ahead than we really were. The next year at a crucial showdown between British and American scientists in Washington, the British Aldermaston team persuaded Edward Teller's men from Los

Alamos that Britain was just as far advanced in the theory of nuclear weaponry. Teller conceded that the laws of physics seemed to apply on both sides of the Atlantic and for a brief time the cooperation of 1940–5 was resumed although, after Suez, any illusion of equal partners working together was an obvious sham. Perhaps Britain, like France, could have broken away from the American-run military command of Nato and returned to developing her own nuclear weapons and strategy, joining full-heartedly with the new Europe. It would have been expensive and altered the shape of the post-war world but an entirely different path was available to Britain after Suez, even if it seemed a stony and unattractive one. Macmillan never considered it.

The stony path was the terrain of a politician to whom Macmillan was almost allergic. One morning in 1962, the Foreign Secretary, Lord Home, walked into the cabinet room in Number Ten to find the Prime Minister quietly shuffling the place-names around the table. He asked the cabinet secretary what has going on. Had someone died? No, came the reply, it was all to do with Enoch Powell: ' "The PM can't have Enoch's accusing eye looking at him straight across the table any more." And poor Enoch was put way down the left where Harold couldn't see him.'[24] It is not a bad symbol for the age. Avoiding eye contact with unpleasant choices was part of the art of governing and for much of this time governments got away with it rather successfully. Powell, a brilliant romantic driven by a cold, intense logic, was tormented by the choices ahead, from the economic effect of an ever-growing state, to the consequences of the loss of Empire and the effect of immigration on traditional

Englishness. His answers to these questions would change over time and some would destroy his political career, but he never stopped following his agonized conscience. Macmillan, by contrast, was perfectly well aware of hard choices ahead. His diaries are full of foreboding and he could write crisp, clear-sighted private papers. He pushed decolonization hard and struggled to get Britain into the European Economic Community. But confronted by the most dangerous questions, such as whether union power and state spending needed to be reversed, he seemed rather more interested in staying in office and reassuring the people that all would be well. He was a great actor, a wonderful showman. And he put Powell so far out of eyeline that he couldn't see him.

Much though they disliked one another, Macmillan and Powell had several important things in common. They had both been soldiers and both carried a certain guilt that they had not been killed fighting Germans. Harold Macmillan had fought exceedingly bravely in the First World War. He was wounded repeatedly. He survived without ever forgetting how many of his friends and the soldiers serving under him had not. He had a shuffling walk, much mocked when he became Prime Minister as some kind of aristocratic affectation. It was, in fact, caused by shrapnel from a German shell. Powell, a much younger man, had been an intelligence officer with the Eighth Army in the Second World War and said much later, with a touch of the characteristic Powellite emphasis: 'I should like to have been killed in the war.' Both men were haunted. Both also came from humbler families than Macmillan's marriage and pheasant-shooting, or Powell's perfect diction and fox-hunting, might have suggested. Macmillan's family had been Scottish crofters before going into the book trade, which bought him his privileged upbringing. Powell was the son of a Birmingham schoolmaster who rose through mental power and ferocious hard work. Both men were well read, particularly in the classics, and gifted at languages, though Macmillan lacked Powell's brilliance and preferred English novelists and political biographies. They shared a belief in Britain's unique destiny. The differences between them were chemical – and generational.

Harold Macmillan was a high-minded Victorian reformer, who grew up to the sound of horse-drawn carnages and the spectacle of the old Queen's Diamond Jubilee. A young Tory, his conscience was stirred by the awful poverty of the Depression, notably in his Stockton constituency. His politics in the thirties became radical to the point of extremism. He hired the former secretary of Oswald Mosley's New Party, a former Marxist. He called for widespread planning of the economy, including the abolition of the Stock Exchange and the bringing of the trade unions into the heart of economic decision-making. He was remarkably close to the politics of Tony Benn fifty years later. He might well not have stayed with the Tories had the war not intervened. After it, he was still a stirrer, suggesting renaming the Conservatives the New Democratic Paity. By the time he returned to government in 1951, his ideological wildness had matured into a paternalistic mildness, a horror of right-wingers and left-wingers both. Like Winston Churchill the son of an American mother, he hoped to show that in an American world, Britain could still play the role of a wise if wobbly parent, 'Greece to America's Rome.'

Enoch Powell, eighteen years younger, was no less romantic. But he was formed by the university study, the Indian army and the last days of the British Empire. Unlike Churchill or Macmillan he loathed the Americans to the point where he seriously believed, during 1944–5, that the next war would pit Europe and Russia on the one hand against the anti-imperialist United States on the other. Greece to their Rome? Had Powell not been a distinguished Latinist he would probably have preferred to torch Rome. Where Macmillan was vague and paternalistic in his thinking, Powell had a disconcerting habit of beginning with first principles and then following his logic wherever it led, which was often to uncomfortable places. Sovereignty, independence and race were not woolly abstractions for him. He distrusted wit and showmanship – though like his Labour doppelgänger and friend Michael Foot, he was always more of a showman and a personality politician than he admitted. Enoch Powell came relatively late to hunting. But compared to Macmillan, he was the wilder horseman, notorious among friends for throwing himself off while leaping unwisely over high fences with unknown drops. Macmillan was the ultimate master of staying in the saddle and would rule for years. Powell never would, but his anger matters as much for the British story as Macmillan's affectation that things were under control. Together, these two men make up the inner argument that animates the thirteen Tory years, even when looking the other way. Macmillan

240

had the power but not the ideas. Powell lacked the power, most of the time. But he would find the ideas.

The Revolt of the Chicken Farmer

Ideas matter. And because ideas matter, so too does the story of an Old Etonian Christian Scientist, former RAF fighter pilot, chicken farmer and unsuccessful turtle rancher called Antony Fisher. In the high years of socialism and planning, from 1945 onwards, Fisher stood out as an utterly self-certain individualist and anti-socialist. 'Communism is the poison offered to the people; socialism is the cup in which it is given; and the welfare state is the tempting label on the bottle,' he liked to say. In the Britain of the forties and fifties these views made him an eccentric. Once this country had been the world centre for liberal economics, famous for its people's distrust of big government – a land without identity cards or intrusive central government. Now even its Liberal Party was a keen supporter of the post-war consensus (the party, after all, of Beveridge and Keynes). There were some standing out against it. Not many, but some. Their unlikely spiritual teacher was Friedrich von Hayek, an exiled Viennese economist, who came from the very heart of cosmopolitan intellectualism where socialism, communism, Freudianism and fascism contended. A cousin of the daunting philosopher Wittgenstein, he would help reconvert the British to their old doctrines of economic liberalism.

Hayek had arrived in London to teach economics

241

in 1931 and developed a close rapport with another economist Lionel Robbins, the son of a London market gardener who had been taken up by that creator of the Welfare State, William Beveridge. Hayek and Robbins formed a crucial partnership at the London School of Economics, a subversive friendship which would help, eventually, to change the intellectual climate of Britain. Hayek's *The Road to Serfdom,* published in 1944, was one of the most influential books of the age, a full-throated attack on socialism which was received with contempt by many but admired – with reservations – by both George Orwell and Keynes himself. But a book is not a movement. Liberal economists did begin to meet regularly in Switzerland from 1947 but for Britain the key moment came with the arrival on the scene of Fisher, now an almost entirely forgotten man. He had been traumatized by watching the death of his brother during the Battle of Britain and rebuilt his life as a Sussex farmer. A staunch individualist, he had been entranced by Hayek's book and managed to meet his hero after the war. Hayek told Fisher not to try to become a politician but instead to try to win the battle of ideas by forming some kind of institute or organization to fight the rotting influence of the State. It was a message Fisher never forgot. Luckily for him, the State stepped in to help him spread it. In 1952 his herd of cattle contracted foot and mouth disease and had to be destroyed. Fisher used his compensation money to visit the United States.[25]

There he not only picked up the latest free-market thinking but visited a huge experimental 'broiler chicken' farm at Cornell University, where

15,000 birds were being raised under one roof. This, thought Fisher, was exactly what the meat-starved British needed. It was illegal to import the chunky American poultry central to the new factory farming, so the (anti-regulations) Fisher was reduced to covering two dozen fertilized White Rock eggs with silver foil and bringing them through in his hand luggage as 'Easter Eggs'. Back in Sussex he built sheds with gas heating systems and an overhead rail system to bring in food. Soon twenty-four chickens became 2,400 and then 24,000. Within a few years, his family were raising 1.25 million birds, Buxted Chickens had been formed, and Fisher was a very rich man, the most successful poultry farmer in Europe. Across Britain, affordable roast chicken became a staple of the Sunday lunch table, thanks to Fisher. And with the money they made him, he was able to fund the Institute for Economic Affairs, undoubtedly the most influential think tank in modern British history. Set up by Fisher and the eccentric ex-paratrooper and Liberal, Oliver Smedley, the IEA was intended to combat the socialist influence of the Fabians.[26] Soon they would be joined by others, Ralph Harris and Arthur Seldon. Hayek would be proved right. It was the seeding of ideas that mattered most, not conventional political careers.

The IEA first touched British politics during the winter of 1957–8 when inflation was rising above 4 per cent and wage settlements were in double figures. Like so many political crises of the time this one occurred in deepest private. The question was whether government spending should be cut back as part of a wider drive to curb the amount of money in the economy. Banks were also to be instructed to cut back credit. Macmillan was far more worried about confrontation and unemployment than he was about rising prices. His Chancellor, Peter Thorneycroft, disagreed. He was insistent that savings had to be made to squeeze inflation and save the pound. His enemies thought Macmillan an unprincipled coward. He was certainly driven by a ruthless enthusiasm for staying in office. But there was another side to the Prime Minister. Brought up in the intellectual shadow of Keynes, he thought that seriously painful cuts were perhaps not necessary and that the economy was already slowing. Though Macmillan was inclined to dither, haggle and to split the difference, this was a shrewd call. And around him he had many spending ministers, looking after the armed forces, the hospitals and welfare, who were bitterly against cutting back. He feared some of them might resign.

On the other side of the argument, as it turned out, were the real resigners, Thorneycroft and his two junior Treasury ministers – the wealthy, sarcastic, ruthlessly logical and nearly blind Nigel Birch, and Enoch Powell. Their insistence that it was vital to control the money supply was not just a technical position, but was intertwined with a personal suspicion of corporatism and the big state that was close to the more intellectual economic case now being pushed by the newly formed IEA. Lionel Robbins had been advising the three ministers, despite much sucking of teeth by more consensus-minded officials, and Fisher's men would come to see Thorneycroft and his fellow rebels at Macmillan's Treasury as heroes. They provided the intellectual ammunition and connected through Powell to younger Tories, and gained them as converts. Powell had already been introduced to Hayek's thinking. In the months before the three Treasury ministers resigned, they had been dropping in on one another for a rolling conversation which showed they had all concluded the same thing – that government spending was too high and had to be severely reined back. Against the instincts of their own officials as well as their colleagues, they put together a planned series of cuts, including a 50 per cent increase in the cost of school meals, freezes on pay rises and the removal of family allowances for the second child. It would have hit five million families, including millions of the very middle-class mothers whose support the Tories most needed.

It was a deliberately tough and provocative package, and battle was duly joined in the cabinet. If there was ever a moment before the great political smash-ups of the seventies when ministers could have gripped the issue of inflation and asserted themselves against the consensus of Whitehall and the unions, this was it. Day after day, the arguments raged back and forward. Compromises were offered, partially accepted, and then rejected again. Tempers grew shorter. The Treasury team trooped in and out of Number Ten. A special cabinet was held on Friday, then again on the Sunday. But Thorneycroft, despite being accused of 'Hitler tactics' by irate colleagues, would not budge. Macmillan, anxious to get away for a tour of the Commonwealth, would not concede the cuts. All three ministers then resigned. Thorneycroft would later become chairman of the Tories under Margaret Thatcher.

Birch would struggle with his growing blindness and never return. Powell's stormy career had many more crises in it yet. In apparently throw-away but actually carefully considered words, Macmillan dismissed the whole matter as 'a little local difficulty', appointed a new team, and swanned off abroad exactly on schedule. It seemed stylish, insouciant, masterly. From it, immediately, nothing flowed. Some cuts were made by the new Chancellor. The economy was in fact turning down, which suggests Thorneycroft's medicine would have been grim indeed.

Yet this was a turning point – away from the ideas of free marketeers and towards the last phase of the planning economy which would end in disaster. That, in turn, would eventually produce Thatcherism, the IEA's final triumph and the time when Antony Fisher's eggs came home to roost. Before that could happen, another pre-election boom was engineered in 1959 and a new idea for improving British economic performance began to take hold, the central plan used by the French. By 1961 there was a 'pay pause' to try to hold down inflation, and then the establishment of a grand chat-in, the National Economic Development Council, or Neddy, which brought industrialists, civil servants and trade unionists around a table to discuss how to produce more. Reggie Maudling virtually ordered the carmakers to build new factories in Scotland, Merseyside and Wales in order to combat rising unemployment. The following year saw a 4 per cent growth target. The run-up to the 1964 election under a new Prime Minister featured a giveaway budget by Maudling, by now Chancellor, which would later be blamed by

246

Labour for leaving an atrocious economic crisis. Almost all the weapons used by Labour to try and plan their way out of economic decline, from pay and incomes targets to national plans and regional directives, were already in place under Macmillan and his successor Alec Douglas-Home. All would fail. Antony Fisher knew why.

Things that Fall on your Feet

The best answer was clearly for British industry to produce more that the rest of the world wanted to buy, reliably and at the right price. Was that impossible? In the fifties there were plenty of successful British corporations. There were the oil giants such as Royal Dutch-Shell, product of a merger in 1906 and by then a vast international business, headquartered in London. There were the consumer combines, notably Unilever, another Dutch and British joint venture dating from 1928 which squatted across everything from soap powder to sausages, toothpaste to frozen food, and which was run on the latest principles of market research, ruthlessly targeted advertising and properly trained managers. There was the privatized-again steel industry. The Steel Company of Wales whose vast Port Talbot works in South Wales ('the city of steel which never sleeps') employed 20,000 people and could boast one of the most modern mill systems in the world. Other private steel firms, at Consett for instance, were also working at full pelt and seemed competitive with their European rivals. There was ICI, the chemical combine created in the twenties, which enjoyed a near-monopoly in many products, which employed 6,000 research workers and by the end of the fifties was spending more on R&D than all Britain's universities combined. There were electronic companies like Ferranti's and the sprawling engine-making, light bulb, fridge and washing machine group AEI; the still-successful engineers such as Rolls-Royce and Vickers and tightly run metal-bashers like Guest, Keen and Nettlefolds.

These and other groups were not allowed to sit pretty, or lack for competition. The fifties had seen the start of ruthless 'corporate raiding' by tycoons who took over, broke up and reorganized flaccid and poorly managed firms. There was much talk of learning the latest American management techniques; the big US advertising companies were already growing in London and influencing British thinking; better design was being eagerly sought out from Italy, Denmark and France. In his *Anatomy of Britain* (1962) the journalist Anthony Sampson paints a vivid picture of one of the new property tycoons who was making a fortune by breaking up the inner city portfolios of great old companies and putting up new developments – what he called his 'Canalettos', the new skylines of booming Britain.

Jack Cotton, a Birmingham boy made good, was living in a suite in the Dorchester Hotel, surrounded by surveyors, maps and paintings by Renoir, a jaunty business impresario – 'short, red-faced, fifty-nine, with smooth black hair, shrewd eyes, a pointed handkerchief in his pocket with a bow tie to match ... His cars are called JC1 and JC2.' Then there was Hugh Fraser, the Glasgow draper's son who was building a huge network of stores and other businesses across the country. In 1948 he floated House of Fraser and created a private company Scottish and Universal Investment Trusts (SUITS) which became a mighty force in the fifties; by 1957 he had bought London's John Barker group, and two years later, Harrods. Then, another outsider, the Italian-born Charles Forte who had emigrated to Alloa in Scotland was quietly building a modest chain of roadside cafes into a huge hotel and catering business. He opened Britain's first motorway cafe and his Little Chef and, from 1958, Happy Eater restaurants, which, while not necessarily the finest examples of continental cuisine, kept generations of travelling Britons fuelled. These men are also part of the story of the fifties, alongside the more familiar images of tweed-suited Old Etonians ambling around grouse-moors. Even in government the rumbles of modernization could be heard. The hyperactive Tory minister Ernie Marples, a self-made businessman and rare working-class *arriviste* in Macmillan's cabinet, a fireball of energy in the Jack Cotton mould, was busy recasting Britain's ancient transport system; the first parking meters, for instance, went up in London in 1958 in Grosvenor Square. Under his appointee and friend Dr Beeching, brutal cuts in the rail network would soon follow. Investment went instead to new roads and traffic management systems. During those thirteen Tory years, car ownership quadrupled to eight million and huge amounts of commerce was diverted from rail to lorries.

Britain's car industry, which would later become the ultimate symbol of industrial failure, was

249

looking strong. The tangle of small competing companies that had marked the pre-war industry had been radically pruned. In 1952 the two great rivals, Austin and Morris, came together to form the British Motor Company. Herbert Austin's company at Longbridge, Birmingham, which traced its history to 1906, had dominated the inter-war years with its Austin Seven. This was the first British car which could be bought in large numbers by the less wealthy: good enough to be built under licence by BMW and copied by Nissan, it had sold nearly 300,000 by the outbreak of war. By 1948 a new range of Austins, the Princess and Sheerline, were spattered across magazine and newspaper adverts, and the A40 Somersets and Devons were arriving. Lord Nuffield, over at Oxford, had been one of the great industrial pioneers of modern Britain, building his first car just before the First World War, and still going strong enough at the time of the merger to become president of the new BMC. His Morris Eight and Morris Ten had won pre-war devotees. After the war, it was the Oxford company which produced the first great British car of the age of mass motoring, Alec Issigonis's revolutionary Morris Minor of 1948. This would become the first British model to sell over a million, and would still be in production as late as 1971. Lord Nuffield had not been an immediate fan, describing the car as 'that damned poached egg designed by that damned foreigner'.

The Great Arragonis

Alec Issigonis deserves a short aside in the narrative, a space for himself. He not only designed the Morris Minor but in 1959, the year Macmillan, at the height of his reputation, called a particularly successful election, he produced the Mini too. This was the nearest thing to chic Macmillan's age produced, though of course Macmillan himself would never have bought anything so small and vulgar. Issigonis can lay claim to being one of the more influential figures in the history of the car in Britain as well as being about the only industrial designer anyone has heard of. The son of a Greek engineer living in Turkey who had taken British citizenship, and a German brewer's daughter, his early years had been lived on the site of his father's marine engineering business, watching the drawings transform themselves into engines.

He is as good an example as any of the benefit that immigration brought to the country. He was a war refugee: the First World War peace treaties had carved up the Ottoman empire and given Smyrna, the port where Issigonis lived, to Greece. The Turks won it back and many foreigners fled. Issigonis's father died on the way and he arrived with his mother in London in 1922, virtually penniless. He learned engineering and industrial drawing in London before getting work first for Humber, then Morris. An unconventional designer, he loathed teamwork and mathematics, describing the latter as the enemy of every truly creative man.

He learned in part by hand-making his own racing car, which he raced himself before the war; later he would ridicule such innovations as car radios, seatbelts and comfortable seats.

Issigonis's Morris Minor had been radical in design and structure; it was the nearest of any British car to the Hitler-era Volkswagen Beetle. His Mini-Minor was commissioned in the immediate aftermath of the Suez crisis when petrol shortages had focused attention on the case for cheap, economical cars. The country was already latching on to the cheap bubble cars being imported from Italy and Germany, and soon being made in Britain too, at a Brighton factory. Issigonis's brief was to produce something for the British Motor Corporation that could take them on, but was also a proper car, not a motorbike with pretensions. He not only made it look good, but by turning round the engine and placing it over the wheels, he found a way of packing far more space for passengers into a smaller area than any previous car. His design was so radical it needed a complete set of new machine tools to produce; Issigonis designed them, too. The Mini would become an icon of British cool, a chirpy, cheeky little car we liked to think represented the national character at its classless best. Yet the true story of the Mini is not quite as flattering to British industry. The early Minis were shoddily built, with a series of mechanical problems and poor trim; more importantly they leaked so badly people joked that every car should be sold with a free pair of Wellington boots and one journalist said he was keeping goldfish in the door pockets. Issigonis was short-tempered and intolerant with more junior design and production colleagues, who called him Arragonis and Issigonyet? He had spoken before about building a 'charwoman's car' but the lower-income families the Mini was aimed at initially took against its unfamiliar shape, small size and austere lack of trim.

In fact, for a while, the car looked as if it would be a thundering disaster. The economics behind it were also, to say the least, obscure. The basic model sold at £350, much cheaper than rival small cars such as the Triumph Herald (£495) and the Ford Anglia (£380) and indeed BMC's own old Morris Minor (£416). Yet it had been very expensive to develop and required its own machine tooling to make. How was this possible? Ford tore one apart to cost it and decided it would cost them more to build than BMC were selling it for.[27] It seems unlikely there was any profit: in their urge to undercut its competitors, the makers of the Mini were ignoring the development costs and selling the car at a loss. (Company people say they continued to sell it at a loss for years.) BMC would eventually sell more than five million Minis but its success only came about thanks to what we would now call celebrity endorsement, and even spin. Issigonis happened to know Princess Margaret's new husband, the photographer Lord Snowdon, and presented the glamorous couple with one as a birthday present. They were duly photographed whizzing round London in it. The Queen tried one out, and soon Steve McQueen, Twiggy, the Beatles and Marianne Faithfull, Mick Jagger's girlfriend, were seen in them too. This was completely the opposite image to BMC's and Issigonis's original idea of a cheap, no-frills car for the working classes;

253

conservative-minded people found their car taken up as a chic emblem of youthful impertinence. In the end, of course, whatever works, works. Yet the mechanical problems, lack of good teamwork and unbusinesslike pricing strategy show that there was a darker side to the Mini story from the first. Issigonis's biographer concluded that 'far from being a business triumph for the shaky British Motor Corporation, the Mini was the first nail in their coffin.'

Issigonis was a naif in the world of business but he was prescient in one respect. He hated mergers. The Austin-Morris one produced huge internal pain with two mutually hostile company bureaucracies locking horns. The results were not immediately obvious. Through the fifties BMC rationalized its cars and cut the number of engines used, while keeping its old Austin and Morris dealers happy. With fast economic growth and an insatiable appetite for affordable cars, the domestic industry did well. There was American competition but then, there always had been – General Motors had been a big player in the UK since it took over Vauxhall in 1928, and Ford had chosen Britain as its European base even earlier. By the sixties, German and French imports were also frequent sights on British roads.

Still, there were few signs of a domestic car industry in crisis. Other producers were marketing long-lived and successful models, from the sleek Jaguars to the stolid and stately Rover Eights and Rover 50s. Issigonis was not the only free spirit of the times – Rover went far down the road (at 152mph) towards a commercial jet-powered car. Yet industrial action was growing, despite managers who bought off the unions with generous settlements in an era when they could easily sell every car they made. There was a particularly bad strike at BMC in 1958. There were some strange management decisions, egged on by politicians. Ministers trying to bring employment to run-down parts of Scotland and the North of England persuaded BMC to create a cumbersome and expensive empire of new factories which it did not have the expertise to manage properly. Little of this was apparent to the ordinary observer then, the first years of popular motoring mania.

The Growth of Car Mania

Britain was slow to catch the motorway addiction. There had been a spate of road-building in the thirties but it was not until 1936 that the government took national responsibility for a network of major roads. All building then stopped when war began three years later. But America's vast highways were an inspiration to British engineers; and Hitler's Germany had been known for its gleaming new autobahns. With Britain's cramped, slow, badly congested roads full of military vehicles, in 1941 a cabinet committee was being urged to consider 'motorways' as a vital part of post-war construction. The man responsible was Frederick Cook, a gifted and pushy highways engineer, though his committee included Attlee, Ernie Bevin and the founding Director General of the BBC, Lord Reith. Lord Leathers, the wartime transport minister, duly announced that Britain had been converted to the idea of 'motorways to be reserved exclusively for fast-moving traffic' while warning that they must not be developed on too grand a scale as advocated 'by some enthusiasts who are perhaps unduly influenced by continental analogies'. No Nazi speed mania here, in other words. The result was a Special Roads Act in 1949 which led eventually, when money allowed, to the motorways which began to carve up and transform the country.

In theory, motorway Britain had been only one of two possible options. The world's first industrialized nation was still wired tightly together with a massive railway network. By the end of the fifties, British Rail controlled 17,800 miles of track linking most small towns and every city. It ran more than 7,000 stations and a million freight wagons, all of it worked by a massive staff – 475,000 people in 1961. But the system was making an equally massive loss and needed major investment. With cars becoming the dream of middle-class families, perhaps the railways at that scale needed some pruning. Instead an affable, moustachioed former ICI manager called Dr Richard Beeching came along and cut them to ribbons. Beeching was greatly admired at the time as a living symbol of thrusting new Britain. In the early sixties to 'do a Beeching' became flattering shorthand for ruthless management efficiency. Hired as the chairman of the railways, he conducted a 'reshaping plan' which proposed the closure of 2,361 stations and 5,000 miles of track – and that was just for starters. It was one of the most extreme liquidations in the history of British commerce, on a par with the collapse of the car industry a decade later, or the end of shipbuilding on the Clyde.

Suspicions have been heard ever since that the Beeching cuts were politically motivated. They had been prepared for by a secret committee on which sat industrialists but no railway people. They came a few years after a savagely effective strike by two railway unions which had reminded Conservative ministers that while a country could be closed down if it was linked by trains, this was very much harder if it was a lorry and car economy. The Tories had already denationalized road transport, putting 24,000 lorries back into the hands of private hauliers; everything from fish to potatoes, newspapers to engine parts, seemed to be transferring from rail. This was what 'modern' meant. And to cap it all, the minister in charge who had given Beeching his mandate to cut the railways until they made a profit, without taking social or wider economic interests into account, was hardly neutral on the issue.

Ernest Marples was a bouncy, chirpy Manchester engineering worker's son who had won a grammar school scholarship and gone on to work as a miner, a postman, an accountant and a chef before his war service. A Labour activist in his youth, he was demobbed as a keen Tory and after becoming an MP, served as one of the few real modernizers in the 1951 – 64 governments. He brought in 'trunk' or automatic dialling, designed to make telephones more popular – until the late fifties, everyone had to call up a telephone exchange, give the number and wait to be put through by an operator. He had launched Britain's Premium Bonds too, denounced by Harold Wilson as a 'squalid raffle' but instantly popular. Marples's enthusiasm for the new extended most dramatically, however, to roads. He charged around the world looking for examples of the traffic systems of the future, and brought in the first yellow lines, the first parking meters, the first major roundabouts. He had formed his own civil engineering company, which would soon be responsible for West London's Hammersmith flyover, and much else. Marples was not keen on railways, though. When challenged about the conflict of interest in having his motorway construction company, he simply passed the shares to his wife. Under him, Britain finally embarked on its motorway age.

Those were the days. The first was opened on 5 December 1958, an eight-mile bypass of Preston. No major road had been built for twenty years. British engineers had yet to learn the intricacies of prestressed concrete design, precision and bearing ratios from colleagues in the United States. It was all something of an experiment for the man in charge, John Cox of Tarmac, who had made his name building instant airstrips during the war. The Preston bypass had to be closed forty-six days later because of frost damage. Though the central reservation later allowed it to be widened for levels of traffic undreamed-of in the late fifties, it was still too narrow and its rather beautiful bridges, which had been designed to last for 120 years, were knocked down and replaced after thirty. Still, it worked and the experience was vital for the first long stretch of British motorway, a 67-mile stretch of the M1 linking London and Yorkshire, opened the following year. Built in only nineteen months, it had three lanes in either direction and that now humdrum novelty, the first motorway service stations. Marples opened the Watford Gap service station, run by Blue Boar, on 2 November 1959. Newport Pagnell opened six months later.

Britain has never been the same since. From then on, motorway building spread at a brisk pace. Stretches of the M60 and M6 appeared during 1960–3; the first section of the Al(M) was completed in 1961 and the M5 the following year. Scotland's first motorway building, the M8 outside Glasgow, came in 1967. The early seventies saw a dramatic expansion, with the M4 linking London and Bristol, the M40 reaching towards Oxford and Birmingham and the cities of Liverpool, Leeds, Manchester and Sheffield all being interconnected. The first five-lane dual carriageway arrived outside Belfast in 1973 and it was only after the completion of the M25 round London in 1985 that the pace of building faltered. In the early years of the new century it virtually stopped. By then the network had grown from eight miles to 2,200 miles – and the A-roads servicing it greater still.

The creation of the motorway network has been called the first centrally planned roads system in Britain since the Romans left. It makes a pattern the Romans would have recognized, with London the hub, radial routes spinning out from it, and only the further West Country, rural Wales and northern Scotland ignored. The Romans might have been surprised at the absence of motorways across East Anglia, and the quantity of civil engineering lavished on the north and Midlands of England; but that is a consequence of the industrial revolution. Today's motorways are more curved than the legions would have found acceptable, avoiding hills and towns – though the straightest stretch of all, part of the Al(M) near Stilton, is so because it follows the old Roman street for seven miles. The system is rational and heavily used, heavily policed, heavily taxed and has engorged a swathe of rural England. Even as late as 1985–2001, transport projects (mainly roads) took up a further tract of sparse land equal to three times the area of Nottingham. If usage equals success, then few acts of post-war political decision making have been as popular as the designing and building of what Margaret Thatcher called 'the great car economy'. For every car or van on the roads of Britain in 1950 – 2.3 million of them – there were twice as many by the end of the decade and more than three times as many by the early sixties. By 1970 there were 12 million and by the end of the century, more than 24 million, ten times as many in half a century. This only gives part of the picture, because these cars are also used much more, going further and for longer. In the last fifteen years of the century, car journeys increased by nearly 30 per cent. Year by year, despite propaganda for a healthier lifestyle, high fuel taxes, congestion charging and widespread worry about global warming, the British drive more and walk, cycle or use buses less.

In the days of Marples it was believed that such an increase would also mean vastly more Britons being killed and maimed on the roads. This is one gloomy prediction that has been robustly disproved. Safety campaigns from the Tufty Club of the fifties to the Green Cross Code have had their effect but the real reason is that the British, who think of themselves as lovers of liberty, have allowed their freedom to be drastically curtailed on the roads.

From the first general speed limits in the thirties to today's ubiquitous metal snoop-force of remote cameras, Britain has developed a driving culture which kills proportionately far fewer people than most comparable countries. If there is a single heroine of that part of our motoring history it is Barbara Castle. A non-driving minister in her rather glamorous mid-fifties, Castle had been disappointed to be offered Transport by Harold Wilson in 1965. She had hoped to be Home Secretary. But she was formidably ambitious and media-savvy and quickly turned the job into a great personal success. When she arrived some 8,000 people a year were dying on Britain's roads. Figures produced at the time suggested there would be half a million such deaths by the year 2000.

Castle's Road Safety Act brought in the breathalyser to combat drunk driving, extended the trial 70mph speed limit and made it compulsory for all new cars to have seat belts. There was already a bill prepared but she toughened it up, rejecting random breath tests but making the penalty a year's automatic disqualification. Castle revved up a storm. The Formula One racing driver Stirling Moss attacked 'socialist hypocrisy'. Letters came in reading 'You've ballsed our darts matches up, so get out you wicked old B' or wishing her 'evil Christmas and a whole year of unhappy days. These are the views of the public, you bitchy old cow.'[28] Her long-suffering husband Ted, who did drive, was pursued by journalists eager to catch him over the limit, and had to confine himself to tonic water at public events. But in the test's first year road deaths fell by 1,200. As Castle wrote in her autobiography, she was soon afterwards introduced to a London

261

ambulance driver who told her that before the breathalyser, 'their night's work had followed a regular pattern. As soon as the pubs closed the accident figures shot up and they were operating at full stretch. Now, he said, they spent the night playing cards.' Seatbelts, which saved the looks of thousands of people, and the lives of others, were equally vigorously opposed as an infringement on liberty and a diabolical liberty for women with large bosoms. But they helped stem the deaths. By the end of the century, with nearly three times as many cars on the road as when Mrs Castle took office, the numbers killed each year were less than half the toll in 1965. Compared to most similar countries, Britain's roads are congested, but safe.

Slipping Through Our Fingers

To the ordinary observer, there was plenty to be cheerful about throughout British industrial life. The coal industry, though nationalized, was nevertheless at last rationalized and modernized. In these years, some 200,000 miners' jobs went and super-pits were developed using newer and safer technology, while on the other hand, around Britain the first nuclear power stations came on stream. When Calder Hall was connected to the national grid in 1956 it was the world's first nuclear power station providing energy commercially, and its Magnox gas-cooled reactor incorporated British technology. A further ten similar nuclear power stations followed. Here, as in the car industry – and lesser-known examples, such as industrial glass, chemicals and jet engines, not to mention the beginnings of the offshore gas industry – British technology was as good as any in the world. In an entirely different area, P&O was then the largest shipping line in the world with 366 vessels, seemingly dominating commercial traffic across the oceans. This was not, in short, the basket-case industrial economy that is sometimes misremembered. But during the fifties overseas competition was quietly surveying the British market and its complacent industrial giants, planning to attack.

The story of motorbike manufacturing can stand for other industries, too. In the early years of the decade, Harley-Davidson in the United States were complaining (unsuccessfully) to Washington about the unfair competition from the better, cheaper, British-made Triumph motorbikes – one of which starred in *The Wild One,* featuring Marlon Brando, in 1954. Another American manufacturer, Indian, gave up and began importing Royal Enfield bikes; rock stars and Hollywood actors were seen on British machines; there were more than 300 Triumph and BSA dealers in the United States. Yet in 1955 Yamaha began producing their first motorbikes, followed by Suzuki, using wartime aircraft manufacturing kit. At the end of the decade, when British motorcycle sales were at their all-time peak, Honda entered its first bike in the TT race. British executives toured Japan in 1960 and were horrified by the scale of production by the three rival companies: Japan was making more than 500,000 motorcycles a year, compared to a maximum UK output of just 140,000. Two years later these Japanese bikes were winning key races in

Europe and a new manufacturer, Kawasaki, appeared on the scene. It was a story that would be repeated in electronics and cameras. In this period, West Germany's share of world trade grew nearly four times as fast as Britain's, while the Japanese were already in another league for growth. The Americans were racing ahead in starved, post-war markets all round the world.

It was the structure of Britain's working world that was the problem, not the lack of hardworking people or enterprising companies – not even, at this stage, inflation or industrial militancy. On one side, the industrial companies were dwarfed by the vast nationalized corporations, sucking capital and talent away from the consumer industries that were becoming so central to people's lives. ICI was vast, as has been described; but every three years, the Electricity Board spent enough capital to create a new ICI.[29] On the other side, there were simply too many tiny companies, inefficiently and traditionally run without any knowledge of new management styles, product designs or marketing. By the middle of the fifties, of the nearly 300,000 British companies that existed, only around one in a hundred was actually listed on the Stock Market; the vast majority were under-capitalized traditional private businesses. The economic historian Keith Middlemass describes a business ecology dominated by 'the continued survival of a mass of small firms, reliant on sheltered domestic markets, which were unable or unwilling to reform their practices or their low productivity'.[30]

Was there any direct connection between this national failure and the kind of people running the country? Industrialists and entrepreneurs were not part of the Tory magic circle and were not socially much regarded. Macmillan and Eden both suffered from a pseudo-aristocratic and sentimental attitude to class. With their First World War service and their inter-war worries about the effect of unemployment, they were inclined to admire the working classes from a decent distance and to disdain the 'common' speech and attitudes of upwardly mobile entrepreneurs such as Sir Bernard Docker. They lived privileged and upper-crust lives themselves, set in landed homes and surrounded by literature and art. It was a way of life to which the self-made would aspire too: Michael Heseltine would begin by mixing margarine and butter as he built his low-rent property business, and end with a grand country home and an arboretum. For the ruling class of the fifties, the businessmen, the engineers, the factory organizers were vulgar, vulgar, vulgar. Diplomacy; country sports and farming; the arts; high politics; even journalism were all interesting, but industry was a bore. As we have seen this did not stop large companies thriving or hold back individual entrepreneurs, very often immigrants unintimidated by class barriers. But it was hardly surprising that fewer bright British students went to work for the British motor industry or the chemical giants, compared to the best of the Germans and Americans going into their equivalents. In the fifties, foreigners were not yet talking pityingly of 'the British disease' but there was talk of the 'stagnant society'. No one grasped the nettle.

The Egg-heads and DufFel-coat Rebels

One group of society was equally opposed to the Tory magic circle and the industrial entrepreneur. Its supporters wore heavy blue or beige duffel coats – the coarse, toggle-fastened woollen coats designed in Victorian Britain but which became truly popular on the Atlantic and Arctic convoys of the Second World War – and roll-necked pullovers, baggy tweed jackets, stout shoes. The men would be vigorously bearded. Their look proclaimed the opposite of stylishness or American influence. Their chosen music, too, was very different from the skiffle bands and the rock and roll beginning to infiltrate teenagers' lives. For most politically minded left-wingers folk music was the sound of the times, heard in smoke-filled and beery clubs across the nation.

Folk music became popular throughout the UK in the fifties, though it has been swamped in memory by the eruption of pop soon afterwards. It was particularly strong in Scotland where singing traditions among farm-workers and miners, and the vast popularity of Robert Burns, underpinned an audience for 'the people's music'. Edinburgh had been chosen at the end of the forties as the site of a new annual international festival of the arts (selected just ahead of Bath because it had rather less bomb damage) focusing on the traditional elite arts – opera, classical drama, ballet and fine arts. By 1950 there was growing irritation among the poets and singers at the centre of the Scottish literary revival at the way Scotland was being excluded and, by 1951, an alternative people's festival was established. Trade unions, the Communist Party, left-wing councillors and others backed the project, which in turn kicked off the post-war folk scene in Scotland. There were lectures about the danger of American culture swamping British culture, concerts and get-togethers with Gaelic musicians, films, choirs and specially written plays – but, within three years, at the height of the Cold War, the Edinburgh people's festival was closed down by the trade union movements on the grounds that it was a Communist plot. (It was Communist-tinged but it was hardly a plot.)

Outside Scotland the folk movement was strongest in the Northern and Midland regions of England and the West Country, though folk clubs spread everywhere and by 1957 there were supposed to be some 1,500 of them in Britain. There was something over-defensive about their self-proclaimed independence from American music, since the United States was undergoing its own folk revival at the same time, also strongly linked to left-wing politics and also defiantly 'authentic' in the face of the rising power of commercial music. Jimmie Miller, the best-known leader of the movement, had been born in Salford into a Scottish socialist family of militants and musicians and had had dozens of jobs in the 1930s before marrying the left-wing actress Joan Littlewood, and setting up experimental radical theatre projects with her. Later they split up and Miller wrote his best-known song 'The First Time Ever I Saw Your Face' for an American folk musician, Peggy Seeger, when they fell in love. A committed Marxist, he changed his name to Ewan MacColl as he became central to the folk revival. Among his songs was 'Dirty Old Town', later made famous by the London-Irish band the Pogues. Other key figures were the former soldier and poet Hamish Henderson, who first began collecting traditional songs and stories from across the Western Highlands and Islands; and Norman Buchan, the Labour MP. There was great talent, great energy and great optimism. For a time it seemed that Britain might produce a music radically different from the raucous new noises of North America.

Folk continued to be much enjoyed by a minority. Stars like Billy Connolly cut their teeth on folk. But outside the Celtic nations, the revival was pretty much doomed from the beginning. Any movement so suffused with nostalgia and gentle humour, played on instruments with minimal amplification, is unlikely to cut the mustard in an age of urban consumerism, when the commercial drive is to record and sell short, fast songs for a young and fickle audience no longer interested in the struggles of their grandparents. Any movement so resolutely unfashionable, so tousled, hairy and serious, was unlikely to defeat styles and songs efficiently marketed for the new teenage market. The parallel enthusiasm for modern jazz, which excited the English middle-class youth at the same time, and which seemed so rebellious in a land still contemptuous of 'negro' culture, fizzled away for similar reasons. Live performance in small clubs and songs that went on for too long, and were simply too complicated for everyone to enjoy, surrendered to quick, easy music. In a battle between the 'authentic' and the cool, when the fight is pitched for young urban consumers, it is easy to see what will happen. In the end, for all its beauty and vigour, Britain's folk music revival of the fifties was another exhibition of impotent local revolt against the coming age of America.

So was the political cause which so many of the folk and jazz enthusiasts cherished, the Campaign for Nuclear Disarmament. One of its leading figures, the popular historian A. J. P. Taylor, later reflected that CND, like the Establishment politicians it opposed, simply over-rated Britain's position in the world: 'We thought that Great Britain was still a great power whose example would affect the rest of the world. Ironically, we were the last imperialists.'[31] For a while, the campaign sent a jolt through politics and seemed to all those contemplating the swift extinction of life on the planet far more a moral act than politics as usual. It had begun with a campaign to end the radiation-spreading testing of nuclear weapons, which was causing great alarm. Popular writers, notably J. B. Priestley, and the elderly mathematician and philosopher Bertrand Russell, wrote influential articles proclaiming the moral necessity of renouncing such world-destroying weaponry entirely. The *New Statesman* appealed to Khrushchev to disarm and to its surprise got a reply back from Moscow, albeit an unhelpful one. The Labour left were almost all committed ban-the-bombers as of course was the Moscow-funded Communist Party of Great Britain. These strands, along with Quakers, pacifists and certain journalists, eventually found themselves sitting together in the appropriately named Amen Court, home of Canon John Collins of St Paul's Cathedral, where on 15 January 1958 the new organization was created. A month later, more than five thousand people turned up for the inaugural meeting at Westminster; some were arrested when they went on to protest at Downing Street.

Though CND would fail to persuade any major British party to renounce nuclear weapons throughout the Cold War and failed as well to halt, never mind reverse, the build-up of American nuclear weaponry on British soil, it did succeed in dividing the Labour Party and seizing the imagination of millions of people. For a ramshackle left-wing organization, it behaved in a thoroughly modern and media-savvy way. Its symbol, designed by a professional artist, Gerald Holtham, in 1958, and based on semaphore, became an international brand almost as recognizable as Coca-Cola: suddenly, all those duffel coats and black jumpers had some decoration. The Aldermaston marches, first from Trafalgar Square towards the base and later in the opposite direction, were never enormous but they did attract massive press coverage. Its more militant wing, the Committee of 100, using direct non-violent action, managed to get the 89-year-old Lord Russell arrested by police, a considerable act of public relations. Yet it was as Taylor described it, a movement of egg-heads for egg-heads. Another historian reflected that it was a classic 'anti-political movement of the educated, the affluent and the disaffected, a movement rooted in the leafy suburbs of the middle classes, not the slums or council estates'.[32] Its members tended to be liberal on other issues too, and to be contemptuous of the organized and stodgy routines of politics, Labour politics in particular. By the end of the fifties, radicals found Labour entirely unappetizing. Now, why was that?

Labour Destroys its Future

When the Conservatives have been out of power, they have tended to think and work hard to change themselves and win it back, the six or seven years after 1997 being an exception. When Labour has lost power it has tended, after due thought and consideration, to tear itself into small pieces. This was the case in the fifties, in the seventies and again most spectacularly in the eighties. In each case it was essentially a fight between the Labour left and right but as befits a party of altruists it was often also highly personal and vicious. Labour has not had grand family, old school tie or clubland cliques as the Tories have. It has had gangs instead. Through most of his time, Attlee had kept the socialist gangs apart and quiet, though he began to lose control when Britain rearmed at the time of the Korean War. From then on, it was mostly gang war. On one side, there were always left-wing true believers who believed the country could be dragged to a pure version of socialism – romantics, generally in love with English and Scottish revolutionary socialism, or with Marxism, or both. They were the 'if only' faction. If only the trade unions could be won by the left, then true socialist policies could be imposed on the party. If only the gang at the top could be kicked out. If only we could force Labour MPs to do what their

271

constituency parties told them to. If only we could capture the national executive committee, or the conference arrangements committee, or some committee or other. If only we could get in, we could nationalize the top 200 companies and then everything would change for ever.

Few of them, unfortunately for their cause, were working class. Michael Foot was educated at fee-paying boarding schools and came from a family of Cornish puritans and nonconformists, drunk on books – his father, a solicitor and a Liberal MP, left a collection of 52,000 books, including 240 bibles, which gives some indication of the family tone. Dick Crossman, whose diaries would later lift the lid on the Wilson years, was a wealthy lawyer's son and Oxford academic. Barbara Castle was from lower down the social tree, a tax-surveyor's daughter who nevertheless went to Bradford Grammar School and Oxford. Ian Mikardo was unusual in being the child of poor Polish immigrants – his father's command of English was so poor he is said to have thought for a while he was living in New York, not London – who trained as a rabbi. The great exception was certainly working class. The first leader of the If Onlies was Nye Bevan, the former miner and the minister who had created the National Health Service, before his 'health before guns' resignation. By the mid-fifties his great years were behind him. Though he made some wonderful speeches in Opposition and was tough enough to break with his closest supporters over the issue of nuclear weapons, much of his behaviour seemed petulant and self-regarding. Of his great enemy Hugh Gaitskell, he would spit that the man was 'nothing – nothing – *nothing*' or assert, 'He's an intellectual, I'm a miner.' Barbara Castle, who never had an entirely easy relationship with Bevan, noted when she was sitting beside him on a conference platform: 'I have made a perturbing discovery about him. His favourite doodle is writing his own name.'[33] Like a political Dylan Thomas, his lavish talents were only matched by his skill in lavishly squandering them. As we have seen, in office he had been a great reforming minister. The bigger the job, the bigger the man he became. In Opposition, his charisma was less well employed and his vanity was more damaging. He became smaller.

He seemed to carry round with him a kind of portable audience, essential to his well-being, foils to his wit, witty though many were themselves. Yet Bevan had a bewitching charisma that made him the focus for the left, whose positions included an increasingly reflexive anti-Americanism and a doctrinaire insistence on nationalization and central planning. Bevan was as distrustful of the Soviet Union as the rest of the Labour leadership. There were no illusions about Moscow, particularly after an angry dinner in the Commons at which Khrushchev warned Labour that they must ally with Russia 'because if not, they would swat us off the face of the earth like a dirty old black beetle'.[34] Though he was easily beaten by Gaitskell in the leadership battle in 1955, Bevan's supporters were a formidable crowd in the party throughout this period. In 1952, fifty-seven Labour MPs abstained in a motion on Tory defence spending, which was a measure of their size. The 'Keep Left' group had become the 'Bevanites', votaries even as they protested their sturdy independence. They were a clique, with their own newspaper, *Tribune,* and their own social gatherings in the Commons, at Crossman's London house, at a country house, Buscot Park in Oxfordshire, and in Soho restaurants. They saw themselves as the romantic, rackety and principled opponents of the upper-class traitors who were taking over Labour. Soon, inevitably, they were being called a party within a party.

As suspicions grew, Bevan attacked Gaitskell personally and in public. With support from such unlikely and untrustworthy sources as the right-wing press magnate Lord Beaverbrook, Bevan and his gang started to seriously scare other Labour leaders. Gaitskell told a particularly bitter conference that it was time to stop attempted 'mob rule by a group of frustrated journalists'. A half-hearted attempt to expel Bevan from the Labour Party was matched by a half-hearted discussion among his followers about setting up a new socialist party of their own. Eventually Bevan returned to the front line as shadow foreign secretary and later deputy leader before dying of throat cancer in 1960. He did not read the new Britain well. His last party speech in 1959 predicted that when the British 'have got over the delirium of television', realized they were mortgaged to the hilt, and understood that consumerism had produced 'a vulgar society', they would turn to true socialism and 'we shall lead our people where they deserve to be led'.[35]

On the other side of the divide were Gaitskell and his gang, variously described as the Frognal Set or the Hampstead Set, after the suburban north London house where the Labour leader entertained

274

and, the Bevanites believed, plotted to abolish socialism and lead the people to a hell of television sets and home ownership. Gaitskell was another public schoolboy, who had been radicalized by the General Strike of 1926 and the Nazi thugs on the streets of Vienna in the late thirties. Like Harold Wilson he was an economist, who had served in government during the war. As Attlee's Chancellor of the Exchequer, he had proved tough. It was his decision to fund rearmament partly by making savings by introducing NHS charges that provoked Bevan's resignation from the cabinet and began that feud. (Gaitskell was probably wrong on the numbers, and Bevan right.) In public Gaitskell could come over as a prig, with little of Bevan's champagne fizz. All his life he had been keen on uncomfortable truths. When a small child he had apparently once startled a passing woman who looked down at him by singing from his pram, 'Soon shall you and I be lying / Each within our narrow tomb'. In later life he did not lose the disconcerting style. To become Labour leader after only nine years as an MP, replacing the venerable Attlee, without a strong base in the trade unions or on the left of the party, was nevertheless a remarkable achievement. Gaitskell's mettle was soon tested over the Suez crisis when his party political point-scoring after earlier supportive noises made him hated on the Tory benches. For those who think the Commons has become too much of a bear-pit in recent decades, it is worth recording that Gaitskell contemplated giving up within a couple of years because the booing and shouting from the Conservative side was such that he felt he could not get a hearing in Parliament.

Gaitskell has been fondly remembered by historians partly because of the vivid enthusiasm of his young supporters who later rose to prominence themselves, Roy Jenkins and Tony Crosland in particular, and partly because he died suddenly at fifty-six. He had many admirable qualities, including infectious enthusiasm for literature, music, dancing and life in general. He was stubborn, brave and loyal but his record as a party leader was not unspotted. He seriously contemplated loosening the party's links with the unions, dropping nationalization and changing its name. This was bold but Gaitskell's tactics were nearly disastrous. Against the advice of the young bloods, he attempted to remove the pro-nationalization clause four from the party's rulebook as Tony Blair would do much later. In the more socialist fifties it was a fight too far over a matter of symbolism. Gaitskell retired hurt, in confusion. Beaten, at the high point of CND's first crusades, on the issue of whether Britain should have her own nuclear weapons, he famously promised to fight, fight and fight again to save the party he loved, turning the defeat into a personal public relations triumph. But having rallied the right of the party, he then confounded them by his equally passionate hostility to British membership of the European Common Market. And he had a tendency to flirt with Tory England which did not endear him to the party faithful.

Yet what made Gaitskell truly interesting as a politician of this era was that he accepted and even revelled in the new consumerism. Bevan and his friends deplored the 'affluent society' and the 'crass commercialism' of the time and claimed to feel nostalgic for the colder if nobler vision of the forties. Gaitskell danced, and listened avidly to jazz records, and liked good food and clothes. He had few hang-ups, ideological or otherwise. Gaitskell and those in his set believed you could have a more equal society without it being cheerless or lacking in fun. The essence of this was set out in a hugely influential book *The Future of Socialism,* published in 1956. Its author, Tony Crosland, was one of the wilder spirits of Frognal who had fought in the war as a paratrooper and was busy rebelling against the harshly puritanical standards set by his well-off parents, who belonged to the Plymouth Brethren sect. Crosland argued that increasing individual rights should be as great an aim for reformers as abolishing capitalism, which was already mostly tamed. Education, not nationalization, was the key to changing society. Socialists must turn to issues such as the plight of the mentally handicapped and neglected children, to the divorce and abortion laws, and women's rights in general, to homosexual law reform and the end of censorship of plays and books. Many of these things would dominate the Home Secretaryship of his friend Jenkins. He was against 'hygienic, respectable, virtuous things and people, lacking only in grace and gaiety'. He concluded with a famous swipe at the puritanical Webbs, those Edwardian saints of Labourism: 'Total abstinence and a good filing-system are not now the right sign-posts to the socialist's Utopia; or at least, if they are, some of us will fall by the wayside.'[36] This was a message that would prove popular with the new middle-class voters Labour needed, if not with the intellectuals and journalists around the party's fringes. It was the moment,

277

really, when for Labour the forties ended and, with no intermission, the sixties began.

Gaitskell himself was forgiven by the party for losing the 1959 election. Had he survived to lead Labour into battle in 1964 he would surely have won then and the story of Labour politics would have been strikingly different. By 1962 he was utterly dominant inside his party and increasingly seen outside it as a fresh start – letter-writers and newspaper journalists used language about him which anticipated what was said about Tony Blair before the 1997 election. Like Blair, he managed to come across as less of a party man, and more 'normal' than his great rival, a truly interesting Prime Minister in waiting. None of this was to be. In January 1963 after years of grossly overworking, suffering from a rare and little-understood disease of the immune system, he suddenly died. Though there were rumours afterwards that he had been killed by the KGB as part of a plot to put in Harold Wilson, whom the conspiracists believed was a Soviet agent, it seems more likely that this was mere biology interfering with politics, as it does. With a little more medical and other good-fortune, the prime ministers of post-war Britain could well have included Herbert Morrison, Rab Butler, Hugh Gaitskell and Iain Macleod, rather than Attlee, Macmillan, Douglas-Home and Harold Wilson. But Wilson it would be. The long-lasting significance of the struggle between the Bevanites and the Gaitskellites was that when he became Prime Minister, he was so crippled by trying to placate the various gangs that he could offer no clear direction for the country.

Leaving Mayhem:
the British in Africa

A year after Macmillan's triumphant re-election, he made a speech unlikely to be forgotten. One of the bitterer ironies of Suez had been that London, accused by both the Americans and Russians of being a nest of reactionary imperialism, was actually in the middle of frantically trying to get rid of the Empire. Indian independence was followed by swift dismantling in two other places, Africa and the Middle East. The Sudan, scene of British cavalry charges in an early war against militant Islamists, had become independent in 1956. The Gold Coast, one of the most prosperous African colonies, followed a year later as Ghana and they were followed in turn by a bewildering stream of former African possessions during the sixties – Somaliland (Somalia), Sierra Leone, the Gambia, Nigeria, Kenya, Tanganyika (Tanzania), Zanzibar, Northern Rhodesia (Zambia), Uganda, Nyasaland (Malawi), Swaziland and Basutoland, as well as the islands of Mauritius and the Maldives. Some of these countries had been British only for a short time, others had had large white settler populations who either returned home or tried, uneasily, to accommodate themselves to the new governments, but the scale and speed of the British scuttle produced remarkably little debate at home. On the far right of British politics, the League of Empire Loyalists protested but most of the country regarded it all with boredom or amusement.

In the late forties it had been felt both that Africa

279

might become the core of Britain's new world position and that her countries were far from ready for independence. Within ten years all this was forgotten. There was a rush to independence, urged on from London. No single speech made more of an impact in seeming to settle the argument than the one Harold Macmillan made in Cape Town in 1960, known for ever as his 'wind of change' speech. It was brave not because of what he said, but because the British Prime Minister chose to make it in the white supremacist South African parliament, in front of men who would be architects of apartheid, horrifying them and appalling a large swathe of Tory opinion back in England, where the right-wing Monday Club was formed in protest. Macmillan announced that there was an awakening national consciousness sweeping through Africa. He told his startled audience; 'the wind of change is blowing through this continent' and like it or not, this was simply a fact. Hendrik Verwoerd, the South African Prime Minister retorted that the Englishman was appeasing the black man, adding that they had enough problems in Africa without his coming to add to them.

Why had London lost its nerve? Partly, it was the mere experience of looking about. The French were getting out of Africa. So too were the Belgians, leaving behind an appalling and very bloody civil war in the Congo. Private correspondence of Macmillan's suggests that he also thought the two world wars had made a fundamental change in the position of the whites around the world: 'What we have really seen since the war is the revolt of the yellows and blacks from the automatic leadership and control of the whites.'[37] It need not, however,

280

be a bloody revolt. The experience of the Gold Coast, which became independent under Dr Kwame Nkrumah in 1957 with relative ease, suggested to London there was a gentler way of quitting.

On the other side the vicious war of terrorism against white settlers and blacks who supported them in Kenya, a revolt by the mysterious organization Mau Mau, showed the dangers of hanging on. The Mau Mau rebellion was not an attractive liberation war. It lasted for years, and involved gruesome mutilation, dismemberments, rape and bizarre oaths, claimed to be linked to black magic. Very few whites were killed, but there was a terrible black toll. It did not help that the more experienced leaders such as Jomo Kenyatta, whom we will meet later in a less heroic role, was then locked up, leaving Mau Mau to be run by the young and the angry. The white settlers of the area, who had been among the richest and most self-confident colonials in Africa, responded with vicious militia tactics, taking cash bets for the number of Africans shot or 'bagged', and keeping scorecards, as if they were grouse. The security forces came between the two and suppressed the revolt with classic anti-subversion tactics, though its general found the settlers shady people: 'I hate the guts of them all; they are middle-class sluts,' he told his wife. By the end of the fifties, government forces had killed around 10,000 Kikuyu tribesmen and hanged another thousand. Some 80,000 had been put into grim so-called rehabilitation camps. Eventually only a hard core of Mau Mau were left and at one camp, Hola, eleven were murdered by the guards. The story went round the world and caused extreme embarrassment to the government; Enoch Powell made what some thought the greatest parliamentary speech of the century denouncing British behaviour. Meanwhile in Nyasaland, another bout of violent repression was going on, with fifty-one black protesters killed. So by the time Macmillan made his speech, it seemed that trying to hold on, to protect white settlers he anyway despised, was even more dangerous than getting out.

Macmillan and his liberal Colonial Secretary Iain Macleod, have had a good press ever since. They have been seen as liberal, fair-minded and realistic politicians, who realized that the time had come to push ahead even faster with decolonization, to hit the accelerator and forget the brake. They were undoubtedly influenced by the humiliation of Suez. It was the way the world was going. Yet the story of modern Africa should make anyone look harder at the timing and methods of British decolonization. This is the failed continent. Lines drawn on the map by British imperial administrators were left to help provoke appalling civil and tribal wars. Men trained at Sandhurst, brought up inside the British Empire, turned into corrupt dictators and in the worst case, that of Uganda's Idi Amin, a monster. Few of those liberal, highly intelligent liberation leaders feted in London by the left during the fifties and sixties turned into great progressive figures back home in Africa – perhaps the only great exception being Nelson Mandela himself. Military coups, the imprisonment of opposition leaders, tribal feuds and famines followed and for all this, the former British rulers must take some responsibility. Did the British scuttle from Africa happen too fast, in a mood of political hysteria and without proper thought for what would follow? The sheer speed may not be as admirable as we have been taught to think.

Was there no example of successful British action in withdrawing from old commitments? Luckily for national pride, there is another story. It is not simply the tale of the other former colonies, from Singapore to the Caribbean, which thrived, or the prosperity of the so-called White Commonwealth nations. Not all wars were lost; in Korea, for instance, though Kim 11 Sung survived to create a bleak and murderous dictatorship behind the armistice line, Mao was frustrated. But the best example of a war eventually won through intelligence, in every sense, is the one known simply as the 'emergency'. It ran from 1948 to 1960 – which must make it the longest emergency ever.

Malaya had become a crucial part of the world's industrial system thanks to seeds from a single tree, brought from Brazil to Kew Gardens in London and grown in a tropical plant house. From there, the rubber plants were taken to Malaya in the 1870s, and grew very nicely. By the post-war years, Malaya was producing a third of the world's supply of rubber. With tin, this made it Britain's most profitable colony, a rare exception to the rule. But by the late forties there was, almost inevitably, a Communist and nationalist insurgency against British rule. It went on for a dozen years and was, to all intents and purposes, a war. It has not been remembered as the Malayan War for a curious reason. The insurance policies of local businesses had clauses in them suspending cover in time of war; hence 'emergency'.

After a bad start during which the Communists tied down a huge British force, murdered many rubber planters and their workers, and when atrocities were committed on the other side including by the Scots Guards against Chinese villagers, a new strategy was developed. It was the achievement of one of the British Empire's last and least-known heroes, a clipped and driven soldier called General Sir Gerald Templer. He used helicopters as they had not been used before in warfare. He also moved entire villages away from the jungle to keep them from supporting insurgents and imposed curfews. But beside the unpopular measures Templer introduced a new 'hearts and minds' approach to win over Malaya's Chinese villagers. Roads, clean water, schools, medical centres, elected village councils and relatively restrained policing did more to confound a Communist insurgency than the machine guns and helicopters. Eventually after the Communists were defeated, Malaya became independent under a friendly government. As Malaysia it has thrived. It showed what could be done by a thoughtful and intelligent departing imperial power. After Malaya, no Communist insurgency succeeded against British forces in Africa or Asia again. Had the Americans studied Malaya a little more closely, who knows what might have followed in Vietnam.

Right. New Dawn: Denis Healey
and Roy Jenkins in uniform at Labour's
1945 party conference.

Below. Clement Attlee, driven by
his wife Violet, was advised to jump
in his car and head for Buckingham
Palace to be made prime minister
before plotters could put in
Herbert Morrison instead.

UNOFFICIAL ECONOMIC ADVISER TO GREAT BRITAIN : *John Maynard Keynes in His Study in Bloomsbury*
It was he who foresaw the evil results of Versailles while that treaty was still under construction—and resigned an important job to make them known. To-day, at the age of 56, he has produced a plan for financing the war and avoiding its most disastrous economic consequences.

MR. KEYNES
HAS A PLAN

To carry on a war successfully we must spend over £2,000 millions a year. How are we to pay? How are we to avoid inflation ? In this article Kingsley Martin, Editor of "The New Statesman and Nation," writes of the man who has given an answer to these questions, describes the answer which he gives.

WHEN "The Economic Consequences of the Peace," by John Maynard Keynes, was published in 1919 it caused a prodigious sensation. Here was an important member of the British delegation at Versailles, who had resigned his post in order to tell the truth about the Treaty. The sensation was due at least as much to the book's literary quality as to its expert substance. Those who knew nothing of economics could appreciate, if only from quotations in the press, Mr. Keynes's brilliant picture of M. Clemenceau, Mr. Lloyd George and President Wilson at Versailles. It successfully put over the point that the American President had kept his Puritanical conscience clear by insisting on verbal consistency with the Fourteen Points, while allowing cunning men to find ways of getting round them. It convinced us all that, whatever the other merits or evils of the Treaty, its real vice was its failure to treat Europe as an economic whole and to reconstruct it for the benefit of the common people. It was a treaty of strategy and national greediness—with the League of Nations thrown in to make it look pretty.

John Maynard Keynes, possibly the cleverest man in Britain, died after struggling desperately to save his country from bankruptcy. But he could not do a deal with the Americans good enough to avoid the grim austerity of the post-war years, including bread rationing, the subject of the 1946 demonstration in Trafalgar Square shown below.

Go through your wardrobe

Make-do and Mend

Right. British women were hectored constantly about their clothes, and would soon revolt.

Below. Temporary pre-fab homes, often built using German and Italian prisoners of war, were one answer to the huge housing shortage. Some were still being used in the seventies.

Despite Labour's triumph, and fearing socialism, the old order quickly reasserted itself: Cecil Beaton poses on the set of *Lady Windermere's Fan* in 1946.

Hero of the working classes: Joan Littlewood (*right*) was one of the most radical voices in British theatre. But her influence in conveying the spirit and dilemmas of a new Jerusalem was far less than that of Ealing Studios, with films such as *Passport to Pimlico* (*below*).

Bitterly disappointed by his 1945 rejection, Churchill endured his exile writing, speaking, painting – and hunting, here, four days before his seventy-fourth birthday. He would be back in 1951 (*below*), proclaiming a new Elizabethan age.

Old Labour's greatest prophet? Nye Bevan in full Welsh flow, presumably unaware that he's being mimicked by a small boy.

The comprehensive vision, pushed by Tories too: a new school in Anglesey, 1954.

The Skylon at the 1951
Festival of Britain: people
said that it, like the country,
was suspended without
visible means of support.

Simpler pleasures:
a honeymoon couple
at Billy Butlin's hotel
near Brighton, 1957.

In the Tory years, there were dreams of a super-technological British future: just along from Parliament, this is the planned London Heliport, complete with passenger helicopters, as pictured in 1952. Instead, 'the great car economy' was getting underway: in 1964 London's Chiswick flyover (*below*) was an early glimpse of the real future.

Alec Issigonis, an immigrant from Turkey, was the design genius of post-war British car-making.

His first huge success, the 1948 Morris Minor, was condemned by his company boss as 'that damned poached egg designed by that damned foreigner'.

As the mass car market developed, Issigonis worked on sketches for
an even more radical car (*above*), which would become the Mini.
Later sketches (*below*) for 'the small car of the future' are
strikingly like the rounded city runabouts of today.

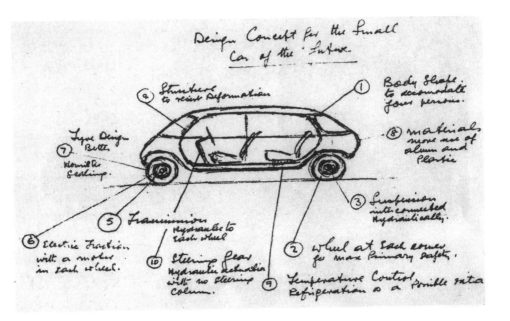

Above. Cold war: RAF crews practise a scramble for their Vulcan nuclear bombers in Lincolnshire, 1960. The V-bombers were Britain's first line of attack but they were quickly made obsolete by improved Russian defences.

Below. By 1958, the anti-nuclear marches were mobilized and CND's logo was on its way to becoming one of the most recognizable symbols of all.

Opposite page. The working classes begin to be heard: Shelagh Delaney's 1958 *A Taste of Honey* was a breakthrough play set in Salford, and written when she was just nineteen.

Chaps dapper and chaps disgraced:
the well-connected Soviet spy Kim
Philby (*above, left*) and the man
who split Britain over Suez,
Anthony Eden (*above*), knew how
to put on a good front. Stephen
Ward (*left*), the man
at the centre of the greatest scandal
of the early Sixties, barely
bothered. Christine Keeler
is to his left.

Opposite page. If the reality
is disappointing, weave a
different one: Ian Fleming,
James Bond's creator, at
the card table, 1962.

The enigma and the optimist: Harold Wilson, reflective, with pipe, in 1963, and Edward Heath, campaigning in exuberant mood, 1966.

British cool?
The actor David
Hemmings in
Swinging London,
1966, and the Kinks,
struggling with
trousers and ruffles.

The Liberal Hour: the flamboyant MP Leo Abse (*left*) was one of the Labour backbenchers who led reform, in his case to legalize homosexual acts between men.

Below. In 1971, the editors of the underground magazine *Oz* were prosecuted for obscenity. A libidinous cartoon Rupert Bear was at the centre of the case; the significance of the whip is unclear.

Violence becomes a
theme: Catholic
demonstrators (*above*)
in Londonderry / Derry
after the killing of
thirteen civil-rights
marchers on 'Bloody
Sunday', 1972, and (*right*)
the nearest Britain came
to
left-wing terrorists,
the Angry Brigade,
outside the Old Bailey,
a few months later.

When the country failed:
a boy stands outside his school,
closed because of a lack of fuel
during the miners' strike of 1972.
The miners (*below*) were badly paid,
and went on to humiliate Heath
and the Conservatives.

Opposite page. It's the beans, stupid.
In the 1975 referendum on British
membership of the European Common
Market, both sides campaigned more
about the cost of food than about the
constitutional implications of
surrendering sovereignty.

Two men as influential as
most prime ministers.
Enoch Powell (*left*),
opponent of immigration,
and (*below*) Denis Healey,
chancellor during Britain's
economic storm, making
a characteristic point to
his opponents.

Punk gets cheeky: Vivienne Westwood (centre), Chrissie Hynde (left) and Jordan advertise Westwood's King's Road punk shop Sex, in 1976.

But nothing was sexy about the economy: rubbish piles up in London during the 'winter of discontent', 1979.

Michael Foot, the most literate and radical man to lead Labour,
points in the general direction of the political wilderness. But his harshest
critics, the SDP's Gang of Four, failed to return to power, either.
Bill Rodgers, David Owen and Roy Jenkins plot over a glass or two in 1982.
The fourth member of the gang was not, as this photograph below suggests,
surprisingly well-endowed but was Mrs Shirley Williams.

Notting Hill

From 1948 until 1962, roughly the period of the Malayan emergency, there had been virtually an open door for immigrants coming into Britain from the Commonwealth or colonies. The British debate over immigration had been hobbled by contradiction. On the one hand, overt racialism had been discredited by the Nazi enemy. Britain's very sense of herself was tied up in the vanquishing of a political culture founded on racial difference. This meant that the few unapologetic racialists, the anti-Semitic fringe or the pro-apartheid colonialists, became outcast. Official documents would refer to the handful of MPs who were outspokenly racialist as 'nutters'. So unthreatening were they thought to be that Oswald Mosley, who had been funded by Mussolini before the war and would have been a likely puppet-leader had Germany invaded Britain, was promptly allowed out of prison after the war, to strut on the back of lorries and yell at his small number of unrepentant fascist supporters. Ignoring him, the public propaganda of Empire made much of a family of races under the British flag all cooperating, loyally together.

In Whitehall, the Colonial Office strongly supported the right of black Caribbean people to migrate to the Mother Country, fending off the worries of the Ministry of Labour about the effects on unemployment during downturns. When some 500 Caribbean immigrants arrived in 1948 on the converted German troopship SS *Windrush,* the Home Secretary declared that though 'some people feel it would be a bad thing to give the coloured races of the Empire the idea that, in some way or the other, they are the equals of people in this country,' the government disagreed: 'we recognise the right of the colonial peoples to be treated as men and brothers with the people of this country.'[38] Britain, in short, believed herself to be the logical opposite of Nazi Germany, a benign and unprejudiced world-connected island. The Jewish migration of the thirties had brought one of the greatest top-ups of skill and energy that any modern European state had ever seen. The country in fact already had a population of about 75,000 black and Asian people and labour shortages suggested it needed many more. The segregation of the American Deep South, and the arrival of the ideology of apartheid in South Africa were treated alike with high-minded contempt.

And yet everyone knew this was not really the whole story. Prewar British society had never been as brutal about race as France or Spain, never mind Germany, but it was riddled with racialism nevertheless. Anti-Semitism had been common in popular novels and obscure modernist poetry alike. The actual practice of the British upper and middle classes had been close to the colour bar practised by Americans. Africans were tolerated as servants and musicians while in Britain, little more. White working-class people hardly ever came across someone of another colour: during the war, black GIs, though welcomed, had been followed around by awestruck locals simply wanting to touch them or hear them speak. Almost as soon as the first post-war migrants arrived from Jamaica and other islands of the West Indies, popular papers were reporting worries about their cleanliness, sexual habits and criminality: 'No dogs, No blacks, No Irish' was not a myth, but a perfectly common sign on boarding houses. The hostility and coldness of native British people was quickly reported back by the early migrants. And Hugh Dalton, a cabinet colleague of the high-minded minister quoted earlier, was also able to talk of the 'pullulating poverty stricken diseased nigger communities' of the African colonies.

For most people, questions of race were obscure and academic. The country remained overwhelmingly white and only tiny pockets of colour could be found until the sixties, most of them in the poorest inner-city areas. A quarter of the world was in theory welcome to come and stay. There were debates in the Tory cabinets of the Churchill, Eden and Macmillan years but for most of the time they never got anywhere. Any legislation to limit migration would have kept out white people of the old Commonwealth too; and any legislation which discriminated would be unacceptably racialist. Conservatives as well as socialists regarded themselves as civilized and liberal on race. By this they meant pick-and-choosy. For instance in the fifties, the Colonial Office specifically championed 'the skilled character and proved industry of the West Indians' against 'the unskilled and largely lazy Asians'.[39] Immigration from the Indian subcontinent had begun almost immediately after independence and partition, as a result of the displacement of Hindus and Muslims, but it had been very small. Sikhs had arrived, looking for work particularly in the industrial Midlands, and in the west London borough of

287

Southall, which quickly became an Asian hub. Indian migrants created networks to buy and supply the corner shops which required punishingly long hours, and the restaurants which would almost instantly become part of the 'British' way of life – there were more than 2,000 Indian restaurants by 1970 and curry would become the single most popular dish within another generation. Other migrants went into the rag trade and grew rich.

So immigration continued through a decade without any great national debate. Much of it was not black but European, mostly migrant workers from Poland, Italy, France and other countries who were positively welcomed in the years of skill and manpower shortages. There was a particularly hefty Italian migration producing a first-generation Italian community of around 100,000 by 1971 to add to the earlier migrations which went back to the 1870s. There was constant and heavy migration from Ireland, mainly into the construction industry, three-quarters of a million in the early fifties and two million by the early seventies, producing little political response except in the immediate aftermath of IRA bombings. There was substantial Maltese immigration which did catch the public attention because of violent gang wars in London between rival Maltese families in the extortion and prostitution business (though to be fair to Malta, many of these people had arrived there from Sicily first). There was a major Cypriot immigration, both of Greek Cypriots and Turkish Cypriots, as the divided island became more politically violent. Again, apart from the enthusiastic adoption of plate-smashing and moussaka in 'Greek' restaurants in British cities, there was no discernable public fuss. Chinese migration, mainly from the impoverished agricultural hinterland of Hong Kong, can be measured by the vast rise in Chinese fish-and-chip shops and restaurants, up from a few hundred in the mid-fifties to more than 4,000 by the beginning of the seventies.[40] The Poles, carefully resettled after the war, were joined by other refugees from Stalinism, Hungarians and Czechs, again without any national response other than warm enthusiasm.

Thus, if there were clear rules about how to migrate quietly to Britain, they would have started first, be white, and second, if you cannot be white, be small in number, and third, if all else fails, feed the brutes. The West Indian migration failed each rule. It was mainly male, young and coming not to open restaurants but to work for wages which could, in part, be sent back home. Some official organizations, from the National Health Service to London Transport, went on specific recruiting drives for workers, nurses or bus-drivers or cleaners, with cheery advertisements in Jamaica for ticket-clippers on London buses. Most of the population shift, however, was driven by migrants themselves desperate for a better life, particularly once the popular alternative of migration to the United States was closed down in 1952. The islands of the Caribbean, dependent on sugar or tobacco for most employment, were going through hard times. As word was passed back about job opportunities, albeit in difficult surroundings, immigration grew fast to about 36,000 people a year by the late fifties. One historian notes the scale of the change: every two years 'a number equivalent to the total non-white national population in 1951 was arriving in Britain'.[41] The black and Asian population had risen to 337,000 by 1961. And it was concentrated, rather than widely dispersed. Different West Indian groups clustered in different parts of London and the English provincial cities – Jamaicans in the south London areas of Brixton and Clapham, people from Trinidad in west London's Notting Hill, islanders from Nevis in Leicester, people from St Vincent in High Wycombe, and so on.

The way these people migrated and made their way had a huge impact on the later condition of post-war Britain and deserves analysis. The fact that so many of the first migrants were young men who found themselves living without wives, mothers or children inevitably created a wilder atmosphere than they were accustomed to in their island homes. They were short of entertainment and short of the social control of ordinary family living. A chain of generational influence was broken and a male strut liberated. Drinking dens, the use of marijuana, ska and blues clubs, and gambling were the inevitable result. A white equivalent might be the atmosphere of the Klondike gold-rush communities, not in general notable for their sobriety and respect for law. Early black communities in Britain tended to cluster where the first arrivals were, which meant in the blighted inner cities. There, as discussed earlier, street prostitution was more open and rampant in the fifties than it would later become; it is hardly surprising that young black men away from home often formed relationships with white prostitutes, and that some then went into pimping. This would feed the press and white gang hysteria about blacks

290

(unsportingly well-endowed, it was thought) stealing 'our women'. The combination of fast, unfamiliar music, the illegal drinking and drugs and the sexual needs of the young migrants combined to paint a lurid picture of a new underworld. It was no coincidence that the Profumo affair had involved a West Indian drug dealer alongside its cast of aristocrats, politicians, good-time girls and spies.

More important for the longer term, a rebelliousness was sown in black families which would be partly tamed only when children and spouses began arriving in large numbers in the sixties, and the Pentecostal churches reclaimed at least some of their own. Housing was another crucial part of the story. For the immigrants of the fifties, accommodation was necessarily privately rented since access to council homes was based on a strict list, dependent on how long you had been living in the area. We have already seen how the early squatting revolt was ended by the threat of participants being moved to the back of the council housing queue. So the early immigrants were cooped up in crowded and often condemned old properties – the gaunt Victorian speculative terraces of west London, or the grimy brick terraces of central Leeds. Landlords and landladies were often reluctant to rent to blacks. Once a few houses had immigrants in them, a domino effect would clear streets as white residents sold up and moved. The 1957 Rent Act, initiated by Enoch Powell in his free-market crusade, perversely made the situation worse since it allowed rents to rise sharply, but only when tenants of unfurnished rooms were removed to allow furnished lettings. Powell meant this to allow a cushion of time before rents rose. Its unintended consequence was that unscrupulous landlords such as the notorious Peter Rachman (an immigrant himself) could buy up low-value rented properties, usually with poorer white tenants in them and then – if only he could oust the tenants – pack in new tenants at far higher rents. Thuggery and threats generally got rid of the old. New black tenants, desperate for somewhere to live and charged much higher rents, were then imported. The result was the creation of instant ghettos, in which three generations of black British would live. The Brixton, Tottenham and Toxteth riots of the eighties can be traced back, in part, to the moral effects of early young-male migration and the housing practices of the fifties.

The other side to the story is the reaction of white Britain. As one Caribbean writer ironically put it, he never met a single English person with colour prejudice.[42] Once he had walked down a whole street, 'and everyone told me that he or she 'ad no prejudice against coloured people. It was the neighbour who was stupid. If only we could find the "neighbour" we could solve the whole problem. But to find 'im is the trouble! Neighbours are the worst people to live beside in this country.' Numerous testimonies by immigrants and in surveys of the time show how hostile local people were to the idea of having black or Asian neighbours. The trade unions bristled against blacks coming in to take jobs, possibly at lower rates of pay, just as they had campaigned against Irish migrants a generation earlier. Union leaders regarded as impeccably left-wing lobbied governments to keep out black workers. They were successful enough for a while to create employment ghettos as well as housing ones, though in the West Midlands in particular black migrants gained a toehold in the car-making factories and other manufacturing. Only a handful of MPs campaigned openly against immigration. Powell raised the issue in private meetings though as a health minister he had been keen enough to use migrant labour. But anti-immigrant feeling was regarded as not respectable and not to be talked about. The elite turned its eyes away from the door-slamming and shunning, and escaped into well-meant if windy generalities about the brotherhood of man and fellow subjects of the Crown. Most of the hostility was at the level of street and popular culture, sometimes the shame-faced 'sorry, the room is taken already' variety and sometimes violent. The white gangs of the Teddy boy age went 'nigger-hunting' or 'black-burying' and chalked the 'Keep Britain White' signs on walls. They may have been influenced by the small groups of right-wing extremists, such as the Union for British Freedom, or Mosley's remaining fascist supporters, but the main motivation seems to have been young male competition and territory-marking. These were, after all, the poor white inhabitants of the very same areas being moved into by the migrants.

All this came to a head in the Notting Hill riots of 1958. Rather like Suez a couple of years earlier, Notting Hill was more a symbol of change than a bloody slaughter. In fact, nobody was killed in the rampaging and by the standards of later riots, there was little physical damage. Furthermore, the trouble actually started far away from London, in the poor St Ann's district of central Nottingham and only spread to Notting Hill a day later. Yet it was a large and deeply unpleasant outbreak of anti-immigrant violence which ran for a total of six days, across two late summer weekends. It was no coincidence that Notting Hill was the area where the rioting happened as distinct from, say, Brixton, which also had a very large and visible black population by the mid-fifties. It had the most open, well-known street culture for black people, near enough to Soho at one side, and the new BBC headquarters on the other, to be advertised and even celebrated by hacks, broadcasters and novelists. It was known for its gambling dens and drinking clubs. It had a resentful and impoverished white population but also, as two historians of British immigration put it, 'It had multi-occupied houses with families of different races on each floor. It had a large population of internal migrants, gypsies and Irish, many of them transient single men, packed into a honeycomb of rooms with communal kitchens, toilets and no bathrooms.'[43]

Into this honeycomb poured a crowd first of tens, and then of hundreds of white men, armed first with sticks, knives, iron railings and bicycle chains, and soon with petrol-bombs too. They were overwhelmingly young, mostly from nearby areas of London, and looking for trouble. They began by picking on small groups of blacks caught out on the streets, beating them and chasing them. They then moved to black-occupied houses and began smashing windows. The crowds swelled until they were estimated at more than 700 strong, whipped up by the occasional fascist agitator, but much more directed by local whites. Racist songs and chants of 'Niggers Out', the smash of windows – though some local whites protected and even fought for their black neighbours, this was mob violence of a kind Britain thought it had long left behind. It shrunk away again partly as a result of black men making a stand, and fighting back with petrol bombs. There were 140 arrests, mainly of white youths, and though far-right parties continued to organize in the area, there was no discernible electoral impact, or indeed any more serious trouble. The huge press coverage ensured, however, that Britain went through its first orgy of national introspection about its liberalism and its immigration policy, while overseas racist regimes such as those of South Africa and Rhodesia mocked the hand-wringing British.

After the riots, many black people did 'go home'. Returns to the Caribbean soared to more than 4,000. There, West Indian governments expressed outrage at the riot and made it clear that there would be no action by them to restrict migration in order to appease lawless white thugs. Indeed the Commonwealth, whose usefulness has been questioned elsewhere in this history, clearly functioned as a kind of doorstop to maintain immigration. It retained a loose association between Crown, obligation and common citizenship which felt real to politicians of both parties. Pressure to close the open border for Commonwealth citizens hardly increased in the Tory Party after the Notting Hill riots, though extra-parliamentary campaigns, such as the Birmingham Immigration Control Association, did spring up. Of course, given that the violence was directed against immigrants by whites, it would have been grotesquely unfair had the first reaction been to send people home. Labour was wholly against restricting immigration, arguing that it would be 'disastrous to our status in the Commonweath'. The Notting Hill Carnival, begun the following year, was an alternative response, celebrating black culture openly. For many black migrants, the riots marked the beginning of assertion and organization. They were looked back on as a racial Dunkirk, the darkest moment after which the real fightback would start.

Only after Macmillan's stunning 1959 general election victory did pressure really begin to build up for some kind of restriction on immigration to Britain. Opinion polls were now showing strong hostility to the open-door policy. Perhaps as important in Whitehall, both the Ministry of Labour and the Home Office wanted a change to help deal with the new threat of unemployment. This was a case of the political class being pushed reluctantly into something which offended their notion of their place in the world, the father-figures of a global Commonwealth. One study of immigration points out that what was truly remarkable was the passive acceptance by politicians and bureaucrats of Britain's transformation into a multicultural society: 'Immigration was restricted a full four years after all measures of the public mood indicated clear hostility to a black presence in Britain, and even then it was only done with hesitation.'[44] And when the 1962 Commonwealth Immigrants Act finally passed into law, it was notably liberal, at least by later standards, assuming the arrival of up to 40,000 legal immigrants a year with complete right of entry for their dependants. Even so, it had only gone through after a ferocious parliamentary battle, with the Labour leader Hugh Gaitskell making emotional and passionate attacks on a measure which was still privately opposed by some of the Tory ministers involved. One particularly contentious issue was that the Republic of Ireland was allowed a completely open border with Britain. This may have seemed only practical politics given the huge number of Irish people living and working there already but it offended in two ways. By discriminating in favour of a country which had been neutral in the war with Hitler and declared itself a republic, but against Commonwealth countries which had stood with Britain, it infuriated many British patriots. Second, by giving Irish people a better deal than Indians or West Indians it seemed frankly racialist.

The new law created a quota system which gave preference to skilled workers and those with firm promises of employment. In order to beat it, a huge new influx of people set out in 1961 for Britain, the biggest group from the Caribbean but also nearly 50,000 from India and Pakistan and 20,000 Hong Kong Chinese. This 'beat the ban' phenomenon would be repeated later when new restrictions were introduced in the seventies. One historian of immigration puts the paradox well: in the three-year period from 1960 to 1963, despite the intense hostility to immigration, 'more migrants had arrived in Britain than had disembarked in the whole of the twentieth century up to that point. The country would never be the same again.'[45]

Incident at Birch Grove

Yet it was Britain's post-war relationship with Europe, not the fate of the Empire, immigration or the Cold War, which produced some of the deepest cracks in British public life. Why should that be? This was not of prime importance to the people of the country, certainly no more so than the cost of living or the building of a multiculture. What gave it added importance in the corridors and lobbies of the Palace of Westminster was that 'Europe' was about them – the importance of MPs and ministers, of mandarins and ambassadors. Britain was fading as head of the Commonwealth and had little leverage with the Washington of Eisenhower and Kennedy. Joining the European Economic Community would either (depending on your point of view) give Britain's elite a new, well-appointed and large theatre to try to dominate; or it might push them aside in a Babel of competing and alien politicians. By the late fifties, this choice was becoming urgent. The distant echoes ignored by Attlee and Churchill had become a deafening proposition. Across the channel, they had had the builders in.

After the iron and coal community, which the Durham miners were supposed to have been so against, the six founding EU nations – France, West Germany, Italy, Luxembourg, Belgium and the Netherlands – had kept designing and laying out bigger structures. The European Defence Community had foundered. But in 1955 a breakthrough had happened in the unlikely setting of a small and undistinguished coastal town in Sicily called Messina. Here the foreign ministers of 'the Six' had agreed to move towards a customs union, and combine in transport, atomic know-how and energy policy. The driving force behind this was a squat, pro-British Belgian now formally revered as a European founding father, called Paul-Henri Spaak. Later, he stolidly recalled how the ministers had worked through the night to complete the proposal: 'The sun was rising over Mount Etna as we returned to our rooms, tired but happy. Far-reaching decisions had been taken.'[46] The first view from London was that, at any rate, Etna had not erupted. As the negotiations continued in Brussels about what would eventually become the EU, Britain refused to send a minister to take part, choosing instead a formidably bright but middle-ranking civil servant, a trade economist called Russell Bretherton.

This fox-like little man with a clipped moustache soon realized two things: he was being treated like a very important person by the Europeans and, second, they were deadly serious about trying to build a new political system. Bretherton was regarded by the French, Belgians and Germans as national negotiator when in truth he was a mere observer with written notes about what he could and could not say. In the mythology of the European Union, there is a wonderful story about Bretherton. It tells us that at the end of the negotiations this starchy representative of Her Britannic Majesty stood up and informed the room: 'Gentlemen, you are trying to negotiate something you will never be able to negotiate. But if negotiated, it will not be ratified. And if ratified, it will not work.' He is then supposed to have walked out, no doubt clutching his rolled umbrella. Sadly, it seems unlikely that this ever happened as reported, though it has poetic truth. The continental negotiators were disappointed and shocked by Britain's lack of serious interest and Bretherton had been given a loftily dismissive brief by his political masters; it was simply less crisp than myth tells us. At any rate the Six shrugged off Britain's attitude. They were still rebuilding shattered cities and healing torn economies, and for them the coming Union was manifest destiny. The Treaty of Rome duly followed in 1957. Coming so soon after the humiliation of Suez it was greeted by increasingly agitated head-scratching in Whitehall.

And for Britain, the world was differently shaped. The Commonwealth then meant more than a worthy outreach programme for the Royal Family. Its food and raw materials poured into Britain and there was an illusion that Britain's manufacturing future would be secured by selling industrial goods to kith and kin in Durban, Dunedin, Canberra and Calgary. In came butter, oil, meat, aluminium, rubber, tobacco and woodpulp. Out would flow engines, cars, clothing, aircraft and electronics. The poorer members of the sterling club kept their reserves in London, so Britain was banker as well as manufacturer for much of Africa and parts of Asia too. Most people believed that to cut adrift the Commonwealth and join a new club would be economically ruinous as well as immoral. For Labour, Wilson told the Commons that 'If there has to be a choice, we are not entitled to sell our friends and kinsmen down the river for a problematical and marginal advantage in selling washing machines in Dusseldorf.' Later Hugh Gaitskell told the Labour conference that membership of the European Economic Community would mean the end of a thousand years of history: 'How can one seriously suppose that if the mother country, the centre of the Commonwealth, is a province of Europe ... it could continue to exist as the mother country of a series of independent nations?' Yet at just this time the European market, thirsting for new consumer goods, was growing spectacularly fast, while the Commonwealth trading group was by comparison falling behind. As we have seen, most of the poorer countries did not want Britain anyway. The richer nations of the old Commonwealth – Australia, New Zealand, Canada and even semi-detached South Africa – would soon turn to the United States for their consumer goods. Rileys would not long compete with Cadillacs.

Yet membership of the EEC would subordinate Britain in important ways to foreigners. This was recognized from the first. There was no illusion. Independence would be lost. Other forms of subordination and loss of independence had already happened. The foundation of the United Nations, the post-war economic system and the establishment of Nato involved relinquishing traditional freedoms of action. Those could be painful, as Suez and the various financial crises had been. Yet there seemed to be good military and security reasons there. Europe was something different. Those who had looked clearly at the Treaty of Rome were struck by its overwhelming ambition. Lord Kilmuir, Harold Macmillan's Lord Chancellor, told him that Parliament would lose powers to the Council of Ministers whose majority vote could change British law; that the Crown's power over treaties would partly shift to Brussels and that British courts would find themselves in part subordinate to the European Court of Justice.[47] He made it all clear in later parliamentary debates though this truth was hardly rammed home to the millions outside the world of high politics. Macmillan himself tended to obscure it in windily reassuring words, the old actor-manager trying to keep the whole theatre happy; but Kilmuir spoke out and so did Lord Home, the future Prime Minister.

Had Britain been involved from the start as even the French wanted, the EEC, eventually the EU, would have developed differently. There would certainly have been less emphasis on agricultural protection and more on free trade. 'Europe' might have been a little less mystical and a little more open, perhaps more democratic, though this is difficult in so many languages. At any rate, the moment passed. Even after the shock and humiliation of Suez, the Commonwealth and relations with the Americans took precedence for London. The struggle to keep in the nuclear race meant private deals with Washington which infuriated Paris. After the Treaty of Rome took effect at the beginning of 1958, French attitudes hardened. General de Gaulle, who had felt humiliated by Churchill during the war, returned as President of France, too late to stop the new European system which he had opposed on traditional nationalistic grounds, and therefore determined that it should at least be dominated by France. In the words of diplomats and journalists

302

at the time there could not be two cocks on the dunghill.

Macmillan, always a keen Europeanist, became worried. Various British plots intended to limit the Six and hamper their project had failed. London had tried to rival the new Common Market with a grouping of the excluded countries, Britain, Austria, Denmark, Portugal, Norway, Switzerland and Sweden, calling it the European Free Trade Association (EFTA) or 'the Seven'. This was a poor arithmetical point, since the Seven had a smaller population than the Six, were geographically scattered and far less determined. EFTA was a petulant minuet of the wallflowers. Roy Jenkins, always an ardent pro-European, described it as 'a foolish attempt to organise a weak periphery against a strong core'.[48] By 1959 Macmillan was worrying that 'for the first time since the Napoleonic era, the major continental powers are united in a positive economic grouping, with considerable political aspects' which might cut Britain out of Europe's main markets and decisions. Soon in his diaries he was sounding even more alarmed, talking of 'a boastful, powerful "Empire of Charlemagne" – now under French, but bound to come under German, control'. There was much self-deception about the possible deal that could be struck. Macmillan's team, centred on Edward Heath, hoped that somehow the trading system of the Commonwealth supporting English-speaking farmers across the world could be accommodated by the protectionist system of Europe. They seem to have thought that any loss of sovereignty would be tolerable if this deal could be struck. Macmillan might have seemed as safely

303

steeped in tradition as country houses and the novels of Trollope but he had nothing like the almost spiritual reverence for the House of Commons felt by Enoch Powell or, on the other side of politics, Gaitskell.

In the early Sixties the battle over Britain's coming loss of sovereignty was postponed because British entry was blocked – brutally, publicly and ruthlessly. Two scenes tell the story. The first occurred in November 1961 at Birch Grove, Macmillan's country house in Sussex, a substantial pile with stunning views to the South Downs. De Gaulle was due to come to Britain for talks and told the Prime Minister that, rather than visit Downing Street, he would prefer to come to his private home, two old comrades together. And they were in some ways old friends. During the war, as the leading British minister in North Africa, Macmillan had been crucial in helping de Gaulle through an immense crisis. De Gaulle, leader of the Free French, was struggling to dominate the coming government-in-exile which would take power in France after its liberation. His opponent was a right-wing general who had tolerated pro-Vichy allies but de Gaulle's arrogance and refusal to compromise with him so infuriated Roosevelt and Churchill that they wanted him kicked out of the exiled administration. Macmillan, realizing de Gaulle's huge potential, had worked frantically to soften Churchill and to shore up the general's position. De Gaulle was grateful to Macmillan personally but he left North Africa more than ever convinced of the danger to France of a coming Anglo-American alliance which would try to dominate the world.

This was the background to his arrival in Sussex, one of the oddest summits in Franco-British history. To the annoyance of local gamekeepers and farmers, the woods surrounding Birch Grove had been filled with French and British police and their dogs though, to the Prime Minister's delight, one of the Alsatians did bite a *Daily Mail* reporter on the bottom. Lady Dorothy, Macmillan's wife, had been warned by the Foreign Office that she would have to find space in the fridge for the French President's blood since he travelled with a stock for transfusion in case of an attempted assassination. Mrs Bell, the family cook, then refused to have it in the kitchen fridge which was 'full of haddock and all sorts of things for tomorrow'; another fridge was set up in a squash court. When the talking finally started, the two leaders were interrupted by an angry gamekeeper, who protested that the police dogs were ruining the prospects for shooting that weekend. De Gaulle was perplexed, Macmillan hugely amused. After apologizing to the gamekeeper, they exchanged blunt views. Macmillan argued that European civilization was threatened from all sides and that if Britain was not allowed to join the Common Market, he would have to review everything, including keeping British troops in Germany. If de Gaulle wanted an 'empire of Charlemagne' it would be on its own. The French President replied that he didn't want Britain to bring in its 'great escort' of Commonwealth countries – the Canadians and Australians were no longer Europeans; Indian and African countries had no place in a European system; and he feared Europe being 'drowned in the Atlantic'. In short, he simply

305

did not believe that Britain would ditch its old empire; and if it did, he thought it would be a Trojan horse for the Americans.

These seem formidable objections, points of principle that should have been seen as a clear warning. Yet the detailed and exhaustive talks about British entry chugged along despite them. Edward Heath clocked up sixty-three visits to Brussels, Paris and other capitals, covering 50,000 miles as he haggled and argued. But by then Macmillan was a fast-fading figure. A natural intriguer who had risen to power on the bloodied back of Eden, he was obsessed by possible political coups against himself, and increasingly (and rightly) worried about the weak state of the economy. He was failing in Europe and looked old when seen with the dapper young President Kennedy.

After an unpopular budget Macmillan drafted an alternative policy based on more planning, and decided to sack his Chancellor, a close friend, Selwyn Lloyd. The news was leaked to the papers, and over a brutal and panicky twenty-four hours in July 1962 Macmillan expanded the circle of his sackings ever more widely, removing a third of his cabinet ministers from their jobs without notice. In what became known as 'the Night of the Long Knives' Macmillan called in and dismissed a succession of bewildered, then outraged, colleagues. One protested that his cook would have been given more notice. Macmillan's official biographer described it as 'an act of carnage unprecedented in British political history'. The press portrayed him as a somewhat crazed executioner. In the Commons Jeremy Thorpe, the Liberal leader, told him, 'greater love hath no man

than this, that he lays down his friends for his life'
The reaction seems odd decades on, when ruthless
cabinet reshuffles have happened so often, though
never again on this scale. Many of those sacked
deserved to lose their jobs and Macmillan, far from
relishing the butchery, found it made him vomit.
But it was the final failure of sangfroid.

In November, Macmillan returned to his
argument with de Gaulle, this time in the grand
chateau of Rambouillet, a Renaissance confection
south of Paris which has been used by French
presidents for scores of summits, as well as summer
holidays. The circumstances were almost as odd as
at Birch Grove and again centred on the issue of
pheasant shooting. Though de Gaulle did not shoot
himself, he organized a fairly comprehensive
welcoming slaughter, standing behind Macmillan
and other guests and commenting loudly every time
they missed. There was much use of trumpets and
the beaters were soldiers; Macmillan shot seventy-
seven birds.[49] But now, on his home turf de Gaulle's
objections to British membership were even more
aggressively expressed. If Britain wanted to choose
Europe, she would have to cut her special ties with
America. At one point, Macmillan broke down in
tears of frustration at the Frenchman's
intransigence, leading de Gaulle to report cruelly
to his cabinet later: 'This poor man, to whom I had
nothing to give, seemed so sad, so beaten that I
wanted to put my hand on his shoulder and say to
him, as in the Edith Piaf song, *"Ne pleurez pas,
milord"*.'

Cruel or not, it was a significant moment for
Macmillan, for the Tories and for Britain. The
Edwardian act now seemed weak and old, not

impressive. When a few months later, in early 1963, de Gaulle's 'Non' was abruptly announced in a Paris press conference, causing huge offence in Britain. A visit by Princess Margaret to Paris was cancelled. At the England-France rugby international at Twickenham a few days later, England won six-five and the captain assured Heath, the failed negotiator, that he had had a word with the team and told them 'this was an all-important game. Everyone knew what I meant and produced the necessary.'[50] Macmillan himself bitterly recorded in his diary that 'the French always betray you in the end'.

Tales of Yankee Power

In 1962 the world had come to the brink of nuclear war during the Cuban missile crisis. The people living round Scotland's Holy Loch, where Macmillan had allowed the Americans to base the first nuclear submarines, immediately realized the gravity of the Cuban crisis when they awoke in the night to the unfamiliar sound of silence. The humming of motors on the loch they had become so used to had suddenly ceased and when morning broke they saw that the US submarines had slipped away to prepare their nuclear attack on Russia. In Whitehall the historian Peter Hennessy believes that Macmillan was preparing for a cabinet meeting which would have authorized the first stage of hiding his government underground. There were no illusions about what a missile strike would mean. In 1955 secret government papers on the impact of hydrogen bombs stated that the effect 'on dense populations would remain beyond the imagination until it happened. Whether this country could withstand an all-out attack and still be in any state to carry on hostilities must be very doubtful.'[51] How many H-bombs would it take to wipe out the British military state? At an eerie encounter in 1961 between the Russian leader Nikita Khrushchev and the British ambassador Sir Frank Roberts, who found themselves together at a ballet performance in Moscow, exactly this issue came up. Khrushchev asked Roberts how many it would take and he replied, loyally hoping to limit the scale of any planned strike, that Britain would be destroyed by six H-bombs. The Soviet leader told him that 'optimists' at the Soviet forward command headquarters in East Berlin had reckoned Britain would take nine. In fact, said Khrushchev, the Soviet general staff had a higher opinion of the UK's capacity to resist and had earmarked 'several scores of bombs for use' against Britain.[52]

In the face of this horror, the British government had built huge networks of bunkers, with food and water supplies, emergency generators, communications systems, decontamination suits and the rest in order to maintain some vestigial State alive after the holocaust. Plans for regional command centres and what has been described as a form of Cromwellian military dictatorship with martial law and the shooting of civilians who resisted, were well advanced. By the early sixties, Macmillan had his post-nuclear government system ready. Whitehall had earmarked 210 people who would run the remnant of a country, from chiefs of staff and intelligence officers to typists and clerks.

They would be rushed to TURNSTILE, the top secret underground bunker system with sixty miles of tunnels, built deep under the Cotswolds at Corsham. Everyone else, including the wives, husbands and children of those ordered to the bunkers, would have been left to burn, die of radiation poisoning, or otherwise expire. Sir Rodric Braithwaite, later Chairman of the Joint Intelligence Committee, said of all this planning that 'It was inescapable, it was necessary and it was lunatic.'

Something of the same mix of fatalism and fascination underpinned the determination of successive British governments to persevere with un-independent nuclear weapons, something to chuck back in the final hour. We have seen how, under Attlee and Churchill, Britain struggled to create her own nuclear deterrent, and did so hoping to maintain her independence from America. For a brief period of five or six years Bevin's belief in the possibility of a genuinely independent British bomb was vindicated but in the Macmillan years all this changed. It is striking that the original clinching argument for British nuclear weapons, which was that they would give Britain's politicians special status and leverage to influence Washington, so quickly collapsed. Leverage and dependency rarely go together. And it is even more striking that when the argument collapsed there was no radical rethinking of Britain's nuclear posture. In government nobody seemed to notice.

The RAF had been assembling a great fleet of V-bombers – Valiants, Victors and finally Vulcans – intended to fly over Russia and drop free-falling nuclear bombs. Like the bombers, the bombs had been developed independently at Aldermaston. They continued to grow in destructive power, giant squat tubes with wings and names such as Blue Danube, Yellow Sun or Red Beard. But the V-bomber fleet had been running late. So in 1958 as a stop-gap Macmillan allowed sixty huge American Thor missiles to be stationed in Britain. The UK's intercontinental ballistic missiles, Blue Streak, used liquid propellant which had to be stored separately, creating too long a preparation period in a nuclear emergency. British planners believed they would have as little as two and a half minutes' warning of a Soviet missile attack. To defend Blue Streak while the fuel was prepared would have meant building sixty vast silos deep in the ground, an epic project too expensive for Whitehall to contemplate.

Two years later in 1960 when the Soviets shot down an American U2 spy plane, flying far higher than any Victor, Vulcan or B52 could manage, the age of the bombers was over. At first that wasn't clear and Macmillan began negotiating to buy American air-launched Skybolt missiles, which it was thought could be used by the V-bomber fleet to fire at the Soviet Union from a safe distance. At Camp David, Eisenhower's Spartan retreat in Maryland outside Washington, Macmillan struck his deal. Britain could buy Skybolt and in return the United States would be allowed a deep-water base for its latest top-secret missile system, the submarine-launched Polaris, which was to be tested that year. Yet again, events overtook Macmillan. Skybolt turned out to be a dud, or at least too unreliable for the United States. The age of the nuclear submarine had arrived.

To stay in this race, Britain would need Polaris

instead. Impossible to trace underwater, the submarines carrying them could cruise the oceans for months. Each submarine sailed with sixteen missiles. Each missile, once launched could not be stopped. Each carried more destructive force than all the bombs dropped in the Second World War. 'Polaris' was the ultimate doomsday fish. Thanks to Macmillan's deal at Camp David, the first American version arrived a short drive away from Glasgow. Macmillan originally talked to Eisenhower only about some base in Scottish waters, though sites in England and Wales were also considered. He had been nervous from the start, noting in his diary that 'A picture could well be drawn of some frightful accident which might devastate the whole of Scotland.'[53] The US Navy, however, searching for suitable sites, rejected the north-west Highlands as too remote. They fixed on the Holy Loch, a steep-sided inlet close to Glasgow. It had deep water, it was easy for navigation, quiet and yet submarines would quickly be able to hide themselves in the heavy marine traffic leaving and entering the Clyde. It was also close to Scotland's only international airport, Prestwick, which would be handy for American sailors. Macmillan became increasingly alarmed at the promise he had made, writing to Eisenhower that, 'It would surely be a mistake to put down what will become a major nuclear target so near to the third largest and most overcrowded city in this country. As soon as the announcement was made, Malinovsky [the Soviet defence minister] would threaten to aim his rockets at Glasgow and there would not only be the usual agitation of the defeatists and the pacifists but also genuine apprehension among ordinary folk.'

Eisenhower was blandly dismissive: they had discussed merely a Scottish base, had they not? The details would be worked out by naval people. But that was the trouble. The Royal Navy was desperate to get its hands on Polaris. Its status was crucially affected. If it became the nuclear delivery system, then after decades of air power supremacy, the navy would finally edge ahead of the RAF as the most important, as well as the senior, service. So the naval lobbyists were adamant that Macmillan must be accommodating about the Holy Loch. Macmillan was impaled. The same went for a government suggestion that the US Navy might agree to joint control over the American missiles stationed in Scotland. Again, this was vetoed. Again, the Navy was with the Americans. Macmillan buckled and allowed the deal to stand. The now inaptly named Holy Loch would welcome America's nuclear submarine fleet. When the first US nuclear supply ship arrived in the Clyde, the captain faced a tiny demonstration by Scottish CND members in canoes and kayaks – which he dismissed as the protest of a few 'damn Eskimos'. Both his ship, the *Proteus,* and the first nuclear submarines into the Clyde, were targeted by protesters who managed to hold onto the bows of the supply ship, climb its side and generally win a little publicity. There was a demonstration in Glasgow and marches to the gates of the new US base but CND's plan for a blockade by dinghy and canoe was defeated by rain, choppy waters and energetic policing by local bobbies.

A few years later, Macmillan did a further deal, this time with the new US President John F. Kennedy; and the Royal Navy duly got its own

Polaris fleet. Britain would build the submarines, at Barrow-in-Furness and Birkenhead, including the nuclear power systems, and would produce her own nuclear warheads. But America would supply the Polaris missiles themselves. Work started in 1963 on a new British nuclear submarine base at Faslane, just along the coast from the Holy Loch, the first new naval base since 1909. It had become perfectly obvious after the Cuban missile crisis that if Armageddon happened, it would have been triggered by some miscalculation or accident involving the US or the USSR. Every other nation, nuclear or not, would be a mere observer. And if the independent deterrence was not independent, and far from giving Britain leverage, made her a supplicant, why did Britain press on? The mixed motives of Macmillan and Alec Douglas-Home included a whiff of the old Churchillian fantasy about great power status. There was also a vague sense that the Western alliance should include more than just one nuclear power. Russia was a real threat, and if deterrence worked then Britain needed it as much as anyone. With a large British Army of the Rhine and this country the first in line for any pre-emptive Soviet missile strike, there was a remarkably wide political consensus on the need for submarines and missiles, with the Union Jack on top. Polling and voting shows that most of the time a large majority of voters agreed with this despite the campaigns of the disarmers. Labour never went anti-nuclear, even though so many of its supporters were so passionately committed to CND.

By the early sixties Britain was essentially in the same global rictus that she would adopt until the end of the Cold War. Once she had stomped the globe, imposing her will on subject peoples. Now she was stoically preparing for her own destruction, burrowing deep and buying the wherewithal for a final act of retaliation. She was sloughing off the Age of Empire, until only a few scattered dots would remain. She was America's unsinkable carrier and ally, not an independent European power. Her main commitment was to the fight against Communism and on it she was spending proportionately more money than any comparable country. This required a great rearrangement of the mental furniture, but it was rearranged by both main parties. They all struggled with it. In the Attlee years it had been the struggle for financial survival and to achieve an independent British bomb. In the sunset Churchill administration it was his forlorn attempt to make peace between the Americans and Russians. Eden suffered the disillusioning smash of Suez and Macmillan came to terms with the Americans finding that even the smallest expressions of independence, as over the Holy Loch, were brushed aside. All through these years with steadily shrinking armed forces, Britain had been fighting somebody somewhere. Any British citizen reviewing life in these islands since 1945 would conclude that they have enjoyed one of the longest periods of peace ever. Yet from outside, and in secret corners, the story had been very different. Fighters then, fighters now.

Small Worlds Collide

How might one sum up the love-hate relationship between the British Establishment and their allies in Washington, at the height of the Cold War? What metaphor might you choose? They were like competitive gamblers trying to outwit the wicked Soviets, yet constantly wary of one another. The self-assured Englishman, who moves between the world of espionage and high society, is out there taking the risks, but he simply doesn't have the cash to keep playing. The Americans, whom he treats with a mixture of condescension and admiration, are watching half-contemptuously, ready to help at the last minute. The British agent is cultured, well educated and stylish but fated to be the junior partner. He is prickly about his politics. Obsessively, he defends his country's underlying greatness despite the appearance of weakness. For one to the manner born, it is a kind of torture and he ends up naked, with his testicles hanging out of the bottom of a cane chair, having them beaten – a nasty but undeniably powerful image of the humiliation of British power. All this comes, of course, from the first ever James Bond novel, *Casino Royale,* published in 1953.

Its author was in his way at least as influential a commentator on the Anglo-American relationship as most politicians. Ian Fleming is also a fine example of how British society was tightly twisted at the top. He was yet another Etonian, and yet another character who flitted between journalism, intelligence and high society. Of a Scottish banking family, he had tried Sandhurst, foreign reporting – including in Stalin's Moscow – and the City – where he was no good – before joining Naval Intelligence during the war. There his wild schemes for sabotage and dirty tricks were widely considered more fit for novels. After the war he ran a network of foreign correspondents from London and, like so many other Britons, tried to work out ways of moving out of the dreary reality of austerity London. He eventually built a house in Jamaica, then a British colony, which he called Goldeneye.

It turns out to be Ian Fleming's wife Ann, admired by her friends for her 'sharpness, determination and lack of pretence'[54] who really gives us the feel of how interconnected politics and society life were in the 1950s. Ann had originally been married to a newspaper magnate, Esmond Rothermere, owner of the *Daily Mail* and London *Evening Standard.* She had had a high old time in the years after the war, living like an old-fashioned society hostess while making and unmaking editors and journalistic careers – it was one of her protégés who broke the story of Princess Elizabeth's engagement to Philip Mountbatten. But she had been enjoying a long affair with Fleming and eventually divorced the devastated Lord Rothermere to marry him, taking off in new directions, politically and sexually. She was a close friend of Eden's wife, Clarissa, who had in turn been loved by the novelist Evelyn Waugh, a friend of Ann's. The latter two were great letter-writers, which is how we can picture Clarissa Eden in Number Ten practising with a snorkel – for it was to Ian Fleming's Goldeneye that the Edens fled after Suez to recuperate.

317

Ann was dubious about the idea, writing to Waugh in November 1956 that the Prime Minister's wife 'seemed disconcerted to hear that if one wished a bath, one had to give two days' notice and that I did not know if there was a dentist on the island and that all the doctors were black. I warned her that shoes must be worn while bathing and that the reef abounded with scorpion fish, barracuda and urchins. I forgot to tell her that if [Eden] is impregnated with spines he should pee on them ... I think Torquay and a sunlamp would be more peaceful and patriotic.' The governor of Jamaica was equally concerned, but the Edens, like Noël Coward and many others, did make for the island and the Flemings' exotic home. When wounded you stick with your own, and these were tight little circles: Ian and Ann Fleming had originally heard about Burgess and Maclean's defection to Moscow, for instance, while staying with the Edens at Chequers. The memory stayed with them; defending the honour of the British secret service at a time when it was stained by treachery was one of Fleming's purposes in his novels.

It was not only the worlds of newspapers, Tory politics and writing that Ann Fleming pulled together. A few years after the Edens had visited she was describing another politician on the island, someone who had become one of her favourite dance-partners and lovers. She paints a vivid portrait of the Labour leader Hugh Gaitskell swimming, then disappearing underwater for a worryingly long time before breaking surface 'like an amiable hippo'. In her letters to friends, she was discreet about her love affair with Gaitskell, though the affectionate animal metaphors slightly give the

318

game away – later, he is 'a very inquisitive man, he has a long inquisitive nose like the ant-eating tapir'. Gaitskell was one of the upper-crust socialists, distrusted by the Labour left. Even so, for such a Tory hostess to have an affair with him would have horrified her friends. It only matters because it shows how small and tight-woven the top of British society still was. You should have seen: everybody, darling, was there.

The history of Britain in the fifties is the history of unconscious conspiracies. The private language of upper-crust diaries and letters is mocking but nervous. The London drinking clubs remain from prewar times but the grand houses are shutting down and the Americans are taking over. In different ways, all these people, from Noël Coward to the newspaper barons, Gaitskell to the Flemings, are struggling with timewarp lives and challenged patriotism. Morals are becoming more fluid. New kinds of pleasure are seeping in. One of his biographers wrote of the Labour leader, 'Britain was changing, growing more affluent, beginning to enjoy the peace, and Gaitskell relaxed a little alongside everyone else.'[55] Gaitskell himself, meanwhile, was able to appreciate both Flemings, writing of the Bond books in the *New Statesman* that 'I am a confirmed Fleming fan – or should it be addict? The combination of sex, violence, alcohol and – at intervals – good food and nice clothes is, to one who lives such a circumscribed life as I do, irresistible.'[56] It is hard to think of a couple of sentences which explain so well how the austerity years gave way to the Swinging Sixties. Gaitskell was one of the most intensely patriotic men in British public life, deeply wary of America, yet he was being tugged that way too.

James Bond would become one of the most successful if mildly ironic symbols of defiant British pride as the years rolled on, not least through the endless films. Gadget-packed Aston Martins; imperturbable and apparently competent Whitehall mandarins; parachutes opening to display the Union Jack; and above all Bond himself, with his self-confidence in everything from cocktails and sex to scuba-diving and skiing – this was truly a glorious fantasy for a nation in trouble. The Americans were shown as friendly and powerful but slightly slow on the uptake, while in the early novels Fleming worked to satisfy the almost pornographic lust of the British for the richer, more colourful consumer culture over the Atlantic – Gaitskell's wistful 'good food and nice clothes'. American cigarettes, nylon shirts and food are indeed lovingly described: in a characteristic passage from *Live and Let Die,* Bond leaves a 'bitter raw day … the dreary half-light of a London fog' to go to New York, where his hotel serves him crabs and tartare sauce, 'flat beef Hamburgers, medium-rare, from the charcoal grill, french-fried potatoes, broccoli, mixed salad with thousand-island dressing, ice-cream with melted butterscotch' and Liebfraumilch wine. That a burger-and-chips with Blue Nun menu, which would soon become common in suburban lounge bars across Britain, clearly seemed so mouth-wateringly exotic in 1954 is eloquent and, in its way, touching. Though Fleming was a connected member of the elite, Bond's route to a mass audience would be through rougher trade. Fleming had pictured his agent as an

Old Etonian but a working-class Scottish bodybuilder and former milkman, Sean Connery, was chosen to play the first James Bond, and he was followed by a range of shapes and accents, including an Irishman. This appeared to suggest that Bond was something of an outsider, which in turn expanded the films' appeal. In a further twist, the films were only ever made because of the financial backing of America's United Artists and the ex-Hollywood producer Albert or 'Cubby' Broccoli. He had been working in London, as had his Bond partner, a Canadian called Harry Salzman, whose earlier work included films of grittier subjects such as John Osborne's *Look Back in Anger.* James Bond would pay rather better.

Was it all a bit too much? Not really: the political scandal that happened at the fag-end of the Tory years was more highly coloured and more unlikely than much of what Ian Fleming poured into his early 'shockers'.

This tall tale began on a hot summer evening around the swimming pool of a grand house, Cliveden, in Buckinghamshire. Now a hotel for the very rich, the Italianate mansion overlooking the Thames in one of the finest locations in southern England, had once belonged to the Duke of Westminster. Its architecture has an exuberant opulence that makes you laugh out loud even now, and its original style can be summarized by the fact that it contained a dining room taken wholesale from the French palace of Madame de Pompadour. Cliveden was already notorious as a place of cliques and plotters. It had been the home of the first Lord Astor, a newspaper magnate, and his famous wife, politician and hostess, Nancy, a woman who could have given Ann Fleming a run for her money. Before the war, Nancy Astor's gatherings had been attacked by the left-wing journalist Claud Cockburn as the very epicentre of pro-appeasement thinking. At Cliveden, Cockburn insisted, Lords Halifax and Lothian and the pro-appeasement *Times* editor Geoffrey Dawson, gathered with the Astors to undermine Eden and Churchill, and plot a deal with Hitler. The evidence of actual plotting at Cliveden is scanty but the Communist Party took up the story of an upper-class conspiracy, involving highly placed Americans and members of the Royal Family ready to sell out democracy to the Nazis. Soon the 'Cliveden set' was being talked about from Berlin to Washington. Nancy Astor, then an MP, complained that she was portrayed as the centre of 'a vicious and degenerate gang' and received letters saying that she and her family 'should be taken out and shot'. When she eventually confronted Cockburn at a party she spat in his face. Remarkably, political lightning now struck the same house again. Cliveden, or rather its swimming pool, helped finish off Tory reputations a generation later.[57]

The next Lord Astor, known as Bill, was trying to live a relatively apolitical and social life. Amiable, thrice-married, he was turning Cliveden again into a party palace where well-off and eminent guests enjoyed themselves. One of his friends was a slightly sinister osteopath of extreme left-wing affectations (rather than views) called Stephen Ward. He had massaged the backs of Winston Churchill, Gaitskell, many Royals and Elizabeth Taylor. It was said of him that 'he enjoyed "handling" people's lives as he enjoyed handling their dislocated limbs or damaged muscles.' Ward, also a talented artist, kept a collection of pretty young girls whose careers he vaguely promoted in the modelling and sex business. One was called Christine Keeler. She had run away to London from her railway carriage home at the age of fifteen and lived a wild teenage youth afterwards. On the night in question, she was staying with Ward and two others at a grand, vaguely Germanic 'cottage' in the Cliveden grounds. Astor allowed Ward and his guests to use his swimming pool. On the muggy evening Keeler shed a borrowed bathing costume and was naked in the pool when Astor wandered down with one of his guests, the Secretary of State for War, John Profumo. Handsome, flirtatious, Profumo had had a good war in a cavalry regiment and was married to a then-famous actress, Valerie Hobson. The only obviously exotic thing about him was his name, which came from an aristocratic Italian grandfather. But hot summer nights are hot summer nights. The men chased Keeler around the pool and later invited her and Ward back to the main house, where Keeler and Profumo began to flirt. He contacted her later and they were soon having an affair. This would probably have remained unknown, in the discreet codes of the time, except for a rotund, cheerful Russian military attaché, and spy, called Yevgeny Ivanov. Ward knew him too (Ward knew 'everybody') because he had been introduced to Ivanov by the editor of the *Daily Telegraph* (who else?) at lunch in the exclusive Garrick Club (where else?). Ivanov also wanted to hire a cottage at Cliveden, which might have struck others as being a tad suspicious. He met Profumo at the pool too. The two men were soon engaged in a childish swimming race. A couple of years later, neatly completing the circle, Ivanov was sleeping with Keeler.

This tangled connection of minister, spy, call-girl, peer and masseur might not have hit the headlines at all, except that among Keeler's other men was a West Indian dope-dealer who was accused of firing a gun at Ward's flat. During his trial, rumours started to spread. Keeler became a minor celebrity. There was the famous photograph, attributed by many to David Bailey, of her sitting naked as she looked back from a trendy Arne Jacobsen chair. (In this story nothing should be taken at face value: the photographer was Lewis Morley, the chair was a copy and Keeler was not naked, just cleverly posed.) *Private Eye* printed a knowing cartoon and article though in fact the cartoonist and writers were largely using guesswork. Keeler had been hanging round the same crowd as the satirists and her connections were widely known in London. The *Private Eye* story so alarmed Stephen Ward, however, that he turned up at the magazine's grimy Soho offices and confirmed the lot. Political London is a village and soon the story was raised in the Commons by George Wigg, an unpleasant ex-army Labour MP and friend of Harold Wilson's, who happened to loathe Profumo. The panicking minister was hauled in and interrogated late at night by the government whips. He hotly denied that he had had sex with Keeler, a lie he then repeated to the Commons. The Prime Minister, like the rest of the Tory hierarchy, believed him.

Jack Profumo was tormented by what he had done. As the Labour opposition leader, Harold

Wilson, sent Macmillan further lurid allegations that Ward had tried to get nuclear secrets from Profumo, using Keeler and pillow-talk, the minister fled on holiday to Italy. He there admitted the truth to his wife and returned to make a public confession. He was instantly ruined, spent the rest of his life in private voluntary work in London, atoning for what he had done, and ended his life widely respected and officially honoured for his charity work. But you never escape a name that memorable. More than forty years on, newspaper billboards announced: 'Sex Scandal Minister Dies'. Back in 1963 the press was in particularly vengeful mood. During his trial for living off the earnings of prostitution, Ward killed himself with an overdose. In the most famous words uttered as the tale unfolded, Mandy Rice-Davies, Keeler's friend, was asked in court about Lord Astor's denial that he had had sex with her. She replied: 'He would say that, wouldn't he?' The frankness of her assumption that yes, of course, rich and powerful men were liars, caught the nation's mood. Most such scandals simply end. The headlines yellow, the victims limp off to try to rebuild their lives and politics thunders on as usual. The Profumo affair was different. There was a famous inquiry into it by the judge Lord Denning. His report was a bestseller when published by the government, rivalling the Beveridge Report of twenty years earlier. (The different subjects and tone tell us something about Britain's journey.) Denning cleared MI5 of failure, minimized any security aspect and concluded that Ivanov and Profumo were not sharing Keeler's bed. Yet very shortly afterwards, in a very tight race, Labour would win the 1964 general election by just four seats. It is a tiny margin. The Profumo affair caused such national interest that it might well have tipped the balance against the Tories.

If so, it was a vote against a closed world of interconnecting relationships from which too many British people felt excluded. Macmillan himself had led a blameless, indeed celibate, life in late adulthood after his wife's long affair with a fellow politician, Bob Boothby. But the tight connections between a small number of powerful political and social players were particularly intense in the fifties, before the democratizing effect of the sixties' educational and cultural revolution. The Profumo affair brought both worlds together, in collision. Astor and Profumo, the mistresses and the discreet introductions in London clubs, all came from the old world. The drug-smuggling boyfriend with a gun and the good-time girls from working class backgrounds, unshockable and impossible to intimidate, were characters from the new Britain taking shape around Macmillan. Universes collided. Energy was released. Its noise was heard as the 'satire boom'.

Beyond the Fringe

Political satire, which had been exuberantly popular in Georgian times, had become duller during the noontide of Empire, and now returned in full force, from savage cartoons in the newspapers, staged lampoons, and the fortnightly mockery of the magazine *Private Eye*. It can be tempting to treat comedy like a ball being passed down the line in a game of rugby. Among the two million regular listeners to *The Goon Show* in the mid-fifties were key members of the next generation of comics, who would sting more, men such as Jonathan Miller and Peter Cook. The Goons pass to *Beyond the Fringe*; *Beyond the Fringe* passes to *Monty Python's Flying Circus*; they pass to *Little Britain,* and so on until the touch-judge puts a flag up and stops play. Each generation does indeed catch the humour of the previous one, changes it and throws it on. Peter Cook, who is Spike Milligan's only rival as the outstanding comic genius of the age, as a schoolboy sent a script to the BBC good enough for Milligan to invite him up to London for lunch. In turn, the generation of comedians who created *Monty Python's Flying Circus* were transfixed by Cook and his friends. But the origins of the comedy keep changing. The real difference between Milligan and Secombe, and indeed many other war-trained comedians making names for themselves in post-war London, and the next lot, was public school. Had R. A. Butler acted on his original instinct and broken down the ancient class divide in British education, the country's humour would have been very different. By the 1960s, the flow of lower-middle-class and working-class children through grammar schools and into the universities was strongly affecting the atmosphere of the whole country. But in the decade after the war, the private schools still dominated things. They were often bleak institutions. The austerity years meant little heating, poor food and few modern facilities, a life decorated by brutal customs and petty hierarchies often dating back to the reign of Queen Victoria.

Peter Cook's school, Radley in Oxfordshire,

deployed a private vocabulary, frequent beatings, cold showers, complicated rules about which buttons which boys were allowed to do up, compulsory star-jumps, thumpings with hockey sticks for minor transgressions, and of course a great deal of bullying, undeterred by the staff. This forced bright but vulnerable children like Cook to develop mimickry and mockery to deflect bullies – which in his case included the England cricket captain to be, Ted Dexter. Cook's biographer, Harry Thompson, himself a noted comic, quoted Cook explaining how he would make people laugh in order that they would not hit him. Thompson asked: 'How many times, over the years, has the British comedy industry had cause to be grateful to generations of public school bullies?'[58] Richard Ingrams, editor of *Private Eye,* cut his comic teeth at Shrewsbury School, sitting high above the River Severn, and at least as weird as Radley. Its new boys were called 'douls' after the Greek for slave; its day started with cold baths; it too had a byzantine dress code, involving different colours of scarf, tie and waistcoat, buttons done up or not, and the rest; when the whole school was sent on cross-country runs, the boys were chased by men with whips. Ingrams's humour was less about mimickry; instead he, Paul Foot and Willie Rushton, who would join him at *Private Eye,* turned to writing mock school magazines.

At Radley and Shrewsbury as in scores of other similar schools, such as John Cleese's Clifton College in Bristol, or indeed Prince Charles's Gordonstoun in Scotland, boys developed underground languages to cope with their aggressive and closed communities. They knew little of women, which meant the humour that emerged from this was often toe-curlingly juvenile about sex. They were rarely politically radical. They were from a privileged elite, after all. Cook's father had been a colonial civil servant in Nigeria and Gibraltar. Ingrams was the son of an eccentric banker and intelligence agent, a one-time member of the pro-Nazi Anglo-German Fellowship Society, and a Catholic mother whose father had been Queen Victoria's doctor. Both men were brought up to look down on the working classes as essentially inferior and comic, though Ingrams would have his perspective shifted as a soldier during the Korean War. Their satire would be biting, with underlying layers of anger and hurt. But it would be very public-schoolboyish too, tittering and often snobby.

The brightest then went on to Cambridge or Oxford, still then mostly male societies, and where in those days there was a direct line from the world of Oxbridge student reviews to the West End. Future satirists mingled with fellow students who would go on to become politicians and business leaders. Thompson points out that this too would affect the style of comedy soon to sweep middle-class Britain. Peter Cook's generation at Cambridge in 1957 would include the later Conservative cabinet ministers Michael Howard, Kenneth Clarke and Leon Brittan, as well as numerous actors and impresarios: 'One reason that Oxbridge has traditionally produced so many political satirists is that its undergraduates come face to face with their future political leaders at an early age, and realise then quite how many of them are social retards who join debating societies in order to find friends.' (Though in fairness it should be added that the same can apply to those joining student theatre companies and satirical magazines.) At Cambridge, Cook simply transferred his monotone sketches about the Radley school butler, to the new environment and eventually had half the undergraduates mimicking him and repeating his one-liners. Sometimes comic success is just a voice. Cook found his voice as a schoolboy and essentially never lost it; the same deadpan, bathetic philosophy swept from public school to Cambridge to Edinburgh's *Beyond the Fringe* review, to London, New York and immortality. Ingrams and Rushton, similarly, transferred their jokes and cartoon characters from a school magazine to a student one, and then, with others, to *Private Eye*. Around these people were many others from different backgrounds who would become just as important in the story of British comedy – Alan Bennett, the Yorkshire grammar school boy; Dudley Moore, the working-class boy from Dagenham; David Frost, the Methodist preacher's son from Kent. But the dominant personalities of Cook and Ingrams gave them a particular hold over the satire boom.

The day when the traditional Establishment decided it had to acknowledge its critical cousin, the comedy establishment, was 28 February 1962. The Queen visited *Beyond the Fringe* in London's Fortune Theatre to see the vicious caricature of her prime minister by Peter Cook. Cook had done his Macmillan at Cambridge and at the Edinburgh Festival Fringe already. In London he had been playing to packed houses since the previous May. There had been protests and walk-outs by people outraged at seeing the Queen's first minister lampooned in public. But the Queen herself roared with laughter. After this Macmillan, determined to show he was a good sport and could take a joke, decided to go along too. This was a mistake. Other Tory cabinet ministers had seen it already but when the Prime Minister arrived, Cook spotted him in the audience and deviated from his script. In an Edwardian drawl, he told Macmillan: 'When I've a spare evening, there's nothing I like better than to wander over to a theatre and sit there listening to a group of sappy, urgent, vibrant young satirists, with a stupid great grin spread all over my silly old face.'

The crueller the political comedy, the greater its success. Shortly afterwards, Cook opened the briefly famous Establishment Club in Soho as the capital of the new satire movement. Every night comedy and music would be offered, along with trendy new foods and a bar. It was mobbed and its membership included much of the old Establishment. Everybody, it seemed, wanted a part of the new comedy, including some who weren't very funny themselves. A spin-off revue, where David Frost was doing his own version of Cook's Macmillan, was visited by the gangsters of the moment, the Kray twins. A few months after the Queen's visit, Cook bought the fledgling *Private Eye* too, where Richard Ingrams would soon become editor. The BBC was just holding its breath to see whether the satire boom could survive on-screen, with *That Was the Week That Was,* again compered by Frost. It ran for a short season until hurriedly taken off the air as the 1964 election approached. For a short time it seemed that a small bunch of university comics had created a republic of laughter strong enough to change the country.

331

This was an illusion, never shared by the key players themselves. Cook had had the idea for his club many years earlier visiting West Germany, and would refer wryly to the 'great tradition of those satirical clubs of the 1930s that had done so much to prevent the rise of Adolf Hitler'. He said different things at different times about Macmillan and the Tories. Right-wing friends tended to think he was right-wing, and socialists thought he was one of theirs, but if Peter Cook had any politics they were never consistent and always took second place to a good punchline. Richard Ingrams was certainly no socialist; his independent-minded Tory radicalism allowed him to flay party placemen from all sides and he was compared to that great nineteenth-century radical Tory William Cobbett. Harold Wilson, observing with delight the satirical onslaught on Macmillan and Alec Douglas-Home, later tried to ingratiate himself with *Private Eye* when he became Prime Minister, inviting Ingrams to Downing Street and professing himself a great admirer of satire. His reward was to become one of the magazine's most loathed and aggressively pursued targets as the Labour years rolled on.

There were politically minded people at the edges of the satire movement of the early sixties, many of them radicalized by CND and on the left of the Labour Party. Fluck and Law, who would go on to create the latex puppetry of *Spitting Image,* were socialist friends of Peter Cook's. Richard Ingrams' closest friend was probably Paul Foot, nephew of the Labour politician Michael Foot, who became a leading light in the Socialist Workers' Party and a fine investigative journalist. But there was no organic link between the left of British politics and the wave of comedians, mimics and journalists who tore down the facade of Tory Britain fifteen years after the war. There could not have been. Too many of the satirists were public schoolboys, getting their own back on the nation's authority figures just as they tried to get their own back on schoolmasters and bullies. Macmillan was for them, in essence, just the head of a decaying prep school. Labour was full of lower-middle-class and working-class people with their funny accents and limited little lives. If there was any alliance, it was very short and entirely one of convenience.

Conclusion: A Country of Cliques is Over

The story of Britain in the years after the fall of Attlee's New Jerusalem, and before the sixties really began to swing is the story of a country still run by cliques and in-groups, rather than by visionary individuals, still less the masses. Understand the networks, the clubs and the personal associations and you understand the system. For the Tories, public school and Oxbridge links, even family ones, had provided the fusebox of power. Post-war growth had given clique politics a good run. But this Britain eventually failed. It failed over Suez, over the growing signs of economic failure, in its late attempt to copy French central planning and in its inability to grasp the new culture and society growing up all around it. The symbols of that failure were the spy scandals, the Profumo affair and the rising froth of satirical laughter. Macmillan had finished it off, bloodily, on 'the Night of the Long Knives'. Before this act of almost domestic butchery there was still a notion that the chaps at the Turf Club, the old families with their stalking and salmon rivers, that web of Old Etonian cronies, could maintain British authority and self-confidence, despite the local difficulties of a disintegrating Empire and a weak economy; that they could hang together. Patently, they could not.

The final stage in the collapse of the old authority came with Macmillan's illness and resignation, and the stitch-up which eventually put the bony, amiable, slightly bemused Lord Home of the Hirsel into Number Ten as the fourth Tory Prime Minister in a row. Much of British politics still came down to class, which threw up many ironies. In this case it was the long, ultimately successful legal fight by a Labour leftwinger, Lord Stansgate, better known as Anthony Wedgwood Benn, better known still as Tony Benn, to disclaim or throw off his peerage. His success in court electrified the Tory struggle. There were Tories in the Commons who were popular candidates to replace Macmillan, above all Rab Butler. Yet the new ability to fling off a coronet and become a commoner and thus possibly an MP in the Commons, meant two other prominent Conservatives could now take part in the race. One was Lord Hailsham, a clever, popular but ultimately rather undignified man, favoured by Macmillan. The other was Lord Home. Macmillan was far less ill than he thought but the news that he would go turned the Tory conference of October 1963, normally a placid and deferential gathering, into wild and hysterical seaside hustings. Lord

Hailsham made it clear he would renounce his peerage but then discredited himself with a display of crude and exhibitionistic self-promotion. Macmillan quickly dropped him as favourite, some suggest because he did not want a successor who would be there for long, just in case he could manage a comeback. Rab Butler made a poor speech, leading some to wonder if he really wanted to be prime minister; he was a great mind, and much admired by the brighter Tories, but he lacked the slightest evidence of killer instinct. Enoch Powell, one of his supporters, said they had put the gun in his hands, but he refused to fire it. Macmillan coldly dismissed him as lacking 'the last six inches of steel'. Up in London, Macmillan was still ill in bed and arranged for the various grandees of the party to 'take soundings' among the MPs, party workers, peers and constituency chairmen. This highly unscientific survey produced Lord Home's name and he was duly proposed by Macmillan, invited by the Queen, accepted, renounced his peerage, won a by-election in a then-tame Scottish Tory constituency and duly entered Number Ten. Fast work milord.

Widely liked but self-effacing, Lord Home, Macmillan's Foreign Secretary, had a political career which led right back to the Chamberlain government and the Munich appeasement of Hitler. This did not and should not have counted against him entirely. Butler had also been an appeaser; so had, for a while, Hailsham; indeed, so had most of the Tory Party at the time. But Home seemed utterly against the spirit of the new decade. He was the ultimate grouse-moor Tory, but without Macmillan's wily toughness. Not just a toff but worse, a nice toff. The idea outraged many Tories, notably Hailsham and the liberal Iain Macleod. Powell was equally livid and both men refused to serve under Home, who was described by press commentators at the time as 'a cretin' and 'this half-witted Earl'. In a famous article in the *Spectator,* Iain Macleod as editor attacked the choice as a stitch-up by the Conservative Party's 'magic circle'. He narrated the key soundings, involving Macmillan and functionaries such as Lords Dilhorne, Poole and St Aldwyn, pointing out in a devastating aside: 'Eight of the nine men mentioned in the last sentence went to Eton.'

As it happened, Alec Douglas-Home went on to be a tougher opponent than Harold Wilson had expected. An Etonian schoolboy contemporary, the writer Cyril Connolly, had described the new Prime Minister as 'the kind of graceful, tolerant, sleepy boy who is showered with favours and crowned with all the laurels ... In the eighteenth century he would have become prime minister before he was thirty: as it was he appeared honourably ineligible for the struggle for life.' Home proved Connolly wrong, at least in getting to the premier position and in being ready to fight for it. Later, he would return as Heath's Foreign Secretary in 1970–4 and lived long to be a much-liked grand old man of Toryism. Yet he never overcame the handicap of being a symbol of the old ways. As Prime Minister in the early sixties he was out of time, an immaculately turned out anachronism. Macmillan unwittingly pointed this out in a draft of his resignation letter to the Queen, in which he cheerfully described Home as 'clearly a man who represents the old, governing class at its best'. By

1964, that class was bust. Wilson put it well: 'We are living in the jet age but we are governed by an Edwardian establishment mentality.'

Though in theory opposed to this fusty clique-ridden world, behind the clothing and language, Labour leaders were not quite as different as they liked to appear. That party too was a cluster of competing clubs and networks, whose own connections to business were chance friendships which would later cause much embarrassment. The trade unions were still mostly in the hands of the old right-wing leaders who manipulated and wire-pulled to stay in office; Whitehall was run by a tiny elite of clubmen, the hyper-educated classicists from Oxbridge in their striped trousers and stiff collars who knew they were cleverer than any elite, anywhere else. The Liberals, under their charismatic leader Jo Grimond, stood outside the inner clubs of fifties power which was no doubt why they began to have some spectacular by-election successes towards the end of the Tory years, particularly in Cornwall, Wales and Scotland. They were seen as somehow modern and classless, though in fact Grimond was another Old Etonian who was intertwined in the once-grand family alliances of strangely dead Liberal England. In Scotland and Wales, the Nationalist parties were just beginning to challenge the paternalists. But when Anthony Sampson published *Anatomy of Britain* he had illustrated it with a sprawling diagram of intersecting circles to show the closed and nepotistic system under which the country was organized. It was probably the most influential piece of journalism of his long career and as potent in its way as the coining of the word 'Establishment' by another journalist, Henry Fairlie, at around the same time.

Of course, all advanced societies have Establishments. France swapped her great Catholic families for the intellectual elites of the de Gaulle era; German industrialists cooperated cosily together in their assault on world markets; even the United States has its Ivy League colleges and grand families interlinked from Wall Street to Washington. But in democracies elites require prestige to survive. They need to have spread their successes widely enough to retain authority. The British elites of the early sixties failed this test. Despite the new tycoons and the cluster of truly innovative big companies, Britain's output was growing far more slowly than other comparable countries and her share of world markets was shrivelling at a terrifying speed. Despite outside shocks, from Indian independence to Suez, from the sterling crises and the failure of weapons systems, to France's rejection of her application for Common Market membership, the country had made no radical change of direction. Privately, civil servants and politicians acknowledged that there were profound problems, and agonized about what should be done. Publicly, under Macmillan and Douglas-Home, there was a complacent front of self-congratulation and business as usual.

Was this because we had been happier than other nations in our age of lost content? No revolution, invasion or wartime defeat had shaken the British as they acquired their new cars and explored their new supermarkets; British political scandals were a branch of light entertainment compared to the darker struggles convulsing Italy, France or Eastern

Europe. And when Britain finally made a change, it turned out to be a surprisingly modest and ineffective one. Outside politics and the economy, a new country was breaking through – brightly coloured, fashionable, less masculine. For a brief flicker, it seemed to be matched by the arrival of a new government too. An alternative assessment came from Crossman as he contemplated the funeral gathering for Sir Winston Churchill in Westminster Hall at the end of January 1965: 'But, oh, what a faded, declining establishment surrounded me. Aged marshals, grey, dreary ladies, decadent Marlboroughs and Churchills. It was a dying congregation gathered there and I am afraid the Labour Cabinet didn't look too distinguished, either. It felt like the end of an epoch, possibly even the end of a nation.'[59]

PART 3

HAROLD, TED AND JIM:
WHEN THE MODERN FAILED

The thirteen years of Tory rule, wasted according to Harold Wilson, were followed by fifteen years when modern Britain rose and failed. 'Modern' does not simply mean the look and shape of the country formed during 1964–79, most of which is still here around us, essentially unaltered – the motorways and mass car economy, the concrete architecture, the rock music, the high street chains. It also means a belief in planning and management. This was the time of practical men, educated in grammar schools, sure of their intelligence, rolling up their sleeves and taking no nonsense. They were going to scrap the old and fusty, whether that meant the huge Victorian railway network, the grand Edwardian government palazzos in Whitehall, the historic regiments, terraced housing, hanging, theatre censorship, the prohibitions on homosexual behaviour and abortion, the ancient coinage and the quaint county names. Bigger in general would be better. Huge comprehensive schools would be more efficient than the maze of selective and rubbish-dump academies. The many hundreds of trade unions would resolve themselves into a few leviathans, known only by their initials. Small companies would wither and combine and ever-larger corporations would arise in their place, ruthless and managed on the latest scientific, American lines. Britain herself would cease to be a small independent trader and would merge into the largest corporation then available, the European Community. This was managerial self-confidence which would be smashed to pieces during the seventies and never recover.

Just seven men dominate the politics of these thirteen years. They are the three prime ministers, Harold Wilson, Edward Heath and James Callaghan; two other Labour politicians so important they stand alongside the premiers, Roy Jenkins and Denis Healey; and two men who stood increasingly outside the management consensus, leading attacks on it from right and left – Enoch Powell, and Anthony Wedgwood Benn. All have appeared briefly in this history already but these were the years when they truly mattered. Of the five insiders none was born into remotely rich or powerful families. Four of them, Wilson, Heath, Jenkins and Healey, were grammar school boys, who had elbowed their way to an elite university education. The fifth, Jim Callaghan, had a rougher start. All of them had served in the armed forces during the war, except for Wilson who had been a civil servant. All were exceptionally clever men of wide experience brimming with the energetic certainty of those trained to hold power, not merely born to the role. Though they had many differences of outlook, in broad terms they could agree that Marxism destroyed freedom, and that the discredited liberal free market brought chaos and unfairness. For them, enlightened state management was the last big idea left standing.

So these were men more abrasive and less interested in pleasing the media than later, more nervous politicians. They were hurrying men, prepared to be rude, particularly to each other. Their language was blunt in private, sometimes in public. Heath would denounce 'the unacceptable face of capitalism' and Healey would promise to make the richest in the land 'howl with anguish'. In one important way these men did represent the Britain of their time. These were years of increased social mobility. The country was full of little Harolds and lesser Teds, bright men and women from lower-middle-class or working-class families who were rising fast through business, universities and the professions, who hugely admired such leaders. When Wilson talked of the scientific revolution that would transform Britain, his audience included tens of thousands of managers and engineers, in their off-the-peg tweed jackets and flannel trousers. When Heath promised that Europe would open up great new vistas for British industry, boardrooms and offices contained impatient self-made people ready to get cracking. Callaghan's beefy working-class patriotism and conservative instincts were shared by millions of Labour voters, pro-trade union but staunchly monarchical.

But in other ways, they were already out of date. In the sixties and seventies, Britain was becoming a more feminized, sexualized, rebellious and consumption-addicted society. The political class was cut off from this by their age. They would rely on their children to keep them a little in touch. They might manage eventually, a brownish kipper tie or daringly wider lapels on their suits but they looked and sounded what they were, people from a more conservative and formal time.

For the vast majority the early sixties were experienced as a continuation of the fifties. Britain remained an industrial society and apparently a world power, whose future was believed to depend on factories churning out cars, engines, washing machines and electrical goods for export, and whose major cities were relics of the industrial revolution. Authority figures, police, teachers, judges and above all parents, were still clothed in the semi-military sense of order that derived from wartime experience. They were the butt of widespread mockery, in Alan Bennett's early plays, in newspaper cartoons by Giles of the Daily Express, in television sketches by John Cleese and David Frost or in film comedies about bus-drivers and diplomats. The cross-looking men with moustaches and short back and sides were losing ground. But they were visibly still in power. Little islands of change were all around. Immigration was changing small patches of the country, the textile towns of Yorkshire and parts of west London, though it had barely impinged on most people's lives. There was a growing snappiness and lightness of design, in everything from clothes to the shape of cars, an aesthetic escape from the seriousness of the immediate post-war period, which took different form year by year, but was experienced as a continuum not a revolution.

For some the country was just becoming more childish and less dignified. The refined, highbrow, purist modernism born among Europe's intellectuals before the war, had had its last throw. Benjamin Britten's musical austerities, Eliot's Anglo-Catholic seriousness and the formal stillness of the sculpture of Barbara Hepworth were falling from fashion. Classical music was receding before ear-splitting tidal advance of rock and pop, driven by radio. In poetry, politics and incantation were returning. In painting, pop art and the pleasure principle were on the attack. Though it is a huge generalization, it can fairly be argued that simpler and more digestible art forms, suitable for mass market consumption, were replacing elite art which assumed an educated and concentrated viewer, listener or reader. Throughout these years there would be self-conscious moves to create new elites, to keep the masses out. There always are. They might come from the portentous theories of modern art or the avowedly difficult atonal music arriving from France and America, but these would be eddies against the stream, tiny whirlpools in the metropolis or at universities. The general move was for easier, brighter, sweeter stuff.

The two great rebels mentioned earlier, Enoch Powell and Tony Benn, were neither easier nor sweeter. They had shared much with the five insiders and, indeed, would remain insiders through part of this era, Powell until he was finally expelled from the Tory shadow cabinet for his anti-immigration speech of 1968 and Benn until his increasing radicalism made him the silly socialist Satan of the later seventies. They both rejected the consumer society growing around them in favour of a higher vision. Powell's was a romantic dream of an older, tougher, swashbuckling England, freed of continental and imperial entanglements, populated by spiky, ingenious, hard-working (and white) people rather like himself. Benn's was of a socialist commonwealth, equal, republican, dominated by scientifically minded people thinking everything through from first principles, rather as he saw himself.

Both visions required British independence, a self-sufficient island, which ran entirely against the great forces of the time. Both were fundamentally nostalgic. If Powell harked back to the energetic Victorians, Benn dreamed of Puritan revolutionaries. Both drew sustenance from people around them who seemed to be excluded from mainstream politics. For Powell, it was the Wolverhampton constituents who had immigration imposed on them, and the small shopkeepers drowning under red tape and taxes. For Benn it was the radical shop stewards' committees on the Clyde or in Midlands factories, and his children's generation, protesting against Vietnam. In return, viewed from Fleet Street or the pulpits of broadcasting, each man was seen as an irrelevance, marching off to nowhere. Yet Powell was the prophet after whom Margaret Thatcher would stride into power while Benn represented a militant leftism which very nearly seized control of the Labour Party itself.

The Little Spherical Thing

No period of British parliamentary history has been as well and copiously described by those who were there as have the Wilson administrations of 1964–70. Two of the key ministers, Roy Jenkins and Denis Healey, wrote autobiographies which rank as the finest such books ever. The governments contained three diarists of superb quality and rare descriptive honesty. Richard Crossman blew the lid off cabinet confidentiality. Barbara Castle was the most effective female politician in Labour history. Benn's diaries are simply unparalleled descriptions of the age. Wilson himself was no great writer. He nevertheless produced a monumental tome on the governments which sets out his side of the story, in wearisome detail. James Callaghan did the same. Two of the best biographies in modern politics, by Ben Pimlott and Philip Ziegler, were devoted to Wilson. Other very fine accounts of the time include biographies of all the key players, as well as a small bookshelf of further memoirs by aides, press officers, lawyers, newspaper-men, diplomats and backbenchers. There is also a large literature devoted to the various theories about whether Wilson was a Soviet spy and whether MI5 agents and assorted extremists really tried to remove him from office. As a result we know more about what individual ministers were thinking and doing, and more about their internal feuds with officials and each other, than is the case for any previous government. Among later ones, only the Thatcher years have been as carefully chronicled, though its diarists were never top-rankers.

Yet the figure bobbing at the centre of this oceanic ebb and flow of words remains strangely obscure. It was said of Stalin during his rise through the Soviet power game that he was a grey blur. Wilson too can seem a grey blur, moving from a stolid lower-middle-class boyhood in Huddersfield, where his main enthusiasms were school learning and the Boy Scouts, through a quiet fact-grinding career at Oxford, winning prizes but keeping well clear of the politically glamorous set, until he became an academic economist and wartime civil servant. In letters and contemporary descriptions he comes over as doughy, cautious, priggish – immensely able but not likeable. Early in his career he was used by others, from Beveridge to Cripps and Dalton, as a superior office-boy, there to gather the figures, marshal the arguments and snib the door each evening. He was old-young, growing a moustache in his twenties in order to look more mature, and living in bulging suits, with his famous pipe. Yet as we have seen he was rarely trusted. An early piece of exaggeration, when he claimed to have gone to school with children too poor to afford shoes, which was untrue and exposed as untrue, gave him a public reputation for slipperiness.

When he resigned with Bevan in 1951, many people saw this as a piece of pure opportunism – he could see Attlee was finished and thought the party would shift to the left. He was disparaged as 'Nye's little dog' but his resignation speech was shrewd enough to leave the door open to a cabinet return. Then, having infuriated the right, he infuriated the left-wing Bevanites by waltzing back into a position very quickly. Later, pressed by the left to stand against Gaitskell, he was overcome with fear. The diarist Crossman recorded: 'They all bullied Harold and threatened him and pushed at him and tugged at him and the little spherical thing kept twirling round in dismay ...' In Labour's internal feuds he ratted, then re-ratted, then ratted again. In the early sixties he was a lonely figure at Westminster. The Labour right loathed him; the left merely despised him. Yet his sheer ability with numbers and increasingly with words kept him always in contention. When Gaitskell died suddenly, the left, without Bevan, had no other candidate than Wilson.

Sir Alec Douglas-Home became Prime Minister because Harold Macmillan was ill and conspiratorial. Harold Wilson became Labour leader because George Brown was a drunk and not nearly conspiratorial enough. Brown had assumed he would succeed, as Browns do. He was a richly talented working-class man, a lorry-driver's son from south London who rose through the trade union movement and entered Parliament in the Attlee landslide of 1945. With huge black eyebrows, a round red face, charm and a killer glare, he established himself as a forthright and at times brilliant speaker and an able young minister. He could be famously rude but also delightful and winning, and when Gaitskell died was the obvious person to take over, at least from the point of view of the right and centre of the party. The trouble, as Tony Crosland put it, was that Brown was also 'a neurotic drunk'. The party's choice, he went on, was now between 'a crook and a drunk'.[1] Brown's drinking was heavy and his personality mercurial. Later, his rants and self-pitying outbursts, his sudden disappearances, heroic sulks and astonishingly regular threats to resign from the Labour government would become legendary. A typical story about him, probably apocryphal, has him attending an official reception in Peru and, very inebriated, approaching a willowy figure in scarlet for a dance. Brown is repulsed and protests grandly that he is Her Britannic Majesty's Secretary of State for Foreign and Commonwealth Affairs; why could he not have a nice dance? The reply comes: for three reasons, Mr Brown. First because you are disgustingly drunk, second because that music is not a dance but our national anthem, and third because I am the cardinal-archbishop of Lima. The story, at least, demonstrates why Brown's reputation would

351

entertain, as well as appal, the Westminster village. Yet the drunk might well have beaten the crook, had not James Callaghan decided to stand as well. He had been encouraged by Wilson's team, so splitting the anti-Wilson vote and losing Brown vital momentum. In the end, Wilson won easily, by the votes of 144 Labour MPs to Brown's 103 – these were the days before trade unions or party activists were allowed a say.

Having won, Wilson's reputation soared in a way which today seems hard to explain. All his weaving, double-crossing, opportunism and deceptions were now forgiven, or at any rate forgotten. The press hailed him as a youthful master of his craft, a devastatingly witty speaker, man of the hour. Wilson's speeches had certainly improved immensely and he was an acknowledged maestro of the put-down and witty aside, essential in an age of open meetings and hecklers. He developed an acid line of attack on the easy targets of Macmillan and then Douglas-Home, and was full of vague but inspiring sounding thoughts such as 'the Labour movement is a crusade or it is nothing' and 'we need men with fire in their belly and humanity in their heart'. Yet his political thinking, as distinct from his political tactics, was stodgily conventional. He thought Britain was badly run and old-fashioned but believed more central planning, preferably by grammar school-educated technocrats like himself, would solve the problem. He was hardly young, an old-looking forty-six, whose image was comfortingly respectable. He harped on about preferring beer to champagne, tinned salmon to smoked salmon, HP sauce to any other sauce, and being a quiet, provincial sort. He seemed prudish about sex, still the Methodist Boy Scout at heart, and in many ways out of kilter with the fashionable, risk-taking, youthful Britain all around him. So why did he seem so good?

Partly it was a simple matter of class. He might send his children to private schools and live in Hampstead, but Wilson came across as a simple and ordinary man, a breath of fresh air compared to the Old Etonians whose fumbling rule was ending. He was the political equivalent to the men breaking through elsewhere in public life – the tweed-jacketed lecturers of Kingsley Amis novels or David Frost with his nasal vowels on television or Richard Hoggart, the plain-speaking lecturer called at the 'Lady Chatterley' trial. He lacked deference. His calm impertinence delighted millions. Here, in a world still run by the old lot, was a clever new man who took it for granted that he was better than the old lot. In Frost's off-the-cuff summation, it was smart Alec against dull Alec. Of course Wilson was not really any kind of outsider in politics. As an old Whitehall hand who had worked in the Cabinet Office and with Beveridge, who had visited Moscow and Washington for complex trade and business talks, he was formidably experienced by the time he took office, simply a different brand of insider. Yet he turned this to his advantage too. Britain had been going through a time of self-doubt, partly because of the seedy revelations of the Profumo affair and fears of moral decay among the old ruling class, but more importantly because of economic decline. Wilson's propaganda triumph was to bring the two themes together. The country needed to sweep away privilege and cobwebbed aristocracy, and replace it with ruthless and 'purposive' modern planning. Faced with the choice between socialists of the far left variety and the capitalist toffs, Wilson found a third way that would have appealed to Tony Blair thirty years later. It sounded unanswerable, exciting, yet vague. It was science.

In his speech to Labour's 1963 conference, the most famous he ever made, Wilson promised a scientific revolution which would require wholesale social change. 'The Britain that is going to be forged in the white heat of this revolution will be no place for restrictive practices or for outdated methods ... those charged with the control of our affairs must be ready to think and speak in the language of our scientific age.' It was a time, after Sputnik, when the awesome power of Communist Russian science mesmerized and terrified the West. Wilson said he had studied 'the formidable Soviet challenge in the education of scientists and technologists and above all, in the ruthless application of scientific techniques in Soviet industry'. As a democrat he rejected their methods but 'we must use all the resources of democratic planning, all the latent and underdeveloped energies and skills of our people, to ensure Britain's standing in the world'. If one replaces the archaic fear of Soviet power and replaces it with the contemporary fear of the rising economies of China and India, then Wilson's rhetoric, with its emphasis on wasted and under-educated skills, is strikingly similar to the language of New Labour in the twenty-first century.

For Wilson, the real answers were the same ones that the Attlee government had tried. State ownership and state planning would end the inefficiencies of the private system. There would be a huge expansion of university places, new state direction of R&D, even a state-sponsored chemical engineering consortium. He was offering an answer to the stop-go demand management of the Tory years. Instead, Labour would grow the economy through the supply-side reforms of better education and higher investment in science. This was the man who had been in the wartime ministry of mines, plotting the rationalization of the coal industry, who had been President of the Board of Trade in the late forties. It was the vision of an old-fashioned civil service man. But it sidestepped the weary ideological battles inside the Labour Party between right and left, and it sounded modern. From the late seventeenth century, 'science' always has done.

The problem Wilson would soon face was how to achieve a successful planned economy in a capitalist world. For all his abuse of them, the Tories had already set out on the same road. In 1962 suitably modern, scientific British businesses, such as Dunlop and Ferranti, were represented at the table alongside trade union leaders and Whitehall mandarins at the first meeting of the National Economic Development Council, or 'Neddy'. As Labour would also discover, simply talking and making optimistic forecasts was entirely useless. The Tory industrial experience of the early sixties, from the failed attempts to get voluntary agreements on prices and incomes, to the direction of entire industries in order to combat regional unemployment, were there to be learned from. But the tactical fun of teasing a Tory regime to death meant more to Wilson than carefully studying how to be a success in Downing Street.

Wilson's zigzagging through Labour factions had hardly been glorious but it had made him ruthless.

He turned this ruthlessness against the Conservatives, making unfair but funny attacks on Douglas-Home's inability to understand economics except with matchsticks, and his archaic background as a Fourteenth Earl. (Though the Prime Minister famously hit back by mildly replying that he supposed – when you thought about it – he supposed Mr Wilson was the Fourteenth Mr Wilson.) Wilson's chutzpah and increasingly self-confident style have been ascribed by many people to his political secretary Marcia Williams. Later she would become a byword for clique and scandal but she was a brilliant and loyal if unpredictable player in Wilson's inner team. She was described by another member of it, the press secretary Joe Haines, as possessing 'a brilliant political mind – probably better than any other woman of her generation'. She would rant and rail at Wilson and treated him at times like a naughty schoolboy. Many believed she had had an affair with Wilson. 'Funny fellow, Wilson,' said Macmillan. 'Keeps his mistress at Number Ten. Always kept mine in St John's Wood.' By another account, she once confronted Mary Wilson and told her she had had sex with her husband several times years before 'and it wasn't satisfactory'. She and he always denied this and would set libel lawyers (successfully) on journalists who repeated such stories. Even so, since Wilson's death some have gone much further, asserting that the Russians had blackmailed him about Marcia, persuading him to work for them. This seems highly unlikely. The Mitrokhin archive seems to clear him. What can safely be said is that she helped build up his morale, challenged his complacency and, until her apparent

356

bullying became intolerable, probably made him a better politician than he would otherwise have been.

Some Bad News, Minister ...

Labour came to power confronted by economic choices which would torture it in office and come close to destroying it for good when it was finally defeated at the end of the seventies. From the first weekend in October 1964 when Wilson, his Chancellor Jim Callaghan and the other senior ministers picked up their briefing papers, appalling dilemmas stared them in the face. On the face of it, the economy was not doing so badly. Inflation was still low, though rising. Unemployment was relatively low. Productivity was respectable, though falling behind Britain's competitors. Strikes were a problem. Britain's falling share of world markets was a problem. But these were all issues voters might have expected a fresh, vigorous, forward-looking new government to be able to grip. A darker story was laid bare in the official briefings. Britain under the Tories had been wildly overspending. It was living on borrowed money. Britain's balance of payments was eyed with increasing worry and suspicion by its creditors, the Americans above all. Longer term, the only solution was for the British economy to become more successful, growing faster without sucking in inflation. Labour had ideas about that – more investment, more planning, a better educated workforce. But this would take time. And there was no time.

When Callaghan arrived in Downing Street on the Friday evening after the election, his predecessor, the easy-going Tory Chancellor Reggie Maudling, is said to have passed him on the way out, stopped with his coat on his arm and apologized: 'Sorry to leave such a mess, old cock.' He wasn't talking about the furnishings. Callaghan's Treasury officials presented him with 500 typed pages, arranged into forty-nine sections. They showed that the deficit the Tories had left him was far worse than previously thought, some £800m and that he would have to begin with a programme of savage spending cuts and tax rises. Even then the pound, still a world 'reserve' currency, would be under constant pressure. This was bad enough. Labour had been elected promising a more generous welfare system, better pensions, spending on schools and much more. That was immediately in jeopardy. Prized national projects including the supersonic airliner project jointly developed with the French, Concorde, were under threat of being axed. The Governor of the Bank of England, Lord Cromer, regarded by Labour ministers as a Tory reactionary, was quickly insisting that the deflationary squeeze must be tighter still and that other pet Labour projects such as the renationalization of steel must be dropped. He only desisted when Wilson warned him that, in that case, he might have to hold an immediate election on the theme 'who governs Britain?' – familiar later on, but in the 1964 context meaning, elected politicians or bankers? It was hardly surprising that the new team felt shocked and

358

somehow betrayed. Callaghan, who had lost his Baptist faith years before, began to pray again.[2]

Cuts and tax rises apart, there was one other obvious policy choice, which was to devalue the pound and in effect try to start again. Initially devaluation was entirely ruled out by Wilson, Callaghan and Brown who met privately on the Saturday following the 1964 election. They saw it as humiliating for Britain, cruel to poorer nations keeping their money in sterling, and possibly deadly for the Labour Party which was still saddled with the memory of devaluation in 1949. Beyond that, buffeted by the pressures on the pound and the brusque demands to cut and to tax, their only answer was – more planning. As we have seen the Conservatives had already been taken by the idea. Beeching's brutal reshaping of the railways had been an early example of the new ruthlessness. Meanwhile 'Neddy' had begun work three years before Labour came to power. Industrialists and trade unionists were sitting round large tables, creating working groups and setting plans for growth – in exports, personal consumption, government spending, capital investment. Under Maudling, the Tories had also tried voluntary restraint in prices and incomes and a National Plan.

This was all meant to be French. In the early sixties, Paris was in vogue among the politicians, just as Parisian philosophers, film-makers and singers were in vogue among the beatniks in their black turtlenecks who frequented the coffee bars a mile north of Westminster. France's system did not use production quotas or targets like the Soviet bloc. Instead 'indicative planning' meant the state directing money and materials into particular industries, regions and products, while obliging French banks to invest in new factories and techniques. This had begun in the shattered post-war nation of 1947 under the brandy merchant's son and father of the EU, Jean Monnet. Fifteen years on, France was connected by new rail and road systems, her town planning seemed radical and effective compared to the mess of British cities, and from jet fighters to cars, engineering to plastics, she appeared more technologically successful than her old adversary. But Britain did not have the crisp centralism of the French political elite, nor the self-confident young technocrats being churned out of the new system of elite education created by President de Gaulle's post-war revolution, the *enarques*. Britain had mutually suspicious captains of industry and union barons, plus a few economists and a highly independent, rather anti-manufacturing City. Under the Conservatives cheerful growth figures were duly agreed, and bore absolutely no relation to what then transpired. There were no levers.

It might have been thought that Labour, preparing for power, would have taken note. Nothing of the sort. George Brown, after swallowing his bitter disappointment at failing to become Labour leader, was soon dreaming of a dramatic new role for himself as knight commander of the British economy. The Tories' trouble, he told the Labour conference, was that they didn't really believe in planning, which was why it was not working. Faith was needed, said Brother George. Whether or not it still moved mountains, then faith would at least move factories and output figures. It was the same vague, cheerful, fairies-in-the-garden

360

faith in science and professionalism articulated by the wartime planner Harold Wilson. Yet professionalism, never mind science, was sadly lacking. Brown wanted to run a new ministry which would oversee everything, dominating even the Treasury. Like many Labour people he believed that the Treasury was rigidly conservative and therefore to blame for economic failure. As he later wrote, 'we were all ... expansionists at heart.' To take on the self-confident Treasury, as well as the Bank of England and by implication the City, might be regarded as rash. To succeed it would certainly need wily and careful preparation. Yet in a hurried, amateurish way the home policy committee of the Labour Party drew up its plans in 1963 to create a new department to run the economy. This would be known variously as the Ministry of Economic Expansion, the Ministry of Production, and eventually the Department of Economic Affairs, or DEA. No single document was ever produced giving details of how the DEA would work; its relationship with the Treasury; or its ultimate powers. The final agreement to go ahead with it was completed by Brown and Wilson late at night in the back of a taxi during the short journey between a London hotel and the Commons. Brown later conceded with uncharacteristic understatement: 'I think it is a pity that we didn't produce a "blueprint" setting out precisely what we wanted to achieve.'[3]

Meanwhile over at the Treasury some of the brightest minds were planning how to frustrate Brown's intended coup. In scenes which might have come from the post-1980 television satire *Yes, Minister,* a new dividing line was drawn through the building which left George Brown's DEA with a scattering of empty rooms and almost no staff. To find out about the economy Brown's newly appointed private secretary, Tom Caulcott, had virtually to steal the key economic briefing papers and smuggle them to Brown at his home. Many of the key staff Brown had hoped to use in the DEA were hurriedly switched to jobs in Downing Street or the Treasury itself before he could get his hands on them. In this stiff-collared boycott of facts, people and equipment, Caulcott even had to snatch a typewriter. Bullying and hectoring, Brown would eventually get his department up and running. In a blaze of energy he would then write another and more detailed National Plan. Yet without the oversight of taxation and spending controls operated by the Treasury machine his authority was not based on much beyond personality. Increasingly desperate, Brown went charging off round Whitehall on unexpected and often tempestuous personal visits, storming at other ministers. Breaking Whitehall protocol, he insisted on a private phone line that went directly to his desk, avoiding his private office. But the civil service is harder to beat than that. Caulcott simply arranged with the Post Office to have Brown's phone bugged. And to ensure his private office knew when he was setting off on another personal mission, they had a discreet buzzer attached to his door which would alert them as he left so he could be followed.

Unaware, Brown drew together the usual industrialists, trade union leaders and civil servants and hammered out proposals for a British economic miracle, more detailed than the

Tory version, but equally lacking in levers. His first move was to create a 'Declaration of Intent' committing both sides of industry to voluntary wages and prices controls and within his first year he had a full-blown National Plan, with economic planning councils set up across Britain. One sympathetic biographer called this 'a huge personal achievement, the result of working immensely long hours, breaking every convention to get his own way and successively bullying and charming and ultimately exhausting those whose support he required'.[4] There was much shouting at officials, much searching for key documents hidden by the Treasury, which had by now taken to calling its would-be rival the Department for Extraordinary Aggression. The trouble was that by the time Brown's deal-making marathon had been completed, the economy was in such trouble voluntary controls were impossible. The Treasury had squeezed the DEA into irrelevance before it properly got going.

Crossman, the cabinet minister and diarist, was worried as early as December 1964 at the absence of economic strategy as the pound came under increasing pressure. Both Callaghan and Brown were routinely describing the situation privately as desperate; Labour's promises to its supporters, including pensioners, were already impossible to fund. Crossman recorded: 'The pound is still being nibbled away and I feel the cabinet isn't very firm or very stable because the central leadership isn't there, the sense of priorities, the sense of grip that you need. Yes, we've got a remarkable man in Harold Wilson and a good man in George Brown ... But what we still lack is that coherent, strong control which is real policy.'[5] Roy Jenkins, later to become Chancellor himself, recorded a similar assessment. So long as the pound remained expensive compared to the dollar, 'there was hardly an event in the world which did not produce a British currency crisis. And the only way of dealing with such a crisis was a new package of hastily approved deflationary measures which seemed bereft of any strategic framework.'[6] This left the DEA a marooned and rudderless creature once the cuts had destroyed its growth targets. Brown was moved to the Foreign Office in 1966 and the department was passed around until eventually it came under the personal control of Wilson, an idea that came to him in the middle of the night after he had been woken by his adored but delinquent labrador, Paddy. That did no good, and the DEA died.

Empty Pots and Magic Boxes

In other areas, Labour was on the move. Tony Crosland, a dashing ex-paratrooper and admirer of Hugh Gaitskell, has featured earlier in this history for his rebellion against socialist puritanism and his seminal book *The Future of Socialism,* which called on the left to accept the consumer society and the mixed economy. By 1965, as MP for Grimsby, he was a rising Labour star, a glamorous, cheroot-smoking, rough-tongued man known for his ferocious attacks on the public school system. He had recently married the exceptionally beautiful divorced American journalist Susan Catling, acquired two stepdaughters and moved into a house in London's Notting Hill, no longer the scene of riots and not yet the backdrop for glossy films. Wilson had made him Education Secretary after offering the job to Crosland's friend and rival Roy Jenkins, whose children were at private schools. Crosland's next two years would make him one of the most controversial, reviled and admired ministers in the history of British schooling. His wife Susan wrote a book about him which is as tender and eloquent a portrait of a twentieth-century British politician as exists, but in it she also revealed a couple of sentences he uttered to her which have been hung around Crosland's reputation ever since. Luckily for posterity, the journalist in her trumped the pious memorialist. It was late one night in their home when he had been at a wearisome dinner with teachers' associations. Crosland's tread was ominous as he mounted the stairs.

He stopped at our bedroom door.
'Good evening. You'd better come in the study.'
I put my novel aside and got smartly out of our bed, wondering what had caused this latest vexation.
'If it's the last thing I do, I'm going to destroy every fucking grammar school in England,' he said. 'And Wales. And Northern Ireland.'
'Why not Scotland?' I asked out of pure curiosity.
'Because their schools come under the Secretary of State for Scotland.' He began to

laugh at his inability to destroy their grammar schools.[7]

By 1965 the post-war division of children into potential intellectuals, technical workers and drones – gold, silver and lead – was thoroughly discredited. The private or 'public' schools still thrived, with around 5 per cent of the country's children creamed off through their exclusive portals. For the other 95 per cent, ever since 1944, state schooling was meant to be divided into three types of school. In practice, however, there were just two. For roughly a quarter of children there were the grammar schools, offering traditional academic teaching, including much memorizing and strict discipline. The grandest of these were the 179 direct-grant schools, effectively independent of central government and often with strong traditions of their own – schools such as Manchester Grammar, Haberdashers' Aske's, Elstree, and King Edward's in Birmingham. They tended to be long-established schools, town academies or old foundations, with uniforms, badges and school songs to match. Their brighter children would be expected to go to the expanding university sector and to become professionals. Alongside them, also traditionalist in atmosphere but with less independence and status, were some 1,500 ordinary grammar schools, maintained by the local authorities.

For the other three-quarters of state-educated children there were the secondary moderns, frankly second-rate and often in buildings which reflected their lower status. As one writer observed in 1965, 'modern' had become a curious euphemism for 'less clever'. Some of these schools were truly dreadful, sparsely staffed, crowded into ancient and unsuitable buildings and sitting almost no pupils for outside examinations before most were released to start work at fifteen. At A-level, in 1964, the secondary moderns, with around 72 per cent of Britain's children, had 318 candidates. The public schools, with 5 per cent, had 9,838. The third kind of school originally planned in 1944 was to have been the technical school, teaching specific practical skills on German lines, but these had been forgotten. In practice there was therefore a sharp, public, sheep-and-goats division of the country's children which took place at eleven years old through the 'eleven-plus' examination. It in turn was based on an IQ test supposed to scientifically measure intelligence. Among those who made it to the grammar schools, many hated being separated from their old friends – George Best and Neil Kinnock being among the innumerable examples of eleven-plus successes who then bunked off or frittered their school days in a mood of rebellion. Many of the majority who were rejected and sent to the secondary moderns never got over the sense of rejection and failure. John Prescott never forgot that his brother passed, and was given a bicycle while he failed and wasn't. Rifts opened in families. Siblings turned on each other.

Any schooling system has some problems. Most involve unfairness at one stage or another. Academic selection and examinations require children to fail, as well as to succeed. But by the late fifties, there were larger complaints. The IQ tests were shown not to be nearly as reliable as first thought. Substantial minorities, up to 60,000 children a year, were at the 'wrong' school and many were being transferred later, up or down. Different education authorities had wildly different proportions of grammar school and secondary modern places – division by geography, not examination. A big expansion of teachers and buildings was needed to deal with those post-war baby-boom children who were now reaching secondary school. Across Britain, there were rotting buildings and a shortage of around 60,000 teachers. Desperately looking for money, education authorities snatched at the savings a simpler comprehensive system might produce. Socialists who wanted more equality, among whom Crosland had long been prominent, were against the eleven-plus on ideological grounds. But many articulate middle-class parents who would never have called themselves socialist were equally against it because their children had failed to get grammar school places. With all these pressures, education authorities – that is, local councillors, not national politicians – had begun to move towards a one-school-for-all or comprehensive system during the Conservative years. Tory councils were doing this, as well as Labour ones. The Conservative Education Secretary, a man on the left of his party, Sir Edward Boyle, found that ninety of the 146 education authorities in England and Wales were making some moves towards comprehensive schooling by 1962.[8]

So when Crosland took over, the great schooling revolution, which has caused so much controversy ever since, was well under way. There were already comprehensives, on the Swedish model, and they were much admired for their huge scale, airy architecture and apparent modernity. The first had been Kidbrooke in Blackheath, south-east London, which opened for 2,200 girls in 1954. Grammar schools across the country were fighting back, particularly in cities with a strong sense of their history, such as Bristol and Nottingham, but across the country generally they were losing ground. What Crosland did was to hasten their destruction. He did this not by ordering the education authorities to go comprehensive but by requesting them to, in what has been described as the most famous circular in the history of the education department, directive 10/65. He did not say how many comprehensives must be opened nor how many grammar schools should be shut down. But by making government money for new school building conditional on going comprehensive, the change was greatly accelerated.

By 1970 when Wilson was defeated, a third of children were at comprehensives and a mere eight education authorities were holding on to the old division. The revolution simply rolled on. Edward Heath, devoted to his old grammar school, had promised to stop bullying education authorities into destroying grammar schools. Crosland's 10/65 was duly withdrawn, and Heath appointed that ultimate enthusiast for the grammar schools system, Margaret Thatcher, as Education Secretary. She duly announced a presumption against further shake-up and change. But what happened? Out of 3,612 proposals for comprehensives sent to Mrs Thatcher, she turned down just 326 and the proportion of children at comprehensives nearly doubled again, up from 32 per cent under Labour to 62 per cent under this thoroughly Conservative politician. As one of her biographers flatly pointed out, 'for all her strong prejudices against them ... Margaret Thatcher approved more schemes for comprehensive schools, and the abolition of more grammar schools, than any other Secretary of State before or since.'[9] Heath, who fought a tough campaign as Prime Minister to save his local grammar school in Bexley, blamed the desire of Tory-led authorities to save money by replacing boys-only and girls-only grammars with co-ed comprehensives. He also confessed: 'The tide was strong, but I do wish in retrospect, that the many supporters of selection had all campaigned more vigorously before it was too late.'[10]

There had always been a contradiction in the way comprehensives were sold, which was neatly summed up by Wilson when he promised that they would offer 'a grammar school education for all'. Since the essence of grammar schools was that they selected only the brightest children, this was plainly a ridiculous suggestion. Yet Wilson was reflecting back something that was deeply rooted among parents and many Labour voters, which was a simple enthusiasm for 'good' education, meaning traditional teaching in a disciplined environment, popularly associated with grammar schools. Most other countries, after all, had traditionalist, even rote-learning education in a single state system without the division of schools by academic ability. If the Germans and Americans, the French, Russians and Swedes could do it, why not the British?

It was the singular misfortune of the comprehensive experiment that it coincided with a move away from traditional education to what was called child-centred teaching. In the long run, this may well have been more important than any structural reorganization of schools. Instead of viewing the child as an empty pot, happily large or sadly small, into which a given quantity of facts and values could be poured, the new teaching regarded the child as a magic box, crammed with integrity and surprise, which should be carefully unwrapped. Perhaps a more organic metaphor is called for. The young sapling should be watered and admired, not tied to a stick, nor pruned. Here was a fundamental disagreement about the nature of humanity and social order. Philosophically it goes back to the French thinkers of the eighteenth century but it was fought out in concrete form in British classrooms throughout this period. The old rows of desks facing a blackboard began to go, and cosily intimate semicircles of chairs appeared. Children of different abilities were taught in the same room, so that they could learn from each other, causing some chaos and boredom. Topics replaced lists. Grammar retreated and creativity advanced. Teachers began to dress informally and encourage the use of an Adrian or Sara, rather than Sir or Miss. Corporal punishment went from state schools entirely and on the vast, windy sites of the seventies comprehensives, with their modernist airiness, discipline loosened. The elite remained mainly in private schools, taught much as their parents and grandparents had been. But across the country millions of parents shook their heads and wondered. Hostility to comprehensives, which would swell through the eighties and nineties, was much of the time really hostility to trendy teaching, the spirit of the sixties which was being marshalled and organized in scores of teacher training colleges.

Crosland's legacy went far beyond comprehensives. He was a high spender on education, as was Margaret Thatcher, both believing long before Tony Blair that there was no better way of investing taxes than in 'education, education, education'. In particular, he oversaw a big expansion of higher education, the creation of thirty polytechnics to supplement Britain's universities. These were to develop the technical and practical higher education enjoyed by Germans and French students but which was sadly lacking in the fustier and more academic British universities. This offended the universities, not surprisingly, who had been hoping for a major expansion in their own right. The Robbins Report had reminded the country that just 5 per cent of British youngsters went into higher education, as compared to 25 per cent of Americans or 12 per cent of French. There was a major expansion underway, from the trendiest of all, Sussex University at Brighton, to the 'redbricks' which were in fact often concrete, granite or plate glass erections, from Liverpool to Bristol, Aberdeen to Southampton. But Crosland argued the then-fashionable case that Britain needed technical and industrial colleges on the German model far more than universities. Britain had to get away from 'its snobbish, caste-ridden hierarchical obsession with university status'.[11] Later, the wheel would come full circle when the polytechnics and other colleges would simply be allowed to call themselves universities, but at the time the Crosland ideology seemed on a par with his crusade for comprehensives, a vigorous attack on the old and traditional in favour of a more efficient and egalitarian new Britain.

Perhaps the proudest educational achievement of the Wilson years was the Open University. It too was nothing if not new. First proposed in 1962 by the same Michael Young who had co-written Labour's 1945 manifesto, the Open University was hatched in government by Jennie Lee, a Scottish miner's daughter, and Nye Bevan's widow. Originally described as a 'university of the air', the OU was meant to offer higher education to millions who had not had the chance to go to a campus university. Lee was determined that it should offer serious, heavyweight degree courses, taught by academics with a strong reputation. Attacked by the Conservatives at the time as 'blithering nonsense', it aimed to use television and the postal service to teach degree-level courses in everything from the sciences to history and law. It has been one of the most successful and liberating acts by a post-war government in education. Its critics attacked it first for being not elite enough, and later for attracting too many middle-class women but by the mid-2000s, the OU was being ranked in the top five British universities for teaching quality and had given qualifications to some 600,000 of the 2 million people who studied with it. This is often credited as Wilson's great contribution, and he was a great supporter; but Jennie Lee was the heroine of a hundred committee fights to create it.

As for Crosland he would go on to serve as the Environment Secretary who warned the high-spending local authorities in 1975 that 'the party's over' but the destruction of Labour's own high-spending instincts in the economic storm of the seventies blew away the easy optimism of his political philosophy. In 1977, still hoping to be Chancellor and after enduring a dinner sitting beside a woman whose conversation about the EEC he said was killing him, Crosland died of a stroke at the age of fifty-eight.

Roy Jenkins's Britain

The greatest changes of the Labour years were achieved by Roy Jenkins, a man Wilson had always distrusted. Back in the Tory years when he was slim and dashing, Roy Jenkins had set out his case for social reforms which would remove the State's powers over individual freedoms. He argued that the 'ghastly apparatus of the gallows' must go, as well as judicial flogging; that the persecution of homosexuals should end, as Wolfenden had suggested; that the Lord Chamberlain's powers to censor stage plays must also end; that the 'harsh and archaic' law forbidding almost all abortions should be changed; that the divorce laws, which caused unnecessary suffering, should be reformed; and that the immigration laws needed to be made more civilized. Through the mid-sixties, all these changes happened. Hanging went in 1965, before Jenkins became Home Secretary, but there was a softening on immigration in 1966, flogging went in 1967, the same year as the liberalization of abortion law, and the decriminalization of private homosexual acts between men aged over twenty-one. State censorship of plays ended in 1968, and

374

the following year, the divorce laws were liberalized. Jenkins had also called for changes to the laws on suicide and on alcohol licensing, and those came later; but it was a formidable drum-roll of libertarian change, without precedent and never matched. Ever afterwards, Roy Jenkins has been either praised or demonized as the most liberal Home Secretary in British history, the man more responsible for the permissive society than any other. But though he himself called his first spell at the Home Office 'the liberal hour' one of the oddities of this is that Jenkins was personally responsible for few of these measures. They were private members' bills.

The abolition of hanging, on a free vote in 1965 was led by the Labour backbencher Sydney Silverman. He was building on a rising tide of disquiet about judicial death in Britain. The 8 a.m. ritual carried out from condemned cells throughout the country, often using a portable gallows transported from Pentonville Prison in London, with its pinions, white hood, last glass of brandy and unmarked grave in prison grounds, had been followed with intense interest throughout modern times. By the mid-fifties many thought the practice uncivilized. Famous writers such as Arthur Koestler, scourge of the Stalinists who had faced death himself, and famous broadcasters such as Ludovic Kennedy, were gaining a public hearing against capital punishment. That might have remained an elite interest, had it not been for some hangings that caused more general queasiness.

In 1952 two teenagers were involved in the murder of a policeman during a robbery. The one who actually fired the shot, Christopher Craig, was sixteen at the time and therefore escaped the rope. But he was accompanied by Derek Bentley who at nineteen was old enough to be hanged. He was being held by police when the murder occurred and he had the mental age of a child, but was judged guilty. Despite a national campaign for clemency and a letter signed by more than 200 MPs, the hardline Tory Home Secretary Sir David Maxwell-Fyfe, one of the judges at Nuremberg, whom we met earlier busily persecuting homosexuals, ordered Bentley's execution to go ahead. On 13 July 1955 a young mother, Ruth Ellis, was hanged for the murder of her faithless lover, the last woman to be executed in Britain. The following year the man who had killed her, Britain's famous executioner Albert Pierrepoint, pub landlord and member of a family of public hangmen, resigned from his job. He had ended the lives of 433 men and seventeen women, ranging from frightened boys who had been in the wrong place, to some of the worst Nazi war criminals. Many believed he had retired out of a sense of disgust. This was far from the case. Pierrepoint had been having an argument about his last fee when he turned up one cold morning to find the prisoner had been granted clemency. Later he would revise his original view and support abolition.

Though there was still formidable public support for hanging, MPs were becoming increasingly unhappy about it. Silverman formed a national campaign to end the death penalty. In 1957 the Tory government radically slimmed down the offences which demanded capital punishment, to five forms of murder. The number of hangings fell from an average of fifteen a year in the first half of the fifties, to about four a year. The executions still however included some odd decisions, such as the putting to death of Hendryk Niemasz who appeared to have killed while he was sleepwalking. Against this background, the anti-hanging majority in the Commons, which had before been frustrated by the pro-hanging House of Lords, became steadily more assertive. In Silverman, a left-wing pacifist from a very poor Jewish family who had served time in Wormwood Scrubs for his views during the First World War, the anti-hanging movement had a persistent and eloquent leader, able to win over such notable non-liberals as the future Home Secretary and Prime Minister, Jim Callaghan. In two days in August 1964 three men were hanged for murder, a 21-year-old Scot who had killed a seaman, and who was executed in Aberdeen, an Englishman in Walton Prison in Liverpool, and a Welshman in Manchester's Strangeways Prison. They were the last. Hanging was abolished for almost every offence – in practice, ended completely – in 1965. Initially the abolition was for a trial period of five years; it was then formally abolished. This did not make Britain strikingly liberal by Western standards, though executions went on in France, by guillotine, until 1977 and continue in the United States now.

The Sexual Offences Bill which ended the indictment of homosexuals, was led by another Labour backbencher, Leo Abse – also as it happens a Jewish left-winger, from a poor background and, like Silverman, a passionate lawyer, regarded with a mixture of admiration and suspicion by the Labour front bench. Here too, politicians were reacting to a changing mood, if not among the whole public, then at least among what would later be called with easy disparagement, the chattering classes. John Wolfenden, whose report in 1957 had called for the decriminalization of homosexual acts in private between consenting adults, was a public school headmaster. His committee included the whole card-deck of great and good professionals, from presbyterian clergy and a professor of moral theology to Tory MPs. After his conclusions were rejected by the Conservative government, the campaign spread, though it was a cliquish affair. It opened with a letter to the *Spectator* followed by another to *The Times.* Lord Attlee was a supporter, as was A. J. Ayer, the philosopher. When the Homosexual Law Reform Society was formed in May 1958, its founders included clergy, publishers, poets and MPs, few of them homosexual themselves; its first full-time worker was a married vicar, Andrew Hallidie Smith. Its first big public meeting at London's Caxton Hall attracted a thousand people.

Harold Wilson's government was privately divided about legalizing homosexuality; in general the more conventional working-class members of the cabinet were least enthusiastic and the liberal intellectuals, such as Crosland and Jenkins, were most supportive. If anything, the Conservative benches, packed with former public schoolboys, were privately more tolerant than the Labour ones. Wilson was judged to be privately hostile to reform. Yet as with hanging, the tacit support of the Home Office and its guarantee of enough parliamentary time to get the measure through, helped to win the day. And as with hanging, in Abse the measure had a hyperactive and persistent advocate. A factory worker and communist sympathiser before the war, who fought in the RAF before becoming a lawyer, Abse would go on to show time and again that backbenchers need not be lobby fodder but can affect real change. He was a curious, peacock character whose application of Freudian analysis to other politicians caused much mirth and offence later on: a whiff of his style can be had from the title of his book *Fellatio, Masochism, Politics and Love,* published in 2000. In time the Sexual Offences Act of 1967 would be criticized by gay activists for not going nearly far enough in giving equality before the law. The age of consent was higher and 'privacy' was judged very narrowly indeed, leading to a spate of indecency convictions after the law was passed. But it was a landmark nevertheless, building on the shifts in attitude that had begun in the fifties and perhaps even earlier, during the war.

If the anti-hanging movement can be traced to the executions of Bentley and Ellis, and the homosexual reform movement to revulsion against the purge of the fifties, the abortion law reform movement can be traced to two unrelated, horrible stories. The first was the rape of a fourteen-year-old girl by some guardsmen in a West London barracks shortly before the war. After one doctor refused to perform an abortion, on the grounds that since her life was not in danger he would be breaking the law, another doctor, Alick Bourne, stepped in. He performed the operation and was duly prosecuted. Bourne defended himself on the grounds that the girl's fragile mental health meant that the abortion was, in practice, essential. He won and became an instant hero to the small female campaign which

379

had been set up to reform the abortion law in 1936. (From their point of view, this was a mistake: Bourne would later recant, declaring that mass abortions would be 'the greatest holocaust in history' and in 1945 he would become a founding member of the anti-abortion group, the Society for the Protection of the Unborn Child, or Spuc.) The second event was much more widespread. It was the Thalidomide drug disaster of 1959–62. This alleged wonder drug, which helped sleeplessness, colds, flu and morning sickness, was responsible for huge numbers of badly deformed children being born, many missing all or some of their limbs. Opinion polls at the time showed large public majorities in favour of abortions when the foetus was deformed. This was far more influential than the actions of the Abortion Law Reform Association, which had just over 1,100 members at the time.

Abortion was also clearly a class issue. In the early sixties an estimated 10,000 private abortions were taking place in Harley Street and other West End clinics, where relevant paperwork had been obtained and plenty of cash had changed hands. At the other end of the social scale, horrific back-street abortions with coat-hangers, chemicals and rubber pumps were causing injuries and some deaths. Around 35,000 women a year were being treated in National Health Service hospitals for botched abortions. Even if one takes a middle figure between the 100,000 and quarter of a million illegal abortions then taking place (vagueness about numbers is inevitable, given the hidden and private nature of the abortions) this suggests very large numbers of young women were exposing themselves to terrible risk. By the mid-sixties, botched abortions were the main cause of avoidable maternal death. It was a theme that would be crucial to the MP who took on this reform, the next in the series of backbench nation-changers.

David Steel, a Scottish Liberal who had just been elected to the Commons in a by-election, was still in his twenties and just two years out of law school. 'The Boy David' would go on to lead his party and be the first Presiding Officer of the Scottish Parliament, but his dogged battle to legalize abortion was the most controversial fight of his life. He had come third in the ballot for private members' bills in 1966 and initially thought he would try to pilot through homosexual law reform, until he realized the level of hostility in Scotland (where the law would remain unchanged for years to come) meant it could only be an English and Welsh measure. A serious-minded young man, Steel had been much impressed by the Church of England's recent report on abortion, arguing the Christian case for its moderate use, and attended an abortion for himself before deciding. But essentially, he was put up to it by Roy Jenkins. Like Silverman and Abse, he had much expert opinion on his side – not a Wolfenden Report or the passionate books of philosophers, but the World Health Organization, which had declared in 1946 that health meant 'complete mental, physical and social well-being'. This implied that mental suffering to the woman could be grounds for abortion. It was written into the bill and today of the 180,000 abortions taking place each year in Britain, all but 2 per cent of them are on just such grounds.

Though these were the most famous, or

infamous, moments of Roy Jenkins's 'liberal hour' they were not the only ones. The old law on divorce, which generally required evidence that one party had committed adultery, and therefore the whole jig of private detectives, cameras, hotel rooms and often staged 'in flagrante' moments, would finally be ended in 1969 by the Divorce Reform Act. This was also part of the Jenkins agenda, and he had wanted to see it through two years earlier. The new law allowed divorce if a couple had lived apart for two years and both wanted it, or if they had lived apart for five years and one partner wanted divorce. This 'irretrieveable breakdown' clause, often oddly called 'no-fault divorce', was followed by a rocketing rate of divorces rising from around 7 per cent of marriages in the late fifties to close to 50 per cent now. The causes of this domestic revolution are many, and include greater publicity about sexual gratification, domestic violence and greater female financial independence. But the 1969 Act was a huge factor.

Then there was the Theatres Act of 1968, again taken through by a Labour backbencher, George Strauss, one of the founders of *Tribune,* which finally ended the Lord Chamberlain's censorship role after a particularly controversial verdict against a play at the Royal Court, *Saved* by Edward Bond. The Lord Chamberlain of the time, Kim Cobbold, was privately grateful for the end of his role. Though shows like *Hair* and *Oh, Calcutta!* quickly exploited the new freedoms of the stage to the disgust of Middle England, there was hardly a tide of filth spewing across the stage. Over the next decade or two, the plays which were genuinely controversial would be rare enough to produce media cyclones; yet hardly anyone called for the return of the Lord High Censor and his blue pencil.

Jenkins turns out to be the single most influential politician of the sixties, though never Prime Minister himself. All of these measures were given vital help by him, following a personal agenda he had set out years earlier and vigorously pursued by exercising personal decision-making and persuasive powers in the cabinet and Commons. Most private members' bills fail because they run out of time for debate (something controlled by the government). Jenkins ensured there was plenty of time. He helped pick and coach backbench leaders for reform. On numerous occasions he spoke for them. So why had he not led the charge himself? The simple answer is that Wilson's cabinet was a lot less liberal than Jenkins was, with three or four ministers utterly opposed to each of these measures. Wilson was hostile, for instance, to the ending of stage censorship, partly because he was nervous about the forthcoming stage version of *Private Eye*'s satirical 'Mrs Wilson's Diary'. The Secretary of State for Scotland, Willie Ross, was hostile to almost all the reforms. And often, backbenchers who supported one liberalization would be against another. So Jenkins proposed what he called a 'stratagem' whereby he would give backbenchers time and freedom to attack first, while allowing himself the liberty to speak in their support. This allowed his cabinet critics to vote against the changes, which were carried after very long and highly emotional late-night debates.

All transpired just as Jenkins had hoped. He felt he was at the cutting edge of a war about what it meant to be civilized. Against him and the reformers were many clergy, including the Roman Catholic Church; millions of quietly conservative-minded citizens; and much of the political Establishment. When he arrived at the old ministerial rooms of the Home Secretary (long since gone) he found an air of gloom and some very suspicious officials. There was an indicator board in one corner of his office with the names of prisoners awaiting execution. Hanging was only suspended, as it were. Originally the board had shown the names moving steadily towards the date fixed for their hanging. Jenkins had it moved out and replaced with a fridge for white wine and soda.

After supporting the abolition of hanging, and after refusing to authorize the birching of a prisoner, he became a hate-figure among many ordinary policemen as well as for the grassroots of the Tory Party, something he seemed to regard as an honour. Yet he was not liberal on everything. He believed that crime would be cut more effectively by catching more criminals and getting more guilty verdicts, than by horrific punishments. One of his most important changes was to bring in majority verdicts for English juries (Scotland had always allowed them) rather than the old rule that they must be unanimous. Many of Jenkins's critics on the right opposed this. As he noted with a certain smugness much later, seventy-four Conservatives voted against, 'including Mrs Thatcher, who went into the lobby against the change which has contributed more to the conviction of professional and dangerous criminals than any measure which was introduced by her four Home Secretaries'.[12]

The social changes were rarely argued through with clarity, or indeed honesty. Abse later described the arguments he used about homosexuality, accepting that it was a pitiable medical condition that required treatment, as 'absolute crap'. Despite endless public debate, the abortion reformers entirely played down the significance of psychological health as a reason for a termination, passionately arguing that the bill was not a charter for abortion on demand – which it certainly became. The use of separation as ground for divorce, rather than proof of adultery, was said to be a measure which would strengthen marriage; if so, it was clearly a failure. It was argued and assumed that the end of hanging would not increase the rate of murder or violent crime. Both would soon rise sharply.

All these measures had the backing of small and dedicated campaigns, generally only a few thousand strong. Each depended on celebrity intellectuals of one kind or another, to finally slaughter legislation which went back to Victorian times – and in the case of hanging, far earlier. Whether it was the philosopher Bertrand Russell inveighing against the anti-homosexual laws, or Laurence Olivier giving evidence against theatre censorship, or the British Medical Association helping turn the mood on abortions, this was a social revolution led by eggheads and experts. It showed just how influential apparently marginal people could be in the Britain of the late fifties and mid-sixties. Liberals, though unimportant politically, indeed at their low point of the century, were particularly influential – not only Steel on abortion and Ludovic Kennedy on the death penalty, but through the parliamentary enthusiasm of their leader Jo Grimond. The left-wingers and intellectuals around *Tribune,* who were being elbowed aside by Wilson, also had a real influence on these non-economic issues.

The model for egghead-led change had been the famous court case of October 1960, Regina *v.* Penguin Books Ltd at the Old Bailey, better known as the 'Lady Chatterley' trial. Again, Jenkins was there: he had been the only MP on the committee of liberalizers whose work eventually produced the Obscene Publications Act of the previous year, now about to be tested. Defending Penguin's right to publish an unexpurgated text of Lawrence's novel about the love affair between a lady and a gamekeeper, with its phallic romps through the undergrowth, its scenes of copulation and buggery and, not least, its use of the words fuck and cunt, had brought together a coalition of the permissive. From the Bishop of Woolwich to E. M. Forster, these were the people who might be expected to append their names to letters to *The Times* about the evils of colonialism, or turn up at a pro-homosexual rights meeting, or support CND – the people who would be satirized mercilessly by Michael Wharton of the *Daily Telegraph* in his Beachcomber column, and by the cartoonist Osbert Lancaster. The list of witnesses for the 'Lady Chatterley' defence included Oxbridge professors, clergymen, famous writers, a future Tory MP, and a poet laureate. It was a unique coming together of liberal and intellectual strands in British public life. Left-wing and liberal Christian thought had been in the ascendant in the Church of England during and after the war, as we have seen; the wartime Archbishop William Temple was still being quoted at the 'Lady Chatterley' trial. The big publishing houses were often in the hands of men of the high-minded liberal and centre-left, Sir Allen Lane himself or Victor Gollancz. The leftish newspapers such as the *Observer, Manchester Guardian* and *News Chronicle,* not to mention the resurgent *Daily Mirror,* were at the height of their influence. As with abortion or the divorce law, expert advice was used to intimidate and mock the self-appointed guardians of tradition; and to good effect.

The tactic of finding irreproachably serious and well-regarded authority figures to front radical change, so confusing the forces of tradition, was first tested over 'Lady Chatterley'. Mervyn Griffith-Jones QC, an Old Etonian, ex-Grenadier Guard, summing up for the prosecution, was explicit about the historic nature of the choice before the jury. There must be, he pleaded, 'some standards of morality, some standards of language and conversation, some standards of conduct which are essential to the well-being of our society'. Since the war the country had been suffering from increasing sex obsession, a lack of restraint and moral discipline. The jury had heard a long list of experts, Griffith-Jones concluded: 'Members of the Jury, you will not be browbeaten by evidence given by these people … You will judge this as ordinary men and women, with your feet, I trust, firmly planted on the ground.'

But what was ordinary now? His question as to whether male jurymen would permit their wives or servants to read such a book caused hoots of laughter round the country. Their verdict against him concluded what had been a kind of genteel liberal carnival, the opening act of the permissive society that was coming. It would mean the publication of books which, unlike Lawrence's, were mainly to be read with one hand – John Cleland's eighteenth century porn-novel, *Fanny Hill,* Pauline Reage's sado-masochistic novel *The Story of 0,* and much else. In this sense the high-mindedness of the anti-censorship brigade would be quickly confounded. They had stood their ground on Lawrence, or James Joyce, elite writers. Doing so, they ushered in freedoms which would swiftly be exploited in ways they had not intended or foreseen. That, however, is the nature of freedoms.

Thus, small groups of the upper orders changed the rules of British life and found themselves unprepared for the torrent of change that followed. Some of the fastidious homosexual rights campaigners of the fifties and sixties were appalled by the shameless exuberance of the gay-lib movement. Many of the abortion rights campaigners, including David Steel himself, said later that they had not expected the sheer number of terminations that were then permitted. The argument about hanging raged more strongly, if anything, after abolition than it had before it. There were still strong conservative voices expressing unease and anger. In the Lords, the war hero Viscount Montgomery of Alamein said he favoured the age of homosexual consent being fixed at eighty. The Chief Scout protested about England going the way of ancient Greece and a bishop warned that the country was rife with 'buggers' clubs'. A world away, in a Midlands secondary school, an art teacher with strong Christian principles began planning her campaign against lewdness. Mary Whitehouse's Clean Up TV campaign would, from 1964, make her a major national figure who spoke for millions. Judges, local councils and hundreds of clergy who did not agree with the Bishop of Woolwich, would later be joined by journalists who had had second thoughts about the sixties – men such as Malcolm Muggeridge, Christopher Booker and Bernard Levin.

It is always dangerous to define an era by a few high-profile events taking place in London; yet, across Britain there is no doubt that traditional values were under attack and falling back in confusion. The reforms of the Jenkins era could all be regarded as denationalizations or 'social privatizations' in that they involved the State giving up powers that it had once had, backing away from its old authority. They can be seen as the social and moral equivalent of the industrial privatizations of the Thatcher years, when the State surrendered economic powers and ownership. The left tended to think people's private lives should be their own, even if they made choices traditional Christian society regarded as immoral; but that people's working lives, from how much they earned to where they worked, were fit for State interference. The right had a reverse view, that the State should uphold traditional moral codes with the full rigour of the law, but keep out of the economy as much as possible. The lasting changes made by each side are the ones in which politics did pull back, leaving the State smaller both morally and economically.

Did they make the country more civilized, as Jenkins and his supporters believed, or did they make it coarser and more dangerous, as right-wing commentary has alleged? Despite serious rises in violent crime, there is little campaigning for a return to hanging. Censorship too, seems something few modern Britons are keen on. Though divorce has become commonplace, causing great unhappiness as well as liberation, tougher laws to force people to remain married are on no political party's agenda. Homosexual rights have been increased; again, the movement seems all one way. Abortion, affected by changes in medical technology and by the influence of evangelical organizations, is probably the most disputed of the sixties reforms, and the one most likely to be revisited. A fair verdict is that the changes allowed the British to be more openly themselves, and that while the results are not always pretty, the apple of self-knowledge cannot be uneaten again and returned to the tree.

The Democracy of Narcissism

Much the same divided response still resonates about the whole decade. Why do the sixties seem to matter so much? Why is it that on television, in magazine articles, net debates, in books and in conversation, so much time is spent on a few events, involving a tiny number of people in a few places? There is almost autistic repetitiveness to our scratching of the images, from Minis to minis, Beatlemania to Biba, as if there are secrets still hidden there for us to uncover, some hidden pattern that gives order to history. The truth is that we have never really left the sixties. We have simply repeated them, and that goes for those who were only born later. Sixties music, shopping and celebrity culture have been spread far beyond their first makers and participants, to almost everybody in the land.

The essence of British culture in the early twenty-first century, from drug abuse to the background soundtracks of our lives, the 'celeb'-obsessed media to swift changes in fashion, the pretence of classlessness, the car dependency, was all set down first between around 1958 and 1968. We are still living then, or at least in a slightly tired copy of how the sixties were for the elite. There was a brief political interruption in the mid-seventies when Britain was said to be ungovernable and punk pogo'd past, but it was only a pause. As the eighties' economy revived, the sixties' basic preoccupations – escapism, personal fulfilment, and shopping – returned with full force. This was a time when the mass consumer culture first arrived, our democracy of narcissism. First time round, of course, it was fresher. Pioneers have an innocence their imitators lack. Sixties culture was made by people who had no idea they were setting patterns for the future.

The pop songs of the early Beatles or the Kinks were not foremost neatly packaged commodities as all pop songs later became. When Mary Quant set up her shop she was a rotten businesswoman. The fun was in the clothes. No business with so little grip on cash could be cynical. When the protest poets first howled, or artists staged happenings, there was just a fragment of a flicker of a hope that it might change something. This innocence extends even to the mistakes – the belief that drugs can make urban life more benign, rather than dirtier and more dangerous; or that tower-blocks would bring a bright, airy future to the urban working classes. And it extends to that desperate search for alternatives, other ways of living. These included anarchist Utopias, Jungian analysis, Eastern religion, radical feminism, all tumbling one after another with the speed of changes in musical fashion. This 'counter-culture' was discredited and left behind. It survives as fragmented sub-cultures only. But the push back against the great force of the shopping age was, like so much else in these years, vigorous and gripping. No new ideas have come since.

At the time, of course, the sixties were a minority sport. The King's Road and the Royal Court were as foreign to most Britons in 1965 as the King and Royal Court had been in 1765. The majority who lived through the decade have personal memories of rather conventional suburban and provincial lives. Though city centres were being torn up and new housing replacing old, from Manchester's dreadful Hulme estate to the government-award-winning Broadwater Farm in Tottenham, most working-class people were living in old-fashioned housing, brick terraced houses in the English industrial cities, tenements in Glasgow or Dundee. There were brighter coloured new cars on the roads, but much of the traffic was still the boxy black, cream or toffee-coloured traffic of the fifties. People did have money in their pockets but it was still being spent on holidays at Butlin's and the seaside rather than on decadent parties. The great working-class prosperity of the Midlands, based on the last fat years of manufacturing industry, was only just paying dividends in holidays in Spain. Wilson might be promising the white-hot heat of technological revolution, but British factories were the sprawling, dirty, assembly-line centres of class conflict they had been for decades. For children the authority figures of the wartime era, the formally dressed fathers, teachers with short haircuts and shorter tempers, remained all too visible. Schools still used corporal punishment. Mothers tended to cook and clean at home. The Britain which proudly displayed volumes of Churchill's war memoirs on bookshelves, and stood up in cinemas for the national anthem, did not disappear when Ringo Starr grew his first luxuriant moustache.

So in one way the story of 'the sixties', in inverted commas, is elitist. A relatively small number of musicians, entrepreneurs, writers, designers and others created what the rest now study and talk about. If you weren't listening in the Cavern Club in the early days, or at the Isle of Wight when Dylan went electric, if you never dodged the police horses at Grosvenor Square, or heard Adrian Mitchell and Allen Ginsberg in the Albert Hall, or sashayed out of Bazaar with a bright bag of swirly-patterned clothes ... then sorry, Babe, you missed it, and you missed it for ever. Most of us did miss it – too young, too old, too living-in-the-wrong place. But then most people missed the Wild West and the French Revolution, and the rest of the events that come with capital letters.

Yet apart from its small number of players the new culture was far from elitist: it was shaped by working-class and lower-middle-class people who had never enjoyed this level of cultural power before. The northern cities of England, Liverpool above all but also Newcastle and Manchester, were sending their sons and daughters south to conquer, even if it was only on radio and television shows. It is hard to recall now, but the Beatles' voices, and the Geordie accents of the Animals, sounded almost shocking to the metropolitan and Home Counties listeners of the mid-sixties. The children of lorry drivers and dock workers, cleaners and shop assistants, found themselves being lionized in expensive new nightclubs and standing in line to be introduced to the Queen.

This combination of racing consumerism and pop democracy matters as much as the old debate about the sixties – whether this was a time of liberation and hope, or the devil's decade when respect for authority collapsed. The consumer market as we live it now requires constant surface change, throwing out the almost-new in favour of the newer-still. At a deep level, it needs to be shallow. It also requires almost everyone to be part of it. It both trivializes and democratizes: look around. Compared to that the political significance of pop and the youth rebellion of the sixties was insignificant. The years of insolence destroyed much about traditional Britain but not in order to usher in some kind of anarcho-socialist paradise full of hairy people in boiler suits dropping acid, indulging in free love and cultivating allotments. No, that older Britain with its military traditions, its thousands of slow industrial and village backwaters, its racism, its clear divisions of class and geography, was being pushed aside so that our current democracy of shopping and celebrity could nose its way smoothly in. The people would not liberate themselves with class war, but with price war, not hippy communes but Happy Eaters. Even the old fixed patterns of male and femaleness could get in the way of a self-pleasuring economy. Androgynous fashion, long hair, the Pill, a new interest in the inner psychological life – an unabashed soppiness, if you will – really marks the sixties. It was when Britain went girlie. And what do girls do? Girls shop.

Equal rights and feminism were only touching the surface. There was still a long road to travel. Too many wry memoirs recount the gross sexism of the new rock stars, the innocence of their 'chicks' and the hypocrisy of male student revolutionaries. The Pill might be on the way, and the Abortion Act would become law in 1967 but this is still a time of pregnant girls and knitting needles, the public shame of unmarried mothers, and gross domestic violence administered by drunken men. Equal pay was a long way away; many workplaces, from newspaper offices to engineering works, solicitors' practices to bus depots, were utterly unwelcoming to women wanting work. From the early to middle sixties, egalitarianism was not a real social change but – as often happens at times of change – a philosophical one first. The shift was in what it might mean to be properly human. The old virtues of stoicism, buttoned lips and obedience were retreating. Traditions of submission and obedience, hierarchies of class inherited from medieval landowning, industrial capital and imperial administration, began to wobble and dissolve into something very different, a society which was dilute, porous and mushily self-forgiving. This took place not because bad people corrupted good people or, if you are 'pro-sixties', because noble revolutionaries ushered in an age of personal freedom, but because it suited a new economic system.

Biba, an iconic symbol, promised liberation for

women and girls, but liberation through spending. Its founder Barbara Hulanicki was a girl from an exiled Polish family, born in Warsaw before the war, brought up in British-controlled Palestine until her father, a UN negotiator, was murdered by Zionist terrorists. She too was a kind of outsider, later raised under the influence of a bohemian aunt in Brighton, before the inevitable stint at art school, then the launch of a cheap mail order clothing company with her husband. Biba, named after a younger sister, brought together the new obsessions of glamour and cheap prices. Hulanicki had been mesmerized by Audrey Hepburn ('her shape; long neck, small head, practically jointless') and her first top-selling design was a pink gingham dress like one worn by Brigitte Bardot at her wedding.

Her succession of boutiques were dark, chaotic spaces in which customers could lose themselves, pick up and try on, discard and collect, and sometimes steal, a great gush of new designs which seemed to change every week. The clothes were being run up at speed in the East End and ferried over to the boutique several times a week. Turnover was spectacular and soon the celebrities would be fighting with the off-duty typists and schoolgirls for Biba designs – Mia Farrow, Yoko Ono, Princess Anne, Raquel Welch and even Bardot herself. As one admirer of the Biba experience said, it 'was helping to create the concept of shopping as an experience, a leisure activity for the young'.[13] The trumpeter, cartoonist and writer George Melly called it a democratic version of Mary Quant and Hulanicki herself said: 'I always wanted to get prices down, down, down, to the bare minimum.' The cheapness and disposability of the clothes was shocking to an older Britain in which millions of families made their own clothes, buying patterns from Woolworths and sewing them up by hand or with a machine, and knitting sturdy school jerseys or woollen dresses.

This was the beginning of the buy-and-throw-away consumer culture applied to clothing, and though it would brim with moral dilemmas later, in the sixties it seemed simple freedom for millions of women. This was underscored by the Biba look, that Audrey Hepburn gawkiness. These were clothes for girls without much in the way of breasts, girls who were not defined by motherhood and marriage, the girls who would soon be on the Pill, career girls about town, girls who felt free in ways revolutionary French philosophers would never quite understand. Biba would be destroyed by the inflation of Edward Heath's Britain and by over-ambitious expansion into a giant department store selling everything from meals to Biba-branded baked beans – the greed and cynicism of its new owners, who thought it could be just another big shop. So, poor Biba: misunderstood by the left, as we will see, and by big business too.

A History of British Pop

By the beginning of the sixties all the essential ingredients of an urgent new market were in place. The commodity was music. Most histories of golden-age sixties rock groups follow a familiar pattern. There are the opening pages in which the kids discover Chuck Berry and Elvis thanks to the unreliable but glamorous Radio Luxembourg, the commercial station broadcasting to the UK from 7 p.m. onwards by the early fifties. (Its famous 208 signal concealed a strange history: the station had been built by French entrepreneurs, taken over as an organ of Nazi propaganda during the war, passed to the US forces and finally revived, funded by Ovaltine and football betting adverts, the only known contribution of the Grand Duchy to modern British culture.) These early revelations of American rock and pop will quickly be followed by one or more of the future stars suggesting to a friend that they form a skiffle group. Skiffle, credited to a jazz session musician and son of a Glaswegian violinist called Lonnie Donegan, used simple chords and home-made instruments like washboards to produce a brisk, jaunty, jazz-meets-country blues sound, unaffected and often humorous. Unlike jazz you did not have to be much of a musician to play skiffle – as John Lennon and ten thousand others found. Twenty years later, punk fanzines would print the finger positions for three basic chords and urge their readers to go out and form a band. This was precisely the lesson of skiffle. Lonnie Donegan's hits would be faithfully copied in bedrooms and school halls round the country and, singing in a cod American accent, he would become the first British star to make the US hit parade.

Next in this composite history two seminal places would appear. One would be the coffee bar. Whether the El Toro in Muswell Hill or Liverpool's famous Kardomah, or a thousand in between, coffee bars had become vital hang-out places for young people. Often opened by Italian immigrants, they offered a rare space where music could be listened to, away from family-crowded homes or unwelcoming adult pubs. They hosted the first juke-boxes and sometimes live music. The second place to feature was more important still, the art college. In the fifties art schools played a much more important role than simply producing the next generation of designers or sculptors. Many of them were Victorian or Edwardian institutions connected to local technical colleges and originally meant to provide the craftsmen who would help sustain a town's clothing, ceramic, printing or other businesses. Before the arrival of mass university education, therefore, which would not really change things until the seventies, art schools were where bright and imaginative teenagers who failed to conform to the academic disciplines tended to end up.

John Lennon at Liverpool Art College, Ray Davies at Hornsey, Peter Townsend at Ealing, Ian Dury at Walthamstow, Keith Richards at Sidcup, Cat Stevens, the core of Pink Floyd and Roxy Music were just a few of thousands. The coffee bars were essential meeting places but the art schools were the true factories of popular culture. Art students had long been a recognized and much-mocked subsection of national life, in turtle-necked jumpers and CND badges. Such colleges had become vital rallying places and support systems for talented outsiders, relatively few of whom would end up as conventional artists. The great pop art pioneer Peter Blake, a Dartford electrician's son, had begun to create paintings and sculptures out of the wrestlers, popular magazines, pin-ups and music stars around him. Supplementing his income by teaching in three London art colleges, Blake had a huge influence on younger people and was in advance of American pop artists like Andy Warhol. In 1961 he encouraged the young Ian Dury to start depicting what interested him – 'tits and bums, gangsters, Teddy boys, Jayne Mansfield and Marlon Brando' – but Dury was one of many, reaching out hungrily for a brighter, younger culture. Across the country, student designers found themselves working next door to would-be painters, graphic artists and film-makers, so ideas quickly hopped across. The characteristic Bridget Riley op-art lines of sixties dresses and shop windows had been stolen by students from the artists they mingled with; the RAF-style roundels and bold black arrows which appeared on the clothes of bands such as the Who, and became part of the Mods' insignia, had been swiped from graphic designers and pop painters. The way the sixties and seventies looked came out of the fusion that happened in Britain's municipal applied design institutions, places not quite paralleled in America or continental Europe.

This hunger for novelty and readiness to mingle disciplines became a big force in British music, too. For the art schools had early on been bastions of folk and jazz. Why would they not be? Here were gathered thousands of bright middle-class and working-class teenagers looking for fun and hoping not to be sucked into factory design shops or office jobs. By the later fifties, the art students would be listening to skiffle, R&B and the first generation of safely packaged, toothsome and relatively unthreatening British Elvis copies. First there would be grinning Tommy Steele, then Harry

Webb the Hertfordshire pub singer, reincarnated as the eyeliner-wearing Cliff Richard, then the former tug-boat hand Billy Fury. A few years on, and future members of the Rolling Stones, the Kinks and the Who were imbibing radical ideas and new looks, as clearly the product of art school as any watercolour or well-thrown pot. Ian Dury and his friends got into trouble for using their paint brushes as drum-sticks, sending off a rumble through the rest of the building. That works as a metaphor too. The ultimate art school bands would come later still. Roxy Music, led by Brian Eno of Winchester art college and Bryan Ferry, the coalminer's son who had been taught at Newcastle Art College by the original British pop artist Richard Hamilton, pioneered a decadent, clever-clever, intellectually sharp music loved by British audiences in the early seventies. Pink Floyd, the greatest of the concept album bands, is unimaginable without the art school background.

So, let us continue the composite pop star life story. You have been corrupted by Radio Luxembourg, learned to play in a skiffle band, hung around at coffee bars and had your imagination jemmied open in a provincial art school. What happens next? In a word, management. In the early sixties an unlikely sounding name and a pretty-boy face meant you had probably been discovered by 'flash Larry', or Larry Parnes, first of the Svengalis. The Svengalis feature early and often. Suddenly there is money to be made from tousled-headed boys.

Before pop the dominant popular musical styles produced low profits. Most public music was live – the piano and banjo players on music-hall stages, the star singers and then eventually the big bands of the dancehalls and the smoky subculture of jazz. Sheet-music made big money for talented composers like Ivor Novello and stage stars like Harry Lauder. Gramophone record sales had kicked off with recordings of early twentieth-century opera stars but the invention of the modern microphone in the twenties had then changed popular singing, allowing intimacy and variety of a new kind. So the recording industry had brought Gilbert and Sullivan, Louis Armstrong, the Ink Spots, Flanders and Swann, Vera Lynn, the crooners and many West End musicals, to millions of homes long before pop. By the end of the fifties there were four major British recording companies: EMI, Decca, Pye and Philips. Most of their profits came from classical music or comic recordings. Only since the spread of seven-inch 45s had records really been something teenagers could aspire to buying. Though first produced in the US as early as 1948, for working-class British youngsters they were still formidably expensive by the late fifties.

The other essential technological changes arrived at around the same time. First, loud electric guitars, invented by radio repair man Leo Fender in 1948, swiftly followed by his great rival Les Paul. Then transistor radios, originally invented in the mid-fifties to help Americans keep in touch after the coming nuclear war with Russia, and becoming popular for other purposes at the end of the decade. Without the mike, the electric guitar and the seven-inch record, rock and pop would not have happened. Without the radio, the vital cross-current influences would have been unheard. Everything conspired towards the moment. The post-war economic boom was putting money in the pockets of teenagers and young workers. The baby boom had increased their numbers. Better nutrition meant they tended to mature sexually earlier. And the mechanisms for the mass marketing of pop were already in place. Radio Luxembourg had broadcast its first Top of the Pops show in 1952. Within a few years television would follow – Rediffusion's *Ready, Steady, Go,* a crucial show in the story of British pop – then the BBC's *Top of the Pops.*

The earlier generation of American rock and blues pioneers had turned music into short, addictive bites lasting only a few minutes to be purchased anew every week or so. The radio, TV and magazine publicity machine was up and going. The equipment was in every second home, radios and record players turned out by England's then-booming electronics industry. And 'the workers', all those teenagers with stars in their eyes, desperately strumming away at cheap guitars and handwriting lyrics and chords from the radio, were just waiting to be picked up in every major city in the land. Thus, in this fictional sixties success story, the Svengali duly arrives at the back of the coffee bar basement or the private club with a contract, bought from W. H. Smith in one hand and a flash Parker pen in the other; and a decade of argument about who is ripping off whom, is about to begin. Like Parnes and the most famous of all, Brian Epstein, who managed the Beatles, the agents and middle-men were often edgy outsiders too – both those men were gay when homosexuality was illegal, and Jewish, when anti-Semitism was rife.

And so the typical pop band history will roll predictably on – the early dodgy names for the band; the cover songs; the year or two of bouncing around the narrow roads of pre-motorway Britain in hired coaches between gigs at Butlin's camps and provincial theatres; the first chart hit and the first invitation to Rediffusion's headquarters to be filmed for television; the first Bentley and the first joint; the growing tension between the guitar heroes and the drummer, who never really fitted in, the purchase of a grand house in the Home Counties, the tragic early death of a band member, by overdose, car crash or drowning; and then eventually the split followed by the comeback.

Though the stories of British rock and pop bands follow a predictable trajectory, the stories of the earlier bands are more interesting simply because the story had not occurred before. It was freshly extraordinary, that fairy-tale rocket whoosh from backstreet poverty to international fame and huge wealth; so too was the darker tale of abuse and betrayal which almost always followed. Though pop was a business it was also a story about class and morality: almost every band history will describe the tension between the marketing of the music and the attempt by the band to stay in some way authentic or true to themselves. Many of course never tried to be authentic in the first place but the important ones did and it wasn't always easy. The Kinks, four north London boys who affected a camp look and played rough, hard pop, were put into the most extraordinary confections of pink hunting jackets, ruffs and thigh-high suede boots to attract attention. Long before the New York Dolls or Velvet Underground, their gender-bending pose was also something the straighter American market found very hard to accept. The most famous band of all were bullied and cajoled by Epstein into ditching the rough jeans and leather Luftwaffe jackets image they had learned in Hamburg. To get their first recording contract, the Beatles were told to stop smoking on-stage, stop swearing, turning up late, and making spontaneous decisions about which songs they would play at their gigs. Oh yes, and they had to learn to bow smartly, all together, at the audience after every song.[14] They agreed. It would only be later that their success gave them the freedom to tell their managers and advisers where to go.

The degree of control needed to make a band exciting but not too exciting would become one of the most amusing dilemmas in modern management. The harnessing of youth spirit for maximum commercial return proved as tricky and unstable as the early days of harnessing nuclear fission – though it was finally achieved by the eighties, when the death of punk allowed entirely commercial and packaged pop unquestioned dominance. In the early days it was not always quite as obvious that money would always trump vitality. There were still battles to be had. The Who was a west London band which had, like so many others, emerged from skiffle and been kick-started by the success of the Beatles. They were encouraged by their manager, Peter Meadon, to dress stylishly and address themselves to the new audience of Mods. But their violence and guitar-smashing, while delighting their live audience, kept them away from mainstream venues for ages. Throughout a stellar career during which they gave the Beatles a run for their money in the concept-album stakes, the Who were never properly tamed. Nor were the Kinks, whose song-writing genius Ray Davies became involved in a punch-up with an American television union official who had called the band a 'bunch of commie wimps', and managed to get them banned from the States for four crucial years. One band's roughness and ire would provoke the next to go further.

Apart from keeping physical control of the new market, the big battle line was over the subject of the songs, which quickly moved beyond the easy boy-meets-girl and black American rip-offs of the early years. Rock was about escape, mainly from the urban and suburban Britain of its young consumers. For most, the teenage years would end in a conventional working life and marriage, which was more popular than ever in the sixties, with marriage rates peaking in 1972. But drugs, mysticism, gangs and sexual experimentation were some of the alternatives celebrated by pop culture, to the discomfiture of the record companies, the BBC, politicians and the newspapers. Some bands adopted a provocatively camp look, wore make-up and baited the short-haired traditional male. Songs such as 'Lola' and the Who's 'I'm a Boy' discussed transvestites; there was a lolling libertinism in the Rolling Stones' music which shocked watching parents.

Above all, the rate of experimentation and change in sixties pop itself was simply astonishing. A new sound, line-up of instruments, length of song and image seemed to come along every few months, and in 1966–8 every few weeks. It was a classic capitalist market-driven competition, with profits and status dependent on beating the rest, measured by sales, week after week. Among the great experimenters were Paul McCartney, who was feeding back discoveries about tape loops, modern composers and Bach into the music of the Beatles. As they became the ultimate über-group they however found the screaming at their concerts so loud that even they couldn't hear the music and retreated more and more to work in the studio, which in turn produced longer, more complicated and reflective sounds. On it would go. The Stones' blues-rock would challenge Merseybeat pop, the Mods would hit back, early versions of guitar-rock heavy metal suddenly appeared. The amphetamine-fuelled fast and short singles would give way to LSD-inspired albums with looping, hypnotic rhythms and surrealist covers. Acoustic protest songs were plugged in and went electric.

Hairstyles went from slicked to floppy to long to shaved, moustaches flowered and withered, huge mountain-man beards sprouted from the unlikeliest chins. Always the Beatles were pioneers, the first big stars to fall for Indian mysticism, sitars or the next drug craze and ultimately the first to find the pressures intolerable and to break up. The trajectory seemed impossible to beat. A band's success was based on its members' skills but also on their authentic claim to be kids from the streets whose anger, enthusiasm, boredom and wit reflected the actual Britain all round them, the lives of the people who would save up and buy their songs. Pop was music from below or it was nothing. Yet the successful musicians would be cut off from the world they came from by the money and the security needed to keep fans at bay until they were fated to sound introspective and irrelevant.

Ultimately life in the bubble would prove airless and the music, or the band, would choke to death.

Flash, Snip, Smile: the Making of Celebrity

The contemporary cult of celebrity was born in the sixties too. All developed societies lavish attention on a small number of favoured people, rich, beautiful or talented. In eighteenth-century Europe it might be duchesses and court composers, in classical Rome orators and gladiators, in nineteenth-century Japan, warriors and courtesans. Details of their clothing, personal lives, foibles, family successes and disasters are gossiped about and vicariously enjoyed. They form a fantasy extended family, prettier and wickeder and more brightly coloured than the rest of us. What has changed in recent decades is the scale of celebrity devotion, this cargo cult of modern Britain. It has elbowed aside rival forms in television entertainment, invaded and occupied popular newspapers and produced racks of magazines breathlessly following the face-lifts, marital break-ups, boob jobs and births of celebs. All of this originated in the mid-sixties. The cloying, ingratiating tone of contemporary magazines such as *Hello!* and *OK!* when interviewing or describing some frozen-faced doll can be found in the write-ups of the young set in British newspapers, supplements and the arch glossies of the sixties. The origins of 'Big Brother' television exhibitionism are buried in game shows and agony aunt columns half a century old. The raising of footballers and musicians from being tradesmen-servants of the public to misbehaving gods began then too.

Celebrities are often mocked for being talentless. Some are, some are not. A tribute paid to the young and beautiful by the rest of us, the circle of celebrity is paradoxically both very small and very open. From the outside the celebrity world seems to be a closed, charmed place, a marquee guarded by men with shaved heads and sunglasses inside which rock stars and footballers, actresses and princesses, all magically turn out to know one another. Yet what the sixties discovered was that celebrity must be open too in the sense of letting in new people from the streets, or it congeals into a resented elite. Modern celebrity has no time for a Samurai class or for haughty duchesses – it must be a fantasy island we could all paddle our way to, at least in theory. Cultural democracy rules, even while parliamentary democracy struggles.

What was called Swinging London, or the Scene, was simply a small number of restaurants, shops and clubs where a small number of people were repeatedly photographed and written about. In Chelsea, Biba, Granny Takes a Trip, Bazaar and Hung on You were honeypots for the fashionable. In the evening it might be Annabel's or Showboat or Talk of the Town. When in 1969 the *Private Eye* journalist Christopher Booker published his drily hostile look back at the decade, *The Neophiliacs,* he found that by the summer of 1965 there were a mere twenty or so people who seemed to be at the heart of Swinging London. They included the Beatles and Mick Jagger (the other Stones had not yet quite cut through), the model Jean

Shrimpton, the designer Mary Quant, the painter David Hockney, the actors Michael Caine and Terence Stamp, the photographers Lord Snowdon, David Bailey and Terence Donovan, the cartoonist and editor of the *Sunday Times* colour magazine Mark Boxer and the interior decorator David Hicks.

All these 'New Aristocrats', Booker pointed out, were in some way concerned with the creation of images. This list, though it would lose and gain constantly at the edges, had some validity. Bailey himself would pump the publicity machine with his 'Box of Pin Ups' designed by Boxer. Booker takes up the story:

> The list, which was virtually a Debrett guide to the New Aristocracy and their circle included: 2 actors, 8 pop singers, 1 pop artist, 1 interior decorator, 4 photographer/designers, 1 ballet dancer, 3 models, 1 film producer, 1 dress designer, 1 discotheque manager, 1 creative advertising man, 1 'pop singer's friend' and the Kray brothers from the East End who could only be described as 'connected with the underworld'.

The contours of all this had been sketchily apparent a few years earlier, in the Profumo affair. Old money, big business, the traditional arts and politics were edging out of the spotlight, now only to be seen at the side of the stage. Instead working-class upstarts were arriving and stealing the show. Among the photographers, Bailey was an East Ham tailor's son, Donovan a lorry driver's son, also from the East End of London – indeed, the East

End did very well with photography because it also produced Terry O'Neill who made iconic images of Shrimpton, Stamp and the Beatles, and the key British war photographer of the sixties and seventies, Don McCullin. Michael Caine was a Billingsgate fish porter's son, Stamp the son of a tug-boat captain. The female pioneer aristocrats included that Polish asylum-seeker's child, Barbara Hulanicki; Lesley Hornby of Neasden, better known as Twiggy who was the daughter of a carpenter and a Woolworths shop assistant, and Priscilla White, better known as Cilla Black, from one of the rougher ends of Liverpool.

Few of these people would have made it in the London of the fifties, forties or thirties. The same goes for the Beatles, Kinks, and innumerable others. (Jagger would have made it anywhere, any time, as a successful businessman.) The intertwining of Booker's 'New Aristocrats' was as sticky and sinuous as the old Tory cliques of the fifties or New Labour's Whitehall in the nineties. A few were there entirely because of their looks, such as Jean Shrimpton, the supermodel waif (the word 'supermodel' was, inevitably, first used in 1968). But the important thing was the great sucking-in of working-class talent, a transfusion that the old Britain badly needed. The incomers were fascinated by images and they were colonizing the new media opportunities – music, fashion, colour magazines, hairdressing, radio, television, advertising – that were not the property of the City and old money.

There was a DIY spirit that has not been recovered since. Quant had been cutting up lengths of cloth bought over the counter and selling them at Bazaar since the mid-fifties. Her iconoclasm matched and outpaced a Pete Townshend or Keith Moon, as she drew, sliced and sewed up a uniform that mocked the pleated, padded extravagances of the Old New Look designers. Taking on the fashion industry of Paris and the West End from a bedsit and a tiny shop was at least as bold as taking on American rock from a Liverpool basement. Quant's shockingly short mini-skirts (named after the car, which she loved) were offensive enough for her window to be rapped by umbrella-toting male protesters and even the occasional brick to be lobbed. She always maintained she was trying to free women to be able to run for a bus, and to show off the beautifully fit, skinny bodies that post-war rationing had given young womanhood. But the sexual allure was what shocked. Michael Caine later recalled taking his mother down the Kings Road to see what all the fuss was about: 'I said, here's one now, and this girl walks by with a mini up to here. She goes by and my mother looked at her. So, we walk on a bit. She never said a word. So I said, what do you think, mum? She said: If it's not for sale, you shouldn't put it in the window.'[15]

Butterflies and Other Insects

If modern Britain found her soundtrack and her cargo cult in the sixties, she found her special vices too. In February 1967 Mick Jagger and Keith Richards were arrested at the latter's Sussex manor house Redlands during a raid by police which uncovered amphetamines and dope. Richards and

Jagger received jail sentences and heavy fines, though ended up serving no more than two days behind bars in Brixton before their appeals. The whole thing had been orchestrated by the *News of the World* and set off a heated national debate, with *The Times* leading the way to protest about the excessive sentencing. In a famous editorial, 'Who Breaks a Butterfly Upon a Wheel?' its editor William Rees-Mogg questioned the severity of the sentence, calling it 'as mild a drug case as can ever have been brought before the courts'. A month later, *The Times* carried a full-page advert which declared the law against marijuana 'immoral in principle and unworkable in practice'. The sixty-five signatories included medical experts, Nobel laureate scientists, some politicians, the novelist Graham Greene and the Beatles. By then the Beatles had been introduced to cannabis by Bob Dylan, and Paul McCartney was about to cause a further furore by admitting to taking LSD as well.

The purpose of the drugs had changed in the few years since the Beatles and others hit Hamburg. Once they had been used to keep performers awake, and then to calm them down after exhausting days or nights on the road. By the mid-sixties the agenda was rather more ambitious. LSD was a truth-bringer, allegedly opening minds to higher planes and brighter-coloured realities. This delusion was imported from the West Coast of America, though British writers had praised lysergic acid long before. Jeff Nuttall, a counter-culture writer of the time, declared that it was being launched as 'something other than mere pleasure, as a ready window on the Zen eternal, as a short cut back to the organic life, religion and wonderment'.

Neither the raptures of the counter-culture and the druggy atmospherics of Beatles music during the years when they reinvented pop, nor even campaigners, not much different from those who had successfully backed the Jenkins reforms, would manage to shift the State's hostility to such substances. Sex might be packaged and marketed and so might rock, but drugs were something else, the pleasure that would remain forbidden. Rock certainly helped extend the drugs culture. Heroin, the most dangerous example, spread steadily from a small and wealthy entertainment elite, through middle-class would-be rebels, until it finally emerged with gangs, dealers and all the paraphernalia of misery on council estates. In 1953 there were 290 known heroin addicts in Britain and by 1968 there were 2,780. These numbers are bound to be far below the true figure. On the same basis, the figure by the turn of the century was 25,000. Cannabis, a less dangerous and far more widely tolerated drug, was little used in the fifties outside small sub-cultures but by the mid-sixties there were between 2,000 and 3,000 arrests a year. The figure for 2000 was 97,000. Finally, while in the sixties cocaine was little used by comparison with other drugs, an academic survey suggested that by the new century, some 46,000 people in London alone were using the particularly dangerous version, crack cocaine. The sixties introduced mass drug use to Britain as the musical and hippy enthusiasts promoted it as a social and personal good. The authorities decided to destroy the drug culture as a social evil. Both were confounded. Nobody became wiser or more interesting through using heroin, LSD or dope, and the battle against drug use has been entirely lost. The victims began with a steady stream of performers and hangers-on who died from overdoses or drugs-related accidents and, more important by far, are the hundreds of thousands of poorer, less talented children who followed them after having far less fun.

Home Grown?

No sensible person would try to draw a neat line between British pop and its origins in America. For everyone except the Americans, rock is an import and a transplant. Rock and Roll was black American slang for having sex. It derives from the Deep South, via rhythm and blues and eventually mated with the country music of rural white America – which in turn had come from the folk music of Ireland, England, Scotland and France. Accelerated, amplified and sexualized, when it arrived in Britain it was immediately denounced as alien, indecent, anarchic, corrupting 'Negro' music, thoroughly un-British. This was not just the view of the occasional retired squadron leader sitting in his Kent garden. The hugely popular music magazine *Melody Maker* described rock as 'one of the most terrifying things to have happened to popular music ... The Rock-and-Roll technique, instrumentally and vocally, is the antithesis of all that jazz has been striving for over the years – in other words, good taste and musical integrity.'[16]

Modern jazz fans and folk music purists would try to hold the line for years. Yet the diabolic Elvis and all his works, were too big, too mesmeric, to be resisted. Few of the first performers and bands in Britain wrote their own material. Donegan sang in an American voice; thousands of would-be pop stars did endless covers of Bo Diddley, Little Richard and Fats Domino. Again, it was the breakthrough lead given by Lennon and McCartney in singing their own material that persuaded scores of other bands to follow. Even today and after a lifetime of hits, there is little about the music of the Rolling Stones that feels particularly English; Dusty Springfield had one of the loveliest voices of the age, but if you didn't know you could have been forgiven for thinking that she was a black babe from Motown not a Catholic girl from High Wycombe.

Yet the British Isles had traditions which would feed back into the American musical revolution and change it dramatically, both in sound and content. We have discussed the art schools already. But there was also the folk tradition which was being revived even though the pop and rock stars rarely had first-hand experience of it. John O'Leannain (as his name should properly be written) and Paul McCartney both came from musical Irish families but had been cut off from their heritage. Bands such as Fairport Convention, which began in North London in 1967, taking its name from the house where they practiced, and Jethro Tull, founded by the Scottish and Blackpool flautist Ian Anderson in 1968, would incorporate some of the feel of British folk back into rock; others like the Ulsterman Van Morrison would cross the lines repeatedly.

A stronger influence still was the music hall, or variety tradition, discussed earlier and the humorous or sentimental music played on pianos in the home. These can be heard in the brassy, knees-up sound of Beatles songs like 'Strawberry Fields' or through most of the *Sergeant Pepper* album, in which the stomp of the fairground and the wheezing of the circus organ are not far away. As Lennon and McCartney, who both lost their mothers early, put it, 'Let's all get up and dance to a song, That was a hit before your Mother was born.' And beyond the Beatles, with their Liverpudlian nostalgia, a host of bands filled their lyrics with local references. To take just one example, Jethro Tull's *Aqualung* of 1971 name-checks Preston railway station, Hampstead Heath and Piccadilly Circus, while their following album, *Thick as a Brick,* which was a huge hit in the US, not only addresses the mood of post-sixties despair – 'the sandcastle virtues are all swept away in / the tidal destruction / the moral melee' – but manages to ask 'So where the hell was Biggles when you needed him last Saturday?'

The most impressive and sustained attempt to create a distinctively British pop came from the Kinks and was at the time a huge flop. Banned from the US while others were breaking into American stardom, Ray Davies, a cussed observer of modern life, turned back to local subjects. He had always written pop songs about everything from the death of the dance-halls to the joys of the English autumn, but *The Kinks Are The Village Green Preservation Society* of 1968 was on an entirely different scale. As Ray Davies put it himself: 'While everybody else thought the hip thing to do was to drop acid, take as many drugs as possible and listen to music in a coma, the Kinks were singing songs about lost friends, draught beer, motorbike riders, wicked

417

witches and flying cats.'[17] He is not exaggerating. The title song calls for the preservation of, inter alia, Desperate Dan, strawberry jam, the George Cross, the 'Sherlock Holmes English-speaking vernacular', little shops, china cups, virginity, Tudor houses and antique tables, while attacking the new skyscrapers and office blocks. The album which sold in tiny numbers compared to the Beatles, worried and confused the critics who could not decide whether the Kinks were being serious or satirical. Today it is regarded as one of the great achievements of British pop in the sixties, a subtle mix of affection and derision, nostalgia and micky-taking, and no less essentially English for that. The Kinks were hugely influential not just on other bands of the time such as the Who, but on the later waves of 'Britpop'. They showed that it was possible to write inspiring rock music about what was around you, without posturing as a New Yorker or Alabama boy, indeed without pretending to be (just a little bit) black.

Rock was an arena for dreamers or harmless humorists, the fun factory for weekend rebels whose stars were too busy buying country estates, Rolls-Royces and drugs to worry about the condition of the country. Little of it was political. As John Lennon told *Rolling Stone* magazine in 1971 when asked to assess the impact of the Beatles: 'Nothing happened, except we all dressed up. The same bastards are in control, the same people are running everything, it's exactly the same.' That feeling was shared by the counter-culture left who had been attending seminars and protest meetings about Vietnam, marching against capitalist stooges in the Labour Party and ranting about the need for revolution. Like the world of pop, it was essentially an American import. When counter-culture poets had put on an evening of readings at the Albert Hall in 1965, alongside the British contingent which included Adrian Mitchell and Christopher Logue, there were the New York and San Francisco gurus, Allen Ginsberg, Lawrence Ferlinghetti and Gregory Corso. The poets were the most eloquent voices.

The American influence was, not surprisingly, strongest in the anti-war movement. When the Vietnam Solidarity Committee organized three demonstrations outside the US embassy in London's Grosvenor Square, the second of them particularly violent, they were copying the cause and the tactics used to much greater effect in the United States. The student sit-ins and occupations at Hornsey and Guildford Art Colleges, and Warwick University, were pale imitations of the serious unrest on US and French campuses. There was even a (literally) pale imitation of the ultimate US underground movement, called rather pathetically the White Panthers. Their main revolutionary aim seemed to be free access to rock festivals, or what they called 'the People's music'. A two-week gathering to debate 'the dialectics of liberation' was organized at London's Round House in 1967. The star speaker was the American Black Power leader Stokely Carmichael. The event finished with a speech of abject apology from one of the British organizers on behalf of 'we deracinated white intellectuals, we who are bourgeois and colonizing in essence'. The conference's intellectual guru was a Californian exile from Germany, Herbert Marcuse, whose

419

central message was that the affluent society was oppressive, based on the creation of 'false needs' and impossible to change by conventional political revolution.

In the same year a French revolutionary named Guy Debord came to England with a call to arms. When he arrived at a Notting Hill flat to meet the promised group of *twenty* hardcore revolutionaries only three had turned up, and they spent the afternoon drinking cans of McEwan's Export and watching *Match of the Day*.[18] Not surprisingly, Debord gave up on the Anglo-Saxons. British revolutionaries in modern times have been so little real threat that they were easily and cheerfully incorporated into mainstream television comedy through the character of Citizen Smith of the Tooting Popular Front. Debord's followers, however, taking the name 'Les Enragés', were heavily involved in the great Paris and Nanterre student uprisings of 1968. This was on a scale like nothing seen in Britain – nearly 600 students arrested in fights with the police on a single day and, at the high point of the revolt, 10m workers on strike across France. Hundreds of British students went over to join what they hoped would be a revolution, until de Gaulle, with the backing of an election victory, crushed it.

British alternative politics in print had no equivalents to the Beatles, the Who or the Kinks. The underground magazines such as *International Times, Black Dwarf* and *Oz* copied the rhetoric, art work and cartoon style of similar American publications and lacked the salty, surly working-class energy of rock. The greatest confrontation with the state focused on whether Rupert Bear, as manipulated by the pen of Vivian Berger, a fifteen-year-old schoolboy with a particularly lewd imagination, was behaving obscenely. The cartoon strip was central to the long summer trial in 1971 of the magazine *Oz*. At the Old Bailey, despite the best efforts of the publishers' barrister John Mortimer, the priapic Rupert was judged to be behaving disgracefully. Richard Neville, Felix Dennis and Jim Anderson ended up with suspended sentences. Immortally, the young Berger told the jury that though he wanted to shock 'your generation ... also, I thought it was funny.'[19] A teddy bear with a stiffy: it rather sums up Britain's answer to revolution.

The counter-culture would curdle and gurgle away for fairly obvious reasons. It had no practical agenda. It was deeply hostile to organization. It was largely middle class and had no effective links to the working-class socialists who wanted higher wages and perhaps even workers' cooperatives, but were less keen on long-haired students taking drugs, or indeed angry black people. Those parts of the new politics which would stick, would be anti racism; feminism, to the extent that it focused on practical and realistic ideas, such as equal pay and refuges for battered wives; and the gay liberation movement, which also had clear objectives, and also looked to the United States for a lead, particularly after the Stonewall riot. But the great irony is that the counter-culture, disdainful of sell-out pop music, was far less successful than pop at creating an indigenous British movement. It was dependent on passing American fads and voices as, by the mid-sixties, British pop was not.

Rhodesia: Rebellion of the Whites

While the message of the sixties still lives, other stories can dominate the newspapers for months on end, even years, and then are apparently forgotten almost immediately. Perhaps they are too painful to dwell on. The story of Rhodesia's Unilateral Declaration of Independence, or UDI, and of the short-lived Federation that preceded it, obsessed four prime ministers in a row, Macmillan, Douglas-Home, Wilson and Heath. It filled front pages, elbowing out other contemporary crises such as Vietnam that now bulk vastly bigger in world history. It caused deep divisions in both the main parties, with their leaders condemned as race traitors or betrayers of Africa, according to taste. It produced bizarre summits on Royal Navy warships, and dramatic confrontations at the United Nations. It pitched the young Queen Elizabeth into a constitutional fight over the hanging of three Africans. Its cast of characters, Garfield Todd, Roy Welensky, and Sir Humphrey Gibbs, forgotten now, as well as Ian Smith and Joshua Nkomo, were for a time household names. But little of this is recalled in the history of the sixties. It sits uneasily with the war protests and the fashion, the music and the tower blocks. And the final outcome of the Rhodesian crisis, a vicious guerrilla war followed by the rule of Robert Mugabe, one of the most incompetent megalomaniacs to hold power at the beginning of the twenty-first century, was genuinely tragic.

The tragedy can be traced back to the imperial

idealism of High Victorian days. Cecil John Rhodes was a sickly clergyman's son from Hertfordshire whose head was filled with notions of British world destiny and whose bank accounts were filled with the vast profits of prospecting in the South African goldrush. Using diplomacy, threats, bribes and great cunning, Rhodes created a company to take concessions in the heartland of Africa, far north of the British Cape Province, and the Boer republic of the Transvaal. It was an arèa then known as Zambesia, now the nations of Zimbabwe, Zambia and Malawi. In it lived various tribes, notably the warlike Matabele. Cecil Rhodes's vision of a vast British territory running from the far south of Africa to the very north was never accomplished but the central area, soon known as Rhodesia after him, was carved into new settler states. Bizarrely, the British government never took direct control and allowed Rhodes's company effective autonomy, backed always by the threat of British force from outside. The white settlers, mainly from Britain and South Africa, would first use farming and mining concessions and then take complete political control of these vast, fertile and mineral-rich areas. In the north, a full-blown British colony, Northern Rhodesia, would exploit the copper of the area and attempts were made to ensure decent treatment of the dispossessed local Africans. In Southern Rhodesia, however, whose capital Salisbury had been named after the then Conservative Prime Minister, the settlers established a system of relentless racial discrimination much like South Africa's, with a colour bar in employment and a ban on blacks owning land in cities or anywhere of agricultural value.

Though South Africans of British origin, and many Rhodesians, had fought in the Second World War, the overt racialism of the white elite was both a threat and an embarrassment to London. South Africa would eventually leave the Commonwealth in 1961. Malan, like many Boers, had been pro-Nazi and was an anti-British republican; he is generally credited, if that is the word, as the inventor of full-blown apartheid. The Attlee and Churchill governments feared Rhodesia would soon go the same way. To try to bind the stiff-necked settlers into a more benign system, London offered the lure of federation with Northern Rhodesia and what was then called Nyasaland. The latter two colonies were ruled from London, and had less aggressive polices towards native Africans. But Northern Rhodesia had the vast wealth of the copper mines so federation would give the whites of Salisbury access to an economic boom. In essence the deal, worked out by a brilliant Colonial Office civil servant, Andrew Cohen, was that in return for accepting a less 'South African' attitude to the black majority, the white settlers of Southern Rhodesia would be able to become far richer than they could from farming alone. In 1953, after intense haggling and bargaining about voting systems and land rights which depressed, then angered the few black representatives involved, a new country not much smaller than Canada was duly created: the Central African Federation.

To start with, things went relatively well. Embassies opened in Salisbury, tower blocks went up, international companies moved in. The government of Southern Rhodesia (later simply called Rhodesia, today Zimbabwe) fell under the control of a moderately liberal Christian mission school headteacher, Garfield Todd. For four years he nudged and tickled the white settlers towards a fairer system, enough to gain the cautious trust of the leaders of the twelve-to-one black African majority. Could it be that a liberal alternative to South Africa was being built on the continent? The leadership of the full Federation was taken by a railwayman, part-time boxer and anti-Communist union boss called Roy Welensky, the thirteenth child of a Polish Jew and a Boer mother who called himself '50 per cent Jewish, 50 per cent Polish and 100 per cent British'.[20] He was a much rougher character. The contradictions between British Colonial Office hopes for a steady transition to democracy, the profound racialism of the whites of Salisbury, and the increasing restlessness of black people who saw other parts of the continent breaking from the Empire could not be contained for ever. Eventually the well-meaning Garfield Todd was ousted for refusing to back laws banning sex between blacks and whites, and for campaigning for a wider franchise.

The spark that blew the huge Federation to pieces came in the least expected place. Nyasaland, now Malawi, was a comparatively undeveloped area, with strong connections to Scotland through missionaries, dating back to the days of David Livingstone. There were very few whites living there. What its people did have was an independence leader of rare shrewdness and international savvy. Hastings Banda was a poor village boy encouraged by missionaries, who managed to get himself educated in South Africa, then the United States, where he got a politics degree at Chicago and became a doctor of medicine in Tennessee. He then got a medical diploma at Edinburgh, became an elder of the Church of Scotland, and practised as a doctor in Liverpool and London. He moved to newly independent Ghana and then, in 1958, he returned home in triumph to Nyasaland. Banda was a Christian, pro-British, anti-communist and uninterested in military rebellion. He was, in short, a difficult man to caricature as a rebellious extremist.

Yet, in a series of brilliant speeches and deploying the menace of vast, angry crowds, he persuaded Welensky that he was enough of a threat for force to be used. South Rhodesian troops were sent to the area and though the Conservative government tried to impose a news blackout, Scottish missionaries smuggled back news to the *Scotsman* in Edinburgh, causing protests around the world. Banda was imprisoned, as he had hoped he would be, but after wild accusations that he was choreographing a huge murder-plot against whites were proved to be nonsense, he was eventually released at London's insistence. Nyasaland became independent and the Federation soon collapsed. Northern Rhodesia was helped to independence by the Conservative Colonial Secretary Iain Macleod, a genuine liberal who did a deal behind Welensky's back with the man who would go on to lead independent Zambia, Kenneth Kaunda. Macleod was seen by many as the next Tory leader but this double-dealing, in a virtuous cause, led to him being attacked by the Tory grandee Lord Salisbury (grandson of the man after whom the country's capital was then named) as an unscrupulous bridge-playing twister, 'too clever by half'. The accusation of cleverness was of course fatal in the Conservative Party of the early sixties and Macleod's career never recovered.

This left Southern Rhodesia, with its 220,000 whites and 2.5m blacks, standing almost alone. The settlers wanted independence inside the Commonwealth, on the basis of a constitution that excluded the black African majority from any shred of power. Had this been accepted by London, the anger among other Commonwealth states would have been enough to cause mass resignations and, quite possibly, the end of the organization. It was not simply a matter of keeping the Queen happy, or of retaining the last vestige of Britain's formal imperial power-system. Public opinion by the early sixties was strongly hostile to the idea of apartheid being mimicked in a Commonwealth state. So there was an impasse. And to make it more impassive still, the laconic, difficult and wily figure of Ian Smith arrived on the scene as the new Prime Minister in Salisbury. Smith was a right-wing rancher, educated in South Africa, who had served in the RAF during the war and was idolized by his supporters. The old guard, led by Welensky, realized that simply declaring independence from Britain, and setting up a whites-only state, might be tricky. Rhodesia's judges and soldiers had sworn allegiance to the Queen; Rhodesia's finances and much of her trade flowed through the City of London.

Smith had no such qualms. He was quite prepared for UDI – a unilateral declaration of independence. This was hardly a re-run of the

North American rebellion of 1776, but there were uncomfortable parallels. If, in the end, they were ready to go, what was Britain going to do about it? There was at least the option of sending an army and fighting – though in the American case, this had not worked out wholly successfully. But Rhodesia was thousands of miles beyond the reach of the Royal Navy and, in any case, this was a rebellion by whites who professed to be the front line against Marxist insurrection, many of them veterans of the British wartime forces. Would an attack on 'kith and kin' really be acceptable to British voters? Would its threat be taken seriously in Salisbury? On the other hand, would Rhodesian troops who had declared their personal loyalty to the Crown, fire back against British paratroopers if they landed?

This was the dilemma that Harold Wilson inherited when he took office in 1964. Pro-Rhodesian right-wingers had made things very difficult for Macleod and Macmillan as the Tories struggled to grapple with the break-up of the Federation. Now vehemently anti-colonialist left-wingers would make things almost as difficult for a Labour Prime Minister. Wilson began by warning Rhodesia of the serious economic consequences of UDI and by setting out conditions for British acceptance of an independent state, including unimpeded progress towards majority rule, the end of racial discrimination and no oppression of the majority by the minority – none of which was acceptable to Smith and his followers. Meetings in London did not help. Wilson then went on a disastrous trip to Salisbury. While there, he insisted on seeing the imprisoned African leaders, Nkomo and Sithole, and exploded with anger when they were ushered in to him thirsty and hungry. Only after Wilson threatened to lead his own staff into the shops to buy them something, did the Rhodesians offer water and food. Later, he endured rudeness and mockery from Smith's ministers. Fatally, however, Wilson made clear that he would not use force under any circumstances, confirming in a broadcast that if anyone was expecting 'a thunderbolt in the shape of the Royal Air Force, let me say that this thunderbolt will not be coming'. It was a mistake. Smith had been seriously worried by the prospect of Britain using force and believed Rhodesia would be unable even to try to resist. Perhaps Wilson was worried about the effect on the pound, or perhaps he was too mindful of the humiliation of Suez. At any rate, after Wilson's admission, Smith realized he had nothing to fear (sanctions never worried him) and briskly went ahead in November 1965 to declare the country independent.

From then on the policy of trying to squeeze Rhodesia into submission with oil and other sanctions was tried, even though few in Whitehall thought it had a chance of working. There were too many ways in and out of the country, and too many middlemen prepared to trade. Rhodesia developed her own consumer industries and sold her tobacco and other farm produce via South Africa. The oil came in through Portuguese Mozambique. Wilson tried two more summits with Smith, both on warships anchored in the Mediterranean so that neither man would have to step on the other's territory. Britain's conditions for accepting independence became more and more humiliatingly slim, but Smith brushed them aside, secure in his support at home and realizing that Wilson had no effective threat to hold over his head. The British Governor of Rhodesia, Sir Humphrey Gibbs, with the Chief Justice, Sir Hugh Beadle, kept a tiny oasis of loyalty to the Crown in the old Government House, dining in black tie and toasting the Queen, even though his car and telephone had been cut off by Smith's regime. But the brutal reality of UDI was underlined when three Africans sentenced to be hanged for murder were refused leave to appeal to London in 1968. The Queen, advised by Wilson, then used her prerogative of mercy and reprieved the three men. They were hanged anyway, an act described as assassination and murder in the United Nations. Smith went ahead with a new constitution regarded throughout the world as brutally unfair and racist. By the time Wilson left office in 1970 the Rhodesian dilemma was no nearer to being solved, and it would continue to hang over British politics into the Thatcher years, when the black majority finally won power.

The Smith regime, though regarded as a pariah state, would survive through an increasingly violent and complicated guerrilla war until finally giving way to one-party government by Mugabe. Zimbabwe's fate would be an awful one, ravaged by violence, famine and disease, as Marxist leaders tutored in extremism by their white enemies eventually extracted a revenge – less on the whites, many of whom eventually fled, than on their own people. Could any of this have been prevented by a liberal-minded Whitehall which had never exercised real power in Salisbury since the days of Cecil Rhodes? Only, perhaps, by being prepared to go to war in Africa, this time not to win land and treasure but undo the consequences of earlier adventures and to oust the English-speaking white elites. It would have been a huge risk. The bloody experience of other European countries in African wars and Britain's experience nearer to home in Northern Ireland, suggests that such a war might well then have run out of control and lost its original purpose. Harold Wilson, like his Tory predecessors and successors, decided that such a war was unthinkable. Had they had any inkling of the fate waiting for the people of central Africa, it is just possible that they might have thought again.

The Pound and the Viet Cong

Amid this maelstrom Britain, yet again, was close to bankruptcy. How to get a grip? Devaluing the pound might have given the Wilson government and the country the chance of a fresh start. In a world of fewer and floating currencies, the importance of devaluation is harder to understand now, but it was then the single most important issue facing Wilson. On the one hand, cutting the international value of your currency against others was an admission of failure on the world stage, a humiliation for any government. It would mean imports costing more so unless people bought fewer foreign goods it would mean more inflation. On the other hand it would make exports cheaper, giving British companies a chance to win back markets they were losing. If the government devalued and managed to keep a grip on the consequent inflation

431

while industrial exports grew, then the country could in theory leap in one painful stride away from her economic problems. It was a little like dropping out of a race, intensively retraining, sweating out the fat, slimming down, working on the muscle tone, and then starting the next race better prepared – except that in the economy you never actually stop working. As for a racer, the embarrassment of dropping out would be pointless if there was not the sweat and retraining, the greater efficiency and improved productivity. It needed to be a shock to the system, not a rest from reality. Many people, including in the Labour government, seemed not to have realized this. They thought, when eventually they were prepared to consider it, devaluation would avoid the tough choices at home which, in fact, it absolutely required.

This was a choice which went beyond economics. Devaluation and world politics were inextricably linked. To devalue the pound in the mid-sixties meant Britain's overseas spending would have to be dramatically cut back, just as the ROBOT floating pound scheme of 1953 implied. Those smaller pounds would buy fewer gallons of oil, foreign-manufactured guns and accommodation for troops. So it probably meant a further withdrawal from Britain's world role, in particular 'East of Suez', the bases in Hong Kong, Malaya, Singapore, Aden and the Gulf. That would irritate Washington, particularly as communist advance in South East Asia was the issue of the hour. The alternative was to try to keep the global role and borrow from the United States. This was certainly on offer but at a large political price. As President Johnson's special assistant put it at the time. 'We want to make very sure that the British get into their heads that it makes no sense for us to rescue the pound in a situation in which there is no British flag in Vietnam, and a threatened British thin-out both east of Suez and in Germany ... a British Brigade in Vietnam would be worth a billion dollars at the moment of truth for Sterling.'[21]

In the Commons and during the 1964 general election, Wilson had mocked Polaris as being neither independent nor British, and indeed unable to deter. Yet in the later sixties and early seventies, HMS *Resolution, Renown, Repulse* and *Revenge* were duly launched. Their names came from battlecruisers and battleships that had been the pride of an independent Royal Navy; but the new submarines' missiles were American by proxy and the same was true of their successors, the Trident submarines of today. Technological dependence now rendered any idea that this was a truly independent system absurd. In power, Wilson had the option of abandoning the nuclear option, since the submarines being built to take Polaris could have been adapted as conventional hunter-killer boats. He chose not to, and even in the mid-seventies to disguise the economics of the Polaris upgrade, codenamed Chevaline, from the cabinet sceptics. Crossman assessed the dilemma shrewdly, noting in January 1965 that Wilson was committing Britain to defence spending 'almost as burdensome – if not more burdensome – than that to which Ernest Bevin committed us in 1945, and for the same reason: because of our commitment to the Anglo-American special relationship and because of our belief that it is only through the existence of that relationship that we can survive outside Europe.'

For many this was a positive argument for devaluation. The pro-Europeans in the cabinet hoped devaluation would help drive the country towards its destiny as an ordinary member of the EEC, and away from global pretensions. They felt that Britain had to break with America, despite the financial guarantees Wilson had wrung from Washington earlier. She had to change direction, devalue, join Europe. That, according to Barbara Castle, was what George Brown had decided: 'We've got to turn down their money and pull out the troops … I want them out of East of Suez. This is the decision we have got to make: break the commitment to America … I've been sickened by what we have had to do to defend America – what I've had to say at the despatch box.' Castle interjected: 'Vietnam?' and Brown replied: 'Yes, Vietnam too.' Belligerent, contemptuous, he feared that Wilson would simply go over to Washington and 'cook up some screwy little deal'. Brown at least had a clear strategic direction. Wilson did not. Cooking up screwy little deals was his forte. He was the master chef of screwy little deals.

By now the complex nature of the choice facing him was apparent. Devaluation and the future of socialism; Britain's relationship with America and attitude to the Vietnam War; and whether we could and should be in the European Community, were all completely interlinked. Had Britain broken with America during the most testing time in its Vietnamese agony, the story of the Atlantic alliance would have taken a very different turn. We would probably have entered the EEC much earlier and, again probably, have played a role closer to that of France in the following decades, less linked in nuclear defence or intelligence terms to Washington. What this would have meant for the British economy's failing experiment in continental corporatism, and for the stability of the anti-Communist world, is impossible to say. Further, because many Commonwealth countries held their reserves in sterling in London, devaluing the pound would have been a one-off and unilateral cut in the wealth of friendly and often poor countries. Deciding about the value of the pound was also a choice about Britain's place in the world.

Oddly, the thing that would do most to destroy Harold Wilson's reputation on the left was also the policy for which Britain has most cause to remember him gratefully. We have seen some of the pressure he was under to commit British troops to Vietnam. The Australians had committed a battalion, President Johnston constantly reminded him; perhaps the Black Watch might be sent, or at the very least a military band? American hints had been mingled with those American threats about the pound; and Britain's economic position was, as we have seen, weak enough. Whitehall mandarins and some of his own advisers thought he should have committed at least some troops, but though Wilson may have been tempted and though British special forces had been considered, he held back from doing so. He tried to buy the Americans off with words of support and stabs at a diplomatic solution, hoping to use his connections in Moscow and suggesting some intervention directly with the North Vietnamese. He managed to placate nobody. The initiatives infuriated Washington, while the

435

anti-war marchers at home simply heard his supportive words for Johnson.

Wilson was berated in the streets as a murderer. His Secretary of State for Defence who had quickly realized the scale of risk that Vietnam posed and helped keep Britain clear, was rewarded on university campuses with cries of 'Hitler Healey'. When the trade union leader Frank Cousins, briefly in the government himself, asked Wilson why he wasn't taking a firmer stand against American war-making, Wilson furiously replied, 'Because we can't kick our creditors in the balls.' One of Wilson's later biographers made the case for the defence with steely eloquence. Losing all Washington's friendship and financial support would have been devastating: 'Few considered the implications for domestic social, housing, education, arts and science policies, including the probable effect on student grants. Few, indeed of those who attacked the prime minister and his colleagues simultaneously for helping the Americans abroad and not doing more to help the poor at home, ever came to terms with the bleakness of the choice.' Yet, the same writer went on, it was over Vietnam that 'the party of conscience seemed to lose touch with its soul' and over Vietnam too that many who had pinned their trust in Wilson decided his principles were 'a shattered crystal, beyond hope of repair'.[22] Here, for once, he was doing the right thing, or the best thing, and it was over this that he was most denounced. Who said politics was fair?

Even Wilson's close supporters were at times disgusted by his twisting to keep the options open. Tony Benn, a few weeks before Wilson went to the country to try to increase his majority early in 1966, had recorded: 'My opinion of Harold was lower tonight than it has ever been before. He really is a manipulator who thinks that he can get out of everything by fixing somebody or something. Although his reputation is now riding high, I'm sure he will come a cropper one day when one of his fixes just doesn't come off.'[23] At almost exactly the same time, Crossman summed up Labour's wider problem: 'The main trouble is that we haven't delivered the goods; the builders are not building the houses; the cost of living is still rising; the incomes policy isn't working; we haven't held back inflation; we haven't got production moving. We are going to the country now because we are facing every kind of difficulty and we anticipate that things are bound to get worse ...'

Wilson then had his successful re-election in March, when Labour's tiny majority of three was replaced by one of ninety-seven seats. This ought to have ushered in his golden years. His dominance of the Commons had helped finish off Alec Douglas-Home, who was replaced by Edward Heath. The age of the grammar-school boys was truly established. Wilson, whatever his failures of vision, had fought a near-faultless campaign and won a mandate which obliged the British Establishment to accept that Labour truly was entitled to rule. He had shown himself a self-confident showman abroad, in Moscow and Washington, and had pursued frantic diplomacy over the Rhodesian crisis. Now, surely, his time had arrived. Yet there was plenty in the record of that first Wilson administration to give pause for thought – the dithering and manoeuvring over devaluation; the mutual suspicions about screwy little deals already dividing the cabinet; Wilson's own habits of duplicity, notably over deflation and his attitude to British membership of the EEC.

At the centre of all the difficulties the government faced was the dilemma of devaluation. The Chancellor, Jim Callaghan, remained under almost intolerable pressure, as he had been from the day when he took office. At times he seemed close to giving way under the strain. Jenkins recalled a cabinet in July 1966 when Callaghan, later famous for being imperturbable, suddenly started talking away from the agenda about the appalling pressures on sterling. He suggested to the startled ministers around him 'both that the objective situation was desperate and that his own nerve had cracked. Wilson hushed him up and brought the meeting to an end rather like a policeman trying to get a blanket around a nude streaker.'[24] Indeed, Wilson regarded any talk of devaluation, public or private, as indecent. Once he, Brown and Callaghan had decided against it immediately after the 1964 election, it was known as 'the unmentionable'. From then on a complicated three-way dance had been going on in private. Brown turned in favour of devaluation as one way to revive his hopes for expansion and the DEA. Callaghan dithered, but wanted any devaluation to be accompanied by the shock of deflation too. Wilson, against both devaluation and deflation, played the two of them off against each other, always worried that if Brown and Callaghan agreed, he would be scuppered. By July 1966 he was telling Barbara Castle in the Commons tea-room that Brown and Callaghan were plotting to get rid of him: 'You know what the game is – devalue and

438

get into Europe. We've got to scotch it.'[25] This, however, was classic Wilson: Castle was an anti-European, so his words were calculated to flatter her. But at the same time the Prime Minister was telling pro-Europeans in the press that he intended to lead Britain into Europe himself. As the press magnate Cecil King related in his diary months earlier, Callaghan was confidently predicting that Britain would enter Europe: 'the pledges were only given to keep Barbara Castle and her kind quiet … Apparently Wilson thinks that after a successful election he will be able to eat any number of words with impunity.'[26]

Europe had sliced the party horizontally, cutting through the vertical divisions of left and right. Generally the party's activists and left-wing MPs believed that the Common Market was a 'bankers' ramp', a capitalist plot whose rules would prevent true socialism in Britain. The strongest view that Wilson himself had about it all was that he strongly didn't have a view. He had been against on the grounds that Europe would be 'anti-planning', which seems a little odd. But as he moved camp, he told Barbara Castle, according to her diaries, that 'The decision is purely a marginal one. I have always said so. I have never been a fanatic for Europe.' And later, when she accused him of presiding over a messy, middle-of-the-road muddle about conditions for entry, he complacently replied: 'I'm at my best in a messy, middle-of-the-road muddle.'[27] He did not holiday abroad and had a strong sentimental attachment to the Commonwealth and the provincial reassurance of traditional British life. Unlike Jenkins or Heath he had no friends in continental politics. When the referendum finally came in 1975, both Wilson's wife and his political secretary Marcia Falkender voted against staying in, which probably hints at Wilson's private instincts.

Yet in the late sixties British business saw the European Economic Community as an essential escape-route into a more modern and efficient world, words which triggered a response in Wilson. The press was overwhelmingly in favour. Some of his most effective colleagues, notably Jenkins, were vehemently pro. Whitehall opinion, though divided, was leaning that way too. Europe offered Wilson a new theme when he needed it. In 1967 he and the strongly pro-European George Brown gently perambulated their way around Rome, Strasbourg and Paris discussing possible British membership, though de Gaulle was still chilly. Brown spent much of the time insulting and clumsily chatting up secretaries. Soon afterwards Wilson formally announced a renewed British membership bid. De Gaulle, though dismissive in public, privately told the British ambassador in Paris that he envisaged a new kind of Europe, wider but also looser, and led by the strongest military powers, France and Britain, then Italy and Germany. It would allow for more national sovereignty. He implied that this complete reshaping of Europe should be cooked up between Paris and London, then publicly proposed by Britain, after which France would come in to support it. This was not only an early sketch of the kind of Europe that Britain would yearn for but a classic Gaullist swipe at the federal Europe being built from Brussels. It seemed an act of French disloyalty to their German and other continental allies. In London, unsure whether it was a devilish trap, officials urged Wilson to leak the idea to the Germans. The leaks infuriated almost everyone, de Gaulle most of all, and the idea died. Despite all this, and despite warnings that food prices would rise by up to a quarter as a result of British membership, talks went on. Shortly before Wilson finally lost power, the six member states concluded their own pre-British-entry deal which badly tilted the budget system and agricultural support against the UK and the other would-be joiners.

Devaluation and a Coup

Events – dear boy – duly forced the devaluation option into centre stage. Decade by decade, government by government, the impact of energy policy on British politics is a constant theme. One could write a useful political history which did not move beyond the dilemmas posed by energy supply. We can follow it from the winter of 1947 when the frozen coal stocks blew Attlee off course, through the oil-related shock of Suez and the destruction of Eden, to Heath's double confrontation with the miners, ending in his defeat in 1974, the rise of Scottish nationalism fuelled by North Sea oil, and then the epic coalfield confrontation between Margaret Thatcher and Arthur Scargill taking the story up to today's arguments about global warming and gas dependency on Russia. The simple fact of a small and crowded island energy-dependent in an uncertain world has toppled prime ministers and brought violent confrontation to the streets.

It had its effect on Harold Wilson too, when the

441

Six-Day War of June 1967 between Israel and Egypt led to an oil embargo on Britain by Iraq and Kuwait because of an alleged pro-Israel line from London. (Nasser, who made the allegation, of course recalled the Suez plot.) This, combined with war in Nigeria, hit Britain's finances, hoisted prices and produced more selling of sterling. If this was not enough, two months later there was a huge national dock strike, shutting first Liverpool and Hull and then, one by one, most of the rest of the major ports including London. The economic effect was dreadful, the trade figures a national shock. Wilson lashed out at the strikers. A year earlier he had been even more vituperative about striking seamen, suggesting they were being manipulated by communists or, as he called them 'a tightly knit group of politically motivated men' who had failed at the ballot box. Though that strike finished soon afterwards, Wilson's words, reckoned 'bonkers' by some cabinet colleagues, drove a further wedge between him and the left.

In the overheated atmosphere of July 1967 there was renewed talk of a plot to oust Wilson and replace him either with Callaghan or Brown. While the Prime Minister was away in Moscow, the pro-devaluers were talking. George Brown, characteristically, was threatening to resign and trying to persuade others to support him as leader; and characteristically failing. Others, including Benn, felt that if he did resign the whole government would fall. Equally characteristically since he had a weakness for grand hostesses, Roy Jenkins was at the home of Ann Fleming, who has featured earlier in this book. Wilson later told Barbara Castle that the plotting was directed by

442

'Ministers who went a-whoring after society hostesses.' Jenkins responded in his memoirs: 'There was indeed a certain allegorical quality about the behaviour of all of us that weekend ... Wilson kept up his adrenalin by going on an unnecessary trip to Moscow. George Brown went berserk at the Durham Miners' Gala. And I went to stay with Mrs Fleming at Sevenhampton.'

Wilson was still determined to resist devaluation. When he discovered briefing papers on the pros and cons had been prepared by civil servants, he brusquely ordered them to be collected up and burned. This was now a personal fight, corrupted by the rivalries and ambitions which plagued the cabinet. The left-wing devaluers hoped to turn Labour at last into a proper socialist government. They preferred to keep Wilson as leader but would have ditched him if necessary. The pro-European devaluers would have liked to replace Wilson with Roy Jenkins. The ironies are multiple: as the arguments raged, some on the left toyed with leaving Labour and setting up a new left-wing party based on the trade unions to be called the Social Democratic Party. One of them was the young Neil Kinnock, who would later as leader unleash a ferocious war on another 'party within the party'. The title SDP would later be taken not by the left but by Jenkins and many of the pro-Europeans who followed him. Meanwhile the devaluation crisis turned into an ungainly and undignified dance as George, Harold and Jim, with Roy and the rest joined hands, lurched away from each other, formed new sets and jigged towards humiliation. At moments, Callaghan seemed to think devaluation might be such a national catastrophe that it would force Wilson out, and let him in. Brown wanted it for strategic reasons and hoped against the odds it might usher him in as leader. Jenkins may not have been actively plotting, but was much enjoying his stellar reputation in the press and as a leading pro-European. Wilson was determined to fend off devaluation to protect his own position.

Eventually, on the morning of 3 November 1967, the senior economic adviser at the Treasury, Sir Alec Cairncross, told Callaghan at a private meeting that the dance was over. Nothing more could be done, the music had stopped. No further foreign borrowing was available. He would have to devalue. Both knew that Callaghan would have to resign. Though his biographer called this 'the most shattering moment Callaghan was ever to experience in sixty years of public life' he seems to have taken it calmly and set about preparing yet another round of cuts, the deflation without which devaluation would be pointless. This caused cabinet arguments and threats of more resignations. Wilson, after yet another last-minute attempt to borrow more to see Britain through, eventually accepted that the pound was impossible to defend even with American support. In a 6 p.m. broadcast on 18 November Wilson announced that the pound was being devalued by 14 per cent and that defence cuts, restrictions on hire purchase, or credit, and higher interest rates would follow too. Callaghan, as Chancellor, felt utterly humiliated. He wanted to leave the government entirely but was persuaded to take the Home Office instead. Wilson, who had after all just torn up what he had for so long insisted was essential to his strategy, seemed curiously chirpy. Normally an astute reader of the mood, he made an awesomely bad mistake in his broadcast by perkily informing the nation that 'the pound in your pocket' had not been devalued. In terms of its immediate purchasing power in the local shop this was of course true but the suggestion that the pound's international fall in value could be safely ignored was ludicrous and instantly understood to be ludicrous. Wilson was also devalued, possibly by more than 14 per cent.

Roy Jenkins now became Chancellor in Callaghan's place. Under him the Treasury finally regained complete authority. Wilson tried to get his friend and ally Barbara Castle in to run the DEA but Jenkins was having none of that. From then on Labour would become as much a party of Treasury orthodoxy as the Conservatives. After being one of the most energetic Home Secretaries of the twentieth century, Jenkins himself spent a remarkable couple of years as one of its more successful Chancellors. Though he never made it to Number Ten, in terms of personal influence, there is almost a case for renaming the Wilson years the Jenkins years. His 1968 budget increased taxes by twice as much as any previous budget ever, including the wartime ones, and he returned to the attack later in the year, and again in 1969. The last of these, Jenkins pointed out, led to the only excess of revenue over government spending in the period between Baldwin and Thatcher, 'a massive turn-round in the balance of payments and a vast consequent replenishment of our gold and dollar reserves and overseas borrowing capacity'.[28] He was, however, lucky as well as tough, as he generously acknowledged in his memoirs. It turned out that the Inland Revenue and Customs & Excise had dramatically undercounted the value of British exports. With the draconian budgets designed to make the best use of devaluation the mood altered. At last, it seemed, that that elusive 'grip' had been discovered. The trade figures improved. After so long, could it be that Labour had begun to discover a way to run the economy after all? As we will see, the answer was no, and Jenkins, along with Callaghan and most of the rest of the cabinet, must take the blame. For the other great issue was trade union militancy and in particular the rise in strikes. Grip regained on the nation's finances would be grip lost on its industrial climate.

Rivers of Blood

Harold Wilson was always a sincere anti-racialist. He had felt strongly enough about the racialist behaviour of the Tory campaign at Smethwick in the Midlands in 1964 to publicly denounce its victor Peter Griffiths as a 'parliamentary leper'. For Wilson, this was rare vehemence. But he did not try to repeal the 1962 Commonwealth and Immigrants Act, with its controversial quota system and in 1965, he and his Home Secretary, Frank Soskice, tightened it, cutting down the dependants allowed in, and giving the Government the power to deport illegal entrants, offering the first Race Relations Act as a sweetener. This outlawed the 'colour bar' in public places and discrimination in public services and banned incitement to race hatred. It was widely seen at the time as toothless. Yet the combination of restrictions on immigration and measures to better integrate the migrants already in Britain would form the basis for all subsequent policy. There would be a tougher anti-discrimination bill in 1968, and tougher anti-immigration measures to go with it. Never again would the idea of free access to Britain be seriously entertained by mainstream politicians.

One of the new migrations that arrived to beat the 1962 quota system just before Wilson came to power came from a rural area of Pakistan threatened with flooding by a huge dam project. The poor farming villages from the Muslim north, particularly around Kashmir, were not an entrepreneurial environment. They began sending their men to earn money in the labour-short textile mills of Bradford and surrounding towns. Unlike the West Indians, the Pakistanis and Indians were likelier to send for their families. Soon there would be large, inward-looking Muslim communities clustered in areas of Bradford, Leicester and other manufacturing towns. Unlike the Caribbean migrants, these were religiously divided from the whites around them and cut off from the main form of male white working-class entertainment, the consumption of alcohol. Muslim women were kept inside the house and the ancient habits of brides being chosen to cement family connections at home meant there was almost no sexual mixing, either. To many whites, the 'Pakis' were less threatening than the self-confident young Caribbean men, but also more alien.

Had this been all, then perhaps Enoch Powell's

simmering unease would have continued to simmer and his notorious 'River of Blood' speech would never have been made in the apocalyptic terms it was. Whatever the eventual problems thrown up by this mutual sense of alienation Britain's fragile new consensus of 1962–5 was about to be broken by another form of racial discrimination, this time exercised by Africans, mainly of the Kikuyu people of Kenya. After the divisive terror and counter-terror of the Mau Mau campaign, Kenya had won independence under the leadership of Jomo Kenyatta in 1963 and initially thrived as a relatively tolerant market economy. Alongside the majority of Africans, however, and the 40,000-odd whites who stayed after independence, there were some 185,000 Asians in Kenya. They had mostly arrived during British rule and were mostly better-off than the local Kikuyu, well established as doctors, civil servants, traders, business people and police. They also had full British and colonies passports and therefore an absolute right of entry to Britain, which had been confirmed by meetings of Tory ministers before independence. These people have been called the Jews of Africa and the parallels between their position and that of European Jewry in the thirties are striking. Like the Jews they were an abnormally go-ahead, vigorous and prosperous group. Like the Jews they were the object of nationalist and racial suspicion, from black Africans rather than white Germans. They too were often accused of disloyalty. When Kenyatta gave them the choice of surrendering their British passports and taking full Kenyan nationality, or becoming in effect foreigners, dependent on work permits, most of them chose to keep their British nationality. In the unfriendly and increasingly menacing atmosphere of Kenya in the mid-sixties, it seemed sensible. Certainly there was no indication from London that their rights to entry would be taken away.

The pressure on them grew, in ways that also mimicked Nazi treatment of the Jews, at least before the industrial genocide of the Holocaust. The Asians were deprived of their jobs in the civil service. They found they were unable to work or trade in the better-off parts of the country. They faced increasingly unpleasant propaganda. The minority who had opted for Kenyan citizenship found it mysteriously difficult to obtain. And so, inevitably, they began to make for Britain, their obvious refuge. Through 1967 they were coming in by plane at the rate of about a thousand a month. The newspapers began to put the influx onto the front pages and the now-popular television news showed great queues waiting for British passports and for flights. Enoch Powell, in an early warning shot, said that half a million East African Asians could eventually enter which was 'quite monstrous'. He called for an end to work permits and a complete ban on dependants coming to Britain. Other Tories, notably the former Colonial Secretary Iain Macleod, felt the party was entirely bound by the promises it had made when Kenya became independent; the Asians could not be left stateless. This division was echoed in the Labour government too, whose liberals, led by Roy Jenkins, believed the Asian migration could only be halted by pleading with Kenyatta for better treatment at home. The new Home Secretary Jim Callaghan, however, was determined to respond to the

449

apparent mood of worry and anger about the migration. This would mean revoking or cancelling the right of Kenyan Asians to enter. It would be a betrayal of a promise.

Shamefully the same Conservative politician who had made the promise originally, Duncan Sandys, was now leading calls to cancel it. By the turn of the year around 2,000 Kenyan Asians a month were arriving: almost every aircraft seat from East Africa to London, direct or indirect, was booked. Callaghan decided to act. As his colleague Crossman recorded of a crucial cabinet committee meeting in February 1968, 'Jim arrived with the air of a man whose mind was made up. He wasn't going to tolerate this bloody liberalism. He was going to stop this nonsense, as the public was demanding and as the Party was demanding. He would do it come what may and anybody who opposed him was a sentimental jackass.'[29] The Commonwealth Immigrants Act, which effectively slammed the door, while leaving a catflap open for a very small annual quota, was rushed through Parliament that spring. Yet this not only broke the word of the British Government at the time of Kenyan independence, it also left 20,000 people adrift and stateless in a part of Africa that no longer wanted them. The bill has been described as 'among the most divisive and controversial decisions taken by any British government. For some the legislation was the most shameful piece of legislation ever enacted by Parliament, the ultimate appeasement of racist hysteria' while for others it was the moment when the political elite, in the shape of Jim Callaghan, finally listened to their working-class

450

voters.[30] Polls of the public showed that 72 per cent supported the act.

This was the background to Powell's famous speech in Birmingham, at a small room in the city's Midland Hotel, on 20 April 1968, three weeks after Callaghan's bill had become law and the planes carrying would-be Kenyan Asian migrants had been turned round. Powell had argued before that the passport guarantee was never valid originally. He was contemptuous of the Commonwealth by now, seeing it as a high-minded constitutional myth, which stopped Britain from pursuing her self-interest freely. Most of his political fire was directed at the absurdities, as he saw them, of trying to control the level of the currency and direct the economy. Despite Heath's growing despair about his stiff-necked determination to challenge orthodoxy, Powell was still a member of the shadow cabinet. It had just agreed to cautious backing for Labour's tougher Race Relations Bill (the flip side of the Callaghan restrictions). Powell had gone uncharacteristically quiet. He was however quite aware of the size of the political explosion he was about to detonate, telling a local friend 'I'm going to make a speech at the weekend and it's going to go up "fizz" like a rocket; but whereas all rockets fall to earth, this one is going to stay up.'[31] The friend, Clem Jones, the editor of Powell's local newspaper, the *Wolverhampton Express and Star*, had advised him to time the speech for the early evening television bulletins, and not to distribute it generally beforehand. He would regret the advice.

Here is some of what Enoch Powell said. He quoted a Wolverhampton constituent, a middle-aged working man, who told him that if he had the money, he would leave the country because 'in fifteen or twenty years time the black man will have the whip hand over the white man'. Powell continued by asking rhetorically how he dared say such a horrible thing, stirring up trouble and inflaming feelings. 'The answer is I do not have the right not to do so. Here is a decent, ordinary fellow-Englishman, who in broad daylight in my own town says to me, his Member of Parliament, that this country will not be worth living in for his children. I simply do not have the right to shrug my shoulders and think about something else. What he is saying, thousands and hundreds of thousands are saying and thinking . . . ' Those whom the Gods wish to destroy, he reminded his audience, they first make mad. 'We must be mad, literally mad, as a nation to be permitting the annual inflow of some 50,000 dependants, who are for the most part the material of the future growth of the immigrant-descended population. It is like watching a nation busily engaged in heaping its own funeral pyre.' The race relations legislation was merely throwing a match on gunpowder. Powell then quoted another constituent, this time an elderly woman whom he said was persecuted by 'Negroes'. She had excrement stuffed through her letter-box and was followed to the shops 'by children, charming wide-grinning piccaninnies. They cannot speak English, but one word they know. "Racialist", they chant.' He concluded with the peroration which gave the speech its slightly inaccurate popular title: 'As I look ahead, I am filled with foreboding. Like the Roman, I seem to see "the Tiber foaming with much blood".' If Britain did not begin a policy of

452

voluntary repatriation, she would soon face the kind of race riots that were disfiguring America.

The speech was claimed by Powell to be merely a restatement of Tory policy. But its language and Powell's own careful preparation suggest it was both a call to arms by a politician who believed he was fighting for white English nationhood, and a deliberate provocation aimed at Powell's enemy Heath. At any rate, after horrified consultations when he and other leading Tories had seen extracts of the speech on the television news, Heath promptly ordered Powell to phone him, and summarily sacked him. Heath announced that he found the speech 'racialist in tone and liable to exacerbate racial tensions'. As Parliament returned three days after the speech, a thousand London dockers marched to Westminster in Powell's support; by the following day he had received 20,000 letters, almost all in support of his speech, with tens of thousands more still to come. Smithfield meat porters and Heathrow airport workers also demonstrated in his support. Powell also received death threats and needed full-time police protection for a while; numerous marches were held against him and he found it difficult to make speeches at or near university campuses. Asked whether he was a racialist by the *Daily Mail*, he replied: 'We are all racialists. Do I object to one coloured person in this country? No. To 100? No. To a million? A query. To five million? Definitely.'

There can be no serious doubt that most people in 1968 agreed with him.

Plot! Lord Louis and the King Thing

Forty years on, the paranoid atmosphere after only a few years of Wilson's first administration is hard to credit, but there was a rising conviction among some in business and the media that democracy itself had failed. Cecil King, the tall and megalomaniac nephew of those original press barons, Lords Rothermere and Harmsworth, and the effective proprietor of IPC, which owned the *Daily Mirror,* was at the centre of the flapping. He had originally supported Wilson, both in Opposition and in the period immediately after the 1964 election, but was deeply offended when Wilson, who had egalitarian convictions, then offered King only the modish life peerage. King was outraged. He wanted a hereditary title, as befitted the boss of a popular socialist newspaper, preferably an Earldom. Wilson, to his credit, refused to budge. To the Prime Minister's discredit, though, he desperately flattered King, courted him and gave him a string of other baubles, including a damehood for his wife and positions for himself – director of the Bank of England, a seat on the National Coal Board and another on the National Parks Commission, plus repeated offers of junior government jobs and a life peerage. None of it made the slightest impression on the sulking press tycoon, who went round London telling anyone who would listen that Wilson was a dud, a liar and an incompetent who was ruining the country and who should be removed as soon as possible.[32]

454

King's theme, not uncommon in business circles, was that Britain needed professional administrators and managers in charge, not dodgy politicians. He insisted that 'We are coming near to the failure of parliamentary government.' The politicians had made 'such a hash of our affairs that people must be brought into government from outside the rank of professional politicians'. His private views came close to a call for insurrection or a coup, to be fronted by himself and other business leaders. This culminated in a clumsily attempted plot. On 8 May 1968, according to King's brilliant editor-in-chief Hugh Cudlipp, the two of them had a meeting with Lord Louis Mountbatten, whom we have met in his role negotiating India's independence. As a war hero, former Chief of the Defence Staff and close member of the Royal Family, Mountbatten had a unique role in public life. He stood above politics, though many believed he liked the notion of being thought a man of destiny, and he was much discussed by those who dreamed of an anti-Wilson putsch. He had made his worries about the country known to Cudlipp, though denying he wanted 'to appear to be advocating or supporting any notion of a Right Wing dictatorship – or any nonsense of that sort'. Indeed, Mountbatten's idea of the possible leader of some kind of emergency government supplanting Wilson was ... Barbara Castle.

Nevertheless, when King, Cudlipp and Mountbatten met, with the government's chief scientific adviser Sir Solly Zuckerman, the talk was wild. King told the Queen's uncle-in-law that in the coming crisis, 'the government would disintegrate, there would be bloodshed in the streets, the armed forces would be involved' and asked Mountbatten whether he would agree to be titular head of a new administration. According to Cudlipp, Mountbatten then asked Zuckerman what he made of it. The scientist rose, walked to the door and replied: 'This is rank treachery. All this talk of machine guns at street corners is appalling. I am a public servant and will have nothing to do with it. Nor should you, Dickie.' Mountbatten agreed. Later, he recorded that it was he who had told King the idea was 'rank treason' and booted him out. King's account of the meeting is different, though hardly less alarming. He claimed Mountbatten had said morale in the armed forces was low, the Queen was worried and asked for advice. To which the newspaperman replied: 'There might be a stage in the future when the Crown would have to intervene: there might be a stage when the armed forces were important. Dickie should keep himself out of public view so as to have clean hands ...'[33] Whichever account is more accurate, the meeting certainly took place and Mountbatten then seems to have reported the conversation to the Queen. King, unabashed, unleashed a front page attack in the *Daily Mirror* on Wilson, headlined 'Enough is Enough', and calling for a new leader. He was himself putsched by a board which realized he had become a serious embarrassment, shortly afterwards.

Does any of this matter? There is no evidence that the talk of a coup was truly serious, or that the security services were involved, as has been publicly asserted since. Yet the Cecil King story counts in two ways. First, it gives some indication of the fevered and at times almost hysterical mood about

456

Wilson and the condition of the country that had built up by the late sixties – a time now more generally remembered as golden, chic and successful. A heady cocktail of rising crime, student rioting, inflation, civil rights protests in Northern Ireland and embarrassments abroad had convinced some that the country was ungovernable. Because British democracy has survived unscathed through the post-war period, to suggest it was ever threatened now seems outlandish. Perhaps it never was. There is a lurid little saloon bar of the mind where conspiracy theorists, mainly on the left, and self-important fantasists, mainly on the right, gather and talk. The rest of us should be wary of joining them for a tipple. Yet the transition from the discredited old guard of Macmillan-era Britain to the unwelcomed new cliques of Wilson-era Britain was a hard time.

Wilson was a genuine outsider so far as the old Establishment was concerned, and he ran a court of outsiders. The old Tory style of government by clique and clubmen gave way to government by faction and feud, a weakness in Labour politics throughout the party's history. Wilson had emerged by hopping from group to group, with no settled philosophical view or strong body of personal support in the party. Instead of a 'Wilson party', represented in the Commons and country, he relied on a small gang of personal supporters – Marcia Williams most famously, but also the Number Ten insiders Peter Shore, Gerald Kaufman, George Wigg and for, a while in these earlier years, Tony Benn too. Then there were the outside advisers. Some were brought in from academic life, such as the Hungarian-born economists Thomas Balogh and Nicholas Kaldor (popularly known as Buddha and Pest). Some came from business, such as the notorious Gannex raincoat manufacturer Joseph Kagan, or from the law, such as the arch-fixer of the sixties Lord Goodman. Suspicious of the Whitehall Establishment, with some justification, and cut off from both the right-wing group of former Gaitskellites, and the old Bevanites, Wilson felt forced to create his own gang. A Tory in that position might have automatically turned to old school tie connections, or family ones, as Macmillan did. Wilson turned to an eclectic group of one-offs and oddballs, producing a peculiarly neurotic little court, riven by jealousy and misunderstanding.

This anti-court gave easy material to Wilson's snobbish and suspicious enemies in the press, ranging from *Private Eye,* which constantly taunted the insiders with foreign-sounding names, to the MI5-connected 'red conspiracy' merchants, and even scions of the Fleet Street purple. Many in that old Establishment – the top brass, the City grandees, the clubmen – struggled to accept that Wilson was a legitimate leader of the United Kingdom. Wilson was paranoid but plenty of powerful people were out to get him, or at least to get him out.

In Place of Beer

Until the end of the decade the sixties had not been particularly strike-prone compared to the fifties. Strikes tended to be local, unofficial and quickly settled. Inflation was still below 4 per cent for most years and, being voluntary, incomes policies rarely caused national confrontation. But by 1968–9 inflation was rising sharply. Wilson had pioneered the matey 'beer and sandwiches' approach to dealing with union leaders (though he found on his first attempt the sandwiches were too thinly cut to satisfy union appetites). But he was becoming disillusioned. That seamen's strike of 1966 had been a particularly bruising experience. So for once it was Wilson who took a stand. He was supported by an unlikely hammer of the unions, the veteran left-winger Barbara Castle, now made Secretary for Employment. In a homage to her early hero, Nye Bevan's book *In Place of Fear,* she called her plan for industrial harmony 'In Place of Strife'. It proposed new government powers to order pre-strike ballots, and a 28-day pause before strikes took place. The government would be able in the last resort to impose settlements for wildcat strikes. There would be fines if the rules were broken. This was a package of measures which looks gentle by the standards of the laws which would come later. The leading trade unionists of the day, once famous men like Jack Jones and Hugh Scanlon, saw it as an unacceptable return to legal curbs they had fought for decades to lift.

The battle that followed nearly ended Wilson's career, and Castle's. Their defeat made the Thatcher revolution inevitable, though it would not come for a further decade. The failure of 'In Place of Strife' is one of the great lost opportunities of modern British politics. Why did it fail? The easy explanation is that the unions were too powerful and yet also still too popular, not least on the Labour backbenches. Barbara Castle was neither the most tactful negotiator nor the niftiest tactician. Her angry harangues put up the backs of male newspaper commentators and MPs, who compared her to a fishwife and a nag, just as they would Margaret Thatcher. She made silly mistakes, such as going away on holiday in the Mediterranean on the yacht owned by that arch capitalist Lord Forte during one of the most sensitive weeks, lying in the sun and talking of resignation. Later while Wilson sat up companionably with union leaders, quaffing brandies and puffing cigars, she would creep off exhausted to bed. Yet both Wilson and Castle were fully aware that this was a struggle for authority a serious government could not afford to lose.

In a famous confrontation in the summer of 1969 when union leaders were given a private dinner at Chequers, Scanlon had warned the two ministers directly again, that he would not accept any legal penalties, or even any new legislation. Wilson replied that if he as Prime Minister accepted such a position he would be running a government that was not allowed to govern. If the unions mobilized their sponsored Labour MPs to vote against him, 'it would clearly mean that the TUC, a state within a state, was putting itself above the government in deciding what a government could and could not do.' Uttered privately this was just the language which would be heard publicly from Heath and later even more starkly from Thatcher. Scanlon retorted that Wilson was becoming that arch turncoat, a Ramsay MacDonald. Wilson hotly denied it and referred to the Czech reformist leader who had been crushed by the Red Army the previous year: 'Nor do I intend to be another Dubček. Get your tanks off my lawn, Hughie!'

But the tanks stayed resolutely parked under his nose, Scanlon and Jones unblinking, their gun-barrels pointing at Labour's reputation. Wilson and Castle now contemplated a joint resignation. For the Prime Minister also had a weapon of last resort. If he walked away then the Tories would surely return, with tougher measures still. But as the stand-off continued, the unions merely suggested a series of voluntary agreements and letters of intent. They were toughing it out because they had excellent intelligence from inside the government and knew very well that Wilson and Castle were isolated. Not only were the usual forces of the left against reform of industrial relations – all those *Tribune* MPs attacking Castle for betraying her principles, the scores of pragmatic rebels on the Labour benches and the trade union sponsored MPs whose paymasters were jerking the reins – but also some key right-wing ministers too. As so often, below the great issue of the hour, personal vanity and ambition were writhing. Jim Callaghan, with his strong trade union links, was utterly against legal curbs on the unions. Now Home Secretary, a former trade union official himself, he voted against his own government's plans at a meeting of Labour's national executive. His enemies were convinced that he thought the failure of union reform would finish Wilson off. 'In Place of Strife' would become 'In Place of Harold'.

Callaghan's objections to the package went beyond pure self-interest but his own ideas about how to deal with the unions were thin to the point of absurdity. As Prime Minister much later he would be richly and fairly repaid for what he did in 1969. At the time he was reviled by the pro-reform

461

ministers. In a bitter cabinet meeting, Callaghan retorted to Crossman's plea that they must all sink or swim together, with the words, 'sink or sink'. grossman spat back: 'Why don't you go? Get out!' Callaghan's fellow Cardiff MP, later the Speaker, George Thomas, described him as 'our Judas Iscariot'. Other ministers had their own agendas too, of course, and began to peel away from Wilson and Castle. Tony Crosland, another key figure on the Labour right, hoped that if Callaghan succeeded Wilson, he would finally achieve his great ambition and become Chancellor. Jenkins, however, was not mainly motivated by the hope of toppling Wilson. For one thing, no one could tell whether Wilson's fall would mean his success, or Callaghan's. Furthermore, Jenkins knew that since his main criticism of the Prime Minister was lack of principle, to stab him in the back when he did make a stand would look absurd and discreditable. Yet late in the day Jenkins eventually ratted because he said he feared 'a government smash' if the plans were forced through. Tony Benn, who had been warmly backing Barbara Castle before, changed his mind too. After the crucial cabinet meeting, Wilson stormed out, saying to his staff, 'I don't mind running a green cabinet, but I'm buggered if I'm going to run a yellow one!'[34]

It is possible to argue that Castle's plans were too hardline for 1969, though late in life Callaghan eventually recanted and admitted penal sanctions had been necessary.[35] But had the Labour Government been united behind Wilson on this, then legislative reform of trade union practices might have been forced through even the Parliamentary Labour Party of the day, and much

462

subsequent grief avoided. Wilson's reputation, Labour's reputation and the story of British politics would have been markedly different. But with the cabinet as well as the backbenches in rebellion, Wilson had no choice but to give way. His earlier threats to resign were swiftly forgotten. In a brutal aside about Castle which perhaps reflected the strain he was under, he said to an official: 'Poor Barbara. She hangs around like someone with a still-born child. She can't believe it's dead.'[36] The two of them reached a toothless 'solemn and binding' agreement under which unions said they would accept TUC advice on unofficial strikes. Solomon Binding was meant to be a face-saver but instead became a national joke. Hypocritically, the cabinet applauded Wilson for his brilliant negotiating and, hypocritically, he accepted their praise – though Castle, on the edge of physical collapse, gave them a blast of honest contempt. The Tories and the press were rightly derisive. In his memoirs Jenkins admitted that Wilson, whom he generally did not admire, came out of it all with a touch of King Lear-like nobility. 'He did not hedge and he did not whine ... It was a sad story from which he and Barbara Castle emerged with more credit than the rest of us.' The great background question about the Labour governments of the sixties is whether with a stronger leader they could have gripped the country's big problems and dealt with them. How did it happen that a cabinet of such brilliant, such clever and self-confident people achieved so little? In part, it was the effect of the whirling court politics demonstrated by 'In Place of Strife'.

Election Upset

In the end, the Wilson government was felled not by wild-eyed plotters but entirely conventionally by the electorate. When Wilson called the election in 1970 he was feeling optimistic despite the failure of 'In Place of Strife'. He knew his enemy. Heath had been the Leader of the Opposition since 1965, with Tory MPs voting in a secret ballot for the first time. Seen as a ruthless modernizer, he began to reshape the Tory front bench. Out went many of the cod-Edwardian grandees. In came people like Peter Walker, another grammar school boy who had made his money in the City, Geoffrey Rippon, the young former mayor of Surbiton, Tony Barber, the former RAF man and lawyer, and Margaret Thatcher, a grocer's daughter, none of them from rich families. Though a pre-1970 election policy conference at the Selsdon Park hotel outside London was much over-hyped as a lurch to the right (Wilson talked of 'Selsdon Man', as some kind of ape-like throwback), Heath was a staunchly pro-business politician. In the sixties and early seventies, after so many years of the more languid, aristocratic Tory Party, he seemed like a blast of fresh air.

Wilson and Heath cordially detested one another. Perhaps it was because they had so much in common. They came from traditionalist, pious, lower-middle-class, provincial families. They were born in the same year, 1916, Heath four months after Wilson. His family was poorer than Wilson's and his working-class origins stronger. Heath's father was a carpenter who worked for a building contractor and his mother was a lady's maid who later took in lodgers. Like Wilson, Heath rose through fierce academic ability and scholarships. Both seem to have been rather solitary and awkward as young men but benefited from the richness of pre-television community life, Wilson throwing himself into the world of Scouting and Methodist clubs, and Heath into music and choirs. Both arrived at Oxford at much the same time and were on the edge of the glamorous and passionate politics of the pre-war period there, though they never seem to have met. As we have seen, the two of them represented the triumph of the grammar school boy in politics, a class breakthrough comparable to what happened at the same time in business, the arts and the professions. Governing consecutively during 1964–76 they would oversee the near-total destruction of the grammar school in England and Wales. Both would represent moderation in their respective parties, harried by the hard left and the hard right, accused of weakness and appeasement. Each was essentially a believer in managerialism and compromise. Patriots and equally proud men, they would come to be reviled, identified with a time of national collapse and failure. They were certainly easy to caricature, Wilson's pudgy face and pipe, against Heath's vast manic grin and yacht-sailing.

There were good reasons for Labour to think that they would see off the Tories yet again. Jenkins seemed to have pulled the economy around and was self-confident enough not to use his last budget for pre-election bribes. It was in fact quite popular. The opinion polls were onside and the press was generally predicting an easy Labour victory. Even right-wing commentators lavished praise on Wilson's television performances and mastery of debate, though he pursued an avowedly presidential style and tried to avoid controversy.

Heath was regarded as a dull dud by comparison and harried by Powell who had returned to the attack again and again before the 1970 election, provoking Heath to denounce him as inhumane and unchristian, and to make it clear that he would never be asked to serve in a Conservative government. At the height of their battle for the soul of the party, in summer 1969, a Gallup poll suggested 54 per cent agreed with Powell on grants to repatriate what it called coloured immigrant families. By early 1970, 66 per cent of those polled said they were either more favourable to Powell or felt the same about him and only 22 per cent said their view of him was less favourable. Powell was by now attacking Heath over a broad front of policy, over the need for tax cuts, privatization and freer markets in economics; over Northern Ireland, or Ulster; and over British membership of the EEC, which Powell opposed as strongly as Heath supported it. So Powell's battle-cry for repatriation and an end to immigration was taken by the Tory leadership as part of his campaign to unseat Heath and then replace him.

There were plenty in the party and the country who yearned for just that. Apart from the dockers and other marchers, wealthy backers wanted to fund a campaign for Powell's leadership. Marcel Everton, a Worcestershire industrialist, raised money for a national federation of Powellite groups and talked of a march on Conservative headquarters to oust Heath. Wilson's call for an election, however, created an obvious trap which Powell could see very clearly even if his supporters ignored it. His best chance by far would be if Heath lost the election. Then he could attack him openly and perhaps even seize control of the party. Everton, like others, openly said that it would be better for right-wingers to vote Labour so that the Tory party would 'fall into Enoch's lap like a ripe cherry'.[37] Yet if Powell seemed to toy with this, he would be forever branded a traitor by tens of thousands of loyal Conservatives. Either Heath would win and Powell would be finished, or he would lose and Powell would be blamed by so many Tories the party might split.

The campaign was characterized by huge coverage of Powell, in the case of some newspapers, engorging half their reporting of the Tories' entire campaign. It has been described as the only general election campaign in British history in which immigration and race have played a significant part. Conservative meetings were full of home-made 'Enoch' signs. Heath and his colleagues were constantly irritated and embarrassed by being asked whether or not they supported their fallen angel in Wolverhampton. Unsurprisingly, Powell was portrayed by Labour and Liberal politicians as the right-wing ideologue behind whom Ted Heath anxiously waddled. Tony Benn went furthest in this, calling him 'the real leader of the Conservative party. He is a far stronger character than Mr Heath. He speaks his mind ... Heath dare not attack him publicly even when he says things that disgust decent Conservatives.' Benn went on to assert that 'the flag hoisted at Wolverhampton is beginning to look like the one that fluttered over Dachau and Belsen.'

Late in the campaign Powell, who had been hounded by left-wing protesters, finally gave a clear and unequivocal endorsement to the official Tory campaign. Because there was indeed a late surge of support for Heath, it has been argued that Powell was responsible for his victory. But the evidence is thin to prove it and Powell himself fastidiously declined to claim such a thing. Just before the campaign had begun Jenkins learnt, too late, that yet more bad balance of payments figures were to be published along with bad inflation figures. This helped tip things away from Wilson. When the results were in the Tories had won an overall majority of thirty. Polls afterwards scotched the idea that Jenkins's pre-election budget had lost Labour the election. In fact it was quite popular. Powell, according to his biographer, once he realized the consequences of Heath's victory, 'sat around on his own with his head in his hands, deep in gloom. He had realised immediately that, after Wilson, he had been the great loser of the election.'[38]

And Wilson was bitterly disappointed. He was also surprised. With no home of his own on the mainland, he had to take up Heath's offer of a last weekend in Chequers while he desperately searched around for somewhere to live.

Blood and Shame:
the Irish Tragedy Begins

Of the great crises that link Wilson and Heath together, that of Northern Ireland had as much effect on the tenor of mainland British life as any. It brought surprise and embarrassment to millions watching the violence on the streets of the province. It brought bombings, murder and shame. The longer origins of the conflict, from the settlement of Ulster by Scots Presbyterian farmers to the Partition of Ireland in 1921 and the civil war are outside the limits of this book. In the fifties and through most of the sixties, Northern Ireland barely appeared on the Westminster radar. There was a devolved Northern Ireland government, with its own prime minister and a distinct party system, along with the contingent of grey, reliable, conservative-minded Unionist MPs who rarely made ripples in London, never mind waves. The bigotry of the Protestant majority was the butt of jokes and official disapproval.

Yet there was limited English or Scottish sympathy for the cause of Irish unification – hostility to Catholicism and memories of the inglorious role played by the Republic during the war against Hitler remained strong. If the Belfast shipyards of Harland & Wolff were barred to Catholics, then too were some well-known concerns on the mainland. If there was unfairness in the allocation of housing in Londonderry, so there was in Leicester or Nottingham. There was, admittedly, a blatant form of anti-Catholic constituency-rigging, the gerrymandered boundaries designed to maximize Unionist representation. As early as 1964, when Wilson first met the Stormont Prime Minister Captain Terence O'Neill, who had been elected the previous year on a programme of mild reform, he was pressing him to end gerrymandering. Mostly, though, this was a time of dozy neglect which turned out from 1969 to have been a terrible failure of imagination & malign neglect, whose effects would haunt Britain for the next thirty years.

For under the surface, the unfairness and discrimination in jobs, in housing and in politics, had taken the temperature in the Catholic ghettos to simmering point. The changed international climate had something to do with this. Rebellion against injustice was in the air, or at least in the newspapers. Rising protests about apartheid in South Africa and the struggle for equal rights in the southern states of the US had focused attention on the squalid half-secret on Britain's doorstep. O'Neill's cautious moves towards reform had produced a hardline Protestant backlash, led by demagogues including a young and turbulent preacher called Ian Paisley. In 1967 a civil rights movement had been formed, using the language and tactics of the Deep South, and the following year, marches and demonstrations were being met with police violence. A largely Catholic and nationalist party, the Social Democratic and Labour Party, was formed. Bernadette Devlin of the more radical Ulster Unity Party was elected in 1969 to the Commons, the youngest ever woman MP, on a civil rights ticket. She treated MPs to what one of her listeners described as 'the authentic, bitter and resentful voice of Catholic Ulster'.[39] Wilson told O'Neill he thought he should go further and faster, both on housing and on local government boundaries. O'Neill replied that this would require an election. During it, his Unionist Party split and he received a bloody nose, handing over to another, though less effective, moderate, James Chichester-Clarke. At this stage, apart from occasional raids on arms dumps, the ageing and sparsely manned Irish Republican Army was little heard of.

Then, in the summer of 1969, the politics of Northern Ireland erupted. The Apprentice Boys of Derry, a Loyalist anti-Catholic organization, had planned their annual march at Londonderry on the same day and over the same route that a civil rights march was planned. There had been civil rights marches before, but they had been peaceful. This time, ordered not to march, they did so and were attacked by the police. Members of the so-called B-Specials, an unpaid and part-time but armed 12,000-strong wing of the Royal Ulster Constabulary, were particularly brutal. Among the seventy-five marchers injured that day were leading political figures, such as Gerry Fitt who would become an MP and a peer, and a powerful anti-IRA voice for moderation. The bloodied heads and the vengeful use of batons horrified millions watching that evening's television bulletins. In response the Stormont government promised reforms to local elections, housing lists and parliamentary boundaries. This sparked off Loyalist protests. More civil rights marches followed, and more attacks on them, until at the beginning of August, there was a serious pitched battle between Catholic

471

residents, Loyalist extremists and police in the middle of Belfast. Hundreds of houses burned. Harold Wilson, who was on holiday on the Isles of Scilly, flew to Cornwall for a brief talk with his Home Secretary, Jim Callaghan. They agreed to send in the British Army if asked, in return for the abolition of the B-Specials and promises of further reforms. It was a momentous decision, taken without the involvement of the cabinet. As Crossman recorded in his diary: 'Harold and Jim had really committed the cabinet to putting the troops in and once they were there, they couldn't be taken out again, so we had to ratify what had been done.' Tony Benn wrote: 'It looks as though civil war in Ulster has almost begun.'

One of the myths about the moment when Britain sent in the troops to Northern Ireland was that it was done with little understanding of the dangers, no thought about alternatives and no appreciation that, arriving to protect Catholic homes, the troops might find themselves a target for Irish nationalists. This is all untrue. Wilson and Callaghan were acutely aware of the dangers and had put maximum pressure on Chichester-Clarke and the Unionists to hurry through political change, and they got some of what they wanted over the B-Specials and housing. In casting around for alternatives, Wilson even apparently toyed with the idea of a reverse 'plantation', evacuating the entire Ulster Protestant community out of Ireland and giving them new homes in England and Scotland.[40] When Wilson's press secretary, Joe Haines, suggested to him that the troops could be there for months, he grimly replied: 'They're going to be there for seven years at least.' Callaghan, whose handling of the crisis was his finest hour, was under no illusion that the troops would soon be facing both communities, and would indeed become a target. Benn, attending cabinet with a freshly grown beard which caused much amusement around the table, mused whether this was not 'the beginning of ten more years of Irish politics at Westminster which could be very unpleasant'.[41] Meanwhile over in Northern Ireland itself, the hard men were at work. Loyalist mobs reacted with fury to the proposed disbanding of the B-Specials and IRA men were digging into the various civil rights and citizens' defence organizations of Catholic Belfast and Derry. In November, at a tense meeting in Dublin, the IRA split, and the pro-violence Provisional Army Council or 'Provos' came into existence.

Now the nature of the conflict would change. It had begun as a protest about unfairness, bigotry and political corruption. It turned into a fight to force an end to the United Kingdom and to bring about the unification of Ireland. Inspired by a heady mix of Marxism, romantic nationalism and the example of overseas guerrillas from Vietnam to Cuba, the Provos believed that so long as they had the support of most Catholics, they could end the partition of the island. Winning over much of the minority community took time. The IRA's first success was to convince many Catholics living in Belfast, where they were heavily outnumbered, that only they could protect them against the Loyalist thugs and that the British Army was bloodied hand in bloodied glove with their enemies. This was not so but rumour and stone-throwing provocation, followed by over-reaction and army brutality, would

473

soon make it seem that way. In the Irish Republic, many were instinctively with the IRA. In 1970 two Dublin cabinet ministers, Charles Haughey and Neil Blaney, were sacked for being sympathizers with the Provos, though acquitted later of trying to illegally import arms into the Republic. Most of £100,000 voted by the Dail, the Irish Parliament, for the relief of Catholics in the North a year earlier had, in fact, been spent on arms and ammunition. Community defence was morphing into nationalist uprising.

This was the crisis inherited by Heath, the nearly man in Irish peace-making, in 1970. He knew little about Northern Ireland when he arrived in office, though he had once been smuggled across the border under a blanket for lunch in the Republic. In one crucial respect he advanced on the underlying assumption of the Labour ministers. It would not be enough to protect Northern Catholics. Heath thought they would have to be given a stake in the running of Northern Ireland too. Eventually, he hoped, greater prosperity in Ireland, more trade across the border and common membership of Europe would ease the two communities towards an easier relationship. This is what happened, though only after decades of murder had exhausted them, too.

The Yachtsman

Heath's reputation has sunk particularly low. Perhaps this is not surprising. He was defeated as leader in 1975 after losing two generation elections

474

and fell out spectacularly with the new order, Thatcherism. The triumph of Margaret Thatcher's optimistic if divisive free-market politics attracted a blaze of intellectual, media and parliamentary support which saw her success as a refutation of Heath's time. The brighter she burned then, by narrative necessity, the duller he must be. Certainly, his attempts to rein in trade union power and to conquer inflation failed. The cause that excited him more than any other, Europe, also inflamed his enemies who accused him of lying to the country about the true, political nature of the coming European Union. Heath did not help his cause by the implacable sulk that followed his ousting, a huff he managed to maintain for thirty years. His own account of his government is wooden and wearisomely self-justificatory, in prose almost as bad as Harold Wilson's. Further, as a loner who could be extraordinarily rude even to his admirers, Heath never accumulated a team of public defenders. Those who worked with him and thought him a fine leader, such as Douglas Hurd, were rarely able to make themselves heard against the surging self-belief and vituperative journalism of the Thatcher years. Finally Heath had little time in office compared to Wilson's near-eight, just three and a half years.

Almost friendless, Heath is a political leader whose reputation deserves to be revisited. He was the first outsider to break through the class barriers of the old Tory party and he promoted others like him to the cabinet. His European vision came first-hand. Before the war, on a student visit to Germany, he had literally rubbed shoulders with Hitler and met other Nazi leaders. Later he returned as a fighting officer to see their final defeat in 1945 and the war marked him more strongly than it marked Wilson. As Heath wrote later: 'My generation did not have the option of living in the past; we had to work for the future. We were surrounded by destruction, homelessness, hunger and despair. Only by working together right across our continent had we any hope of creating a society which would uphold the true values of European civilisation.' He was a genuinely compassionate and unusually brave politician, whose analysis of what was wrong with Britain in the seventies was far more acute than Wilson's. His struggle with trade union power, conducted at the worst possible time, was relentless but he was up against forces too big to conquer quickly. Like Margaret Thatcher, he believed Britain was in danger of becoming ungovernable. His strategic mistake was to attack union power head-on and in a single act, rather than piecemeal, as her wilier government would. Like her, he cut taxes and even began privatization. Unlike her, he was ruling at a time when public sympathy was more with unions than with government, and when huge rises in the price of oil and other commodities were knocking Western economies sideways. His 1972 U-turn on incomes policy and industrial intervention was indeed a humiliating moment for parliamentary democracy but, while stiff-necked and difficult, mostly Edward Heath was plain unlucky.

He had risen through the Tory Party in Parliament as a tough chief whip and then as an equally tough negotiator on Europe in the Macmillan years. But Heath's greatest achievement as a minister had come in 1964 when, as President of the Board of Trade, he abolished Resale Price Maintenance, or RPM. This is one of those reforms which sound dull and are now largely forgotten but which really did reshape the country. RPM allowed manufacturers to order shops to sell their products at a particular price. A shop which cut prices would be breaking the law. It therefore discriminated heavily in favour of small, relatively expensive shops rather than superstores; under RPM the supermarket revolution would have been much less dramatic and the 'Tesco-ification' of Britain impossible. Heath believed it stood in the way of proper competition and choice, and was inflationary. Yet were not small shopkeepers natural Conservatives? Many in the party and government opposed him, but he carried the day, a crucial defeat of producer interest by the new consumerism.

Ugandan Asians

Heath in power showed that he was desperately worried about the anti-immigration mood revealed in this most bitter of elections. While denouncing Powell, he moved quickly to pass a highly controversial and restrictive piece of legislation which removed any right to immigrate to Britain from anyone who did not have a parent or grandparent born in the country. Heath's manifesto had promised 'a new single system of control over all immigration from overseas'. Nobody had spelled out that this system would be designed to exclude blacks but not whites, yet the grandparent rule was transparently designed to allow Australians, Canadians, South Africans and New Zealanders of white British origins to return to the UK, while keeping out the black and coloured people of the Commonwealth and colonies. Powell himself likened the distinction to a Nazi race purity law; he wanted a new definition of British citizenship instead. The grandparent rule was defeated by the right and the left combining for opposite reasons, though restored two years later. Had this been all, then Heath would go down in history as being yet another panicked Establishment man, slamming the door to keep his party happy.

It was not all. For the Kenyan crisis was about to be replayed, at speed, in Uganda. Here the anti-British Prime Minister, Milton Obote, had just been replaced in a coup by the fat, swaggering, Sandhurst-educated Idi Amin who announced that he had been told in a dream he must expel that country's Asians, just as the Kenyans had theirs. Amin was clearly a monster, whose thugs clubbed his enemies to death with staves, who threatened to kill British journalists, who was rumoured to keep human flesh in his fridge and to feast on it, and who enthused about the way the Nazis had dealt with the Jews. Though Powell argued angrily that Britain had no obligation to allow the trapped Ugandan Asians into her cities, Heath acted decisively to bring them in. Airlifts were arranged, with a resettlement board to help them, and 28,000 people arrived within a few weeks in 1971, eventually settling in the same areas as other East Africans – even though Leicester, becoming the 'least white' city in England, had published adverts in Ugandan newspapers pleading with migrants not to come there.

Within a few years Powell would no longer be a Conservative. Heath had confronted him head-on and beaten him. Once seen as a future prime minister, or at least as a brilliant chancellor-to-be, Powell would spend the rest of his life far from even the fringes of power. His ideas, however, would continue to grow in power and influence. His hostility to European union would inspire the biggest revolt in the modern Tory Party, one which kept Britain out of the euro. His belief in rigorous free-market economics would powerfully influence Margaret Thatcher and her circle so that he would be treated as a prophet, Old Testament Enoch. On race and immigration, the picture is more mixed. His views frightened many and made him one of the most detested as well as admired politicians of post-war times. Those who knew him best insist he was not a racialist. The newspaper editor Clem Jones, who tried and failed to track down the little old lady chased by 'piccaninnies' from Powell's speech nevertheless said 'he was never a racist'. Jones thought he had been affected by the anger of white Wolverhampton people who felt they were being crowded out; even in Powell's own street 'of good, solid, Victorian houses, next door went sort of coloured and then another house, and he saw the value of his own house go down'. But, added the newspaperman, Powell would work very hard as an MP for constituents of any colour: 'We quite often used to go out for a meal, as a family, to a couple of Indian restaurants, and he was on extremely amiable terms with everybody there, 'cos having been in India and his wife brought up in India, they liked that kind of food.'[42]

On the numbers migrating to Britain, and the consequences for the population of non-whites living in the country, Powell's figures which were much ridiculed at the time were not far out. Just before his 1968 speech, he suggested that by the end of the century, the number of black and Asian immigrants and their descendants would number between five and seven million, or about a tenth of the population. According to the 2001 census, the relevant figures were 4.7 million people identifying themselves as black or Asian, or 7.9 per cent of the total population, though with large-scale illegal immigration since then, the true numbers are certainly higher. Immigrants are far more strongly represented, in percentage terms as well as raw numbers, in London and the English cities than in Scotland, Wales or Northern Ireland. It can also be argued that Powell did British democracy a kind of service by speaking out on an issue which had been up to then cloaked in elite silence and so provoking a debate which needed to happen at some time. Against that, his language still feels shockingly inflammatory and provocative nearly forty years later. He was talking just after the formation of the racist and fascist National Front in 1967 and though Powell himself was anti-Nazi and indeed had returned from Australia on the outbreak of war to fight the Germans, his words attracted the enthusiastic support of the would-be gauleiters of provincial Britain. Further, his core prediction, of civil unrest comparable to that suffered in the southern states of the United States, has not come about. Five notable outbreaks of inner city rioting

480

since then, and a rise in street crime linked to disaffected youths from Caribbean and other immigrant communities do not add up to the conflagration he predicted.

Immigration has changed Britain more than almost any other single social event in post-1945 Britain – more than the increase in longevity, or the Pill, the collapse of deference or the spread of suburban housing. The only change which eclipses it is the triumph of the car. It was not a change that was asked for by the white population – though the terms and circumstances of 50 million people choosing suddenly to ask such a question are impossible to imagine. The majority of British people did not want the arrival of large numbers of blacks and Asians, just as they did not want an end to capital punishment, or deep British involvement in the European Union, or many of the other things the political elite has opted for. At no stage was there a measured and frank assessment of the likely scale of immigration led by party leaders, voluntarily, in front of the electorate. And while allowing this change by default, the main parties did very little to ensure that mass immigration from the Caribbean and the Indian subcontinent was successful. West Indians got none of the help and forethought lavished on the demobilized Poles, or even the less adequate help given to the Ugandan Asians. There was no attempt to create mixed communities, or avoid mini-ghettos. Race relations legislation did come, but late and only to balance new restrictions: it simply castigated racialism in the white working-class community, rather than trying to understand it.

So this is another example of Britain's history of rule by elite, of liberal politicians acting above their electorates. The real question is whether this neglect of public opinion, and then of the consequences of immigration, not least for the immigrant families, has produced a better or worse country. The scents, flavours, controversies and rawness of Britain in the twenty-first century divide the country from its former self. It is not just those who have come, but the huge numbers of white British who have left, to South Africa, Australia, Canada and New Zealand, well over half a million in the sixties alone. Britain has become a world island, a little America, despite itself. Having once acquired an Empire in a fit of absent-mindedness, the British have become multi-coloured in much the same way. With new migrations from Eastern Europe, Iraq, Somalia and Ethiopia, it is now clear that this is a far bigger story than simply a tidying-up after Empire.

Floating

If Heath is associated with a single action, it is British entry into 'Europe' but throughout his time in office the economy, not Europe, was the biggest issue facing him. British productivity was still pitifully low compared to the United States or Europe, never mind Japan. The country was spending too much on new consumer goods and not nearly enough on modernized and more efficient factories and businesses. Prices were rising by 7 per cent and wage earnings by double that. This was still the old post-1945 world of fixed exchange rates which meant that the Heath government, just like those of Attlee and Wilson, faced a sterling crisis and perhaps another devaluation. It is hard to describe quite how heavily, how painfully, relative economic decline weighed on the necks of politicians of thirty and forty years ago. The unions, identified by Heath as his first challenge, had just seen off Wilson and Barbara Castle. Heath had decided he would need to face down at least one major public sector strike, as well as removing some of the benefits that he thought encouraged strikes. Britain not only had heavy levels of unionization through all the key industries but also, by modern standards, an incredible number of different unions – more than 600 altogether. Leaders of large unions had only a wobbly hold on what actually happened on the factory floor. It was a time of political militancy well caught by the 1973 hit from the folk-rock band the Strawbs, who reached number two with their anthem, 'Part of the Union'. Its chorus ran, 'Oh you don't get me, I'm part of the union' and different verses spelt out why: 'With a hell of a shout, It's out brothers, out ... And I always get my way, If I strike for higher pay ... So though I'm a working man, I can ruin the government's plan.' And so they could.

Almost immediately Heath faced a dock strike, followed by a big pay settlement for local authority dustmen, then a power workers' go-slow which led to power cuts. Then the postal workers struck. The mood of the government was less focused and less steely than it would be nine years later when Margaret Thatcher came to power. Douglas Hurd, later seen as a 'wet' in her cabinet, was Heath's political secretary at the time, and recorded in his diary his increasing frustration. 'A bad day. It is clear that all the weeks of planning in the civil service have totally failed to cope with what is happening in the electricity dispute: and all the pressures are to surrender.' Later, Hurd confronted Heath in his dressing-gown, warning him that the government machine was 'moving too slowly, far behind events'. Things were so bad in the car industry that Henry Ford III, with his right-hand man Lee Iacocca, came to warn Heath that they were thinking of pulling out of Britain entirely. Yet Heath's Industrial Relations Bill of 1971 was meant to be balanced, giving new rights to trade unionists while at the same time trying to make deals with employers legally enforceable through a new system of industrial courts. It was the Tories' first stab at the kind of package which had been offered to the unions by Wilson. There were also tax reforms, meant to increase investment, a deal with business on keeping price increases to 5 per cent, and even some limited privatization – the travel agents Thomas Cook and Lunn Poly were then state owned, and sold off, along with some breweries.

But the Tory messages were still, to put it gently, mixed. Cuts in some personal taxes encouraged spending and inflation. With European membership looming, Barber, Heath's Chancellor, was dashing for growth, which meant further tax cuts and higher government spending. Perhaps the most significant move in the long term was the removal of lending limits for the high street banks, producing a vast surge in borrowing. Lending had been growing at around 12 per cent a year already but in 1972 rose by 37 per cent and the following year by 43 per cent. This, obviously, further fuelled inflation but it also gave a fillip to the ancient British fetish for house price ownership and borrowing. The huge expansion of credit and the unbalanced amount of capital sunk in bricks and lawns in modern-day Britain can be traced back partly to this decision, then the new credit boom of the Thatcher years. It is not even mentioned in Heath's memoirs.

At the same time one of the historic constraints on British governments had gone. In the summer of 1971 President Nixon unilaterally tore up a key part of the post-war financial system by suspending the convertibility of the dollar for gold and allowing exchange rates to float. His problem was the awesome cost of the war in Vietnam (though it would cost only 60 per cent in real terms of the later post-September 11 conflicts in Afghanistan and Iraq), combined with rising commodity prices. The effect on Britain was that the government and Bank of England no longer had to be quite so obsessed by sterling reserves, though this remained a problem until 1977. But it opened up new questions, about how far down sterling could go and how industrialists could be expected to plan ahead.[43] Heath's instincts on state control were quickly tested when the most valuable parts of Rolls-Royce faced bankruptcy over the cost of developing new aircraft engines. Heath briskly nationalized the company, saving 80,000 jobs and allowed it to regroup and survive, to the relief of the defence industry. Rolls-Royce duly did revive and returned to the private sector, making this a clear case of one nationalization that with hindsight clearly 'worked'.

Into Europe, with the Peasants

We have seen how deeply the cause of Europe had marked Heath, and how hard he had struggled as a negotiator in the early sixties in the face of President de Gaulle's 'Non'. He had done the time, served in the tobacco-smoked rooms, haggled over the detail. As a keen European he knew his French partners better than any other senior British politician. Long before winning power as Prime Minister, he had identified Georges Pompidou who replaced de Gaulle as President as his likely interlocutor. At a meeting at Chequers, Heath later revealed, Pompidou had told him, in French, 'If you ever want to know what my policy is, don't bother to call me on the telephone. I do not speak English, and your French is awful. Just remember that I am a peasant, and my policy will always be to support the peasants.'[44]

This was fair warning about the vast expense of the Common Agricultural Policy but it was not a true reflection of Pompidou's wider vision. In fact, he wanted a Europe of large manufacturing companies able to take on the United States and the Far East. By 1970, after a decade during which Britain had grown much more slowly than the Six members of the Common Market, Heath was in some ways in a weaker position than Macmillan had been. On the other hand, Heath had some advantages. He was trusted as a serious negotiator. Britain's very weakness persuaded Paris that this time, 'les rosbifs' were genuinely determined to join. Pompidou also thought the time

486

was right. A 'Oui' would get him out of the great dead general's shadow. France like the rest of the Community had for years been struggling to understand what Britain really wanted. This had been particularly difficult in the Wilson years, when the British left had been riven by the issue.

Heath had only promised to negotiate, not to join. His enthusiasm, however, was in total contrast to Wilson's wiggling. The best historian of Britain's relations with the rest of the EU described the difference between the two: 'It probably mattered quite a lot to the direction of later events that in early September 1939, as Ted Heath was making it back to Britain from Poland by the skin of his teeth before war was declared, Harold Wilson was motoring to Dundee to deliver an academic paper on exports and the trade cycle, and that later, while Heath was training to run an anti-aircraft battery, Wilson became a potato controller at the Ministry of Food.'[45] Yet opinion polls suggested that Heath's grand vision was alien to most British people and that the former potato controller's warnings about prices had much more effect.

With Heath in power, over eighteen months of haggling in London, Paris and Brussels, a deal was thrashed out. It infuriated Britain's fishermen, who would lose most of their traditional grounds to open European competition, particularly from French and Spanish trawlers. It was a second-best deal on the budget which would later be reopened by Margaret Thatcher. Above all it left intact the previous Common Market designed for the convenience of French farmers and Brussels-based bureaucrats, not for Britain. Vast slews of European law had to be swallowed whole, much of it objectionable to the British negotiators. Only at the very margins, dealing with New Zealand butter, for instance, did the Six make concessions – and the Commonwealth farmers' deal was won at the expense of a worse agreement on the budget. The truth was that the British negotiators had decided it was essential to the country's future to get in at any price. At a press conference at the Elysée Palace in Paris in 1971, Heath and Pompidou, after a long private afternoon of talks between just the two of them, language notwithstanding, revealed to general surprise that so far as France was concerned, Britain could now join the Community. Heath was particularly delighted to have triumphed over the media, who had expected another 'Non'.

Now there would have to be a national debate about the terms of entry and a vote in Parliament. But in Opposition, Wilson was playing true to form. When Heath began negotiations, as we have seen, Wilson was a publicly declared supporter of British membership. But the tactical Wilson soon displaced the statesman. As British accession loomed, he cavilled and sniped. As ever, he was looking over his shoulder. Jim Callaghan, a potential successor, was campaigning openly against Europe, partly on the grounds that a French-speaking institution threatened the language of Chaucer, Shakespeare and Dickens. The left was in full cry. A special Labour conference in July 1971 confirmed how anti-EEC the party had become, voting by a majority of five to one against. Labour MPs were also hostile by a majority of two to one. Wilson now announced that he would oppose British membership on the Heath terms. He was not against in principle, he insisted, just here-and-now. After the long and tortuous journey this disgusted the Labour pro-Europeans. It did not much enthuse the Labour anti-Marketeers, who simply did not believe Wilson's apparent change of heart and assumed he would sign up if he returned to Number Ten. So even Wilson's great cause, Labour unity, was lost.

When the Heath proposals for membership were put to the Commons sixty-nine Labour pro-Europeans defied the party and voted with the Conservatives. They were led by Roy Jenkins, though to his later embarrassment he did not continue voting against his party on every detail. The left, led by Barbara Castle, Michael Foot and Benn, were livid with the rebels. A divide which would eventually lead to the breakaway SDP was just beginning to be visible. For the Labour conference majority, staying out was a matter of principle. For the sixty-nine, going in was a matter of principle. Forms of words, pious evasions and bluster might patch over the cracks in opposition but this quite clearly had the potential to destroy Labour should it return to power. Caught between the moral self-belief of the Castles and Benns, and the steely self-certainty of Jenkins, Wilson protested to the shadow cabinet that 'I've been wading in shit for three months so others can indulge their conscience' and threatened to quit as party leader: 'They can stuff it as far as I'm concerned.' It was only a tantrum but as he struggled to hold things together, the left-wing *New Statesman* delivered a withering verdict on 'the principal apostle of cynicism, the unwitting evangelist of disillusion ... Mr Wilson has now sunk to a position where his very presence in Labour's leadership pollutes the atmosphere of politics.'[46]

After winning his Commons vote on British membership of the Community, Heath went quietly to Downing Street to play Bach on the piano in a mood of triumph. For the Labour party it had been a dreadful night, with screaming matches in the voting lobbies and ghastly personal confrontations between the sixty-nine rebels and the rest.

The hero of the hour turned out to be Tony Benn, then haring leftwards at a keen lollop. 'Tony immatures with age' said Wilson but on this issue he proved a lot shrewder than the Labour leader. Benn began to argue that on a decision of such importance the people should vote, in a referendum. His constituency was in Bristol, whence the great eighteenth-century MP and writer, Edmund Burke, had sent a letter to his electors explaining that he owed them his judgement, not his slavish obedience to their opinions. In a reversal of the argument, the other Bristol MP argued instead that a democracy which denied its people the right to choose a matter of such importance directly would lose all respect. To begin with Benn had almost no support for this radical thought. Labour traditionalists despised referendums as fascist devices, continental jiggery-pokery not to be thought of in a parliamentary democracy. Though at this stage Benn was ambivalent about the Common Market, pro-Europeans also feared this was the first move towards committing Labour to pulling out.

Harold Wilson had committed himself publicly

and repeatedly against a referendum. Slowly and painfully, however, he came to realize that opposing Heath's deal but promising to renegotiate, while offering a referendum could be the way out. This could be sold to the anti-Marketeers as a swerve against Europe but the pro-Marketeers would realize he was not actually committed to withdraw. And the referendum promise would gain some political high-ground. He would 'trust the people' even if the people were, according to the polls, already fairly bored and hostile. When Pompidou suddenly announced that France would have a referendum, Wilson snatched at the Benn plan. It was an important moment. The referendum would make the attitude of the whole country clear, at least for the seventies. It was to be a device used again by politicians faced with particularly important or tricky constitutional choices.

A Dream Disintegrates

On the afternoon of May Day 1971 John Evans, the manager of the hugely popular Kensington boutique Biba, walked nervously downstairs into the basement. There had been a series of outlandish phone warnings about some kind of bomb, which to start with had simply been ignored by the girl on the till. Outside on the street were some 500 women and children who had by now been hurriedly evacuated. When Evans pushed open the door of the stock-room, there was an almighty bang, a flash of flame and a billow of smoke. The Angry Brigade, middle Britain's very own terror group, had struck again. In their communiqué explaining the attack, they misquoted Bob Dylan – 'if you're not busy being born, you're busy buying' – and went on: 'All the sales girls in all the flash boutiques are made to dress the same and have the same make-up … Life is so boring there's nothing to do except spend all our wages on the latest skirt, or shirt. Brothers and Sisters, what are your real desires? Sit in the drugstore, look distant, empty, bored, drinking some tasteless coffee? … The only thing you can do with modern slavehouses – called boutiques – is WRECK THEM.'[47] What they did not seem to realize (except for a cadet enthusiast Erin Pizzey, who broke with them over their Biba plan and later went off to found women's refuges instead) was that its customers found Biba not oppressive but liberating.

There are hundreds of dates and events you could pick to date the end of the sixties dream, but the Biba bombing has a piquancy all of its own. Two of the main forces behind the flowering of youth culture were at war. On the one side is the fantasy of revolution, anarchist or Leninist according to taste, the world of Che Guevara on the wall and obscure leftist handbooks by the bed promising a world in which Starbucks would never have got started. On the other side is the fantasy of benign, hippy business as part of the consumer culture, the world of eyeliner, cool clothes and gentle people making money. The two organizations, Biba and the Angries, sum up much of the underlying argument of sixties youth culture.

The small group of university dropouts who made up the grandly titled Angry Brigade would go to prison for ten years after 123 attacks and are little remembered now. But they were the nearest Britain came to an anarchist threat. They took their philosophy from two counter-culture theorists, the Frenchman Guy Debord and the Belgian poet and teacher, Raoul Vaneigem, who argued that capitalism and Soviet Communism were equally repressive. All organizations were eventually taken over by capitalism which turned everything into a commodity for sale. Even attacks on capitalism could be marketed and sold – witness all those commercially produced Che Guevara badges and posters of Mao. Debord in particular extended his attack from old-style Communists, Western politics, the media and other familiar targets, to the drug-taking hippy culture, modern architecture, even tourism. Once people had so many things they were bored of simply possessing, then capitalism would sell them experiences too, such as foreign travel and nostalgia.

So the 'Situationists', as they called themselves, resolved to attack targets such as shopping centres, museums, and the media, where 'scandalous activity' might provoke repression, and therefore help the scales to drop from people's eyes. They staged a little revolution at Strasbourg University, where they took control of the student union and mocked their contemporaries for merely pretending to be radical, while actually being seduced by 'clothes, discs, scooters, transistors, purple hearts', proving them to be merely conventional consumers. It was a shrewd assessment of what would happen to most radical students.

Debord himself was almost a caricature French intellectual. He was disdainful of Anglo-Saxon culture, committed to fine food, drink, free love and philosophical conversation. His work had been badly translated and spread among students in Britain. At Croydon Art School it had influenced a group calling itself King Mob (after graffiti used by the mob in a London riot in 1790). A belief in anarchy and disorder was spread by this and other groups in magazines and handbills whose scrawled writing and cut-out letters look remarkably like the punk fanzines of the seventies. This is not coincidental. Among the British admirers of the 'Situationists' was the young art student Malcolm McLaren, later the creator of the Sex Pistols. Notes for a film he wrote in 1971, insisting 'the middle classes invented the commodity. It defines our ambitious, our aspirations, our quality of life. Its effects are repression – loneliness – boredom' could have come from an Angry Brigade communiqué of the same time.[48] When McLaren and Vivienne Westwood opened their clothes-to-shock shop in Kings Road, they were producing just the rebel imagery dreamed of by political rebels a few years earlier. Punk in England in the seventies had roots in what happened in Paris in 1968.

Nothing might have followed Debord's calls to revolution in London, had it not been for another European influence, this time dating back to the Spanish Civil War. Anarchists who continued small-scale guerrilla attacks on the Franco regime had developed the key techniques which would later be copied by terrorist groups from the IRA to the Baader Meinhoff group, indeed to al Qaeda – the use of a cell structure to make the group harder to break, and public communiqués, issued to the mainstream media with code-words, to explain their actions. They were a little more serious.

From 1966 the First of May group was carrying out machine-gun attacks and small-scale bombings across Western Europe. Within a few years they were in contact with British admirers, in particular former students from Cambridge and Essex Universities. At Essex, a new and bleak place then, Anna Mendelson, from a girls' high school in Stockport, and Hilary Creek, from a private school in Bristol, had been eagerly watching the 1968 revolt. So over at Cambridge had John Barker, from the posh Haberdashers' Aske's School, a journalist's son, and Jim Greenfield, a lorry driver's son from Widnes in Cheshire, studying medicine. They had studied the 'Situationists' and joined the 'Kim Philby Dining Club' in honour of the University's most famous traitor. All of them committed radicals, they got to know each other through communes and the squatting movement in London, then threw themselves into the Claimants Union, an organization set up to try to extract maximum welfare payments for as many people as possible – and successful enough to have eighty branches across the UK by 1971. Through a young Scottish anarchist called Stuart Christie, who had spent three years in a Spanish prison for his part in a bungled plot to blow up General Franco, the university quartet – a strikingly handsome group – made contact with the First of May group. With others, including a petty criminal and heroin addict called Jake Prescott and a Vietnam Solidarity Campaign activist called Ian Purdie, they began to make and use bombs.

As well as Biba their targets included the Miss World contest at the Albert Hall, a Spanish airline plane at Heathrow, the Commissioner of the

Metropolitan Police, Sir John Waldron, the site of the new Paddington Green police station (where IRA and al Qaeda suspects would later be held), the police computer, a Territorial Army centre in Holloway, the home of the chairman of Ford in Britain, a Rolls-Royce showroom in Paris, and two Conservative cabinet ministers – the trade minister, John Davies, and the employment secretary, Robert Carr, who was struggling to get Heath's trade union legislation through Parliament, and whose white stuccoed home was hit by two bombs, one at the front door and one at the back. In all these attacks, no one was actually killed and just one person, a bystander, was hurt. The Angry Brigade issued regular communiqués under names from films such as *Butch Cassidy and the Sundance Kid* or *The Wild Bunch* and announced that their targets had been selected for execution. They would take on 'High Pigs, Judges, Embassies, Spectacles, Property' they said, and attack 'the shoddy alienating culture pushed out by TV films and magazines ... the ugly sterility of urban life'. After nine months the Angry Brigade were picked up by the police after a trip to Paris to collect gelignite. Raiding their squats, guns and bomb-making equipment were discovered and all the key players were given long prison sentences. The judge blamed their actions on 'a warped misunderstanding of sociology' and the English revolution was again postponed for lack of interest. The violent fringe of protest would continue, but always over secondary issues, such as Scottish and Welsh nationalism and the Irish 'troubles'.

Though in many ways the Angry Brigade were a non-event they represent the only direct confrontation between revolutionary protest, supposed to be one of the key ingredients of the sixties, and the evolving economy of pleasure which was the sixties' real story. Other left-wing groups, mainly Trotskyists, would argue with each other and march, protest and publish about employment and foreign affairs. Revolutionary protest was only felt in its full force in Ireland.

Bloody Sunday

Heath had worked closely with the Taoiseach (Prime Minister of the Irish Republic), Jack Lynch, and the new Stormont leader, Brian Faulkner, who, as a middle-class businessman by origin, was more in Heath's image than the Old Etonian landowner, Chichester-Clark, had been. Eventually he had even managed to get the leaders of the Republic and Northern Ireland to sit and negotiate at the same table, something that had not happened since Partition in 1920. A measure of the intricate diplomacy required was that Heath served a bottle of Paddys whiskey, from the Republic, at Lynch's end of the table, and Bushmills, made in Ulster, at Faulkner's, with a bottle of Scotch between them, and considered it a significant sign when they both opted for Scotch. Chichester-Clark had simply demanded more and more troops, more and more repression, but Faulkner was open to a political solution. Inside Downing Street, three options were being studied. Northern Ireland could be carved into smaller, more intensely Protestant areas, with the rest surrendered to the

Republic, thus effectively getting rid of many Catholics. Or it could be ruled by a power-sharing executive, giving Catholics a role in government. Or, finally, it could be governed jointly by Dublin and London, with its citizens having joint citizenship.

Though Heath rejected the first option because it would be crude and leave too many people on the wrong side of borders and the last one, because the Unionists would refuse it, his second option would be followed by the British governments that followed him. A fourth option, advocated by Enoch Powell who continued his political odyssey by becoming an Ulster Unionist MP, was that the UK should fully incorporate Northern Ireland into British structures and treat it like Kent or Lincolnshire, but this was never taken seriously by Heath. His readiness to discuss other radical solutions gives the lie to the idea that London was pig-headed or unimaginative. But before he had a chance to open serious talks, the collapsing security situation had to be dealt with.

Now politics shrivelled.

If there was one moment when the 'troubles' became unstoppable it was 30 January 1972, 'Bloody Sunday', when troops from the Parachute Regiment killed thirteen unarmed civilians in Londonderry. Ordered in from Belfast to put a stop to stone-throwing Bogside demonstrators, they erupted into the Catholic ghetto and began firing, as it turned out, at unarmed people, many of them teenagers. Some were killed with shots to the back, clearly running away. It was the climax of weeks of escalation. Reluctantly, Heath had introduced internment for suspected terrorists. Reprisals against informers and anti-British feeling meant that the normal process of law was entirely ineffective against the growing IRA threat so, despite the damage it would do to relations with other European countries and the United States, he authorized the arrest and imprisonment in Long Kesh of 337 IRA suspects. In dawn raids, 3,000 troops had found three-quarters of the people they were looking for. Many were old or inactive. Many of the real Provo leaders escaped south of the border. Protests came in from around the world. There was an immediate upsurge in violence, with twenty-one people being killed in three days. The bombings and shootings simply increased in intensity. In the first eight weeks of 1972, forty-nine people were killed and more than 250 seriously injured.

This was the background to the events of 'Bloody Sunday' which, despite endless continuing inquiries and arguments, remains disputed territory. Who shot first? How involved were the IRA in provoking the confrontation? Why did the peaceful march split and stone-throwing begin? Why did the paratroopers suddenly appear to lose control? Whatever the answers, this was an appalling day when Britain's reputation was damaged around the world. In Dublin, ministers reacted with fury and the British embassy was burned to the ground. 'Bloody Sunday' made it far easier for the IRA to raise funds abroad, particularly in the United States. The Provos hit back with a bomb attack on the Parachute Regiment's Aldershot headquarters, killing seven people there – none of them soldiers. The violence led to yet more violence and by degrees to the imposition of direct rule by London and the no-jury Diplock Courts. In July 1973, twenty bombs went off in Belfast, killing eleven people. Mainland Britain became a key Provo target. In October the following year, five people were killed and sixty injured in attacks on Guildford pubs and in December, twenty-one people were killed in pubs in Birmingham city centre.

Assassinations would follow, of Tory MPs such as Airey Neave, Mrs Thatcher's close adviser, and Ian Gow, her popular former parliamentary private secretary. Vocal opponents of the IRA such as Ross McWhirter, would be gunned down and in 1975 a couple in London's Marylebone were taken hostage by an IRA gang in the Balcombe Street Siege. Later IRA 'spectaculars' included the murder of Lord Mountbatten of Burma when boating with his family in Sligo in 1979, and culminated in the attempted assassination of Mrs Thatcher and her cabinet in Brighton in 1984. The 'troubles' in Northern Ireland itself would see endless tit-for-tat car bombings and shootings, routine murder, torture and knee-capping of suspected informers and a quiet steady migration of ambitious people from the province. The security services would break the law in their desperate search for suspected terrorists. 'Dirty protests', involving the smearing of excrement on cell walls and fatal hunger strikes, would be used by republican prisoners in their war against the British State. Within a few years, what had been essentially a policing role by the British Army, separating Protestant bigots from rebellious Catholics, had become a full-scale terrorist or counter-insurgency war with all the paranoia, the kidnappings, the apparatus of repression and the corruption of political life that it brings.

In his last attempt to avert what was coming, Heath believed he needed to persuade Dublin to drop its longstanding constitutional claim to the North, and to persuade mainstream Unionists to work with Catholic politicians. He failed, but not through want of trying. His first Secretary of State for Northern Ireland, a new job made necessary by direct rule, was the bluff, amiable Willie Whitelaw. He met Provisional IRA leaders, including Gerry Adams, for face-to-face talks, a desperate gamble which, however, led nowhere: there was no compromise yet available. So, ignoring the IRA, Sunningdale Agreement proposed a power-sharing executive, with six Unionists, four SDLP members and one from the non-sectarian Alliance Party. There would also be a Council of Ireland, bringing together politicians from Dublin and from the North, with authority over a limited range of issues, in return for Dublin renouncing authority over Northern Ireland. It was an ingenious multi-sided deal not so different in essence from what was later proposed by John Major and Tony Blair in the nineties. But too many Unionists were implacably opposed to it, and the moderates were routed at the first 1974 election. Meanwhile, in the Republic, its leader's renunciation of the territorial claim to the North was declared unconstitutional and illegal. Heath concluded, with understandable bitterness: 'Ultimately it was the people of Northern Ireland themselves who threw away the best chance of peace in the blood-stained history of the six counties.'

Authority Undermined

Then the miners struck. At the beginning of 1972 the National Union of Mineworkers began their first national strike since the dark days of the twenties, pursuing a pay demand of 45 per cent. The government, with modest coal stocks, was quickly taken by surprise at the discipline and aggression of the strikers. A young unknown militant, a miner from Woolley colliery, organized some 15,000 of his comrades from across South Yorkshire in a mass picket of the Saltley coke depot, on which Birmingham depended for much of its fuel. Arthur Scargill, a rousing speaker, former Communist Party member and highly ambitious union activist, later described the confrontation with Midlands police at Saltley as 'the greatest day of my life'. Soon he would be catapulted up as agent, then president of the Yorkshire miners. Heath blamed the police for being too soft. Scargill's greatest day was, for the Prime Minister, 'the most vivid, direct and terrifying challenge to the rule of law that I could ever recall emerging from within our own country ... We were facing civil disorder on a massive scale.' It was clear to Heath that the intention was to bring down the elected government but he decided he could not counter-attack immediately. Confronted with 'the prospect of the country becoming ungovernable, or having to use the armed forces to restore order, which public opinion would never have tolerated', Heath turned to a judge, Lord Wilberforce, for an independent inquiry into miners' wages. From his point of view, it was a terrible mistake. Wilberforce said they should get well over 20 per cent, nearly 50 per cent higher than the average increase. The NUM settled for that, plus extra benefits, in one of the most clear-cut and overwhelming victories over a government that any British trade union has ever enjoyed.

Heath and his ministers knew that they might have to go directly to the country with an appeal about who was in charge but before that, they tried a final round of compromise and negotiation. Triggered by the prospect of unemployment: hitting one million, there now follows the famous U-turn which afterwards so scarred Heath's reputation. It went by the ungainly name of 'tripartism', a three-way national agreement on prices and wages, investment and benefits, involving the government, the TUC and the CBI. The Industry Act of 1972 gave a Tory government unprecedented powers of industrial intervention, gleefully cheered by Tony Benn as 'spadework for socialism'.[49] There was much earnest wooing of moderate trade union leaders. Money, effort and organization went into Job Centres as unemployment rose steadily towards a million. The industrialists did as much as they could, sitting on yet more committees when in truth they might have been more usefully employed trying to run their companies. The unions, however, had the bit between their teeth. By first refusing to acknowledge Heath's industrial relations court 'as really legitimately a law of the land' and then refusing to negotiate seriously until he repealed the Act, they made the breakdown of this last attempt at consensual economics inevitable. Within a year the CBI too would be calling for it to be scrapped.

By now Heath had leaned so far to try to win the unions over that he was behaving like a Wilson-era socialist. He was reinstating planning, particularly regional planning. He was bailing out failing companies such as Upper Clyde Shipbuilders, partly because of the work-in discussed elsewhere – something Heath later believed was a mistake. He was offering the unions a privileged place in the running of the nation. From his perspective this was a last attempt to run the economy as a joint enterprise of British patriots, in which individual roles – trade union leader, company director, party politician – took second place behind a general belief in the common good, the wider politics of 'Buy British'. Individuals followed the logic of their own interests instead. Trade union leaders had got their jobs by promising their members higher wages and better conditions. They could hardly be blamed for doing everything they could within the law to carry out the role they had been given. Industrialists, similarly, would live or die by profit margin and return to investors. They were not auxiliary politicians. Thatcherites later criticized Heath's government for doing things which a government ought not to do, and not doing things it ought to. Governments should not try to run businesses, or do the wage bargaining of trade union officials and companies for them. They should not tell factories where to go. They should not attempt to control prices.

All these things, said Tories of ten years later, were better left to the market. What government should do instead was set tough and clear rules by which the other forces in society had to live. Government should ensure low inflation by controlling the supply of money. It should enforce strong laws against intimidation or law-breaking at work. It should allow firms that fail to suffer the consequences. Overall, the Thatcher critique has been applauded, not simply in Britain but around the world, and Heath's tripartism, or 'corporatism' has been derided and forgotten. Yet he started with an almost identical view to her later one. He had been an enthusiast for letting the market decide prices. He promised not to let lame ducks survive. At the time, Thatcher was his fervent supporter and even her outrider Sir Keith Joseph only converted to a full free-market philosophy in the middle of the seventies, after the fall of the Heath government in which he had been a notably high-spending minister. The argument between the two sides of the Conservative Party was not one between toffs and the hard-nosed middle classes, or 'ordinary people', as many Thatcherites would later claim. Heath was no toff and his nose, though famously Concorde-large, was as hard as any.

Heath was blown off course by a political version of the impossible storm that later wrecked his beloved yacht *Morning Cloud.* Much of the country was simply more left-wing than it was later. The unions, having defeated Wilson and Castle, were more self-confident than ever before or since. Many industrial workers, living in still-bleak towns far away from the glossy pop world of the big cities, did seem underpaid and left behind. After the Macmillan, Douglas-Home and Wilson experiences, politicians did not have the automatic level of respect that they had enjoyed when Heath had first entered the Commons. Heath always argued that he was forced to try consensus politics because in the seventies the alternative policy, the squeeze of mass unemployment which arrived in the Thatcher years, would simply not have been accepted by the country. And given the very rocky ride Mrs Thatcher had a full ten years later, after industrial and some social breakdown had softened the way for her radicalism, he was surely right.

What finally finished off the Heath government was the short war between Israel and Egypt in October 1973, the Yom Kippur War. Israel's swift and decisive victory was a humiliation for the Arab world and it struck back, using oil. OPEC, the organization of the oil-producing countries dominated by the Saudis, had seen the price of oil rising on world markets for some time. They decided to cut supplies to the West each month until Israel handed back its territorial gains and allowed the Palestinians their own state. There would be a total embargo on Israel's most passionate supporters, the United States and the Netherlands. And those countries which were allowed oil would pay steadily more for it. In fact, prices rose fourfold. It was a global economic shock, shovelling further inflation into the industrialized world, but in Britain it arrived with special force. The miners put in yet another huge pay claim, which would have added half as much again to many pay-packets. Despite an appeal by its leader, the moderate Joe Gormley, the NUM executive rejected a 13 per cent pay increase and voted to ballot for another national strike. These were the days, just, before North Sea oil and gas were being produced commercially. Britain could survive high oil prices, even shortages, for a while. The country could hold out against a coal strike, for a while. But both together added up to what the Chancellor, Barber, called the greatest economic crisis since the war. It certainly compared to that of 1947. Coal stocks had not been built up in preparation. Now a whole series of panic measures were introduced.

Plans were made for petrol rationing and coupons printed and distributed. The national speed limit was cut by 20 miles per hour to 50 miles per hour to save fuel. Then in January 1974 came the announcement of a three-day working week. Ministers solemnly urged citizens to share baths and brush their teeth in the dark. Television, by now the nation's sucky-sweet, was ended at 10.30 p.m. each evening. It is remembered as the darkest day (literally) in the story of mid-seventies Britain, and it was an embarrassing time in many ways. Yet it also gave millions an enjoyable frisson, the feeling of taking a holiday from everyday life. The writer Robert Elms recalls that though 'this proud nation had been reduced to a shabby shambles, somewhere between a strife-torn South American dictatorship and a gloomy Soviet satellite, Bolivia meets Bulgaria, a banana republic with a banana shortage ... The reality of course is that almost everybody absolutely loved it. They took to the three-day week with glee. They took terrible liberties.'[50]

Heath and his ministers struggled to try to find a solution to the miners' claim, though the climate was hardly helped when Mick McGahey, the legendary Scottish Communist mineworkers' leader, asked by Heath what he really wanted, answered 'to bring down the government'. Much messing about with intermediaries and many mixed messages, not least from the government's own Pay Board, ensured that no effective compromise could be found. When the miners voted, 81 per cent were for striking, including those in some of the most traditionally moderate areas in the country. In February 1974 Heath asked the Queen to dissolve Parliament and went to the country on the election platform he had prepared two years earlier: 'Who governs?' The country's answer, perhaps taking the question more literally than Heath had hoped, was 'Not you, mate.'

Harold Wilson had expected the Tories to win again, and began the campaign in a depressed mood. A year earlier in Opposition he had prepared his own answer to inflation and the unions, the so-called Social Compact, or Social Contract. Agreed jointly between the union leaders and the Labour shadow cabinet, it was essentially a return to the politics of the forties, with price controls, a complex system of food subsidies, direct redistribution of wealth, controls on housing and investment and the end of the Tory union laws. In return for this Attlee-age manifesto from the politicians, the unions gave vague promises of voluntary pay restraint. It was a one-way deal but it was in Wilson's interests to pretend that he could find practical agreements where Heath could not. It was in the unions' interests to pretend they were signing up to a new era, if that would help expel the Tories and destroy their legislation. Outside observers saw it more plainly as a recipe for inflation which also offered the TUC a privileged place in government in return for very little.

But what was the alternative? The three-day week was not, it later turned out, quite the economic disaster it seemed. Industry had maintained almost all production – which shows how inefficient five-day working must have been – and relatively few jobs had been lost. But politics is half symbol, and Heath's authority had gone. In the election campaign a public fed up of chaos and desperately looking for good news clutched at the Social Contract. Wilson was able to appear as the calm bringer of reason and order. This time, he was lucky as well. A slew of bad economic figures arrived during the campaign. Enoch Powell, Heath's ancient nemesis, suddenly announced that he was quitting the Conservatives over their failure to offer the public a referendum on Europe, and called on everyone to vote Labour. A mistake by the Pay Board suggested that the miners were in fact relatively lower paid than had been recognized. And a surge in Liberal support, which took them from single-figure support to the backing of a quarter of those voting, turned out to help Labour more than the Tories. All this helped produce a late surge in Wilson's favour. By the end of the campaign he had recovered some his old chirpiness and bounce. Having decided that Heath should not rule, however, the country seemed unsure that Wilson should either. Though Labour had won the most seats, 301 against the Conservatives' 297, no party had an overall majority. Heath hung on, trying to do a deal with the Liberal leader Jeremy Thorpe, who had 14 MPs, but eventually conceded defeat. Rather fatter, greyer and more personally conservative than he had been ten years earlier, Harold Wilson was back.

So Mick McGahey and friends had brought down the Heath government, with a little help from the oil-toting Saudi Royal Family, the Liberals and Enoch Powell. A more bizarre coalition of interests is hard to imagine. Edward Heath's three and three-quarter years in Number Ten will be remembered for the three-day week, a rare moment when politics actually shakes everyday life out of its routine; and for taking Britain into Europe. But other important changes happened on his watch, too. The school-leaving age was at last raised to sixteen. To cope with international currency mayhem caused by that Nixon decision to suspend convertibility, the old imperial sterling area finally went in 1972. The Pill was made freely available on the National Health Service. Local government was radically reorganized, with no fewer than 800 English councils disappearing and huge new authorities, much disliked, being created in their place. Heath defended this on the basis that the old Victorian system could not cope with 'the growth of car ownership and of suburbia, which were undermining the distinction between town and country'. Many others saw it as dreary big-is-better dogma. There was more of that when responsibility for NHS hospitals was taken away from hundreds of local boards and passed to new regional and area health authorities, at the suggestion of a new cult then just emerging – management consultants.

Political cynicism had been provoked in the fifties and sixties by the behaviour of the cliques who ran the country. By the seventies it was driven more by a sense of alienation. To many older Britons these were years of out-of-control change. Much of the loathing of Heath on the right of politics came from

510

British membership of the Common Market which seemed the ultimate emblem of this rage for bigger and untraditional systems. Decimalization was almost as big a change to daily life. Though the original decision had been taken in 1965 during the first Wilson government, the disappearance in 1971 of a coinage going back to Anglo-Saxon times was widely blamed on Heath. Away flew the florins and half-crowns, halfpennies, farthings and sixpences, away went all the intricate triple-column mathematics of pounds, shillings and pence; and in came an unfamiliar if more rational decimal currency. Where would this end? Negotiators in Europe specifically fought to maintain the British pint measures in beer and milk, and the mile continued to keep the kilometre at bay. But in the seventies, the familiar seemed everywhere in retreat.

Wilson

At least Wilson was familiar. His February election victory meant he was governing without a Commons majority. He was trying to do so at a time when the economy was still shaking with the effect of the oil price shock, with inflation raging, unemployment rising and the pound under almost constant pressure. Further, the fragile and implausible Social Contract now had to be tested. Almost the first thing Labour did was to settle with the miners for double what Heath had thought possible. The chances of the new government enjoying easy popularity were nil, though at least an Opposition so internally divided between bruised Conservatives, Liberals, Nationalists and Northern Irish Unionists was unlikely to combine often to defeat it.

The new Chancellor, Denis Healey, introduced an emergency Budget a few weeks after the election, followed by another in the autumn, during which he raised income tax to 83 per cent at the top rate, or 98 per cent for unearned income, a level so eyewateringly high it was used against Labour for a generation to come. In the spirit of the Social Contract Healey also increased help for the poorest, with higher pensions and housing and food subsidies. He was trying to deliver for the unions, as Wilson did in abolishing the Conservative employment legislation. For the time being Heath remained as Tory leader, despite some grumbling from the party. He was convinced that before long Wilson would have to call a second election and his chance for revenge would arrive. In October, however, the second election confirmed the earlier verdict, with Labour gaining eighteen seats and a precarious but quite workable overall majority of three.

The fetid atmosphere of Wilson's new government was like that of the mid-sixties, only more so. Marcia Williams still had him mesmerized. As one young Number Ten aide recalled, her dramatic and sometimes destructive power 'was not only exercised through her bewitching domination of the prime minister himself. Once launched against any human obstacle or perceived personal enemy, her frenzied tirades were very impressive and virtually ungovernable.'[51] It was alleged that she would swear and curse like a trooper at Wilson, storm out of dinners and meetings, and threaten him with terrible revenge if he crossed her. Some sources claimed that in Opposition, she had locked all his personal papers in a garage and refused to let him see them. Desperate to write his account of the 1964–70 governments, Wilson had been forced to team up with her brother Tony, break into her garage, and steal them back, although only the three of them would know if this were true. Now, she gave him a new problem when a press furore broke about land deals. The brother, a geologist, had bought slag heaps and quarries and then moved into land speculation, falling in with dodgy Midlands businessmen. There was a forged letter purporting to come from Wilson. There was no evidence that Marcia knew of the deal, but the close connections between Marcia and her brother, and the Prime Minister, began a media frenzy which prefigured many of those directed at the Labour ministers of the nineties and early 2000s. Wilson stood by his inner circle while the attacks rose in intensity, eventually making Williams a peeress, Lady Falkender. This was described by one of Wilson's biographers as 'a magnificently arrogant gesture, contemptuous of almost everybody'[52] and the whole experience broke for ever his once-good relations with the press. The old rumours about links with Russian intelligence and affairs resurfaced and the mood of bitterness and paranoia inside Number Ten was as grim as anything in the equally harassed administrations of John Major and Tony Blair.

In another way, however, Wilson had changed. He interfered far less and seemed less worried by the manoeuvrings of his ministers. He wasn't planning to stay long. There are many separate records of his private comments about retiring at sixty, after another two years in power. If he had not privately decided finally that he would go in 1976, he certainly acted as if he had. The question of who would succeed him, Jenkins or Callaghan, Healey or even Benn, had become one about the direction of the Labour government, rather than a personal threat to Harold Wilson, so there was less rancour around the cabinet table. Wilson was visibly older and more tired. He seems likely to have known about the early stages of Alzheimer's, which would wreak a devastating toll on him in retirement. He forgot facts, confused issues and repeated himself. For a man whose memory and wit had been so important, this must have been a grim burden. There is therefore no need to assume that dark forces, some nether world of MI5 plotters and right-wing extremists, finally removed him from power with threats of blackmail and dirty tricks.

Wilson himself was as fascinated as ever by Security Service plotting and had Marcia Williams dig out files on Jeremy Thorpe's lover, Norman Scott, to try to show that he was being framed by the South African secret service, BOSS. At other times he would suggest Israel's Mossad were after him. In a famous interview given to two BBC reporters, Barry Penrose and Roger Courtiour, after his retirement, he claimed that right-wing officers in the Security Service had been plotting against him. Wilson's state of mind is vividly evoked by his fantastical language to them: 'I see myself as the big fat spider in the corner of the room. Sometimes I speak when I'm asleep. You should both listen. Occasionally when we meet I might tell you to go to Charing Cross Road and kick a blind man standing on the corner. That blind man may tell you something, lead you somewhere.' The Cecil King plot of 1967 and later memoirs by a wild MI5 man show that Wilson's fears were not completely groundless, but this sounds like the raving of a deluded old man.

The Stairs Were on Fire

If Roy Jenkins had in many ways been the most important minister during the mid-sixties, it was Denis Healey who dominated public perceptions of Labour in the mid-seventies. As a Chancellor of the Exchequer during the worst economic storm of post-war times, through both the Wilson and Callaghan governments, he rivalled each of them as a public icon. His scarlet face, huge eyebrows and rough tongue were endlessly caricatured and mimicked, above all by the TV impressionist Mike Yarwood, who invented 'you silly billy' as Healey's catchphrase, one quickly taken up by the Chancellor himself. Healey was one of the most widely read, cultured, intelligent and self-certain politicians of modern times, whose early Communism, active war service and vast range of international contacts helped mulch and decorate his famous beyond-politics 'hinterland'. But there was little poetry, relaxation or fun about the job he took up in 1974 and would hold, through near-farcical crises and grim headlines, for the next five years. He described the economy he had inherited from Heath and Barber as 'like the Augean stables'.

Much of his energy would be thrown into dealing with the newly unstable world economy, with floating currencies and inflation-shocked governments. In effect, after the great devaluation argument of the first Wilson administrations, this one was quietly devaluing all the time, as the pound sank against the dollar.

Where were the levers of control? Healey was taxing and cutting as much as he dared but his only real hope was to control inflation by controlling wages. Wilson insisted that an incomes policy must be voluntary. After the torture and defeat of Heath there must be no going back to legal restraints. The unions, under the leadership of men who had risen as shop stewards in the great revolt of the fifties and sixties, the Spanish Civil War veteran Jack Jones, the wily and cynical Hugh Scanlon, and the grammar school boy and ex-Communist Len Murray, became increasingly worried that rampant inflation might destroy Labour and bring back the Tories. So for a while the Social Contract did deliver fewer strikes. From 1974 to 1975, the number of days lost to strikes halved, and then halved again the following year. Contrary to popular myth, the seventies were not all about mass meetings and walk-outs. After Heath had been beaten, the real trouble did not start again until 1978–9. But the other half of the Social Contract was meant to deliver lower wage settlements and that was an utter failure. Despite Labour delivering on its side of the bargain, by the early months of 1975 the going rate for increases was already 30 per cent, a third higher than inflation. By June inflation was up to 23 per cent, and wage settlements even further ahead. The unions suggested a new deal of a cash limit of an extra £6 a week for most workers. The government did introduce an element of compulsion, but targeted employers who offered too much, not workers who demanded too much.

Yet persuading people not to make deals about pay is extremely difficult. It cannot last long in a free society. There will always be special cases, and one special case inspires the next. Healey reckoned two-thirds of his time was spent trying to deal with the inflationary effects of free collective bargaining and the rest with the distortions caused by his own pay policy. As he reflected later: 'Adopting a pay policy is rather like jumping out of a second-floor window: no one in his senses would do it unless the stairs were on fire. But in post-war Britain the stairs have always been on fire.'[53] By refusing to allow companies to pass on inflationary wage increases as higher prices, and by endless haggling with union leaders who were themselves alarmed about the fate of the country, Healey did manage to squeeze inflation downwards. He believed that if the unions had kept their promises it would have been down to single figures by the autumn of 1975.

In all this, Healey was under constant pressure to show that he was delivering for socialism. He could not spend more. So he sent what signals he could by skewing the tax system dramatically against higher earners, concentrating any tax cuts on the worse off. Though notorious for warning that he would make the rich 'howl with anguish' and often misquoted as promising to squeeze the rich 'until the pips squeak', Healey argued that it was the only way of making the country fairer. He never accepted the Conservative argument that high taxes stopped people working harder and blamed Britain's poor industrial performance instead on low investment in industry, poor training and bad management. A villain and bogeyman for many in the middle classes, Healey did at least suffer from his own policies: 'As a result of my tax changes and my determination to prevent ministerial salaries from rising as fast as the pay norm, my own real take-home pay as Chancellor fell to only half what I had been earning as Defence Secretary, although I was working harder and longer.'

Referendum

Wilson carried out his promised renegotiation of Britain's terms of entry to the EEC and then put the result to the country in the Benn-inspired 1975 referendum. The renegotiation was largely a sham but the referendum was a rare political triumph for that bleak decade in the story of Westminster. On the continent, the reopened talks were understood to be more for Wilson's benefit than anything else. Helmut Schmidt, the new German Chancellor, who travelled to London to help win round the Labour conference, regarded it all as a successful cosmetic operation. Wilson had needed to persuade people he was putting a different deal to the country than the one Heath had won. This he was able to do, though, when the referendum actually arrived, Wilson's old evasiveness returned and he mumbled vaguely in support, rather than actively or enthusiastically making the European case.

There were plenty of others to do it for him. To

preserve longer-term party unity, he had allowed anti-Brussels cabinet ministers to speak from the 'No' platform and Barbara Castle, Benn, Peter Shore and Michael Foot were among those who did so, in alliance with Enoch Powell, the Reverend Ian Paisley, the Scottish Nationalists and others. But the 'Yes' campaign could boast most of the Labour cabinet, with Roy Jenkins at the front, plus most of the Heath team, and the popular Liberal leader Jeremy Thorpe. It seemed to many people a fight between wild-eyed ranters, the outlandish and the discontented, on the one hand and sound chaps on the other hand, men and women with that curious but apparently essential British quality 'bottom'. More important, perhaps, was the bias of business and the press. A CBI survey of company chairmen found that out of 419 interviewed, just four were in favour of leaving the Community.[54] Almost all the newspapers were in favour of staying in, including the *Daily Mail, Daily Telegraph* and *Daily Express.* So was every Anglican bishop.

A fight between the Establishment and its critics was funded accordingly. Britain in Europe, leading the 'Yes' campaign, outspent the 'No' camp by more than ten to one. In this grossly unequal struggle, both sides used scare stories. Britain in Europe constantly warned of a huge loss of jobs if the country left the Community. The 'No' camp warned of huge rises in food prices. Yet this was also an almost carnival-like participatory argument of a kind post-war Britain has rarely known. There were meetings, several thousand strong, night after night around the country – proper meetings with hecklers and humour. Despite miserable weather, including a showering of June snow, there were

519

stunts of all kinds and the country seemed covered with posters. The spectacle of politicians from rival parties who normally attacked one another sitting down together agreeing was a tonic to those watching.

There were good television arguments, notably between Jenkins and Benn. And on the Labour side there were awkward moments when rhetoric got too fierce, and Wilson had to intervene to rebuke warring ministers. Even Margaret Thatcher was out campaigning, for Brussels of course, in a spectacularly hideous jumper with the flags of the member states knitted across her breasts. In the end, to the simple question, 'Do you think that the United Kingdom should stay in the European Community (The Common Market)?', 68.3 per cent, or around 17 million people, said 'Yes' and 32.8 per cent, some 8.5 million, said 'No'. Only Shetland and the Western Isles of Scotland voted 'No'. Symbolically, Jenkins thought, the sun came out and there followed a baking, almost cloudless few weeks. Benn instantly conceded full defeat though privately considered the vote 'some achievement considering we had absolutely no real organisation, no newspapers, nothing'. Powell, however, warned that the decision was only 'provisional' and might be reopened in the future. As so often, his was a lone voice.

More than thirty years later, the biggest question both about Heath's triumph in engineering British membership and then about the Labour referendum, is whether the British were told the full story and truly understood the supranational organization they were signing up to. Ever since, many of those among the 8.5 million who voted against, and younger people who share their view, have suggested that Heath and Jenkins and the rest lied to the country, at least by omission. Had it been properly explained that Europe's law and institutions would sit above the ancient Westminster Parliament, it is said, they would never have agreed. What is the truth? The Britain in Europe campaigners can point to speeches and advertisements which directly mention loss of sovereignty. One of the latter read: 'Forty million people died in two European wars this century. Better lose a little national sovereignty than a son or a daughter.' Yet both in Parliament and in the referendum campaign, the full consequences for national independence were mumbled, not spoken clearly enough. Geoffrey Howe, as he then was, who drafted Heath's European Communities Bill, later admitted that it could have been more explicit about lost sovereignty. Heath talked directly about the 'ever closer union' of the peoples of Europe but was never precise about the effect on British law, as compared, say, to Lord Denning who said the European treaty could be compared to 'an incoming tide. It flows into the estuaries and rivers. It cannot be held back.' Hugo Young, the journalist and historian who studied the campaign in great detail, wrote: 'I traced no major document or speech that said in plain terms that national sovereignty would be lost, still less one that categorically promoted the European Community for its single most striking characteristic: that it was an institution positively designed to curb the full independence of the nation-state.'

There were, of course, the explicit warnings about lost sovereignty delivered by the 'No' campaigners among the more populist arguments about food prices. They came above all from Enoch Powell, Michael Foot and Tony Benn. Powell's language can be gauged from a speech he gave to political journalists in the Commons while the Bill was being debated. He lamented that the Commons was 'perishing by its own hand. Week by week, month by month, the House of Commons votes to divest itself of what it had gained through a length of time not much shorter than the history of England itself.'[55] Foot, though recovering from an operation and so partly out of action, wrote in *The Times* that the British parliamentary system had been made farcical and unworkable. Historians, he said, would be amazed 'that the British people were urged at such a time to tamper irreparably with their most precious institution; to see it circumscribed and contorted and elbowed off the centre of the stage.'[56] Benn, confiding to his diary his reaction on the possibility of a Europe-wide passport, showed how much the left's instincts could chime with those of the right-wing opponents of European change: 'That really hit me in the guts … Like metrication and decimalisation, this really strikes at our national identity.' All these arguments were made in the press, despite its overall bias, and repeatedly in public meetings and broadcast debates.

So it was not as if people were not told. The truth revealed by opinion polls is that sovereignty as an issue did not concern the public nearly as much as jobs and food prices. By later standards the position of Parliament was not taken terribly seriously in public debates. It may be that sovereignty is always of absorbing interest to a minority – the more history-minded, politically aware – and of less interest to the rest, except when a loss of sovereignty directly affects daily life and produces resented laws. In the seventies, Britain's political class was not highly respected, and Europe seemed to offer a glossier, richer future. Though the pro-Community majority in business and politics did not strive to ram home the huge implications of membership, they did not deceitfully hide the political nature of what was happening, either. It was just that, when the referendum was held, people cared less. The argument would return, screaming, demanding to be heard, fifteen years later.

Power Ages

As to the rest of Wilson's short final government, much of his energy was spent on foreign affairs. Despite American disapproval the Labour government began the final withdrawal from east of Suez, giving up any pretensions of British influence in the Far East. The Empire was formally over. A scattering of individual outposts and impoverished islands too weak to enjoy independence were all that was left, a few last governors in places like Hong Kong and Bermuda. In the Middle East, British pens in British fingers had drawn many of the lines on the map – Transjordan, the new state of Israel, Iraq – and all that uncertainty went. It went after guerrilla war and partition among the lemon groves of Cyprus, after gruesome murders of British soldiers in the

Holy Land, a nasty little colonial war in Aden which left behind a Marxist and Soviet satellite. It left an unstable and unpopular king in Iraq, soon overthrown by military coup, leading to the regime of Saddam Hussein. In Iran, the British-backed Shah was many years later overturned by Ayatollah Khomeni's Islamic revolution. The decades that followed have been awful ones for the region, marked by major and minor wars, the regular use of torture, assassination, repression, censorship and suicide bombings. The Middle East, rich in oil and history, has become the world's most dangerous zone; and many of the decisions that made it so dangerous originated in Europe, including London, as well as in Washington.

There remained that strange half-life empire called the British Commonwealth, an illogical world-straddling organization that embraced republics such as India, despotisms and democracies, slavish admirers of Britain and frank opponents of London, as well as all the former white dominions which retained their loyalty to the Crown. The Commonwealth was not a coherent policy-setting organization, particularly after Britain decided to join the European Economic Community. Her members often had diametrically opposed trading interests. When it came to defence, some were firmly non-aligned, even at times leaning to Moscow or Beijing, while others such as the Australians looked increasingly to the United States not Britain. Time and again, on issues such as apartheid South Africa, or Rhodesia, or the misbehaviour of newly independent rulers, or questions of migration, the Commonwealth would fracture, or embarrass London. Lacking an army, trade agreements or common views, it seemed to many a pointless organization, fit for nothing more than acrimonious summits and regular athletic Games which functioned as a low-rent version of the real ones, the Olympics. Was it kept going merely out of sentimentality or to give the Queen something to do? At least it has done no harm and kept different parts of the world in contact. Outside football, it is also the last English-speaking worldwide organization not dominated by the Americans.

Wilson spent much of his domestic energy on resisting the attempt by Tony Benn (by now his bugbear) to introduce a socialist economy via the National Enterprise Board. Benn hoped that this would be a generously funded body which would take over a large range of companies, successful and unsuccessful, bringing state ownership and direction into the heart of the economy. Wilson, by now clearly to the right of his party, was equally determined that this should not happen. He had his way. When it eventually arrived, the NEB was a weak, ill-funded repository for lost causes, British Leyland in particular. Benn's enthusiasm for workers' control continued to amuse and infuriate most of the other ministers and civil servants he worked with and he confided in his diary that he felt as if he was 'trying to swim up the Niagara Falls'. He was particularly keen about cooperatives and took up the cause of the Meriden motorcycle factory, struggling to survive under workers' control. He was much excited by what he took to be its Chinese Communist atmosphere: 'I described our industrial policy, and then they sang "For he's a jolly good fellow" which was very touching.'

It wasn't only Wilson who thought Benn's socialist affection for cooperatives and nationalization was out of time. Jack Jones pinned him down over lunch at the Westminster restaurant Locket's to warn: 'Nationalization is no good. People don't want it. Management in nationalized industries is very bad.' Benn explained that he wanted to take over other firms, including the *Scottish Daily News* and challenged Jones about British Leyland itself. The fiery trade unionist, to Benn's astonishment, suggested selling it off to General Motors. The final phase of nationalization produced little except heartache, though the struggling Chrysler car factory at Linwood in Scotland was kept going for a while. These were truly the last days for planning and public control, which had been so widespread immediately after the war. We should see Benn as a traditionalist in this, as much as a radical. Later Healey would brutally sum up his contribution as a minister to British industry. There were only two monuments to Benn in power, he said: a uranium mine in Namibia he had authorized as energy secretary, which helped support apartheid; and Concorde, used by rich people on expense accounts and subsidized by poorer taxpayers. The only planning agreement actually existing when he left office was the old Farm Price Review 'chaired in my time by the Duke of Northumberland'.

Monuments for this last Wilson government were few. One was the radical refashioning of the failing pensions system by Barbara Castle and her team, with the State Earnings Related Pension, or Serps, which linked pension to rises in earnings or prices, whichever was higher. It was notably generous, particularly to women whose pension rights had been whittled away by years of caring for children or elderly relatives, and in allowing people to claim a pension based on their best twenty years of earnings, not necessarily their final earnings. Castle had won a reputation as a battler for feminism much earlier, in 1968 during the celebrated women's strike at Ford's plant in Dagenham. The women were operating sewing-machines to upholster car seats but were paid only 85 per cent of men's wages for doing the same job. After Castle intervened directly, the company closed most of the gap, and other women took action round the country too. She had also intervened to stop the Commons voting male MPs better pensions than female ones. Though Castle always jibed at being called a feminist, and had underestimated the cost of Serps, so that the earnings link would eventually be broken again by the Conservatives to keep the price down, it was a rare civilizing reform which stuck, at least for a decade.

Meanwhile Wilson, quietly preparing a scandalous resignation honours list for his cronies, and muttering about moles, plots and the possible activities of South African and British agents, left future British governments with one final gift. Working as secretively as Attlee he authorized a vastly expensive modernization and replacement of Britain's nuclear deterrent Chevaline, the cost of which would rise from a planned £24m to more than £1,000m within a few years. He then retired as he had always said he would, at sixty, leaving much of his cabinet utterly astonished and London awash with rumours. Power ages, as well as corrupts and Roy Jenkins speculated that perhaps he had faked his birth certificate and had been ten years older than he admitted all along. It would certainly have explained his precocious rise and precocious retirement. But Wilson was still wily enough to give his preferred successor Callaghan ('I'm making way for an older man') a tip-off which helped him steal a march on the rest, including Healey, who only heard the news from Wilson in the gents toilet before the cabinet meeting when he formally announced it. Wilson would retire to see his reputation sink steadily downwards as his memory started to go. For such a pugnacious and fundamentally decent man, whatever his political failures, it was a sad way to subside.

Peasants Revolt: One, the Right

The underlying political story of the middle and later seventies would not, however, be played out mainly in Parliament. It is the story of how, across the quivering body of a profoundly sick country, two new rival forces emerged to fight for the future. The first came from the right.

In the middle of June 1974, something unusual had happened. A politician said sorry. He did not say sorry for something in his personal life, an error of judgement or even a failed policy. He said sorry for Everything. He said sorry for what had happened to Britain since 1945, and his party's role in that, and his role in that party. The serial apologist was a haggard, anguished-looking man. The son of a rich London businessman, he had risen to become housing and then health minister, and had been until then a conventional-looking Tory. Under Macmillan he had ordered the smashing down of old terraces for new tower blocks. Under Heath he had spent heavily on a bigger bureaucracy for the NHS and higher social security levels. Now Sir Keith Joseph was quite literally wringing his hands and rolling his eyes with mortification. There had been thirty years of interventions, good intentions and disappointments, thirty years of socialism under both Labour and the Tories: 'I must take my blame for following too many of the fashions.'

Joseph's conversion to free-market, small-state economics had the force of a religious experience. Crucial to it would be controlling the amount of money in the economy to keep out inflation, which meant squeezing how much was borrowed and spent by the State. He had joined the Tories in the early fifties but had not been a Conservative, he said: 'I had thought that I was a Conservative but now I see that I was not really one at all.' This kind of thinking would lead within five years to the Thatcher revolution, and the wholesale rejection of the Heath years, taking the economic ideas of intellectuals who featured earlier in this history right into the centre of British public life. Other fellow travellers were professors, Americans or a few Powellite Tories outside the mainstream of the party. But Joseph was different, a former cabinet minister with close and direct experience of government. With his Centre for Policy Studies, he was the rain-maker, the storm-bringer, the Old Testament prophet denouncing his tribe.

Joseph argued that Britain by the mid-seventies had a fundamental choice to make between a socialist siege economy or a breakaway into proper liberal capitalism – in effect, Benn or Joseph. He could not have formed his ideas without the libertarian and monetarist thinkers of the fifties and sixties, men we met earlier. During the Tories' years in opposition from 1964 to 1970 he had educated himself in free-market economics and was soon using as his speechwriter the violently spoken, irrepressible Alfred Sherman, an East End boy from a left-wing family who had fought as a machine-gunner in the Spanish Civil War before swinging right round later and becoming an insistent right-wing critic of the British way. It was well said of Sherman that by the fifties his enthusiasm for the free market 'put him as much on the fringes of Macmillan's Britain as Communism had put him on the edge of politics in Neville Chamberlain's Britain'.[57] But to Sherman's disappointment, when Joseph returned to office in 1970 as Secretary for Health and Social Security, his radicalism went into hiding again, he forgot his enthusiasm for introducing more private money into health, and Sherman took to describing him dismissively as 'a good man fallen among civil servants'.

But the defeat of 1974 had shaken Joseph. With other monetarists he began a thorough rethink of the Heath years, culminating in a shadow cabinet post-mortem, when they argued that the early radicalism of 1970–1 had been right, and the subsequent U-turn a disaster. Heath blankly refused to listen, or at any rate to heed, the attack. Heath's haughty assessment in his autobiography was that Joseph 'had resumed a friendship with a person called Alfred Sherman, a former communist, and undergone what he liked to call "a conversion" as a result … [this] failed to cut any ice with the great majority of his colleagues, though we did them the courtesy of listening.' In fact, many Tories were beginning to listen. With Joseph were Geoffrey Howe and the quiet, watchful figure of Margaret Thatcher. Early on, Howe warned, 'I am not at all sure about Margaret. Many of her economic prejudices are certainly sound. But she is inclined to be rather too dogmatic for my liking on sensitive matters like education and might actually retard the case by simplification.'[58] There were other new radicals, such as the Powellite Tory MP John Biffen, the young economics writer Nigel Lawson and a crowd of journalists and academics.

Here was an intellectual analysis, hard and uncompromising, which excited a generation of new recruits to the party, while it repelled Tories of the comfortable Macmillan persuasion. Macmillan himself said of Joseph that he was 'the only boring Jew I've ever known' and later there would be much snide muttering about the men Thatcher learned from and worked with – Hayek, Sherman, Joseph, Lawson and Friedman. The truth was that Jews were prominent in intellectual thinking on the right, as on the left, bringing opposite lessons to Britain from the disasters of continental Europe. A serious commitment to ideas and old-fashioned attitudes to education gave them their unique influence in politics. Thatcher was open to the ideas, ready to listen, unprejudiced; many traditional Tories were not.

In the winter of 1974–5 after Heath had lost his second successive election, there was no such thing as 'Thatcherism'. She was expressing her public support for the policies of consensus, whatever her developing inner feelings. She backed intervention in the housing market and had queried council house sales. There was no sign that she would become leader. Heath was anyway stubbornly determined to stay on. He insisted his supporters, who included most of the well-known Tories of the day, back him. Polls suggested 70 per cent of Conservative voters wanted him to stay. Yet there was deep dissatisfaction on the Tory benches in Parliament. A City slicker, Sir Edward du Cann, who chaired the backbenchers' 1922 Committee, began to take soundings about challenging Heath. He was backed by the war hero, Tory MP and arch-intriguer, Airey Neave, but Neave soon pulled out. Joseph stepped up to the plate before making a catastrophically ill-judged and offensive speech in which he seemed to suggest that working-class women were having too many babies and should be stopped because they were degrading the gene pool. This finished the man *Private Eye* was already calling the 'mad monk'. So who could the right find as a candidate?

If Heath had realized that two successive election defeats meant he really had to go, and had he allowed other Tory moderates to prepare campaigns to replace him, Mrs Thatcher would have had no chance. Had Joseph not made a disaster of a speech, she would have been committed to backing him, and so would not have stood herself. Had du Cann stood, the brilliant campaign manager Neave would not have worked for her. Many Tory MPs were persuaded by him to vote for her because she had no chance, as a way of easing out Heath. Then more 'serious' candidates could stand. It was a brilliant ruse. On 4 February 1975, she shocked everyone by defeating Heath in the first ballot by 130 votes to 119. She then went on to beat the also-rans easily. A current of right-wing free-market thinking that had been gurgling almost unnoticed underground since the fifties would break ground in spectacular fashion, changing Britain for ever. 'Josephism' became 'Thatcherism'. Few of the Tory MPs in what was called 'the peasants' revolt' realized quite where their new leader would take them. For the next few years, supercilious smirks and patronizing remarks from Wilson and then the new Prime Minister, James Callaghan, would be her lot. And then she would show them.

Beyond Pop

The seventies was an extreme decade; the extreme left and extreme right were reflected even in its music. Drawing neat lines between popular culture and the wider world of politics and economics is a dangerous game. Any art follows its own internal logic and much of what happened to British music and fashion during the seventies was driven by the straightforward need to adopt then outpace what had happened the day before. Clipped, hard-edged styles appear on the street to mock floppy, romantic ones, and then it happens in reverse. The high-gloss extravagance of the late Teds is answered by the neat, fresh, cool look of the Mods, which will be met by the psychedelic extravagance and hairiness of the

Hippies. They are answered by the super-Mod working-class cool of the first skinheads, though in due course wannabe Ziggy Stardusts will bring androgyny and excess back to the pavement and playing ground. Leather-bound punks find a new trump card to offend the older rockers; New Romantics with eyeliner and quiffs challenge Goths. Huge baggy trousers are suddenly in then disappear as quickly. Shoes, shirts, haircuts, mutate and compete. For much of the time, this game doesn't mean anything outside its own rhetoric, it simply is – and then isn't.

Exactly the same can be said about musical fads, the way Soul is picked up in Northern clubs from Wigan to Blackpool to Manchester; the struggle between the concept albums of the art-house bands and the arrival of punkier noises from New York in the mid-seventies; the dance crazes that come and go. Often the motivation for change is boredom. We have heard enough of that three-minute noise and it's time for something shorter and louder, or longer and quieter. Nothing lasts long. Like fashion, musical styles begin to break up and head in many directions in this period, coexisting as rival subcultures across the country. Rock and roll is not dead, nor is Motown, when reggae and ska arrive. The Rolling Stones and Yes carry on oblivious to the arrival of the Sex Pistols and the Clash. Every individual who drank in popular culture feels a sudden rush of remembrance of days past when a particular band, song or look is revived. But we should not fool ourselves that emotion equals meaning. The life lived and its soundtrack are not quite the same.

Yet in this musical and stylistic chaos, which runs

from the early seventies to modern times, there are moments and themes which stick out. Perhaps the most important statistic to hold in mind is that between the early fifties and the mid-seventies, real disposable income – what people had in their hand to spend, taking inflation into account – exactly doubled. Between Lonnie Donegan and Led Zeppelin, as it were, people became twice as well off. Yet from 1974 until the end of 1978, living standards actually went into decline.[59] The long working-class boom had ended. Broadly speaking, British pop was invented during the optimism of 1958–68, when the economy was most of the time still booming and was evolving in its fastest and most creative spirit. Then the mood turned in the later sixties and seventies towards fantasy and escapism in wider and wilder varieties, as unemployment arrived and the world seemed bleaker and more confusing. This second phase involved the sci-fi ambiguities and glamour of Bowie, the gothic, mystical hokum of the heavy bad-boy bands like Black Sabbath and Led Zeppelin, and the druggy obscurities of Yes. The second half of the seventies were the years of deep political disillusion, strains which seemed to tear at the unity of the UK: Irish terrorism on the mainland, a rise in racial tension and widespread industrial mayhem. The optimism which had helped fuel popular culture suddenly gurgled dry. So it is not perhaps a coincidence that this period is a darker time in music and fashion, a nightmare inversion of the sixties dream. After the innocent raptures of England's 1966 World Cup victory and Manchester United's European Cup triumph two years later, the mid-seventies invent the modern football hooligan and by the eighties, English clubs were being banned from European competitions because of their followers. Vivienne Westwood and Malcolm McLaren turn from creating cod-fifties drape coats and beatnik jumpers to the ripped T-shirts and bondage gear of punk; the Sex Pistols portray themselves as a kind of anti-Beatles; older musical heroes flirt with fascism.

Westwood was in many ways a perfect inheritor of Quant's role a dozen years earlier. Like Quant, she was brought up to make clothes herself and came through art college. Like Quant she had a male partner who had a touch of business genius. Like Quant she was interested in the liberating power of clothes. Like Quant she set herself up in the Kings Road in a shop which first of all had to be braved rather than simply patronized. Her clothes would shock passers-by just as Quant's had horrified Michael Caine's mother. Like Quant she was sardonic and fearless and later on, she out-Quanted Quant as the grand dame of British fashion. Westwood received a Damehood from the Queen whose face she had famously impaled with a safety-pin earlier on, and was honoured with a huge retrospective show at the Victoria and Albert Museum.

Yet this daughter of a Derbyshire mill-weaver and a shoe-making family was also startlingly different from Quant, the Welsh teachers' child. Westwood had first mixed and matched to create a style of her own at the Manchester branch of C&A and said with only a twinge of irony, 'my work is rooted in English tailoring.'[60] Her vision of fashion was anything but uncluttered. It was a magpie, rip-it-up and make-it-new assault on the history of couture, postmodern to Quant's straightforward modern. And in the mid-seventies, working from a shop recently renamed simply Sex, Westwood's vision was a fetishistic, rubbery, vaguely sado-masochistic assault on mainstream decencies. Chains, zips in odd places, rips, obscene slogans and provocative images, referring for instance to a notorious serial rapist, all featured. She once declared that she had 'an in-built perversity, a kind of in-built clock which reacts against anything orthodox'. Her helper and model Jordan (aka Pamela Rooke) used to set off on a commuter train to the shop, wearing rubber clothes, fishnet stockings and a beehive hairdo and attracted so much attention British Rail put her in a first class compartment for her own protection. Quant's vision had been essentially optimistic – easy to wear, clean-looking clothes for free and liberated women. Westwood's vision was darker. Her clothes were to be worn like armour in the street battle with authority and repression, in the England of flashers and perverts.

Nor was her then partner Malcolm McLaren in any way like Plunkett Alexander-Greene, the aristocratic businessman husband of Quant. McLaren was also an art college product and, as we saw earlier, had been influenced by the radical anger of the 'Situationists' and the raw typography of King Mob. The son of a dysfunctional Jewish and Scottish family he had drifted through the worlds of fringe politics, music and film-making but was now remaking himself as a kind of wideboy entrepreneur of street culture, a latter-day Svengali modelled on 'Flash Larry' Parnes. He had already offered style advice to the New York

Dolls and was on the lookout for his anti-Beatles, duly forming the Sex Pistols in December 1975. Steve Jones, Paul Cook, John Lydon and Glen Matlock – who much admired the Beatles – were another working-class quartet in their late teens. But they expressed the self-loathing spirit of the times as the Beatles had expressed the geeky optimism of an earlier Britain. Pock-marked, sneering, spiky-haired, exuding violence and playing with a wild and simple thrash of a sound, they dutifully performed the essential duty of shocking a still easily shocked nation. Their handful of good songs have a leaping energy which really did take the ageing, lumbering rock establishment by storm, but their juvenile side quickly became embarrassing.

Compared to the most self-important assertions of John Lennon, their notorious performance on the London television show *Thames Today* with Bill Grundy, was desperate stuff. (Grundy: 'Go on, you've got another ten seconds. Say something outrageous'. Steve: 'You dirty bastard.' Grundy: 'Go on, again.' Steve: 'You dirty fucker!' Grundy: 'What a clever boy!' Steve: 'You fucking rotter!' It leaves later satirical attempts to depict punk rockers as in the television comedy *The Young Ones* floundering.) But the tabloid papers and stupider backbench MPs duly played their allotted role and helped fan the Sex Pistols' publicity engine. McLaren thrived on outrage and played up to the role of cynical charlatan for all he was worth. The Pistols played a series of increasingly wild gigs, including in the broken-up set of the bankrupt Biba shop (everything connects) and made juvenile political attacks in songs such as 'Anarchy in the

UK' and, in the year of the Silver Jubilee, 'God Save the Queen'. (Jim Callaghan can be accused of many things, but presiding over a 'fascist regime' is not one of them.) Yet punk was the first revival of fast, belligerent popular music to concern itself with the politics of the country, and this was the first time since the brief 'street fighting man' posturing of the late sixties when mainstream society needed to notice rock.

On the other side of the political divide was an eruption of racist, skinhead rock, and an interest in the far right. Among the rock stars who seemed to flirt with these ideas were Eric Clapton, who said in 1976 that 'Powell is the only bloke who's telling the truth, for the good of the country' and David Bowie, who spoke of Hitler as being the first superstar, musing that perhaps he would make a good Hitler himself. Though the Sex Pistols liked to see themselves as vaguely on the anarchist left, their enthusiasm for shocking, particularly after the nihilistic and amoral Sid Vicious joined them, at least left room for ambiguity. McLaren and Westwood had produced clothing with swastikas and other Nazi emblems, if only to outrage people (it worked) while Vicious's contribution to political thought can be summed up by his lyric 'Belsen was a gas / I read the other day / About the open graves / Where the Jews all lay ...'

Reacting to the surrounding mood, Rock Against Racism was formed in August 1976, helping create the wider Anti-Nazi League a year later. Punk bands were at the forefront of the RAR movement, above all the Clash whose lead singer Joe Strummer became more influential and admired than Johnny Rotten or the rest of the Sex Pistols, and bands such

539

as the Jam. Black music – reggae, ska and soul – was popular enough among white youths for it to have had a real influence in turning the fashion in street culture decisively against racism. Ska revival bands such as the Specials and the reggae-influenced Police and UB40 (the latter from the West Midlands, home of Powellism) had an effect which went beyond the odd memorable song. Hard-left politics had often been a joyless business but the seventies produced, in the middle of visions of social breakdown, a musical revival which cheered up the lost generation. The racist skinhead 'Oi' bands found themselves in a violent and uncomfortable ghetto. As one cultural critic of the time put it, 'A lifestyle – urban, mixed, music-loving, modern and creative – had survived, despite being under threat from the NF.'[61] The streets might be dirty and living standards falling, but it was not all bad news.

Sunny Jim, Stormy Winter:
the Callaghan Years

Jim Callaghan has featured already, both as hero in Northern Ireland and as rather a villain when he stabbed Wilson and Castle in the front over trade union reform. In the spring of 1976 he finally entered Number Ten after a series of votes by Labour MPs shaved off his rivals – Denis Healey, Tony Crosland and Roy Jenkins on the right, and Michael Foot and Tony Benn on the left. After three ballots, he beat Foot by 176 votes to 137 and replaced Wilson as Prime Minister. For three turbulent years he would run a government with no overall majority in Parliament, kept going by deals and pacts, and in an atmosphere of repeated, though not quite constant crisis. Callaghan was by now a familiar and reassuring figure in Britain, tall, ruddy, no-nonsense, robust and, by comparison with Wilson, straightforward. He had had all the top jobs in politics, though had not distinguished himself either as Chancellor or as Home Secretary. Latterly he had been Foreign Secretary, deeply involved in the early stages of détente, bringing an end to the Cold War, and forging close personal relations with Germany's Chancellor, Helmut Schmidt, America's Henry Kissinger and the amiable but derided President Ford. At sixty-five he was one of the most experienced politicians to become Prime Minister. After Wilson and Heath he was the third and last of the centrist seekers after consensus, the wartime avoiders of national confrontation. Yet behind the genial, occasionally stubborn-looking face with its protuberant lower lip and owlish glasses there was a man who, in the growing contest between hard left and right, was a Labour leader now instinctively looking to the right.

Churchill apart, all of his post-war predecessors had been Oxbridge men. Callaghan had not been to university at all. The son of a Royal Navy chief petty officer who had died young, and a devout Baptist mother from Portsmouth, he had known real poverty and had clawed his way up as a young clerk working for the Inland Revenue, and then as a union official, before wartime naval service. One of the 1945 generation of MPs, he was a young rebel who drifted right, though always keeping his strong pro-trade union instincts. His wounding experiences as Chancellor during the dark days of 1966–7 had nearly broken him but he had found, as the best politicians do, that what did not kill him made him stronger. He was a social conservative, uneasy about: divorce, homosexuality and vehemently pro-police, pro-monarchy, pro-armed forces, though he was anti-hanging and strongly anti-racialist too. As Home Secretary he had announced that the permissive society had gone too far. As Prime Minister, he would try to initiate a 'great debate' against trendy teaching in schools, calling for an inquiry into teaching methods, standards, discipline and the case for a national curriculum. On the economy, he would become steadily more impressed by the case for monetarism, then raging on the right. Famously, he told a stunned 1976 Labour conference used to the Keynesian doctrines about governments spending their way out of recession, cutting taxes and boosting investment: 'I tell you in all candour that that option no longer exists and that insofar as it ever did exist, it worked by injecting inflation into the economy ... Higher inflation, followed by higher unemployment. That is the history of the last twenty years.'

Yet even if he could read the runes, in the national memory Callaghan is forever associated with failure. There is the humiliating, cap-in-hand begging for help from the International Monetary Fund, the soaring inflation and interest rates of the late seventies and finally the piled rubbish, vast strike meetings and unburied dead of the 1979 'winter of discontent'. There is an arc which plummets through earlier crises under Wilson and Heath, before crashing into final chaos and destruction under Callaghan. Only after the wasteland of his time in office can the bold remaking of Britain under Margaret Thatcher begin. And Callaghan himself had been part of the problem. His sentimental failure to understand the aggression of the union challenge to elected power, and his earlier lack of interest in radical economic ideas, came home to haunt him in Downing Street. But the story of the Callaghan and Healey years, for the two must be taken together, is more intriguing than its body-strewn, gore-splattered final act. It is also a story of comparative success, of wrenching inflation down again, doing the best deals with international bankers that could be done, and facing up to challenges that had been dodged for decades. It did not end well for the protagonists, but then few interesting tragedies do.

Callaghan had a brutal side to him. In remaking his cabinet, he purged much of the left, leaving Michael Foot as his loyal and invaluable leader in the Commons delivering the votes, but sacking Barbara Castle as 'too old' and too left wing. The leader of the right, Roy Jenkins, was out too, off to take up the job of European Commissioner in Brussels. Crosland, briefly Foreign Secretary, died, so Callaghan had no serious rivals left. He responded by constructing the most right-wing Labour cabinet since the war, whose new faces included Bill Rodgers, Shirley Williams and David Owen. All would later join Jenkins in the breakaway Social Democratic Party (SDP). By the standards of New Labour after 1997 this was still a left-wing government, keen on redistribution, still describing itself as socialist, levying high rates of income tax. It believed in nationalization, adding shipbuilding, the new oil industry and the aircraft manufacture to the State's bulging holdings, and in such traditional anti-privilege issues as the abolition of pay beds in NHS hospitals. Some of its cabinet members, including Shirley Williams, joined the picket line during the violent 1977 Grunwick dispute at a film processing laboratory in London – one where Asian female workers, barred from joining the union APEX, had some moral right on their side but which became a bloody mob confrontation. It is hard to imagine New Labour ministers doing the same.

But by the standards of Labour's history, Callaghan's suspicion of liberalism, his admiration for American republicans like Kissinger and Ford, his new faith in monetarism and his increasingly aggressive attitude to high pay demands, put him to the right even of Wilson. In private he toyed with policies which would later make Mrs Thatcher famous, such as selling off council houses. His famous and much-quoted remark to an aide, just as Labour was losing power in 1979, that the country was going through a once-in-thirty-years sea change suggested that he half accepted the consensus years had failed: 'There is a shift in what the public wants and what it approves of. I suspect there is now such a sea-change – and it is for Mrs Thatcher.' About this, he was right. But if as Enoch Powell said, all political careers end in failure, then what happened before Callaghan's final failure is still an extraordinary story of despair, courage, hope and bungled accounting.

Cap in Hand

Jim Callaghan's first few days as Prime Minister in April 1976 must have brought back some grim memories. A dozen years earlier, as Chancellor, he had been confronted with awful economic news which nearly crushed him and ended in the forced devaluation of the pound. Now, on the first day of his premiership, he was told the pound was falling fast (it had been 'floating' since the Heath years but this had become a euphemism). A devaluation by sterling holders was likely. The Chancellor, Denis Healey, had negotiated the £6 pay limit and this would feed through to much lower wage increases and eventually to lower inflation. Cash limits on public spending brought in under Wilson would also radically cut public expenditure. But in the spring of 1976 inflation was still rampant and unemployment was rising fast. Healey now told Callaghan that because of the billions spent by the Bank of England supporting sterling in the first few months of the year, a loan from the International Monetary Fund looked essential. In June standby credits were arranged with the IMF and countries such as the United States, Germany, Japan and Switzerland. What would follow was about as humiliating as peacetime politics gets.

Healey had imposed tough cuts in the summer but by its end, as he returned from a desperately needed break in the Scottish Highlands, the pound was under intense pressure again. On 27 September 1976 Healey was meant to fly out to a Commonwealth finance ministers' conference in

Hong Kong with the Governor of the Bank of England. But so great was the crisis and so panicked were the markets that he decided he could not afford to be out of touch for seventeen hours' flying time. (This was before in-flight phones.) In full view of the television cameras, he turned round at Heathrow airport and went back to the Treasury. There he decided to apply to the IMF for a conditional loan – one which gave authority to the international banking officials above Britain's elected leaders. With exquisite timing, the Ford workers began a major strike. Healey was close to collapse, to 'demoralization', he later said, for the first and last time in his life.

Against Callaghan's initial advice, he decided to dash to the Labour conference in Blackpool and make his case to an anguished and angry party. As we have seen there was a powerful mood at the time for a siege economy, telling the IMF to get lost, cutting imports and nationalizing swathes of industry. Given just five minutes to speak from the floor because of the absurdities of Labour conference rules, the Chancellor warned his party this would mean trade war, mass unemployment and the return of a Tory government. But, he shouted against a rising hubbub, with something of the young Major Healey who had visited the 1945 conference in battledress, he was speaking to them from the battlefront. He would negotiate with the IMF which would mean 'things we do not like as well as things we do like. It means sticking to the very painful cuts in public expenditure ... It means sticking to the pay policy.' As Healey ruefully recorded in his autobiography, he had begun with a background of modest cheers and a rumble of booing: 'When I sat down, the cheers were much louder. So were the boos.' Benn called his speech vulgar and abusive: in fact Healey's final arm-clasp of triumph was a last throw by one of politics' great showmen.

So, with the cabinet nervously watching, the negotiations with the IMF started. Callaghan and Healey naturally wanted to limit as far as they could the cuts being forced on them. The IMF, with the US Treasury standing behind them, was under pressure to squeeze ever harder. The British side was in a horribly weak position. The government was riven by argument and threats of resignation, including from Healey. There were incredibly long and difficult cabinet arguments about what levels of cuts were acceptable and whether there was any real alternative in a leftist siege economy. In deepest secret, Callaghan and the lead IMF negotiator from Washington had bitter private talks, in which the Prime Minister warned that British democracy itself would be imperilled by mass unemployment. When it came to the very end of the tense and complicated haggling, the IMF was still calling for an extra billion pounds' worth of cuts and it was only when Healey, without telling Callaghan, threatened the international bankers with yet another 'Who runs Britain?' election, that they gave way. The final package of cuts was announced in Healey's budget, severe but not as grim as some had feared, and greeted with headlines about Britain's shame.

But the truly extraordinary thing about this whole story is that it was unnecessary from the start. The cash limits Healey had already imposed on Whitehall would cut spending far more effectively than anyone realized. More startling still, the public spending statistics (on which the cuts were based) were wildly wrong. Public finances were stronger than they appeared. The Treasury estimate for public borrowing in 1974–5 had been too low by £4,000m, a mistake greater than any tax changes ever made by a British Chancellor; but the 1976 estimate was twice as high as it should have been. The IMF-directed cuts were more savage than they needed to have been. As to the bloated State, another major issue of the day, the amount of Britain's wealth spent by government was miscalculated too. A government white paper early in 1976 had put it at about 60 per cent – huge by the standards of the West. But this was, as Healey put it, 'unforgiveably misleading'. When Britain's spending was defined in the same way as other countries' and at market prices, the figure fell to 46 per cent. By the time Labour left office it was 42 per cent, about the same as West Germany's and well below that of social democratic Scandinavian countries. Britain's balance of payments came back into balance long before the IMF cuts could take effect and Healey reflected later that 'If I had been given accurate forecasts in 1976, I would never have needed to go to the IMF at all.'

In the end only half the loan was used, all of which was repaid by the time Labour left office. Only half the standby credit was used and it was untouched from August 1977 onwards. During the IMF negotiations Healey had talked about 'Sod Off Day' when he and Britain would finally be free of outside control. That came far sooner than he had expected. Of course, at the time, nobody did know that Britain's finances were so much stronger than they had seemed. Yet all the lurid drama which imprinted itself on Britain's memory – the rush back from Heathrow, the dramatic scenes at the Labour conference, the humiliating arrival of the IMF hard men, backed by Wall Street, a political thriller which destroyed Labour's self-confidence for more than a decade and which was used repeatedly in the Thatcher years as clinching evidence of its bankruptcy – all this could have been avoided. That is only the start. It was the prospect of ever greater cuts in public spending, inflation out of control, and the economy in the hands of outsiders that helped break the Labour Party into warring factions and gave the hard left its great opportunity. Had the IMF crisis not happened would the 'winter of discontent' and the Bennite uprising have followed?

Healey later said he forgave the Treasury for its mistakes in calculating public sector borrowing needs, because nobody had got their forecasts right. He and they were operating in a new economic world of floating exchange rates, huge capital flows and speculation still little understood. It made him highly critical of monetarism, however, and all academic theories which depended on accurate measurement and forecasting of the money supply. He liked to quote President Johnson, who at about this time reflected that making a speech on economics 'is a lot like pissing down your leg. It seems hot to you, but it never does to anyone else.' Healey was bitter, though, about the Treasury's mistakes over the true scale of public spending which so hobbled his hopes of being seen as a successful Chancellor. He said later he could not forgive them: 'I cannot help suspecting that

549

Treasury officials deliberately overstated public spending in order to put pressure on governments which were reluctant to cut it. Such dishonesty for political purposes is contrary to all the proclaimed traditions of the British civil service.'[62]

The Callaghan government is remembered for the IMF crisis and for the 'winter of discontent'. His defenders point out that Callaghan actually presided over a relatively popular and successful government for more than half his time in power – some twenty months out of thirty-seven. Following the IMF affair, the pound recovered strongly, the markets recovered, inflation fell, eventually to single figures, and unemployment fell too. By the middle of 1977, the year of the Queen's Silver Jubilee, North Sea Oil was coming ashore to the tune of more than half a million barrels a day, a third of the country's needs. Britain would be self-sufficient in oil by 1980 and already was in gas. The pay restraint agreed earlier with Healey was still holding, though only just. The new American President, Jimmy Carter, visited for a much-praised summit. Callaghan, for the first time, was getting a good press while the Tory opposition under Margaret Thatcher seemed to be struggling. After having to rely on an odd mixture of nationalist MPs for its precarious Commons majority, Labour entered a deal with David Steel's Liberals from March 1977 to August of the following year, giving Callaghan a secure parliamentary position for the first time. The Lib-Lab pact gave the smaller party, which then had only thirteen MPs, rights only to be consulted, plus vague promises on possible voting system changes: it was much more helpful to Labour. Labour regained a modest majority over the Tories in the opinion polls and the prospect of Callaghan and Labour continuing to govern well into the eighties looked perfectly reasonable. This did not look like a dying government, still less the end of an era.

Peasants' Revolt: Two, the Left

We have seen the peasants' revolt of the right, but there was another too, from the left. This would be publicly associated with Tony Benn, the face of the left in Labour's highest circles. But it was a wide and a deep political force, with complicated roots. The Communist Party of Great Britain had almost collapsed, so great was the disillusion with the Soviet system to which it pledged undying and largely uncritical obedience. By the seventies it was riven by arguments of the kind that split most declining organizations. Further left were a bewildering number of Trotskyist groups, all hostile to the Soviet Union, all claiming to be the true party of Lenin, all denouncing one another over ideological and tactical detail. They tended to be dour and puritan. Only two had any real following: the Socialist Workers' Party, or SWP, and the Militant Tendency. Each had descended by political split and fusion from earlier groups which had first organized in Britain in the forties.

Militant would later cause a huge convulsion in the Labour Party. Wilson complained a lot about 'Trots' trying to take the party over but in the seventies he was largely ignored and Militant built up strong local bases, particularly in Liverpool. The

SWP, outside the Labour Party, campaigned on specific issues such as strikes and racism. Their distinctive clenched fist logo and dramatic typography appears in the background of countless industrial and political marches, pickets and rallies. The SWP's single biggest influence was in combating the rise of the National Front.

The NF, under its tubby would-be führer Martin Webster and the bullet-headed John Tyndall, had been founded in 1967 after the original British National Party and the old League of Empire Loyalists joined together. Electorally it was struggling, though Webster polled 16 per cent in the West Bromwich by-election of May 1973 and in the two 1974 general elections the NF put up first fifty-four and then ninety candidates, entitling them to a television broadcast. More important to their strategy were the street confrontations, engineered by marching with Union Jacks and anti-immigrant slogans through Bangladeshi or Pakistani areas in Leeds, Birmingham and London. A more extreme offshoot of the original skinheads attached themselves to the NF's racialist politics and by the mid-seventies they too were on the march. The SWP determined to organize street politics of their own and bring things to a halt and formed the Anti-Nazi League in 1977. The League drew in tens of thousands of people who had no particular interest in the obscurities of Leninist revolutionary theory, but who saw the NF as a genuine threat to the new immigrant communities. And the young flooded to their rallies, marches and confrontations, during which there were a couple of deaths as the police weighed in to protect the National Front's right to march. Beyond Militant and the SWP, other far-left groups inside and outside the Labour Party would achieve brief notoriety because they were supported by a famous actress, such as Vanessa Redgrave, or through influence in a local party or borough. Eventually the 'loony left' would come to the boil, enjoying enough influence, particularly in London, to shred Labour's credibility. But in the seventies, this was still a slowly developing, obscure story.

Much more important then was the influence of socialists who were not working for secretive Trotskyist or communist parties, but had simply wanted to bring down Wilson and were now gunning for Callaghan and his friends. Like Thatcher and Joseph, they believed the old consensus politics was failing. Some of their thinking was also shared by the right – they were mostly hostile to the European Community, for example, opposed Scottish and Welsh nationalism, and were hostile to America. But that was where the similarities ended. The Labour left wanted to deal with world economic chaos by pulling up the drawbridge, imposing strict controls on what was imported, taking direct control of the major industries, and the City too. The left thought planning had failed because it was too weak, and should therefore be dramatically extended. Any strongly held political view which is excluded from the centre of power tends to develop a conspiracy theory. The Powellites believed Heath had lied to the British people. The Labour left believed Wilson, Callaghan and Healey had been captured by international capitalism, as had many MPs. The answer was to make them accountable to 'ordinary people', as the obsessive meeting-attenders of Labour politics innocently believed themselves to be. So the siege economy or 'Alternative Economic Strategy' and mandatory reselection of MPs became the two main planks of the left.

Tony Benn became the voice and leader of Labour's peasants' revolt. His enthusiasm for workers' cooperatives and a National Enterprise Board had already made him a figure of ridicule in Fleet Street. Later he would become a kind of revered national grandfather, a white-haired, humorous sage whose wry memories of Attlee and Wilson would transfix audiences of all ages and views. His unbending hostility to nuclear weapons, American and British war-making, and market capitalism would inspire hundreds of thousands deep into the years of New Labour. But between the eager-beaver Anthony Wedgwood Benn, champion of Concorde, and the paternal Grandpa Tony, came the turbulent years of 'Bennism', the central phase of his political life. Radicalized by his children towards the politics of feminism, anti-nuclear campaigning and much else, he became increasingly detached from his colleagues as the Wilson–Callaghan government staggered towards collapse. Benn had come close to leaving it over his opposition to Labour's deal with the Liberals, and he fell out badly with the other notably left-wing cabinet minister Michael Foot over parliamentary tactics on Europe.

His general attitude to the party is well caught by his diary entry for 15 January 1978: 'The whole Labour leadership now is totally demoralised and all the growth on the left is going to come up from the outside and underneath. This is the death of the Labour Party. It believes in nothing any more, except staying in power.' Benn was in the curious position of still being a senior member of the government when he wrote this, attending intimate gatherings at Chequers, hobnobbing with visiting Americans, hearing deep military and security secrets, while at the same growing the eyes and ears of an outsider. He was on the side of the strikers who brought much of the country to a halt and his new friend Arthur Scargill, the miners' leader, was telling Benn he could be the next Labour leader himself. Though it seemed a fantasy in 1978, within a few years Benn would come within a hair's breadth of winning the deputy leadership on a left-wing socialist ticket, during the middle of a vicious and deeply damaging Labour civil war.

Then Was the Winter of their Discontent

The 'winter of discontent', a Shakespearean phrase, was used by Callaghan himself to describe the industrial and social chaos of 1978–9. It has stuck in people's memories, as few political events do – the schools closed, the ports blockaded, the rubbish rotting in the streets, the dead unburied. Actions by individual union branches and shop stewards were reckless and heartless. Left-wing union leaders and activists whipped up the disputes for their own purposes. Right-wing newspapers, desperate to see the end of Labour, exaggerated the effects and rammed home the picture of a nation no longer governable. But much of the fault for this was Callaghan's. It was not just that he had opposed the legal restrictions on union power pleaded for by

Wilson and Castle, and then fought for vainly by Heath. It was not even that he and Healey, acting in good faith, had imposed a more drastic squeeze on public spending and thus on the poorest families, than was economically necessary ... though none of that helped. It was also that by trying to impose an unreasonably tough new pay limit on the country, and then dithering about the date of the election, he destroyed the fragile calm he had so greatly enjoyed.

Most people, including most of the cabinet, had assumed that Callaghan would call a general election in the autumn of 1978. The economic news was still good, Labour was ahead in the polls. Two dates in October had already been pencilled in, though 12 October had been ruled out because it was Margaret Thatcher's birthday. But Callaghan, musing at his Sussex farm during the summer, decided that he did not trust the polls. He would wait, soldiering on until the spring. When the Prime Minister invited half a dozen trade union leaders to his farm to discuss the election, they left still thinking he was going in the autumn. Then, at the TUC conference, with the world agog for an announcement, Callaghan sang a verse from an old music hall song, originally by Vesta Victoria:

There was I waiting at the church, waiting at
   the church, waiting at the church
When I found he'd left me in the lurch, Lor'
   how it did upset me
All at once he sent me round a note, here's
   the very note, this is what he wrote,
Can't get away to marry you today, My wife
   won't let me.

While a good enough song in its day, it was hardly a clear message to Britain. Was the jilted bride Mrs Thatcher? The trade union movement? Callaghan's intention was to suggest that he was delaying the election but many trade union leaders and newspaper correspondents assumed just the opposite. When he finally came clean to the cabinet, they were shocked.

This might not have mattered so much had Callaghan also not promised a new 5 per cent pay limit to bring inflation down further. Because of the 1974–5 cash limit on pay rises at a time of high inflation, take-home pay for most people had been falling. Public sector workers had had a particularly hard time. There were the inevitable stories of fat cat directors and bosses awarding themselves high settlements. The union leaders and many ministers thought that a further period of pay limits would be impossible to sell, while a 5 per cent limit, which appears to have come from Callaghan almost off the cuff, was widely considered to be ludicrously tough.

Had Callaghan gone to the country in October then the promise of further pay restraint might have helped boost Labour's popularity, while the unions could have comforted themselves with the thought that it was probably mere window-dressing. By delaying the election until the following spring, Callaghan ensured that his 5 per cent would be tested in Britain's increasingly impatient and dangerous industrial relations market. First up, almost as soon as Callaghan had finished his music-hall turn, were the 57,000 car-workers employed by Ford, the US giant. The Transport & General Workers' Union called not for 5 per cent but for 30 per cent, on the back of high profits (and, it has to be said, an 80 per cent pay rise just awarded to Ford's chairman). Callaghan was badly embarrassed – his son, as it happened, worked for the company – and when after five weeks of lost production, Ford eventually settled for 17 per cent, he became convinced he would lose the coming election.

There was a vale of tears to be endured first. Oil tanker drivers also in the TGWU came out for 40 per cent, and were followed by road haulage drivers, workers at Ford's nationalized rival British Leyland, then water and sewerage workers. BBC electricians threatened a blackout of Christmas television. The docks were picketed and closed down. Blazing braziers, surrounded by huddled figures in woolly hats, with snow whirling round them, were shown nightly on the television news. Hull, virtually cut off, was known as the 'second Stalingrad'. The effects were felt directly by ministers along with the rest of the country. Bill Rodgers, the transport minister, whose mother was dying of cancer, found that vital chemotherapy chemicals were not being allowed out of Hull. Later, when the Health Secretary David Ennals was admitted to Westminster Hospital the local shop steward announced gleefully that he was 'a legitimate target' for action: 'He won't get the little extras our members provide patients. He won't get his locker cleaned or the area around his bed tidied up. He won't get tea or soup.'[63] In the middle of it all Callaghan went off for an international summit on the Caribbean island of Guadeloupe, staying on for talks and sightseeing in Barbados. Pictures of him swimming and sunning himself did not improve the national mood. When he returned to Heathrow, confronted by news reporters asking about the industrial crisis, he replied blandly: 'I don't think other people in the world will share the view that there is mounting chaos.' This was famously translated by the *Daily Mail* and then the *Sun* into, 'Crisis? What Crisis?' The nation's mood grew no sunnier.

As the railwaymen prepared to join the strikes, the worst blow for the government came from the public sector union NUPE, who called out more than a million school caretakers, cooks, ambulance men, refuse collectors on random stoppages for a £60 a week guaranteed minimum wage. Strikes by car workers were one thing. But now the public was being hit directly, and the most vulnerable were being hit the hardest. Children's hospitals, old people's homes and schools were all plunged into trouble. The single most notorious action was by the Liverpool Parks and Cemeteries Branch of the General & Municipal Workers' Union, who refused to bury dead bodies, leaving more than 300 to pile up in a cold storage depot and a disused factory, and Liverpool council to discuss emergency plans for disposing of some corpses at sea. Funeral corteges were met at the cemeteries by pickets and forced to turn back. Strikers were confronted in local pubs and thumped.

In the centre of London and other major cities, huge piles of rotting rubbish piled up, overrun with rats and a serious health hazard. Inside government, ordinary work almost ground to a halt. It must be recorded that most of those striking, the public sector workers in particular, were woefully badly paid and living in relative poverty;

and that they had no history of industrial militancy. Nor was the crisis quite as dreadful as some of the papers and politicians showed it. As with Heath's three-day week, many people gleefully enjoyed the enforced holiday from their public sector jobs. Nobody was proved to have died in hospital as a result of union action, there was no shortage of food in the shops and there was no violence. Troops were never used. This was chaos, and a direct challenge to the authority of the government. It was not a revolution, or an attempt to overthrow a government.

Yet that is the effect it had. The revolution would bring in Thatcherism not socialism, and Labour would be overthrown, plunging quickly into civil war. A 'St Valentine's Day concordat' was eventually unveiled between the government and the TUC, talking of annual assessments and guidance, targeting long-term inflation, virtually admitting the 5 per cent limit had been a mistake. After all the drama, it was a fig-leaf so thin and ragged it was barely worth holding up. By March most of the action had ended and various large settlements and inquiries had been set up. But in the Commons, the government was running out of allies, spirit and hope. The failure of the referendum on Scottish devolution meant that under previously agreed rules, the act would have to be repealed. This in turn gave the Scottish Nationalists no reason to continue supporting Labour. The Liberals, facing the highly embarrassing trial of Jeremy Thorpe for conspiracy to murder (he would later be acquitted), had their own reasons for wanting an early election. In the drink-sodden, conspiracy-ridden, frenetic atmosphere of an exhausted Parliament, in which dying MPs had been carried through the lobbies to keep the government afloat, final attempts were made by Michael Foot and the Labour whips to find some kind of majority – Ulster Unionists, Irish Nationalists, renegade Scots were all approached. Callaghan, by now, was in a calmly fatalistic mood. He did not want to struggle on through another summer and autumn. Finally, on 28 March 1979, the game ended when the government was defeated by a single vote, brought down at last by a ragged coalition of Tories, Liberals, Scottish Nationalists and Ulster Unionists. Callaghan was the first Prime Minister since 1924 to have to go to Buckingham Palace and ask for a dissolution of Parliament, because he had lost a vote in the Commons.

The five-week election campaign started after the Irish assassination of Mrs Thatcher's wily leadership campaign manager, the Tory MP Airey Neave, murdered by a car-bomb on his way into the Commons underground car-park. On the Labour side it was dominated by Callaghan, still more popular than his party, who emphasized stable prices and his deal with the unions, if such it was. On the Tory side, Thatcher showed a new media savvy, working with the television news teams and taking the advice of her advertising gurus, the Saatchis. Callaghan, who had never expected to win, was soundly beaten. The Conservatives took sixty-one seats directly from Labour, gaining nearly 43 per cent of the vote, and a substantial overall majority, with 339 seats.

What of the players in the last act of Old Labour and the Broken Consensus? Callaghan would stumble on as leader before retiring in October 1980. Healey would fight a desperate struggle against the left, as his party did its level best to commit suicide in public. Numerous moderates would form the breakaway SDP. The Scottish Nationalists, derided by Callaghan when they voted him down as 'turkeys voting for Christmas', lost eleven of their thirteen MPs. The unions would eventually lose almost half their members and any political influence they briefly enjoyed. More important than all that, mass unemployment would arrive in Britain. The one economic medicine so bitter that no minister in the seventies had thought of trying it was duly uncorked and poured into the spoon. It was time for Britain to grimace and open her mouth.

NOTES

Prologue

1. See Correlli Barnett, *The Collapse of British Power*, Eyre Methuen, 1972.
2. George L. Bernstein, *The Myth of Decline: The Rise of Britain Since 1945*, Pimlico, 2004.

Part 1: Hunger and Pride

1. William Harrington & Peter Young, *The 1945 Revolution*, Davis-Poynter, 1978.
2. Norman Howard, *A New Dawn*, Politico's, 2005.
3. Ibid.
4. W. K. Hancock & M. M. Gowing, *The British War Economy*, HMSO, 1949.
5. All quotes from Correlli Barnett, *The Lost Victory*, Macmillan, 1995.
6. Robert Skidelsky, *John Maynard Keynes. Volume 3: Fighting for Britain*, Macmillan, 2000.
7. Ibid.
8. See Desmond Wettern, *The Decline of British Sea Power*, Jane's, 1982.
9. Vice Admiral Sir Louis le Bailly, *From Fisher to the Falklands*, Institute of Marine Engineers, 1991; and Eric J. Grove, *Vanguard to Trident: British Naval Policy since World War 2*, The Bodley Head, 1987.

10. Dan Van der Vat, *Standard of Power*, Hutchinson, 2000.
11. N. A. M. Rodger, *The Admiralty*, Terence Dalton, 1979.
12. Peter Hennessy, *The Prime Minister*, Allen Lane, 2000.
13. Quoted often but see ibid.
14. Hugh Dalton, *The Fateful Years*, Muller, 1957.
15. Story recounted to the author by Gordon Brown, who showed me the very same mahogany lavatory.
16. Alan Bullock, *Ernest Bevin, Foreign Secretary*, Oxford U. P., 1985.
17. Ibid.
18. Aneurin Bevan, *In Place of Fear*, Heinemann, 1952.
19. Dean Acheson, *Sketches from Life* (1961), quoted in Bullock, op. cit.
20. For this and further material in the following paragraph, see Paul Addison, *The Road to 1945*, Jonathan Cape, 1975.
21. George Orwell, 'England Your England', from *Inside the Whale and Other Essays*, Victor Gollancz, 1940; repr. Penguin, 1962.
22. Arthur Herman, *To Rule the Waves*, Hodder, 2004.
23. See Peter Hennessy, *Never Again: Britain 1945–1951*, Jonathan Cape, 1992.
24. CAB 134/1315 PR (56)3, 1 June 1956, reproduced in *British Documents on the End of Empire*, ed. David Goldsworthy, HMSO, 1994.
25. Labour Party, *Fair Shares of Scarce Consumer Goods*, London 1946, quoted in Ina Zweiniger-

Bargielowska, *Austerity in Britain,* Oxford U. P., 2000.

26. See Susan Cooper, 'Snoek Piquante', in *Age of Austerity 1945–1951,* ed. Michael Sissons & Philip French, Hodder & Stoughton, 1963.
27. Simon Garfield (ed.), *Our Hidden Lives,* Ebury Press, 2004.
28. See Peter Hennessy, *Whitehall,* Seeker & Warburg, 1989.
29. Most of this information comes from Robert Winder, *Bloody Foreigners,* Abacus, 2004.
30. See Juliet Cheetham, in *Trends in British Society since 1900,* ed. A. H. Halsey, Macmillan, 1972.
31. Jean Medawar & David Pyke, *Hitler's Gift,* Richard Cohen Books, 2000.
32. For instance in adverts warning of the dangers of VD.
33. Quoted in Nicholas Timmins, *The Five Giants,* HarperCollins, 1995.
34. Ibid.
35. Graham Payn & Sheridan Morley (eds), *The Noël Coward Diaries,* Weidenfeld & Nicolson, 1982.
36. See Gyles Brandreth, *Charles and Camilla,* Century, 2005.
37. Ben Pimlott, *The Queen,* HarperCollins, 1996.
38. Richard Chamberlain, et al (eds) *Austerity to Affluence, British Art and Design, 1945–1962,* Merrell Holberton, 1997.
39. See Maureen Waller, *London 1945,* John Murray, 2004.
40. See Paul Addison, *Now the War is Over,* BBC/ Cape, 1985.
41. Zweiniger-Bargielowska, op. cit.
42. Waller, op. cit.

43. See Nigel Walker in Halsey, op. cit.
44. Peter Hitchens, *A Brief History of Crime,* Atlantic Books, 2003.
45. Timmins, op. cit.
46. For all this, Timmins, the best single account of the Beveridge report easily available.
47. See Christian Wolmar, *On the Wrong Line,* Aurum Press, 2005.
48. Barnett, *The Lost Victory.*
49. Godfey Hodgson, 'The Steel Debates' in Sissons & French, op. cit.
50. See Peter Hennessy, *Never Again,* Jonathan Cape, 1992; and Timmins, op. cit.
51. For a full description of the Prefab story, see Greg Stevenson, *Palaces for the People,* Batsford, 2003.
52. Quoted in Miles Glendinning & Stefan Muthesius, *Tower Block,* Paul Mellon Centre/ Yale University Press, 1994.
53. Quoted in ibid.
54. David Hughes, 'The Spivs' in Sissons & French, op. cit.
55. Quoted in Addison, op. cit.
56. Anne Perkins, *Red Queen,* Macmillan, 2003.
57. Susan Cooper, 'Snoek Piquante' in Sissons & French, op. cit.
58. Pearson Phillips in ibid.
59. Ruth Adam, *A Woman's Place, 1910–1975,* Persephone Books, 2000.
60. Quoted in: Addison, op. cit.
61. Interview, *The Stage,* 2005.
62. Dominic Shellard, *British Theatre Since the War,* Yale U. P., 1999.
63. John Osborne, *Almost a Gentleman,* Faber & Faber, 1991.

64. Arthur Miller, quoted in Terry Coleman, *Olivier: The Authorised Biography,* Bloomsbury, 2005.
65. Quoted in Max Hastings, *The Korean War,* Michael Joseph, 1987.
66. Jung Chang & Jon Halliday, *Mao: The Unknown Story,* Jonathan Cape, 2005.
67. Hastings, op. cit.
68. James Cameron, *Point of Departure,* Arthur Barker, 1967; repr. Granta Books, 2006.
69. See Jung Chang & Halliday, op. cit.
70. Tom Hickman, *The Call-Up: A History of National Service,* Headline, 2004.
71. Anthony Farrar-Hockley, *The British Part in the Korean War,* HMSO, 1990.
72. Betty Vernon, *Ellen Wilkinson,* Croom Helm, 1987.
73. B. L. Donoughue & G. L. Jones, *Herbert Morrison, Portrait of a Politician,* Weidenfeld & Nicolson, 1973.
74. Michael Frayn, and Francis Boyd of the *Manchester Guardian.*
75. Michael Frayn, 'Festival' in Sissons & French, op. cit.

Part 2: The Land of Lost Content

1. For these figures, see Anthony Sampson, *Anatomy of Britain Today,* Hodder & Stoughton, 1965.
2. For Balcon see Matthew Sweet, *Shepperton Babylon,* Faber & Faber, 2005; Michael Balcon, *A Lifetime of Films,* Hutchinson, 1969; and

Charles Barr, *Ealing Studios,* Cameron & Hollis, 1998.

3. *The Macmillan Diaries: The Cabinet Years 1950–1957,* Macmillan, 2000.

4. Edward Heath, *The Course of My Life,* Hodder & Stoughton, 1998.

5. Ibid.

6. See Dominic Sandbrook, *Never Had It So Good,* Little, Brown, 2005.

7. D. R. Thorpe, *Eden: The Life and Times of Anthony Eden, First Earl of Avon, 1897–1977,* Chatto & Windus, 2003.

8. Quoted in Peter Hennessy, *The Secret State,* Penguin, 2002.

9. Hugo Young, *This Blessed Plot,* Macmillan, 1998.

10. See Alistair Home, *Macmillan,* vol. 1, Macmillan, 1988.

11. Peter Hennessy, *Having It So Good,* Allen Lane, 2006.

12. R. A. Butler, *The Art of the Possible,* quoted in Hennessy, ibid.

13. Peter Wildeblood, *Against the Law,* Weidenfeld & Nicolson, 1955.

14. Lord Montagu of Beaulieu, *Wheels Within Wheels: An Unconventional Life,* Weidenfeld & Nicolson, 2000.

15. Tom Driberg, *Guy Burgess,* Weidenfeld & Nicolson, 1956.

16. Spike Milligan, *Adolf Hitler: My Part in his Downfall,* Michael Joseph, 1971; Penguin, 1973.

17. In a 1957 interview, quoted by Humphrey Carpenter, *Spike Milligan,* Hodder & Stoughton, 2003. The following quotes are also from this book.

18. D. R. Thorne, *Eden,* Chatto & Windus, 2003.
19. Brian Lapping, *End of Empire,* Granada, 1985.
20. Ben Pimlott, *The Queen,* HarperCollins, 1996.
21. See, for all this, Tom Hickman, *The Call-Up: A History of National Service,* Headline, 2004.
22. Thanks to Rick Richards of Christchurch and Jean Webber of Burghclere, Newbury, for this information to the author.
23. Jean-Raymond Tourneaux, *Secrets d'Etat,* Paris, 1960, quoted in Herman Finer, *Dulles over Suez,* Heinemann, 1964.
24. Quoted in Robert Shepherd, *Enoch Powell,* Hutchinson, 1996.
25. See Gerald Frost, *Antony Fisher, Champion of Liberty,* Profile Books, 2002.
26. Richard Cockett, *Thinking the Unthinkable,* HarperCollins, 1994.
27. Gillian Bardsley, *Issigonis: the Official Biography,* Icon Books, 2005.
28. See Barbara Castle, *Fighting All the Way,* Macmillan, 1993; and Anne Perkins, *Red Queen,* Macmillan, 2003.
29. See Sandbrook, op. cit.
30. Keith Middlemass, *Power, Competition and the State,* vol. 1, Macmillan, 1986.
31. Quoted in Sandbrook, op. cit.
32. Ibid.
33. Quoted in Perkins, op. cit.
34. Crossman's account, quoted in Philip Williams, *Hugh Gaitskell,* Jonathan Cape, 1979.
35. Quoted in Patrick Hannan, *When Arthur Met Maggie,* Seren, 2006.
36. Anthony Crosland, *The Future of Socialism,* Jonathan Cape, 1956; see also Susan Crosland, *Tony Crosland,* Jonathan Cape, 1982.

37. Letter of Harold Macmillan to Sir Robert Menzies, quoted in Andrew Roberts, *A History of the English-Speaking Peoples since 1900,* Weidenfeld & Nicolson, 2006.
38. James Chuter Ede, quoted in Mike & Trevor Phillips, *Windrush: The Irresistible Rise of Multi-Racial Britain,* HarperCollins, 1999.
39. Quoted in Randall Hansen, *Citizenship and Immigration in Post-war Britain,* Oxford U. P., 2000.
40. See Robert Winder, *Bloody Foreigners,* Abacus, 2004.
41. Sandbrook, op. cit.
42. A. G. Bennett, quoted in ibid.
43. Phillips & Phillips, op. cit.
44. Hansen, op. cit.
45. Winder, op. cit.
46. For this, and other material here, see Hugo Young's *This Blessed Plot,* op. cit.
47. See ibid.
48. Roy Jenkins, *A Life at the Centre,* Macmillan, 1991.
49. Horne, *Macmillan,* vol. 2; also for the Birch Grove meeting.
50. Heath, op. cit.
51. Quoted in Hennessy, *The Secret State,* op. cit.
52. Hennessy, ibid.
53. Brian Lavery, *Journal of Maritime Research:* his article on Macmillan, Eisenhower and the Holy Loch affair is by far the best account.
54. Mark Amory, in his preface to *The Letters of Ann Fleming,* Collins Harvill, 1985.
55. Brian Brivati, *Hugh Gaitskell,* Richard Cohen Books, 1996.
56. Ibid.

57. For Cliveden and the following, see Derek Wilson, *The Astors,* Weidenfeld & Nicolson, 1993.
58. Harry Thompson, *Peter Cook: A Biography,* Hodder & Stoughton, 1997.
59. R. H. S. Crossman, *The Diaries of a Cabinet Minister,* Hamish Hamilton/Cape, 1975.

Part 3: Harold, Ted and Jim

1. See Ben Pimlott, *Harold Wilson,* HarperCollins, 1992.
2. Kenneth O. Morgan, *Callaghan: A Life,* Oxford U. P., 1997.
3. Lord George-Brown, *In My Way,* Victor Gollancz, 1971.
4. Lord Rodgers of Quarry Bank, in *Dictionary of Labour Biography,* ed. Greg Rosen, Politico's, 2001.
5. R. H. S. Crossman, *The Diaries of a Cabinet Minister,* vol. 1, Hamish Hamilton/Cape, 1975.
6. Roy Jenkins, *A Life at the Centre,* Macmillan, 1991.
7. Susan Crosland, *Tony Crosland,* Jonathan Cape, 1982.
8. See Nick Timmins, *The Five Giants,* HarperCollins, 1995.
9. Hugo Young, *One of Us,* Macmillan, 1989.
10. Edward Heath, *The Course of My Life,* Hodder & Stoughton, 1998.
11. See Giles Radice, *Friends & Rivals,* Abacus, 2002.
12. Roy Jenkins, op. cit.

13. Alwyn Turner in *The Biba Experience*, Antique Collectors Club, 2004, from where much of this paragraph derives.
14. See Bob Spitz, *The Beatles*, Aurum Press, 2006.
15. *Parkinson*, quoted in Max Decharne, *Kings Road*, Weidenfeld & Nicolson, 2005.
16. Quoted in Dominic Sandbrook, *Never Had It So Good*, Little Brown, 2005.
17. Ray Davies, *X-Ray: the Unauthorised Autobiography*, Viking, 1994; see also Andy Miller, *The Kinks are the Village Green Preservation Society*, Continuum, 2003 and Neville Marten & Jeff Hudson, *The Kinks*, Sanctuary Publishing, 1996.
18. Andrew Hussey, *The Game of War: The Life and Death of Guy Debord*, Pimlico, 2002.
19. See Dave Haslam, *Not Abba*, Fourth Estate, 2005; and Robert Hewison, *Too Much*, Methuen, 1986.
20. See Brian Lapping, *End of Empire*, Granada, 1985.
21. Quoted in Pimlott, op. cit.
22. Pimlott, ibid.
23. Tony Benn, *The Benn Diaries*, Arrow, 1996 (entry in February 1966).
24. Jenkins, op. cit.
25. Barbara Castle, *The Castle Diaries*, Weidenfeld & Nicolson, 1974.
26. *The Cecil King Diaries: 1965–1970*, Jonathan Cape, 1972.
27. Philip Ziegler, *Wilson: The Authorised Life*, Weidenfeld & Nicolson, 1993.
28. Jenkins, op. cit.
29. Richard Crossman, op. cit.

30. Randall Hansen, *Citizenship and Immigration Post-war Britain,* Oxford U. P., 2000.
31. Simon Heffer, *Like the Roman,* Weidenfeld & Nicolson, 1998.
32. See Ruth Dudley Edwards, *Newspapermen,* Pimlico, 2003; and *The Cecil King Diaries.*
33. Dudley Edwards, ibid.
34. Ziegler, op. cit.
35. See Morgan, op. cit.
36. Susan Crosland, op. cit.
37. See Heffer, op. cit.
38. Ibid.
39. Roy Hattersley, *Fifty Years On,* Little, Brown, 1997.
40. See Ziegler, op. cit.
41. *The Benn Diaries.*
42. Clem Jones, quoted in Mike & Trevor Phillips, *Windrush: The Irresistible Rise of Multi-Racial Britain,* HarperCollins, 1999.
43. Nicholas Mayhew, *Sterling: The Rise and Fall of a Currency,* Allen Lane, 1999.
44. Heath, ibid.
45. Hugo Young, *This Blessed Plot,* Macmillan, 1998.
46. Quoted in Ziegler, op. cit.
47. *The Times,* 3 May 1971.
48. See Jon Savage, *England's Dreaming,* Faber & Faber, 1991.
49. See Arthur Seldon in Arthur Seldon & Stuart Ball, *Conservative Century,* Oxford U. P., 1994.
50. Robert Elms, *The Way We Wore,* Picador, 2005.
51. Bernard Donoughue, *Downing Street Diary,* Jonathan Cape, 2005.
52. Pimlott, op. cit.

53. Denis Healey, *The Time of My Life*, Michael Joseph, 1989.
54. See Young, *This Blessed Plot*
55. Heffer, op. cit.
56. Mervyn Jones, *Michael Foot*, Victor Gollancz, 1994.
57. Richard Cockett, *Thinking the Unthinkable*, Fontana Press, 1995.
58. Letter to Anthony Seldon, quoted in Cockett.
59. See Haslam, op. cit.
60. Claire Wilcox, *Vivienne Westwood*, V&A Publishing, 2004.
61. Haslam, op. cit.
62. Healey, op. cit.
63. Quoted in Kevin Jeffreys, *Finest and Darkest Hours*, Atlantic Books, 2002.

PICTURE ACKNOWLEDGEMENTS

Credits are by page number in order from left to right and top to bottom.

1 – Getty Images (both). 2 – Getty Images (both). 3 – The Advertising Archive; Corbis. 4 – National Portrait Gallery. 5 – Jane Bown / Camera Press; Ronald Grant Archive. 6 – Getty Images; Corbis. 7 – *Time Life* / Getty Images; Getty Images. 8 – Getty Images (both). 9 – *Illustrated London News*; Getty Images. 10 – The Advertising Archives; Popperfoto. 11 – Courtesy of British Motor Industry Heritage Trust (both). 12 – Popperfoto; Getty Images. 13 – Arnold Newman / Getty Images. 14 – Getty Images (all). 15 – *Time Life* / Getty Images. 16 – Getty Images (both). 17 – Getty Images; Petra Niemeier / Redferns. 18 – Getty Images (both). 19 – Getty Images (both). 20 – Getty Images (both). 21 – Getty Images (both). 22 – Getty Images; PA Photos. 23 – David Dagley / Rex Features; Getty Images. 24 – Getty Images; PA Photos. 25 – Peter Jordan / Getty Images; PA Photos. 26 – Michael Cummings / *Daily Express*, 6 February 1980, courtesy of the British Cartoon Archive; *Time Life* / Getty Images. 27 – P.J. Arkell; Howard Davies / Corbis. 28 – *Time Life* / Getty Images; Getty Images; PA Photos. 29 – PA Photos; Getty Images. 30 – Don McPhee / *Guardian*; Getty Images. 31 – Stephen Hird / Reuters / Corbis; AFP / Getty Images. 32 – Getty Images (both).